LEVEL

3

HEALTH & SOCIAL CARE DIPLOMA
EVIDENCE GUIDE

Maria Ferreiro Peteiro

HODDER
EDUCATION
AN HACHETTE UK COMPANY

Although every effort has been made to ensure that website addresses are correct at time of going to press, Hodder Education cannot be held responsible for the content of any website mentioned. It is sometimes possible to find a relocated web page by typing in the address of the home page for a website in the URL window of your browser.

Orders: please contact Bookpoint Ltd, 130 Milton Park, Abingdon, Oxon OX14 4SB. Telephone: (44) 01235 827720. Fax: (44) 01235 400454. Lines are open 9:00–17:00, Monday to Saturday, with a 24-hour message answering service. Visit our website at www.hoddereducation.co.uk

© Maria Ferreiro Peteiro, 2014

First published in 2015 by

Hodder Education

An Hachette UK Company

338 Euston Road

London NW1 3BH

Impression number	5	4	3	2	1
Year	2019	2018	2017	2016	2015

Cover photo © fstop123/iStockphoto.

Typeset in Futura Std by Aptara, Inc.

Printed and bound by CPI Group (UK) Ltd., Croydon, CR0 4YY.

A catalogue record for this title is available from the British Library.

ISBN 978 1 471 80657 5

Contents

How to use this book

Assessment and You!

This Evidence Guide has been specially designed to help you gather evidence of the right knowledge and skills for your portfolio, in order for you to achieve the L3 Diploma in Health and Social Care.

Each separate assessment criterion is one page. It explains in simple terms the knowledge and skills you will need to know and demonstrate, and how you might go about generating evidence.

This book is your constant companion and a source of reference whenever your assessor is not available! It covers all the mandatory and 13 optional units.

Key features of the book

The L3 Evidence Guide will help you to understand:

Learning Outcome 1:
Understand why effective communication is important in the work setting

Assessment Criterion 1.1:
Identify the different reasons people communicate

The meaning of each assessment criterion

Understand all the requirements of the qualification with clearly stated learning outcomes and assessment criteria fully matched to the specification

What does AC1.1 mean?

The lead word **identify** means that you must **make clear** the reasons why people communicate.

- Your **list** must make clear **different** reasons why people communicate with others.
- For the key word **people** you can think about all those who you come in contact with in **your work setting**, such as the individuals you provide care for and support to, their families and friends, your colleagues, your manager and other external professionals you liaise with, such as GPs, Social Workers, Speech Therapists, Interpreters and advocates.

The key words included in each assessment criterion

Enhance your understanding of Assessment criteria and key terms, and what you will need to do to evidence each AC

Real Work Setting

Name: Steven

Job role: Senior Support Worker in a residential care home for adults who have learning disabilities

Steven has been working as a Senior Support Worker for eighteen months. His Senior responsibilities include: leading shifts and providing support to a team of six staff; liaising with individuals' families and others involved in their lives.

Communicating with staff: Steven works alongside all staff, undertakes supervision meetings with them, speaks with them during handovers, and provides advice and support when issues and questions arise during shifts.

Communicating with individuals: Steven completes needs assessments and develops support plans with all individuals. He liaises with all individuals with respect to their day-to-day activities, and provides information and support with the decisions they make about their lives.

How each assessment criterion relates to your work setting

See how concepts are applied in settings with real life scenarios. Each AC has a different role, description and case study that links to the AC so you can reflect and apply the scenario to your own role and setting

Evidencing AC1.1 to your assessor:

For AC1.1 you must evidence your understanding of the different reasons people communicate.

Assessment Methods:

Oral/Written Questioning or **Discussion** or a **Spidergram**.

- You can **tell** your assessor the different reasons people communicate.
- *Or*, you can **talk** to your assessor about the different reasons people communicate.
- *Or*, you can complete a **spidergram** showing the different reasons people communicate.

REMEMBER TO:

- Provide the different reasons people communicate.
- Include **varied** reasons why people communicate.
- Think about your work setting and **why** communication is necessary.
- Think about the different people you come in contact with and communicate with in **your work setting**.

The range of assessment methods that you can use to gather evidence

Helpful suggestions for how you can evidence your understanding of assessment criteria including oral, written and discussion assessment methods as well as ways to show your understanding and skills in competence based units

How to ensure that each assessment criterion is fully addressed

Helpful tips and guidance including points to cover in your evidence. Points to remember to help you in the work setting and develop your professional skills are also included.

SHC31 Promote communication in health, social care, children's or young people's settings

Learning Outcome 1: Understand why effective communication is important in the work setting

Assessment Criterion 1.1: Identify the different reasons people communicate

What does AC1.1 mean?

- The lead word **identify** means that you must **make clear** the reasons why people communicate.
- Your **list** must make clear **different** reasons why people communicate with others.
- For the key word **people** you can think about all those who you come in contact with in **your work setting**, such as the individuals you provide care for and support to, their families and friends, your colleagues, your manager and other external professionals you liaise with, such as GPs, Social Workers, Speech Therapists, Interpreters and advocates.

Read the following **Real Work Setting** scenario and think about how it relates to your work setting and role:

Real Work Setting

Name: Steven

Job role: Senior Support Worker in a residential care home for adults who have learning disabilities

Steven has been working as a Senior Support Worker for eighteen months. His Senior responsibilities include: leading shifts and providing support to a team of six staff; leading on support planning and day-to-day living; promoting individuals' independence; liaising with individuals' families and others involved in their lives.

Communicating with staff: Steven works alongside all staff, undertakes supervision meetings with them, speaks with them during handovers, and provides advice and support when issues and questions arise during shifts.

Communicating with individuals: Steven completes needs assessments and develops support plans with all individuals. He liaises with all individuals with respect to their day-to-day activities, and provides information and support with the decisions they make about their lives.

Communicating with families and others: Steven speaks and liaises with individuals' families and others involved in their lives at support planning meetings and when they come to visit their relatives.

Evidencing AC1.1 to your assessor:

For AC1.1 you must evidence your understanding of the different reasons people communicate.

Assessment Methods:
Oral/Written Questioning or **Discussion** or a **Spidergram**.

- You can **tell** your assessor the different reasons people communicate.
- Or, you can **talk** to your assessor about the different reasons people communicate.
- Or, you can complete a **spidergram** showing the different reasons people communicate.

REMEMBER TO:
- Provide the different reasons people communicate.
- Include **varied** reasons why people communicate.
- Think about your work setting and **why** communication is necessary.
- Think about the different people you come in contact with and communicate with in **your work setting**.

Learning Outcome 1: Understand why effective communication is important in the work setting

Assessment Criterion 1.2: Explain how communication affects relationships in the work setting

What does AC1.2 mean?

○ The lead word **explain** means that you must **make clear** how communication affects relationships in the work setting.

○ Your **account** must make clear the **different ways** communication can affect relationships.

○ For the key word **communication** you can think about how both **good** and **poor** communication affects relationships in the work setting.

○ For the key word **relationships** you can think about the different working relationships there are in **your work setting**, such as the individuals you provide care for and support to, their families and friends, your colleagues, manager and other external professionals you liaise with, such as GPs, Social Workers, Speech Therapists, Interpreters and advocates.

Read the following **Real Work Setting** scenario and think about how it relates to your work setting and role:

Real Work Setting

Name: Steven
Job role: Senior Support Worker in a residential care home for adults who have learning disabilities
(See page 1 for a description of the role.)
Work relationships with staff: Steven has built up a strong team and believes that this is because he provides constructive feedback to staff and positive support to identify and address any developmental needs they may have.
Work relationships with individuals: Steven meets with individuals one to one and reviews with them on a regular basis the activities they participate in and any support they require. Steven knows all the individuals who use the service and ensures he seeks their views on the services being provided.
Work relationships with families and others: Steven ensures he always makes time to speak with individuals' families, advocates and Speech Therapists, both over the telephone and in person.

Evidencing AC1.2 to your assessor:

For AC1.2 you must evidence your understanding of how communication affects relationships in a work setting.

Assessment Methods:

Oral/Written Questioning or **Discussion** or a **Personal Statement or Reflection**.

● You can **tell** your assessor about how communication affects relationships in your work setting.

● Or, you can **talk** to your assessor about how communication affects relationships in your work setting.

● Or, you can write a **personal statement or reflection** about your experience of how communication affects relationships in your work setting.

REMEMBER TO:

● Provide an **account** and explain how communication affects relationships in a work setting.

● Include **how** good and poor communication can affect relationships.

● Include the **effects** on different work relationships.

● Think about communication in your work setting.

● Think about different relationships in **your work setting**.

Learning Outcome 2: Be able to meet the communication and language needs, wishes and preferences of individuals

Assessment Criterion 2.1: Demonstrate how to establish the communication and language needs, wishes and preferences of individuals

What does AC2.1 mean?

○ The lead word **demonstrate** means that you must **be able to show** through **your work practices** how to establish individuals' communication and language needs, wishes and preferences.

○ Your **observations** of your work practices must include **different ways** of establishing individuals' communication and language needs, wishes and preferences.

○ For the key word **establish** you can think about the different ways to determine individuals' requirements in relation to their communication and language needs, wishes and preferences.

Read the following **Real Work Setting** scenario and think about how it relates to your work setting and role:

Real Work Setting

Name: Anne

Job role: Senior Support Worker in an independent living scheme for adults who have mental health needs

Anne has been working as a Senior Support Worker for one year. Her Senior responsibilities include: supporting and monitoring a team of Support Workers; supervising the delivery of care; developing, reviewing and updating individuals' care plans and risk assessments; providing support to individuals.

Establishing individuals' communication needs: Anne and her team work with individuals who communicate in different ways; Anne ensures she finds out whether and how they use verbal or non-verbal ways of communicating.

Establishing individuals' language needs: Anne and her team support individuals who express themselves in different ways and communicate using different languages; Anne ensures she finds out how they prefer to express their needs.

Establishing individuals' preferences: Anne and her team ensure that the support individuals require is provided in a way that reflects how they prefer to be communicated with.

Establishing individuals' wishes: Anne and her team communicate with individuals in ways that respect their choices and desires.

Evidencing AC2.1 to your assessor:

For AC2.1 you must evidence your skills to establish the communication and language needs, wishes and preferences of an individual.

Assessment Methods:

Direct Observation of your work practices.

● You can **show** your assessor or an expert witness how you establish with an individual their communication and language needs, wishes and preferences.

● You can also use communication profiles or care plans you have completed with an individual and that indicate how you established their communication and language needs, wishes and preferences as a supporting piece of **work product evidence**.

REMEMBER TO:

● Make arrangements for **observation** of **your work practices**.

● Include evidence of your work practices with different individuals.

● Include evidence of communication and language needs, wishes and preferences.

● Think about how you establish in your work setting how different individuals communicate.

● Think about different individuals in **your work setting**, their different backgrounds, cultures and beliefs.

Learning Outcome 2: Be able to meet the communication and language needs, wishes and preferences of individuals

Assessment Criterion 2.2: Describe the factors to consider when promoting effective communication

What does AC2.2 mean?

- The lead word **describe** means that you must provide an **account** that **details** the factors to consider when promoting effective communication.
- Your **account** must detail **different** factors to take into consideration.
- For the key word **factors** you can think about how the environment, the individuals' needs and approaches to communication must be taken into account.
- For the key words **effective communication** you can think about the individuals you work with in **your work setting** and the different ways you can encourage them to express themselves in ways that are appropriate to their needs, cultures, wishes and preferences.

Read the following **Real Work Setting** scenario and think about how it relates to your work setting and role:

Real Work Setting

Name: Anne

Job role: Senior Support Worker in an independent living scheme for adults who have mental health needs

(See page 3 for a description of the role.)

Communication and the environment: Anne understands how important it is when she speaks with an individual that they feel comfortable and safe to express their needs.

Communication and the individual's needs: Anne believes that her team's communications with individuals are most effective when they have spent time getting to know the individual, including how they prefer to communicate with others.

Communication and different approaches: Anne has observed her team use a range of different approaches when communicating with individuals, depending on the situation, what is being communicated and the individual's needs.

Evidencing AC2.2 to your assessor:

For AC2.2 you must evidence your knowledge of the factors to consider when promoting effective communication.

Assessment Methods:

Oral/Written Questioning or **Discussion** or a **Personal Statement or Reflection** or a **Witness Testimony**.

- You can **tell** your assessor the factors to consider when promoting effective communication.
- Or, you can **talk** to your assessor about the factors to consider when promoting effective communication.
- Or, you can write a **personal statement or reflection** about your experience of the factors you take into account when promoting effective communication in **your work setting**.
- Or, your supervisor or manager can write a **witness testimony** about the different factors you take into consideration for effective communication.
- You can also use communication profiles you have completed or updated with individuals to meet their needs and preferences as a supporting piece of **work product evidence**.

REMEMBER TO:

- Provide a detailed **account** of the factors to consider when promoting effective communication.
- Include **different factors** to take into consideration.
- Think about examples of effective communications in your work setting.
- Think about different individuals you communicate with in **your work setting**.

Learning Outcome 2: Be able to meet the communication and language needs, wishes and preferences of individuals

Assessment Criterion 2.3: Demonstrate a range of communication methods and styles to meet individuals' needs

What does AC2.3 mean?

- The lead word **demonstrate** means that you must **be able to show** through **your work practices** how you use a range of communication methods and styles to meet individuals' needs.
- Your **observations** of your work practices must include the use of **different** communication methods and **different** communication styles to meet individuals' needs.
- For the key word **range** you can think about the different communication methods and styles you use to communicate with different individuals in **your work setting**.
- For the key word **methods** you can think about the different verbal (e.g. vocabulary, linguistic tone, pitch) and non-verbal (e.g. eye contact, touch, physical gestures, body language, behaviour) ways you use to communicate with individuals in **your work setting**, including any communication aids that you use.
- For the key word **styles** you can think about the different ways that communication can be expressed to suit different individuals' needs and situations.

Read the following **Real Work Setting** scenario and think about how it relates to your work setting and role:

Real Work Setting

Name: Anne
Job role: Senior Support Worker in an independent living scheme for adults who have mental health needs
(See page 3 for a description of the role.)
Demonstrating communication methods: Anne and her team work closely with individuals who communicate in different ways; Anne and her team ensure they encourage this and use only the methods that individuals find the most effective.
Demonstrating communication styles: Anne and her team use different communication styles with different individuals, depending on the situation, the type of information that has to be expressed and the individual's needs.

Evidencing AC2.3 to your assessor:

For AC2.3 you must evidence your skills to use a range of communication methods and styles to meet individuals' needs.

Assessment Method:

Direct Observation of your work practices.

- You can **show** your assessor how you use a range of communication methods and styles to meet individuals' needs.

REMEMBER TO:

- Make arrangements for **observations** of **your work practices**.
- Include evidence of your work practices with different individuals.
- Include evidence of using different communication methods.
- Include evidence of using different communication styles.
- Think about the **ways** you communicate with different individuals in your work setting.
- Think about the **styles** of communication you use with different individuals in your work setting.
- Think about different individuals in **your work setting**, their different backgrounds, cultures and beliefs.

Learning Outcome 2: Be able to meet the communication and language needs, wishes and preferences of individuals

Assessment Criterion 2.4: Demonstrate how to respond to an individual's reactions when communicating

What does AC2.4 mean?

- The lead word **demonstrate** means that you must **be able to show** through **your work practices** how to respond to an individual's reactions when communicating.
- Your **observations** of your work practices must include **how** you respond to an individual's different reactions when they are communicating with you or others.
- For the key word **respond** you can think about the different approaches you use when responding to an individual in your work setting.
- For the key word **reactions** you can think about the different feelings that could be experienced by an individual and the different ways individuals may react to different communications.

Read the following **Real Work Setting** scenario and think about how it relates to your work setting and role:

Real Work Setting
Name: Anne
Job role: Senior Support Worker in an independent living scheme for adults who have mental health needs
(See page 3 for a description of the role.)
Responding to positive reactions: Anne supports individuals with arranging different places to visit and supports them on these visits. Anne has noticed that one individual, Ken, enjoys this aspect of his support and is always willing to visit new places.
Responding to negative reactions: Anne has built up a good rapport with Ken and knows him as a person, knows what's important to him and how he wants to be supported. Anne is also responsible for providing Ken with prompts to take his medication and uses different approaches to do so as she knows that Ken does not like to be reminded about activities.

Evidencing AC2.4 to your assessor:

For AC2.4 you must evidence your skills to respond to an individual's reactions when communicating.

Assessment Method:	REMEMBER TO:
Direct Observation of your work practice. • You can **show** your assessor or an expert witness how you to respond to an individual's reactions when communicating.	• Make arrangements for **observations** of **your work practices**. • Include evidence of your work practices of how to respond to an individual's different reactions. • Include evidence of responding to **both** positive and negative reactions. • Include evidence of using **different ways** of responding to an individual. • Think about the ways you respond to an individual when communicating in your work setting. • Think about an individual in **your work setting**, their background, culture and beliefs.

Learning Outcome 3: Be able to overcome barriers to communication

Assessment Criterion 3.1: Explain how people from different backgrounds may use and/or interpret communication methods in different ways

What does AC3.1 mean?

- ○ The lead word **explain** means that you must **make clear** how people from different backgrounds may use and/or interpret communication methods in different ways.
- ○ Your **account** must make clear the **different** ways people from **different backgrounds** may use and/or interpret communication methods.
- ○ For the key word **people** you can think about how individuals, health and social care professionals and others use communication methods.
- ○ For the key word **methods** you can think about the different ways you and others communicate both verbally and non-verbally with individuals from different backgrounds in your work setting.

Read the following **Real Work Setting** scenario and think about how it relates to your work setting and role:

Real Work Setting

Name: Jaz

Job role: Senior Support Worker to people who have learning disabilities living in their own homes

Jaz has been working as a Senior Support Worker for eight months. His Senior responsibilities include: supporting and supervising a team of three Support Workers and two volunteers; monitoring and reviewing all individuals' person-centred plans; monitoring the support provided by the team to ensure that all individuals' needs are met and that all agreed activities are completed. As part of his role Jaz also supports his team to provide a reliable and consistent service to individuals from many different backgrounds.

Communicating with individuals: Jaz leads on the development of communication profiles for all individuals; these are developed with the individual and their family and/or friends so as to fully explain the acceptable ways of communicating with individuals from different cultures; in this way individuals' beliefs are taken into account and respected when communicating with them. Jaz and his team use communication passports that have been developed with individuals, which include specific language, pictures, words and phrases that are familiar to individuals so as to promote effective communication.

Evidencing AC3.1 to your assessor:

For AC3.1 you must evidence your knowledge of how people from different backgrounds may use and/or interpret communication methods in different ways.

Assessment Methods:

Oral/Written Questioning or **Discussion** or a **Personal Statement** or **Reflection**.

- You can **tell** your assessor about how people from different backgrounds may use and/or interpret communication methods in different ways.
- Or, you can **talk** to your assessor about how people from different backgrounds may use and/or interpret communication methods in different ways.
- Or, you can write a **personal statement or reflection** about your experience of how people from different backgrounds may use and/or interpret communication methods in different ways in your work setting.

REMEMBER TO:

- Provide an **account** and explain how people from different backgrounds may use and/or interpret communication methods in different ways.
- Include the use of **different communication methods.**
- Think about communication methods used by people in **your work setting**.

Learning Outcome 3: Be able to overcome barriers to communication

Assessment Criterion 3.2: Identify barriers to effective communication

What does AC3.2 mean?

- The lead word **identify** means that you must **make clear** barriers to effective communication.
- Your **list** must make clear the **different** barriers to effective communication.
- For the key word **barriers** you can think about how these can arise out of the **physical environment** and the **psychological attitude** of those communicating, as well as **cultural and language differences** that may exist.

Read the following **Real Work Setting** scenario and think about how it relates to your work setting and role:

Real Work Setting

Name: Jaz
Job role: Senior Support Worker to people who have learning disabilities living in their own homes
(See page 7 for a description of the role.)
Communicating with individuals: Jaz reviews individuals' person-centred plans with them and supports them to express their needs, views and preferences. Jaz always takes into account that each individual is their own unique person and does not make any assumptions about individuals' communication preferences. Jaz is also aware that individuals may choose to communicate in different ways with different people and in different situations.
Communicating with families and others: Jaz speaks and liaises with individuals' families and others involved in their lives at reviews. Jaz respects each person's views and preferences, and listens carefully to what they are saying and how this relates to individuals' best interests.

Evidencing AC3.2 to your assessor:

For AC3.2 you must evidence your understanding of the barriers to effective communication.

Assessment Methods:

Oral/Written Questioning or Discussion or a Spidergram.

- You can **tell** your assessor about the barriers to effective communication.
- Or, you can **talk** to your assessor about the barriers to effective communication.
- Or, you can complete a **spidergram** showing the barriers to effective communication.

REMEMBER TO:

- Provide a list of **different** barriers to communication.
- Include the barriers to **effective** communication.
- Think about your work setting and the **different** barriers that there are to effective communication.
- Think about **your work setting** and the different staff, individuals, families and others with whom you communicate.

Learning Outcome 3: Be able to reduce barriers to communication

Assessment Criterion 3.3: Demonstrate ways to overcome barriers to communication

What does AC3.3 mean?

- The lead word **demonstrate** means that you must **be able to show** through **your work practices** how to lessen barriers to effective communication.
- Your **observations** of your work practices must include how you overcome **different** barriers to communication that may arise.
- For the key word **overcome** you can think about how you successfully deal with barriers to communication that arise in your work setting.
- For the key word **barriers** you can think about how these can arise out of the **physical environment** and the **psychological attitude** of those communicating, as well as **cultural and language differences** that may exist.

Read the following **Real Work Setting** scenario and think about how it relates to your work setting and role:

Real Work Setting

Name: Jaz

Job role: Senior Support Worker to people who have learning disabilities living in their own homes

(See page 7 for a description of the role.)

Reducing physical barriers: Jaz supports Mark with visiting new places. When planning this support Jaz and Mark take into account whether the place they will be visiting will be busy, as well as its location.

Reducing psychological barriers: Jaz has built up a good rapport with Mark and knows him as a person, knows what's important to him and how he wants to be supported. It is important to Jaz and Mark that they make time to be able to sit down together and discuss and review Mark's support, and that Mark feels comfortable to be able to say what he thinks.

Reducing cultural and language barriers: Jaz reviews Mark's support plan with Mark's brother present; Mark has requested this as his brother is Jewish like him. Mark also uses Makaton to communicate with Jaz and updates new signs of his own choice on a regular basis.

Evidencing AC3.3 to your assessor:

For AC3.3 you must evidence your skills to overcome barriers to communication.

Assessment Methods:

Direct Observation of your work practice.

- You can **show** your assessor or an expert witness how you overcome barriers to communication.
- You can also use communication profiles or care plans you have completed with different individuals that indicate how you've overcome barriers to effective communication as a supporting piece of **work product evidence**.

REMEMBER TO:

- Make arrangements for **observations** of your **work practices**.
- Include evidence of your work practices of how to overcome **different barriers** to communication.
- Think about the ways you overcome barriers to communication in **your work setting**.

Learning Outcome 3: Be able to overcome barriers to communication

Assessment Criterion 3.4: Demonstrate strategies that can be used to clarify misunderstandings

What does AC3.4 mean?

- The lead word **demonstrate** means that you must **be able to show** through **your work practices** how you use different strategies to clarify misunderstandings.
- Your **observations** of your work practices must include how you use **different** strategies to clarify misunderstandings.
- For the key word **strategies** you can think about how you use different methods to clarify misunderstandings.
- For the key word **misunderstandings** you can think about how these may arise when communications are misinterpreted due to the **physical environment** and the **psychological attitude** of those communicating, as well as **cultural and language differences** that may exist.

Read the following **Real Work Setting** scenario and think about how it relates to your work setting and role:

Real Work Setting

Name: Jaz

Job role: Senior Support Worker to people who have learning disabilities living in their own homes

(See page 7 for a description of the role.)

Clarifying misunderstandings: Jaz and Mark make time to sit down together and discuss and review Mark's support. It is during these support meetings that sometimes misunderstandings between what Mark feels about the support and how he is being supported come to light, as Mark at times uses new ways of communicating his views that are not always understood by the team and do therefore lead to misunderstandings. At other times misunderstandings arise when Mark finds himself in different situations and places, as he does not always feel comfortable and therefore finds it difficult to express what he is thinking and feeling to others.

Evidencing AC3.4 to your assessor:

For AC3.4 you must evidence your skills to use different strategies to clarify misunderstandings.

Assessment Method:
Direct Observation of your work practice.
- You can **show** your assessor or an expert witness how you use different strategies to clarify misunderstandings.

REMEMBER TO:
- Make arrangements for **observations of your work practices**.
- Include evidence of your work practices showing how to use **different strategies** to clarify misunderstandings.
- Think about the ways you clarify misunderstandings that arise in **your work setting**.

Learning Outcome 3: Be able to overcome barriers to communication

Assessment Criterion 3.5: Explain how to access extra support or services to enable individuals to communicate effectively

What does AC3.5 mean?

○ The lead word **explain** means that you must **make clear** how support or services to enable individuals to communicate effectively can be accessed.

○ Your **account** must make clear **how** to access different types of support or services.

○ For the key word **support** you can think about the different **communication aids, people and professionals** that can be accessed to enable individuals to communicate effectively.

○ For the key word **services** you can think about the different specialist **external agencies** that can be accessed to enable individuals to communicate effectively. Services may include, for example, translation, interpreting, speech and language, and/or advocacy services, which are independent services that support and enable people to have their views heard, express their concerns, promote their rights, and access information to make informed choices in their lives.

Read the following **Real Work Setting** scenario and think about how it relates to your work setting and role:

Real Work Setting

Name: Jaz

Job role: Senior Support Worker to people with learning disabilities living in their own homes

(See page 7 for a description of the role.)

Accessing support: Jaz and his team use communication passports that have been developed with individuals, and hold regular meetings with all those involved with individuals so as to establish effective communication.

Accessing services: Jaz and the team also welcome the input of their internal speech and language team, as well as the use of external services for BSL Signers and Interpreters when communicating with individuals who use different languages to express themselves.

Evidencing AC3.5 to your assessor:

For AC3.5 you must evidence your knowledge of how to access support or services to enable individuals to communicate effectively.

Assessment Methods:

Oral/Written Questioning or **Discussion** or a **Personal Statement or Reflection** or a **Witness Testimony**.

● You can **tell** your assessor about how to access support or services to enable individuals to communicate effectively.

● Or, you can **talk** to your assessor about how to access support or services to enable individuals to communicate effectively.

● Or, you can write a **personal statement or reflection** about your experience of how to access support or services to enable individuals in **your work setting** to communicate effectively.

● Or, your supervisor or manager can write a **witness testimony** about the different ways you access support or services to enable individuals to communicate effectively.

REMEMBER TO:

● Provide an **account** and explain how to access support or services to enable individuals to communicate effectively.

● Include **how** to access support or services.

● Include how to access **different types** of support or services.

● Think about how you access support or services to enable individuals in **your work setting** to communicate effectively.

Learning Outcome 4: Be able to apply principles and practices relating to confidentiality in own work

Assessment Criterion 4.1: Explain the meaning of the term confidentiality

What does AC4.1 mean?
- The lead word **explain** means that you must **make clear** the meaning of the term confidentiality.
- Your **account** must make clear the meaning of confidentiality.
- For the key word **confidentiality** you can think about how to keep safe personal information that is held, discussed and written about individuals and others.

Read the following **Real Work Setting** scenario and think about how it relates to your work setting and role:

Real Work Setting

Name: Jordan

Job role: Senior Residential Worker to older people

Jordan has been working as a Senior Residential Worker for eight years. His Senior responsibilities include: providing supervision to a team of six Residential Workers; updating individuals' care plans; leading on care plan activities; administering medication. As part of his role Jordan supports his team to provide high quality care and support to all individuals.

Confidentiality: Jordan and his team are soon going to attend a training session about confidentiality at work. In preparation for the training Jordan has asked each member of the team to bring along to their supervisions a list of the different types of personal information about individuals that they come across on a day-to-day basis at work. Jordan has asked the team to think about all types of information they handle, including verbal and written information, paper-based and electronic information and records. Jordan plans to use these as a basis for discussions with team members at their supervisions so as to ensure that they understand the meaning and importance of confidentiality at work.

Evidencing AC4.1 to your assessor:

For AC4.1 you must evidence your knowledge of the term confidentiality.

Assessment Methods:

Oral/Written Questioning or **Discussion** or a **Personal Statement** or **Reflection**.
- You can **tell** your assessor what the term confidentiality means.
- Or, you can **talk** to your assessor about what the term confidentiality means.
- Or, you can write a **personal statement or reflection** about your experience of the meaning of the term confidentiality in **your work setting**.

REMEMBER TO:
- Provide an **account** and explain with examples the meaning of the term confidentiality.
- Include the **meaning** of the term confidentiality.
- Include how confidentiality applies to your work role and work setting.
- Think about what confidentiality means in **your work setting**.

Learning Outcome 4: Be able to apply principles and practices relating to confidentiality in own work

Assessment Criterion 4.2: Demonstrate ways to maintain confidentiality in day-to-day communication

What does AC4.2 mean?

○ The lead word **demonstrate** means that you must **be able to show** through **your work practices** how you maintain confidentiality in day-to-day communication.

○ Your **observations** of your work practices must include **different ways** you maintain confidentiality in day-to-day communication.

○ For the key word **confidentiality** you can think about personal information that is held, discussed and written about individuals and how your work setting's policies and procedures support confidentiality in day-to-day communication.

Read the following **Real Work Setting** scenario and think about how it relates to your work setting and role:

Real Work Setting

Name: Jordan

Job role: Senior Residential Worker to older people

(See page 12 for a description of the role.)

Confidentiality: Jordan arranges supervisions with team members at the main office, where he can book a private room they can meet in. Discussions with individuals and their families respect individuals' privacy and all day-to-day records that are maintained and updated are completed in a private location; care is also taken to return all records back to their agreed private locations. Communications with families and external agencies take place in person, over the phone and at times by email; precautions to maintain confidentiality are also taken in terms of considering where the communications take place and who else might have access to these at the time.

Evidencing AC4.2 to your assessor:

For AC4.2 you must evidence your skills to maintain confidentiality in different ways in day-to-day communication.

Assessment Method:

Direct Observation of your work practice.

● You can **show** your assessor or an expert witness the different ways in which you maintain confidentiality in day-to-day communication.

REMEMBER TO:

● Make arrangements for **observations** of **your work practices**.

● Include evidence of your work practices of how to maintain confidentiality in day-to-day communication.

● Think about the ways you maintain confidentiality in day-to-day communication in **your work setting**.

Learning Outcome 4: Be able to apply principles and practices relating to confidentiality in own work

Assessment Criterion 4.3: Describe the potential tension between maintaining an individual's confidentiality and disclosing concerns

What does AC4.3 mean?

- ○ The lead word **describe** means that you must provide an **account** that **details** the potential tension that exists between maintaining an individual's confidentiality and disclosing concerns.
- ○ Your **account** must make clear the potential tension that exists.
- ○ For the key words **potential tension** you can think about what difficulties there may be between maintaining an individual's confidentiality and disclosing concerns.
- ○ For the key word **confidentiality** you can think about personal information that is held, discussed and written about individuals.
- ○ For the key word **concerns** you can think about worries you may have about an individual's safety and well-being.

Read the following **Real Work Setting** scenario and think about how it relates to your work setting and role:

Real Work Setting

Name: Jordan

Job role: Senior Residential Worker to older people

(See page 12 for a description of the role.)

Potential tensions: One of the individuals Jordan provides support to has told him that she is concerned about her son who comes to visit her as he is becoming increasingly agitated during their visits; although she is worried about her son she does not think that he would ever harm her and so asks Jordan not to say anything as she wants to continue having regular visits from him. Jordan understands how this individual is feeling and is pleased that she was able to confide in him but is also aware that as part of his job role he has a duty of care.

Evidencing AC4.3 to your assessor:

For AC4.3 you must evidence your knowledge of the potential tension between maintaining an individual's confidentiality and disclosing concerns.

Assessment Methods:

Oral/Written Questioning or **Discussion** or a **Personal Statement** or **Reflection**.

- ● You can **tell** your assessor about the potential tension between maintaining an individual's confidentiality and disclosing concerns.
- ● Or, you can **talk** to your assessor about the potential tension between maintaining an individual's confidentiality and disclosing concerns.
- ● Or, you can write a **personal statement or reflection** about your experience of the potential tension between maintaining an individual's confidentiality and disclosing concerns in **your work setting**.

REMEMBER TO:

- ● Provide an **account** and detail the potential tension that exists.
- ● Include **examples** of the potential tension between maintaining an individual's confidentiality and disclosing concerns.
- ● Think about the potential tension between maintaining an individual's confidentiality and disclosing concerns in **your work setting**.

Learning Outcome 1: Understand what is required for competence in your work role

Assessment Criterion 1.1: Describe the duties and responsibilities of your work role

What does AC1.1 mean?

- The lead word **describe** means that you must provide an **account** that **details** the range of duties and responsibilities you have.
- Your **account** must make clear **both** the duties and the responsibilities you have.
- For the key word **duties** you can think about the **activities** you are expected to carry out as part of your job role.
- For the key word **responsibilities** you can think about the different **approaches and qualities** you use to carry out your work activities.

Read the following Real Work Setting scenario and think about how it relates to your work setting and role:

Real Work Setting

Name: Tatiana

Job role: Senior Care Assistant to adults who have dementia

Tatiana has been working as a Senior Care Assistant in the community for three years. Tatiana's Senior responsibilities include supporting individuals to maintain and develop their independence in their communities.

Duties: Tatiana's duties include enabling individuals to prepare meals and carry out household activities, such as laundry and cleaning, as well as leading on the development of individuals' support plans and monitoring their implementation.

Responsibilities: Tatiana's responsibilities include motivating and encouraging individuals to maintain their independence and develop where possible new skills, as well as working as part of a team with her colleagues, individuals' families and other professionals providing high quality care and support.

Evidencing AC1.1 to your assessor:

For AC1.1 you must evidence your understanding of the duties and responsibilities of your work role.

Assessment Methods:
Oral/Written Questioning or **Discussion** or a **Personal Statement or Reflection.**

- You can **tell** your assessor the different duties and responsibilities you have at work.
- Or, you can **talk** to your assessor about the duties and responsibilities you have at work.
- Or, you can write a **personal statement or reflection** about your experience of the different duties and responsibilities you have in **your work setting**.

REMEMBER TO:
- Provide an **account** and detail **both** your duties and your responsibilities.
- Include different examples of the duties and responsibilities you have.
- Think about your **job description, person specification and your work setting**.

Learning Outcome 1: Understand what is required for competence in your work role

Assessment Criterion 1.2: Explain expectations about your work role as expressed in relevant standards

What does AC1.2 mean?

- The lead word **explain** means that you must **make clear** how national standards are relevant to your duties and responsibilities at work.
- Your **account** must make clear a range of national standards that are relevant.
- For the key word **expectations** you can think about your work **duties** and **responsibilities** and what your employer expects about how you carry these out.
- For the key word **standards** you can think about the different national occupational, minimum and quality standards that are relevant. Standards may also include regulations and codes of practice.

Read the following **Real Work Setting** scenario and think about how it relates to your work setting and role:

Real Work Setting

Name: Tatiana

Job role: Senior Care Assistant to adults who have dementia

(See page 15 for a description of the role.)

Expectations: Tatiana's employer expects her to have the skills and knowledge to be able to work in partnership with individuals and use a person-centred approach. Tatiana is also expected to be able to supervise a team of Care Assistants and provide them with guidance and support.

Standards: Tatiana is expected by her employer to carry out her work duties and responsibilities in accordance with the national occupational and quality standards for those who provide and work in services for people who have dementia.

Evidencing AC1.2 to your assessor:

For AC1.2 you must evidence your understanding of how your duties and responsibilities are linked to national standards.

Assessment Methods:

Oral/Written Questioning or **Discussion** or a **Personal Statement or Reflection.**

- You can **tell** your assessor the different standards that are relevant to the duties and responsibilities you have at work.
- Or, you can **talk** to your assessor about the different standards that are relevant to the duties and responsibilities you have at work.
- Or, you can write a **personal statement or reflection** about your experience of the different standards that are relevant to the duties and responsibilities you have in **your work setting.**

REMEMBER TO:

- Provide an **account** and explain **how** standards are relevant to your duties and responsibilities at work.
- Include **different** examples of standards that are in place.
- Think about different standards that are relevant to **your job role** and **work setting.**

Learning Outcome 2: Be able to reflect on practice

Assessment Criterion 2.1: Explain the importance of reflective practice in continuously improving the quality of service provided

What does AC2.1 mean?

- The lead word **explain** means that you must **make clear** the reasons why reflective practice is important.
- Your **account** must make clear how reflective practice can continuously improve the quality of service provided.
- For the key words **reflective practice** you can think about how you develop your knowledge and skills and improve your working practices.
- For the key words **continuously improving** you can think about the different ways that can be used on an ongoing basis to improve the quality of services provided.

Read the following **Real Work Setting** scenario and think about how it relates to your work setting and role:

Real Work Setting

Name: Maria

Job role: Senior Support Worker to people who have physical disabilities living in their own homes

Maria has been working as a Senior Support Worker in the community for three years. The aim of Maria's job role is to support individuals to maintain and develop their independence in their communities.

Importance of reflective practice: Maria is very committed to ensuring that every individual experiences high quality care and support. She believes that one of the most valuable ways to ensure that the team works to consistently high standards with every individual is through reflecting on the impact of their working practices on the lives of individuals and their families. Listening to others' views on what has worked well and what hasn't and why is integral to the team being able to reflect effectively. Learning from each other's mistakes can also make the team more aware of how to continue to improve the service they provide.

Evidencing AC2.1 to your assessor:

For AC2.1 you must evidence your understanding of the importance of reflective practice in continuously improving the quality of service provided.

Assessment Methods:

Oral/Written Questioning or **Discussion** or a **Personal Statement** or **Reflection.**

- You can **tell** your assessor about the importance of reflective practice in continuously improving the quality of service provided.
- Or, you can **talk** to your assessor about the importance of reflective practice in continuously improving the quality of service provided.
- Or, you can write a **personal statement or reflection** about your experience of the importance of reflective practice in continuously improving the quality of service provided in **your work setting**.

REMEMBER TO:
- Provide an **account** and explain the reasons why reflective practice is important.
- Include different **reasons**.
- Think about different examples of ways that reflective practice has continuously improved the quality of service provided in **your work setting**.

Learning Outcome 2: Be able to reflect on practice

Assessment Criterion 2.2: Demonstrate the ability to reflect on practice

What does AC2.2 mean?

- The lead word **demonstrate** means that you must **be able to show** through **your work practices** how you reflect on day-to-day work practice.
- Your **observations** of your work practices must include how you reflect on day-to-day work practice.
- For the key word **reflect** you can think about how you develop your knowledge and skills and improve your working practices.

Read the following **Real Work Setting** scenario and think about how it relates to your work setting and role:

Real Work Setting

Name: Maria

Job role: Senior Support Worker to people who have physical disabilities living in their own homes (See page 17 for a description of the role.)

Reflection: Maria has set some time aside this week to prepare for her supervision with her manager. In preparation for this she has reflected on the different situations that have arisen in her work setting, including those she has managed well and those she has found quite challenging. Maria plans to talk these through her manager and consider how and why these situations arose, what worked well and what didn't at the time, and what further improvements are required should these situations arise again.

Evidencing AC2.2 to your assessor:

For AC2.2 you must evidence your skills in reflecting on day-to-day work practice.

Assessment Methods:

Direct Observation of your work practice.

- You can **show** your assessor or an expert witness how you reflect on your day-to-day work practice.
- You can also use your personal development plan as a supporting piece of **work product evidence**.

REMEMBER TO:

- Make arrangements for **observation** of you reflecting on your day-to-day work practice.
- Include evidence of **how** you reflect on your day-to-day work practice.
- Think about the ways you reflect on your day-to-day work practice in **your work setting**.

Learning Outcome 2: Be able to reflect on practice

Assessment Criterion 2.3: Describe how your values, belief systems and experiences may affect working practice

What does AC2.3 mean?

- The lead word **describe** means that you must provide an **account** that **details** the different ways that your values, belief systems and experiences may affect working practice.
- Your **account** must **make clear** the effects of your values, belief systems and experiences.
- For the key words **values, belief systems and experiences** you can think about what you believe to be of value and important in life and your own experiences, and how these may be similar to or different from what others value, think is important in life and experience.

Read the following **Real Work Setting** scenario and think about how it relates to your work setting and role:

Real Work Setting

Name: Maria

Job role: Senior Support Worker to people who have physical disabilities living in their own homes

(See page 17 for a description of the role.)

Values, belief systems and experiences: Maria and the team of Support Workers work alongside individuals and their families who may be from different backgrounds, have different life experiences, cultures and beliefs. Some of these are shared with Maria and the team of Support Workers, some are not.

Impact on working practices: Maria and the team of Support Workers attend regular training sessions on diversity and inclusion and discuss in their team meetings and supervisions any issues they have come across and find difficult to manage in their day-to-day activities, including when individuals' attitudes and beliefs are in direct opposition to their own.

Evidencing AC2.3 to your assessor:

For AC2.3 you must evidence your knowledge of how your values, belief systems and experiences may affect working practice.

Assessment Methods:

Oral/Written Questioning or **Discussion** or a **Personal Statement** or **Reflection** or **Witness Testimony**.

- You can **tell** your assessor about how your values, belief systems and experiences may affect working practice.
- Or, you can **talk** to your assessor about how your values, belief systems and experiences may affect working practice.
- Or, you can write a **personal statement or reflection** about your experience of how your values, belief systems and experiences may affect working practice.
- Or, your supervisor or manager can write a **witness testimony** about how your values, belief systems and experiences may affect working practice.

REMEMBER TO:

- Provide a detailed **account** of how your values, belief systems and experiences may affect working practice.
- Include **different ways** in which your values, belief systems and experiences may affect working practice.
- Think about the different personal attitudes and beliefs that there are in **your work setting**.

Learning Outcome 3: Be able to evaluate own performance

Assessment Criterion 3.1: Evaluate your knowledge, understanding and performance against relevant standards

What does AC3.1 mean?

- ○ The lead word **evaluate** means that you must **be able to show** how you assess your knowledge, understanding and performance against relevant standards.
- ○ Your **observations** of your work practices must include how you assess your **strengths** and the **areas** of your knowledge, understanding and performance that **require further development**.
- ○ For the key words **knowledge** and **performance** you can think about what values and information underpin the skills you use to practise at work.
- ○ For the key word **standards** you can think about the different national occupational, minimum and quality standards that are relevant.

Read the following **Real Work Setting** scenario and think about how it relates to your work setting and role:

Real Work Setting

Name: Greg

Job role: Senior Personal Assistant to an adult with Asperger's syndrome

Greg has been working as a Senior Personal Assistant for three months. The aim of Greg's job role is to support Jeremy, an adult with Asperger's, to move into his own flat.

Knowledge, understanding and skills: Greg's brother has Asperger's and he has worked alongside adults with Asperger's for ten years. Greg feels that he has in-depth knowledge about what Asperger's is and how it can have an impact on adults' independent living skills. Greg is aware that he is still getting to know Jeremy and needs to gain a greater understanding of Jeremy's strengths, skills and aspirations. Greg would also like to further develop the approaches he uses to interact with Jeremy and so has arranged to spend some more time with Jeremy and his advocate.

Evidencing AC3.1 to your assessor:

For AC3.1 you must evidence your skills to evaluate your knowledge, understanding and performance against relevant standards.

Assessment Methods:

Direct Observation of your work practice.

- You can **show** your assessor or an expert witness how you evaluate your knowledge, understanding and performance against relevant standards.
- You can also use your personal development plan as a supporting piece of **work product evidence**.

REMEMBER TO:

- Make arrangements for **observations** of you evaluating your working knowledge and practices.
- Include evidence of how you **evaluate** your working knowledge and practices.
- Think about the ways you evaluate your knowledge, understanding and performance in **your work setting**.

Learning Outcome 3: Be able to evaluate own performance

Assessment Criterion 3.2: Demonstrate use of feedback to evaluate your performance and inform development

What does AC3.2 mean?

- The lead word **demonstrate** means that you must **be able to show** how feedback from others – such as the individuals you provide care and support to, your colleagues and your manager – helps you to assess how effectively you perform at work.
- Your **observations** of your work practices must include how you use feedback from others to evaluate your performance and inform development.
- For the key word **feedback** you can think about the different people who contribute to your assessment of how effective you are at work, and how you use their comments and views to continue to improve your practices.

Read the following **Real Work Setting** scenario and think about how it relates to your work setting and role:

Real Work Setting

Name: Greg

Job role: Senior Personal Assistant to an adult with Asperger's syndrome

(See page 20 for a description of the role.)

Use of feedback: Greg has regular supervisions with his manager and together they discuss the duties Greg carries out well in relation to the one-to-one support he provides to Jeremy. Greg and his manager have also talked about how Greg's organisational skills could be further improved in relation to coordinating the weekend activities that Jeremy enjoys taking part in. Jeremy's advocate has fed back to Greg that he has witnessed their positive interactions and would like to see Greg increase his confidence around Jeremy when supporting him in accessing community activities and interacting with people he has not met before. Greg has given careful consideration to all the feedback he has received and has agreed with his manager the actions he needs to take to improve his performance at work.

Evidencing AC3.2 to your assessor:

For AC3.2 you must evidence your skills of using feedback to evaluate your performance and inform development.

Assessment Methods:

Direct Observation of your work practice.

- You can **show** your assessor or an expert witness how you use feedback to evaluate your performance at work and to inform your development.
- You can also use your personal development plan as a supporting piece of **work product evidence**.

REMEMBER TO:

- Make arrangements for **observations** of you using feedback to evaluate your performance at work.
- Include evidence of feedback you've obtained from others.
- Think about the ways you use feedback from others to evaluate how you perform and to inform your development in **your work setting**.

Learning Outcome 4: Be able to agree a personal development plan

Assessment Criterion 4.1: Identify sources of support for planning and reviewing your development

What does AC4.1 mean?

- The lead word **identify** means that you must **make clear** sources of support for planning and reviewing your development.
- Your **list** must make clear **different** sources of support.
- The key words **sources of support** may mean formal or informal support. It may, for example, include supervision and appraisals, and can mean sources both within and outside your setting.
- For the key word **planning** you can think about the different sources of support available for planning the skills and knowledge at work that require updating.
- For the key word **reviewing** you can think about the different sources of support available for reviewing the skills and knowledge at work that require reassessing to ensure they remain up to date and effective.

Read the following **Real Work Setting** scenario and think about how it relates to your work setting and role:

Real Work Setting

Name: Nicola

Job role: Senior Residential Support Worker (Nights) to older people

Nicola has been working as a Senior Residential Worker for five years. Nicola's Senior job role responsibilities include: leading the night shifts; providing support and guidance to the staff team; conducting supervisions and care reviews.

Sources of support for own development: Nicola meets regularly with her manager and together they discuss and agree areas of Nicola's knowledge and skills that would benefit from being updated, including mentoring new and existing staff, dementia care, and infection control and prevention. Nicola also learns a lot from the more experienced Support Workers and the dementia care nurses who visit, including how to interact with some of the individuals with dementia and provide support and guidance to their families.

Evidencing AC4.1 to your assessor:

For AC4.1 you must evidence your knowledge of the different sources of support for planning and reviewing your personal development.

Assessment Methods:

Oral/Written Questioning or **Discussion** or a **Spidergram.**

- You can **tell** your assessor the different sources of support for planning and reviewing your personal development.
- Or, you can **talk** to your assessor about the different sources of support for planning and reviewing your personal development.
- Or, you can complete a **spidergram** showing the different sources of support for planning and reviewing your personal development.
- You can also use your personal development plan as a supporting piece of **work product evidence.**

REMEMBER TO:

- Provide the **different sources** of support that enable you to plan and review your development.
- Include **varied** sources of support.
- Think about the different sources of support available **within and outside your work setting.**

Learning Outcome 4: Be able to agree a personal development plan

Assessment Criterion 4.2: Demonstrate how to work with others to review and prioritise your learning needs, professional interests and development opportunities

What does AC4.2 mean?

○ The lead word **demonstrate** means that you must **be able to show** how you work alongside other people to review and prioritise your learning needs, professional interests and development opportunities.

○ Your **observations** of your work practices must include how you **work alongside different people**.

○ The key word **others** may include, for example, individuals, carers, advocates, supervisors, line managers or employers, as well as other professionals.

○ For the key words **review and prioritise** you can think about the different ways you work with other people to identify and reassess your learning needs, professional interests and development opportunities.

Read the following **Real Work Setting** scenario and think about how it relates to your work setting and role:

Real Work Setting

Name: Nicola

Job role: Senior Residential Support Worker (Nights) to older people

(See page 22 for a description of the role.)

Learning needs: Nicola will be attending a mentoring course to help her mentor new and existing staff effectively, and her manager has booked her on two e-learning modules focused on dementia care and infection control and prevention.

Professional interests: Nicola has a keen interest in dementia care and would like to explore different techniques and approaches that can be used when interacting with adults with dementia. Nicola has spoken to the dementia care nurse about her interest in this area and she has suggested some further reading that Nicola can do.

Development opportunities: Nicola plans to work as a manager in the future and has spoken to her manager about what her role involves; her manager has suggested she spend some time shadowing her. Nicola has also been invited to work alongside two recently recruited Seniors and to show them how she mentors new and existing Support Workers.

Evidencing AC4.2 to your assessor:

For AC4.2 you must evidence your skills to work with others to review and prioritise your learning needs, professional interests and development opportunities.

Assessment Methods:
Direct Observation of your work practice.

● You can **show** your assessor or an expert witness how you work with others to review and prioritise your learning needs, professional interests and development opportunities.

● You can also use your personal development plan as a supporting piece of **work product evidence**.

REMEMBER TO:
● Make arrangements for observations of how you work alongside **different people**.
● Include evidence of how these people enable you to review and prioritise your learning needs, professional interests and development opportunities.
● Think about the different people you work with both **within and outside your work setting**.

Learning Outcome 4: Be able to agree a personal development plan

Assessment Criterion 4.3: Demonstrate how to work with others to agree your personal development plan

What does AC4.3 mean?

- The lead word **demonstrate** means that you must **be able to show** how you work alongside other people to agree your personal development plan.
- Your **observations** of your work practices must include how you **work alongside different people**.
- For the key word **agree** you can think about with whom you discuss your personal development plan and how you decide the activities you plan to undertake.
- For the key words **personal development plan** you can think about how you evidence your personal development, including how this is documented. (This may have a different name in your setting, but will record information such as agreed objectives for development, proposed activities to meet objectives, timescales for review, etc.)

Read the following **Real Work Setting** scenario and think about how it relates to your work setting and role:

Real Work Setting

Name: Nicola

Job role: Senior Residential Support Worker (Nights) to older people

(See page 22 for a description of the role.)

Personal development plan: Nicola will be meeting with her manager to discuss her work practices and development over the last three months, as well as her plans for the next three months. Nicola plans to discuss with her manager the input one individual's advocate has provided in terms of helping her to develop her working relationship with him and also the areas in which she feels she requires further support and knowledge to be able to carry out her job role to the best of her ability.

Evidencing AC4.3 to your assessor:

For AC4.3 you must evidence your skills in working with others to agree your personal development plan.

Assessment Methods:

Direct Observation of your work practice.

- You can **show** your assessor or an expert witness how you work with others to agree your personal development plan.
- You can also use your personal development plan as a supporting piece of **work product evidence**.

REMEMBER TO:

- Make arrangements for **observations** of how you work alongside **different people**.
- Include evidence of how these people enable you to agree your personal development plan.
- Think about the different people you work with both **within and outside your work setting**.

Learning Outcome 5: Be able to use learning opportunities and reflective practice to contribute to personal development

Assessment Criterion 5.1: Evaluate how learning activities have affected practice

What does AC5.1 mean?

- ○ The lead word **evaluate** means that you must **be able to show** how you assess how learning activities have affected practice.
- ○ Your **observations** of your work practices must include **how** you assess the strengths of learning activities and the areas that require further development.
- ○ For the key words **learning activities** you can think about how a situation or training you've undertaken has affected practice in terms of improving your knowledge, skills and understanding, such as by giving you greater insight, providing you with an opportunity to learn about new areas or to develop different ways of working and applying the knowledge and skills you've gained.

Read the following **Real Work Setting** scenario and think about how it relates to your work setting and role:

Real Work Setting

Name: Liam

Job role: Senior Care Assistant to adults who have complex needs

Liam has been working as a Senior Care Assistant for two years. His role involves: providing support and supervision to a team of Care Assistants; mentoring new Care Assistants; carrying out risk assessments; updating care plans; ensuring individuals and others involved in their lives are active participants and communicated with on an ongoing basis.

Evaluating learning activities: Liam meets regularly with his manager and together they discuss and evaluate how learning activities undertaken by the team have affected working practices. In terms of a training session Liam attended on mentoring new and existing staff, both agree Liam's confidence has grown in this area. This in turn has meant that the advice and support he provides to the team has enabled individual team members to learn more about their roles and responsibilities and to perform their roles to a much higher standard and provide higher quality support to individuals. Feedback from the team on an infection control and prevention e-learning module completed by them indicated that this was useful for refreshing their knowledge; monitoring the team's practices has shown that this is still an area that requires improvement, however, and Liam discusses with his manager how the team may benefit from completing a more in-depth course.

Evidencing AC5.1 to your assessor:

For AC5.1 you must evidence your skills to evaluate how learning activities have affected practice.

Assessment Methods:

Direct Observation of your work practice.

- ● You can **show** your assessor or an expert witness how you evaluate how learning activities have affected practice.

REMEMBER TO:

- ● Make arrangements for **observations** of you evaluating learning activities.
- ● Include evidence of **how** you evaluate learning activities.
- ● Include evidence of **different** learning activities.
- ● Include evidence of how learning activities have affected practice in **different ways**.
- ● Think about the ways you evaluate how learning activities have affected practice in **your work setting**.

Learning Outcome 5: Be able to use learning opportunities and reflective practice to contribute to personal development

Assessment Criterion 5.2: Demonstrate how reflective practice has led to improved ways of working

What does AC5.2 mean?

○ The lead word **demonstrate** means that you must **be able to show** how reflective practice has led to improved ways of working.

○ Your **observations** of your work practices must include **how** reflective practice has led to improved working practices.

○ For the key words **reflective practice** you can think about how this process enables you to develop your knowledge and skills and to improve your working practices. This might be by giving you greater insight, providing you with an opportunity to learn about new areas or to develop different ways of working and apply the knowledge and skills you've gained to real life scenarios.

Read the following **Real Work Setting** scenario and think about how it relates to your work setting and role:

Real Work Setting

Name: Liam

Job role: Senior Care Assistant to adults who have complex needs

(See page 25 for a description of the role.)

How reflective practice has led to improved ways of working: During his meeting with his manager Liam reflects on the team's practice in supporting an adult with complex needs who has recently moved in to the scheme and who is experiencing some difficulties settling in and getting along with the other individuals who also live there. Liam reflects on how the team he leads managed the transition for this individual from his previous home to this one and reflects on how they provided him with sufficient support and one-to-one time, but perhaps should have spent more time understanding how he was feeling about the move and the differences between his previous home and this one. As a result of this situation the team reviews their procedure for new individuals coming to live at the scheme and they now offer one-week trials, where individuals can either visit or stay over a period of a week and get to know their new surroundings, the people they will be living with and the staff they will be supported by, which has resulted in individuals settling in a lot more easily.

Evidencing AC5.2 to your assessor:

For AC5.2 you must evidence your skills to show how reflective practice has led to improved ways of working.

Assessment Methods:

Direct Observation of your work practice.

● You can **show** your assessor or an expert witness how reflective practice has led to improved ways of working.

REMEMBER TO:

● Make arrangements for **observations** of how reflective practice has led to improved ways of working.

● Include **evidence** from a situation or learning activity you've reflected on.

● Include evidence of how reflective practice has led to improved ways of working.

● Think about **your work setting** and how reflective practice has led to improved ways of working.

Learning Outcome 5: Be able to use learning opportunities and reflective practice to contribute to personal development

Assessment Criterion 5.3: Show how to record progress in relation to personal development

What does AC5.3 mean?

- ○ The lead word **show** means that you must **be able to demonstrate** how to record progress in relation to personal development.
- ○ Your **observations** of your work practices must include **how** to record your progress in achieving the goals of your personal development plan.
- ○ For the key word **progress** you can think about how to record how you are proceeding with achieving your personal development goals – what has been achieved and how, what has not been achieved and why, as well as how you plan to achieve the goals that are still outstanding.

Read the following **Real Work Setting** scenario and think about how it relates to your work setting and role:

Real Work Setting

Name: Liam

Job role: Senior Care Assistant to adults who have complex needs

(See page 25 for a description of the role.)

How to record progress in relation to personal development: During Liam's meeting with his manager both discuss and review his working practices with respect to mentoring new Care Assistants and conducting supervisions with the team. Liam explains that he was pleased to have attended the supervisory training course his manager put him forward for, as he found it very useful to meet other managers and supervisors and listen to the different ways they manage the staff within their teams and various different situations they come across. Liam also feels that he has developed his mentoring skills and is finding it a lot easier now to provide guidance to staff over their working practices in order to encourage their professional development as practitioners. Liam and his manager agree that this personal development goal has now been achieved and move on to discuss Liam's progress with other goals identified in his personal development plan, including whether the timescales in place remain realistic. Both agree to review all development areas in three months.

Evidencing AC5.3 to your assessor:

For AC5.3 you must evidence your skills to record progress in relation to personal development.

Assessment Methods:

Direct Observation of your work practice.

- You can **show** your assessor or an expert witness how to record progress in relation to personal development.
- You can also use your personal development plan as a supporting piece of **work product evidence**.

REMEMBER TO:

- Make arrangements for **observations** of recording your progress.
- Include evidence of the progress you've made.
- Ensure your evidence relates to your personal development.
- Think about **your work setting** and how to record progress in relation to personal development.

> **Learning Outcome 1:** Understand the importance of diversity, equality and inclusion
>
> **Assessment Criterion 1.1:** Explain what is meant by diversity, equality and inclusion

What does AC1.1 mean?

- The lead word **explain means** that you must **make clear** the meaning of the terms diversity, equality and inclusion.
- Your **account** must make clear the **different meanings** of all three terms.
- For the key word **diversity** you can think about what makes individuals different and unique.
- For the key word **equality** you can think about what opportunities can be made available to all individuals.
- For the key word **inclusion** you can think about how individuals can participate fully and actively in their lives.

Read the following **Real Work Setting** scenario and think about how it relates to your work setting and role:

Real Work Setting

Name: Valerie

Job Role: Senior Carer in a residential care home for older people

Valerie has been working as a Senior Carer for three years. Her Senior responsibilities include: promoting high standards of care; developing, reviewing and updating care plans to meet individuals' changing physical, social and psychological needs; supervising staff; leading shifts. As part of her job role Valerie also liaises with individuals' families and visitors and other health and social care professionals.

Promoting high standards of care: Valerie ensures that the whole team maintains high standards of care by ensuring that all the team understand the importance of respecting individuals' differences and ensuring individuals' rights are upheld and that opportunities are made available to them to live their lives as they wish. When delivering training to the team Valerie ensures that the team understands how to respect individuals and make them feel in control of their lives, and how their words and actions towards each other and to individuals can have an impact on how people feel.

Evidencing AC1.1 to your assessor:

For AC1.1 you must evidence your understanding of what is meant by diversity, equality and inclusion.

Assessment Methods:

Oral/Written Questioning or Discussion or a **Personal Statement**.

- You can **tell** your assessor about the meanings of the terms diversity, equality and inclusion.
- Or, you can **talk** to your assessor about the meanings of the terms diversity, equality and inclusion.
- Or, you can write a **personal statement** about the meanings of the terms diversity, equality and inclusion.

REMEMBER TO:

- Provide an **account** and explain the meanings of **all** three terms.
- Include different **examples** to show your understanding of all three terms.
- Think about what is meant by diversity, equality and inclusion in **your work setting**.

Learning Outcome 1: Understand the importance of diversity, equality and inclusion

Assessment Criterion 1.2: Describe the potential effects of discrimination

What does AC1.2 mean?

- The lead word **describe** means that you must provide an **account** that **details** how discrimination can affect individuals and others.
- Your **account** must make clear the **different** effects that discrimination can have.
- For the key word **effects** you can think about the impact of discrimination on individuals and others, on the families or friends of the individual, on those who inflict discrimination as well as on wider society.
- For the key word **discrimination** you can think about how individuals can be treated unfairly or excluded.

Read the following **Real Work Setting** scenario and think about how it relates to your work setting and role:

Real Work Setting
Name: Valerie
Job Role: Senior Carer in a residential care home for older people
(See page 28 for a description of the role.)
Effects of discrimination: Valerie will be meeting with two Carers tomorrow as she has concerns that they are treating one individual less favourably due to his physical disabilities when supporting him to go out to different places. The individual appears upset and stressed after both Carers have provided him with support; Valerie has made her manager aware of her concerns and the current situation.

Evidencing AC1.2 to your assessor:

For AC1.2 you must evidence your understanding of the effects of discrimination on individuals.

Assessment Methods:

Oral/Written Questioning or Discussion or a Personal Statement or Reflection.

- You can **tell** your assessor about the potential effects of discrimination.
- Or, you can **talk** to your assessor about the potential effects of discrimination.
- Or, you can write a **personal statement or reflection** about your experience of the potential effects of discrimination.

REMEMBER TO:

- Provide an **account** and include details of the effects of discrimination on individuals.
- Include different **examples** of the effects of discrimination on individuals and others.
- Think about whether you have witnessed or been told about discrimination in your work setting.
- Think about how discrimination in **your work setting** can affect individuals.

Learning Outcome 1: Understand the importance of diversity, equality and inclusion

Assessment Criterion 1.3: Explain how inclusive practice promotes equality and supports diversity

What does AC1.3 mean?

○ The lead word **explain** means that you must **make clear** how inclusive practice both promotes equality and supports diversity.

○ Your **account** must make clear the **different ways** that inclusive practice both promotes equality and supports diversity.

○ For the key words **inclusive practice** you can think about the work practices that encourage individuals to be full and active participants in their lives.

○ For the key word **equality** you can think about what opportunities can be made available to all individuals.

○ For the key word **diversity** you can think about what makes individuals different and unique.

Read the following **Real Work Setting** scenario and think about how it relates to your work setting and role:

Real Work Setting

Name: Valerie

Job Role: Senior Carer in a residential care home for older people

(See page 28 for a description of the role.)

Inclusive practice: Valerie ensures when reviewing individuals' care plans that she involves individuals fully and asks them about their views and preferences as she recognises that each individual is different and unique; this includes discussing with the team when an individual prefers or requests to take part in an aspect of daily living that is deemed high risk. Valerie is keen to ensure that she and all the Carers provide individuals with information that is relevant and can be understood so that, where possible, informed choices and decisions can be made.

Evidencing AC1.3 to your assessor:

For AC1.3 you must evidence your understanding of how inclusive practice promotes equality and supports diversity.

Assessment Methods:
Oral/Written Questioning or **Discussion** or a **Personal Statement or Reflection.**

● You can **tell** your assessor about how inclusive practice promotes equality and supports diversity.

● *Or*, you can **talk** to your assessor about how inclusive practice promotes equality and supports diversity.

● *Or*, you can write a **personal statement or reflection** about your experience of how inclusive practice promotes equality and supports diversity.

REMEMBER TO:
● Provide an **account** of how inclusive practice promotes equality and supports diversity.
● Include different **examples** to show your understanding of how inclusive practice promotes equality and supports diversity.
● Think about how inclusive practice occurs in your work setting.
● Think about how inclusive practice promotes equality and supports diversity in **your work setting**.

Learning Outcome 2: Be able to work in an inclusive way

Assessment Criterion 2.1: Explain how legislation and codes of practice relating to equality, diversity and discrimination apply to your work role

What does AC2.1 mean?

- The lead word **explain** means that you must **make clear** how current legislation and codes of practice are relevant to your job role.
- Your **account** must make clear the **different reasons** and the **different ways** that current legislation and codes of practice are relevant to your job role.
- For the key words **legislation** and **codes of practice** you can think about different laws and guidance that relate to your job role.
- For the key word **equality** you can think about what opportunities can be made available to all individuals.
- For the key word **diversity** you can think about what makes individuals different and unique.
- For the key word **discrimination** you can think about how individuals can be treated unfairly or be excluded.

Read the following **Real Work Setting** scenario and think about how it relates to your work setting and role:

Real Work Setting

Name: Cora

Job Role: Senior Care Assistant for adults with physical disabilities

Cora has been working as a Senior Care Assistant for four years. Her job role involves leading a team of Care Assistants and deputising for the manager at times. Cora also provides support to individuals, which involves ensuring their physical, social and emotional needs are met.

Relevance of legislation and codes of practice: Cora is inducting a new Care Assistant and together they discuss the reasons why it is important that their work practices promote equality, support diversity and do not tolerate discrimination. Cora makes the Care Assistant aware of the organisation's code of practice and explains how this supports the organisation's aim of providing individuals with high quality support that is free from unequal treatment, promotes equal rights and supports individuals' differences. Cora also makes the Care Assistant aware of the consequences of not complying with current legislation.

Evidencing AC2.1 to your assessor:

For AC2.1 you must evidence your knowledge of the current legislation and codes of practice that relate to equality, diversity and discrimination.

Assessment Methods:

Oral/Written Questioning or **Discussion** or a **Personal Statement** or **Reflection**.

- You can **tell** your assessor about how current legislation and codes of practice are relevant to your work role.
- Or, you can **talk** to your assessor about how current legislation and codes of practice are relevant to your work role.
- Or, you can write a **personal statement or reflection** about your experience of how current legislation and codes of practice are relevant to your work role.

REMEMBER TO:

- Provide an **account** and explain **how** and **why** current legislation and codes of practice are relevant to your work role.
- Include **different** examples of **both** legislation and codes of practice.
- Think about **your work setting** and how legislation and codes of practice apply to your job role.

Learning Outcome 2: Be able to work in an inclusive way

Assessment Criterion 2.2: Show interaction with individuals that respects their beliefs, culture, values and preferences

What does AC2.2 mean?

- The lead word **show** means that you must **be able to demonstrate** through **your work practices** how your interactions with individuals respect their beliefs, culture, values and preferences.
- Your **observation** of your work practices must include how you respect individuals' beliefs, culture, values and preferences.
- For the key word **beliefs** you can think about how you can ensure that your interactions respect different individuals' faiths.
- For the key word **culture** you can think about how you can ensure that your interactions respect different individuals' ideas, customs and behaviours.
- For the key words **values** and **preferences** you can think about how you can ensure that your interactions respect different individuals' beliefs about what is important in life and to them.

Read the following **Real Work Setting** scenario and think about how it relates to your work setting and role:

Real Work Setting

Name: Cora

Job Role: Senior Care Assistant for adults with physical disabilities

(See page 31 for a description of the role.)

Interactions that respect individuals: Cora guides the team to provide support to individuals in a way that respects and values them, and maintains them as the focus of all the support agreed. Cora is a good role model herself and always works in ways that actively involve individuals and where appropriate their representatives.

Evidencing AC2.2 to your assessor:

For AC2.2 you must evidence your skills to show interaction with individuals that respects their beliefs, culture, values and preferences.

Assessment Method:

Direct Observation of your work practice.

- You can **show** your assessor how you show interaction with individuals that respects their beliefs, culture, values and preferences.

REMEMBER TO:

- Make arrangements for **observation** of how you interact with individuals.
- Include evidence of how your working practices show that you respect individuals' beliefs, culture, values and preferences.
- Think about **your work setting** and interactions with individuals that respect their beliefs, culture, values and preferences.

Learning Outcome 3: Be able to promote diversity, equality and inclusion

Assessment Criterion 3.1: Demonstrate actions that model inclusive practice

What does AC3.1 mean?

○ The lead word **demonstrate** means that you must **be able to show** through **your work practices** how you work in ways that model inclusive practice.

○ Your **observations** of your work practices must include how you work in ways that reflect inclusive practice.

○ For the key words **inclusive practice** you can think about your work practices that encourage individuals to be full and active participants in their lives and that show others how to follow these work practices.

Read the following **Real Work Setting** scenario and think about how it relates to your work setting and role:

Real Work Setting

Name: Daniel
Job Role: Senior Personal Assistant for adults who have autism and learning difficulties
Daniel has been working as a Senior Personal Assistant for two years. The aim of Daniel's job role is to provide support to adults who have autism and learning difficulties. Daniel's Senior responsibilities include: co-ordinating a team of Personal Assistants to provide 24-hour care and support; preparing rotas; facilitating group supervision for the team of Personal Assistants; liaising with other health and social care professionals.
Modelling inclusive practice: Daniel works closely with all the Personal Assistants he supervises so that they are able to provide consistent high quality care and support to all individuals. This includes respecting and valuing individuals' unique needs, preferences, culture, beliefs and values. Daniel also works closely with his manager and the trainer who works for a local organisation to ensure that all Personal Assistants receive regular training and support in how to deliver person-centred support and interact with individuals in positive and enabling ways.

Evidencing AC3.1 to your assessor:

For AC3.1 you must evidence your skills to model inclusive practice.

Assessment Method:

Direct Observation of your work practice.

● You can **show** your assessor how you model inclusive practice.

REMEMBER TO:

● Make arrangements for **observations** of how you model inclusive practice.

● Include evidence of how you work in ways that reflect inclusive practice.

● Include evidence of the procedures you follow that reflect inclusive practice.

● Think about the different people you work with **both within and outside your work setting** and how you model inclusive practice.

Learning Outcome 3: Be able to promote diversity, equality and inclusion

Assessment Criterion 3.2: Demonstrate how to support others to promote equality and rights

What does AC3.2 mean?

- The lead word **demonstrate** means that you must **be able to show** through **your work practices** how to support others to promote equality and rights.
- Your **observations** of your work practices must include **how** you support others.
- For the key word **support** you can think about the different ways you can assist others to promote equality and rights.
- For the key word **others** you can think about how you can provide support to individuals' families, friends, colleagues and other professionals to promote equality and rights.
- For the key words **equality and rights** you can think about how you can provide support to others to promote individuals' differences and rights to live their lives how they wish.

Read the following **Real Work Setting** scenario and think about how it relates to your work setting and role:

Real Work Setting

Name: Daniel

Job Role: Senior Personal Assistant for adults who have autism and learning difficulties

(See page 33 for a description of the role.)

Supporting others: Daniel uses supervisions with his team to discuss and reinforce back to each Personal Assistant how they are promoting equality and rights through their day-to-day working practices. This includes respecting and valuing individuals' unique needs, preferences, culture, beliefs and values, and acknowledging that these may be different to the Assistants' own. Daniel ensures that each Personal Assistant also understands that promoting equality and rights is relevant to how they work with their colleagues and others with whom they may liaise as part of their day-to-day work

Evidencing AC3.2 to your assessor:

For AC3.2 you must evidence your skills to support others to promote equality and rights.

Assessment Method:

Direct Observation of your work practice.

- You can **show** your assessor how you support others to promote equality and rights.

REMEMBER TO:

- Make arrangements for **observations** of how you support others.
- Include evidence of how you work to support others to promote equality and rights.
- Include evidence of the **different ways** you support others.
- Think about the different people you work with both **within and outside your work setting** and how you support them to promote equality and rights.

Learning Outcome 3: Be able to promote diversity, equality and inclusion

Assessment Criterion 3.3: Describe how to challenge discrimination in a way that promotes change

What does AC3.3 mean?

- The lead word **describe** means that you must provide an **account** that **details** how to challenge discrimination in a way that promotes change.
- Your **account** must make clear the **different ways** in which discrimination can be challenged to promote change.
- For the key word **challenge** you can think about positive actions you can take when discrimination occurs.
- For the key word **discrimination** you can think about how individuals and others can be treated unfairly or excluded.

Read the following **Real Work Setting** scenario and think about how it relates to your work setting and role:

Real Work Setting

Name: Daniel

Job Role: Senior Personal Assistant for adults who have autism and learning difficulties

(See page 33 for a description of the role.)

Challenging discrimination: Daniel has spent the last week working alongside two Personal Assistants. He has witnessed one of the Personal Assistants using discriminatory practices when providing support to different individuals. Daniel explained to the Personal Assistant the reasons his practices were discriminatory as soon as he witnessed the incident, and explained that he would be reporting the incident to his manager immediately. Daniel also made a record of the incident he witnessed and suggested that this team member requires further training as a matter of urgency around promoting equality and preventing discrimination.

Evidencing AC3.3 to your assessor:

For AC3.3 you must evidence your knowledge of how to challenge discrimination in a way that promotes change.

Assessment Methods:

Oral/Written Questioning or Discussion or a Personal Statement or Reflection.

- You can **tell** your assessor about how to challenge discrimination in a way that promotes change.
- Or, you can **talk** to your assessor about how to challenge discrimination in a way that promotes change.
- Or, you can write a **personal statement or reflection** about your experience of how to challenge discrimination in a way that promotes change.

REMEMBER TO:

- Provide an **account** and include details of **how** to challenge discrimination in a way that promotes change.
- Include different **examples** of how to challenge discrimination in a way that promotes change.
- Think about how discrimination is challenged in **your work setting** in a way that promotes change.

Learning Outcome 1: Understand how duty of care contributes to safe practice

Assessment Criterion 1.1: Explain what it means to have duty of care in your work role

What does AC1.1 mean?

- The lead word **explain** means that you must **make clear** the meaning of duty of care.
- Your **account** must make clear how duty of care is relevant to your **job role**.
- For the key words **duty of care** you can think about what it means to promote individuals' rights and safeguard individuals from danger, harm and abuse.

Read the following **Real Work Setting** scenario and think about how it relates to your work setting and role:

Real Work Setting

Name: Ryan
Job role: Senior Residential Care Worker for people who have complex needs
Ryan has been working as a Senior Residential Care Worker for two years. His Senior responsibilities include: providing high quality care and support to individuals; carrying out risk assessments; completing and reviewing person-centred care plans; carrying out supervisions, as well as training and inducting team members.
Duty of care: Ryan has put together a half-day training session for the new members of the team around duty of care, in order to ensure each team member understands their responsibilities to the individuals to whom they are providing care and support. Ryan has asked each participant to bring along their job description and think about the qualities and skills that are required to carry out their job role and duties on a day-to-day basis. By the end of the training session Ryan's aim is for each participant to have a full understanding of the meaning of duty of care and its importance and relevance to each of their work roles.

Evidencing AC1.1 to your assessor:

For AC1.1 you must evidence your understanding of what it means to have duty of care in your work role.

Assessment Methods:
Oral/Written Questioning or Discussion or a Personal Statement or Reflection.

- You can **tell** your assessor about what it means to have duty of care in your work role.
- Or, you can **talk** to your assessor about what it means to have duty of care in your work role.
- Or, you can write a **personal statement or reflection** about your experience of what it means to have duty of care in your work role.

REMEMBER TO:
- Provide an **account** and explain the meaning of the term duty of care.
- Include what it means to have duty of care in your work role.
- Think about what duty of care means in **your work setting**.

Learning Outcome 1: Understand how duty of care contributes to safe practice

Assessment Criterion 1.2: Explain how duty of care contributes to the safeguarding or protection of individuals

What does AC1.2 mean?

○ The lead word **explain** means that you must **make clear** how duty of care contributes to safeguarding or protecting individuals.
○ Your **account** must make clear **how duty of care** is relevant to safeguarding or protecting individuals.
○ For the key words **duty of care** you can think about how this contributes to safeguarding or protecting individuals.
○ For the key word **safeguarding** you can think about how individuals are protected from danger, harm and abuse.

Read the following **Real Work Setting** scenario and think about how it relates to your work setting and role:

Real Work Setting

Name: Ryan

Job role: Senior Residential Care Worker for people who have complex needs

(See page 36 for a description of the role.)

Safeguarding or protecting individuals: Ryan considers his role as a Senior to be an important one and sees himself as a mentor to the team of Care Workers he manages. Ryan is responsible for ensuring that the team of Care Workers provides high quality person-centred support to all the individuals who are referred to the service. Central to this is establishing good working practices amongst the team to protect individuals from any danger, harm or abuse; Ryan also monitors the service's reporting and recording systems to ensure that these are understood by every member of the team and are being followed accurately and consistently.

Evidencing AC1.2 to your assessor:

For AC1.2 you must evidence your understanding of how duty of care contributes to the safeguarding or protection of individuals.

Assessment Methods:
Oral/Written Questioning or **Discussion** or a **Personal Statement** or **Reflection**.

● You can **tell** your assessor about how duty of care contributes to the safeguarding or protection of individuals.
● Or, you can **talk** to your assessor about how duty of care contributes to the safeguarding or protection of individuals.
● Or, you can write a **personal statement or reflection** about your experience of how duty of care contributes to the safeguarding or protection of individuals.

REMEMBER TO:
● Provide an **account** of duty of care.
● Include how duty of care contributes to the safeguarding or protection of individuals.
● Think about how you safeguard or protect individuals in **your work setting** and how duty of care contributes to this.

Learning Outcome 2: Know how to address conflicts or dilemmas that may arise between an individual's rights and the duty of care

Assessment Criterion 2.1: Describe potential conflicts or dilemmas that may arise between the duty of care and an individual's rights

What does AC2.1 mean?

- The lead word **describe** means that you must provide an **account** that **details** potential conflicts or dilemmas that may arise between the duty of care and an individual's rights.
- Your **account** must detail **different** conflicts or dilemmas that may arise.
- For the key words **conflicts or dilemmas** you can think about how duty of care may be at variance with an individual's rights.
- For the key words **duty of care** you can think about what it means to promote individuals' rights and safeguard individuals from danger, harm and abuse.

Read the following **Real Work Setting** scenario and think about how it relates to your work setting and role:

Real Work Setting

Name: John

Job role: Senior Care Assistant for adults who have dementia

John has recently been promoted to Senior Care Assistant and as part of his job role leads a team of Carers to provide high quality personalised support to adults who have dementia. John is responsible for ensuring the implementation of personalised care planning, as well as maintaining full and accurate records relevant to his job role.

Conflicts or dilemmas: Lynne, an experienced Care Assistant, has approached John for advice around a difficult situation that has arisen with Claire, an individual to whom she provides care and support. Lynne explains to John that although she would like Claire to continue to maintain her independence when walking outside, she feels that as her mobility has decreased it is no longer safe for her to do so. Lynne has explained this to the family but they are still encouraging their relative to walk in the garden on her own when they visit.

Evidencing AC2.1 to your assessor:

For AC2.1 you must evidence your knowledge of potential conflicts or dilemmas that may arise between the duty of care and an individual's rights.

Assessment Methods:

Oral/Written Questioning or **Discussion** or a **Personal Statement** or **Reflection**.

- You can **tell** your assessor about potential conflicts or dilemmas that may arise.
- Or, you can **talk** to your assessor about potential conflicts or dilemmas that may arise.
- Or, you can write a **personal statement or reflection** about your experience of potential conflicts or dilemmas that may arise.

REMEMBER TO:

- Provide an **account** and include **details** of potential conflicts or dilemmas.
- Include examples of **different conflicts or dilemmas** that may arise between the duty of care and an individual's rights.
- Think about conflicts or dilemmas that have arisen in **your work setting**.

Learning Outcome 2: Know how to address conflicts or dilemmas that may arise between an individual's rights and the duty of care

Assessment Criterion 2.2: Describe how to manage risks associated with conflicts or dilemmas between an individual's rights and the duty of care

What does AC2.2 mean?

- The lead word **describe** means that you must provide an **account** that **details** how to manage risks associated with conflicts or dilemmas between an individual's rights and the duty of care.
- Your **account** must detail the **different ways** to manage risks associated with conflicts.
- For the key word **risks** you can think about how conflicts may place an individual in danger of being harmed.
- For the key words **conflicts or dilemmas** you can think about how duty of care may be at variance with an individual's rights.
- For the key words **duty of care** you can think about what it means to promote individuals' rights and safeguard individuals from danger, harm and abuse.

Read the following **Real Work Setting** scenario and think about how it relates to your work setting and role:

Real Work Setting

Name: John
Job role: Senior Care Assistant for adults who have dementia
(See page 38 for a description of the role.)
Managing risks: John agrees with Claire to organise a care review and to invite Lynne, the Care Manager, Registered Nurse and Claire's family to discuss the situation. John reassures Claire that he is sure that she will continue to be able to make use of the garden, as he knows that she enjoys her walks, whilst at the same time ensuring that she is safe when doing so.

Evidencing AC2.2 to your assessor:

For AC2.2 you must evidence your knowledge of how to manage risks associated with conflicts or dilemmas between an individual's rights and the duty of care.

Assessment Methods:

Oral/Written Questioning or **Discussion** or a **Personal Statement or Reflection** or a **Witness Testimony**.

- You can **tell** your assessor about how to manage risks associated with conflicts or dilemmas.
- Or, you can **talk** to your assessor about how to manage risks associated with conflicts or dilemmas.
- Or, you can write a **personal statement or reflection** about your experience of how to manage risks associated with conflicts or dilemmas.
- Or, your supervisor or manager can write a **witness testimony** about how you managed risks associated with conflicts or dilemmas.

REMEMBER TO:

- Provide an **account** about how to manage risks associated with conflicts or dilemmas.
- Include examples of **different ways** to manage risks associated with conflicts or dilemmas between an individual's rights and the duty of care.
- Think about how conflicts or dilemmas that have arisen in **your work setting** were managed.

Learning Outcome 2: Know how to address conflicts or dilemmas that may arise between an individual's rights and the duty of care

Assessment Criterion 2.3: Explain where to get additional support and advice about conflicts and dilemmas

What does AC2.3 mean?

○ The lead word **explain** means that you must **make clear** where to get additional support and advice about managing conflicts.

○ Your **account** must make clear the **different sources** of support and advice about managing conflicts and dilemmas, **how** to access these and **why**.

○ For the key words **conflicts and dilemmas** you can think about how duty of care may be at variance with an individual's rights.

Read the following **Real Work Setting** scenario and think about how it relates to your work setting and role:

Real Work Setting

Name: John

Job role: Senior Care Assistant for adults who have dementia

(See page 38 for a description of the role.)

Support and advice: John arranges a meeting with Lynne, the Care Manager and Registered Nurse, and explains to them all that a care review will be organised to discuss the situation. Lynne suggests the use of a wheelchair when Claire is in the garden; the Care Manager suggests Claire being supported by a member of staff at all times when outside, and the Registered Nurse states that she would like another mobility assessment to be completed with Claire and suggests that it may be worth contacting both the Physiotherapist and the Occupational Therapist. John explains that he also plans to speak to Claire's family, and thanks everyone for their contributions to date.

Evidencing AC2.3 to your assessor:

For AC2.3 you must evidence your knowledge of where to get additional support and advice about managing conflicts and dilemmas.

Assessment Methods:

Oral/Written Questioning or **Discussion** or a **Personal Statement** or **Reflection** or a **Witness Testimony**.

● You can **tell** your assessor where to get support and advice.

● Or, you can **talk** to your assessor about where to get support and advice.

● Or, you can write a **personal statement or reflection** about your experience of where to get support and advice.

● Or, your supervisor or manager can write a **witness testimony** about an occasion where you got support and advice.

REMEMBER TO:

● Provide an **account** of where to get additional support and advice about managing conflicts and dilemmas.

● Include examples of **different sources** of both support and advice as well as why and how to access these.

● Think about conflicts and dilemmas that have arisen in **your work setting** and the different sources of support and advice that are available to manage these.

Learning Outcome 3: Know how to respond to complaints

Assessment Criterion 3.1: Describe how to respond to complaints

What does AC3.1 mean?

- ○ The lead word **describe** means that you must provide an **account** that **details** the process to follow for responding to complaints.
- ○ Your **account** must detail the **process** to follow.
- ○ For the key word **complaints** you can think about how duty of care may be at variance with an individual's rights and may result in an individual being dissatisfied.

Read the following **Real Work Setting** scenario and think about how it relates to your work setting and role:

Real Work Setting

Name: Lynn

Job role: Senior Personal Assistant

Lynn has been working as a Senior Personal Assistant for three years. As part of her job role she meets with individuals to discuss and review with them the care and support being provided. At times this also involves liaising with individuals' families, friends and/or advocates.

Responding to complaints: Lynn is meeting today with Sarah, her sister and her advocate. Sarah is being supported by her sister and advocate to complain about one Personal Assistant who is refusing to support Sarah to go swimming on a Friday evening. The Personal Assistant does not think it is safe for her to support Sarah on her own; as this has been included in the risk assessment the Personal Assistant refuses to support Sarah with this activity. Lynn listens carefully to Sarah, reassures her that her complaint will be taken seriously and that she will try and find a solution to this situation.

Evidencing AC3.1 to your assessor:

For AC3.1 you must evidence your knowledge of how to respond to complaints.

Assessment Methods:

Oral/Written Questioning or Discussion or a Personal Statement or Reflection or a Witness Testimony.

- You can **tell** your assessor about how to respond to complaints.
- Or, you can **talk** to your assessor about how to respond to complaints.
- Or, you can write a **personal statement or reflection** about your experience of how to respond to complaints.
- Or, your supervisor or manager can write a **witness testimony** about an occasion where you responded to a complaint.

REMEMBER TO:

- Provide an **account** and detail the **process** to follow.
- Include details about each stage of the process to follow.
- Provide details that relate to responding to complaints about duty of care.
- Think about complaints relating to duty of care that have arisen or may arise in **your work setting** and how to respond to these.

Learning Outcome 3: Know how to respond to complaints

Assessment Criterion 3.2: Explain the main points of agreed procedures for handling complaints

What does AC3.2 mean?

- The lead word **explain** means that you must **make clear** the main points of agreed procedures for handling complaints relating to duty of care.
- Your **account** must make clear the **process** to follow.
- For the key word **complaints** you can think about how duty of care may be at variance with an individual's rights and result in an individual being dissatisfied.

Read the following **Real Work Setting** scenario and think about how it relates to your work setting and role:

Real Work Setting

Name: Lynn

Job role: Senior Personal Assistant

(See page 41 for a description of the role.)

Handling complaints: Lynn explains the risk assessment in place, as well as the risks and reasons why the Personal Assistant is unable on her own to support Sarah to go swimming. Lynn then talks through the various different options available to Sarah, including funding for two Personal Assistants to support her to do this activity, or accessing support from someone else to accompany the Personal Assistant, such as her advocate, her sister or a volunteer. Sarah decides to go away and discuss the situation further with her sister and advocate, but in the meantime hands Lynn her complaint in writing. Lynn explains that in line with the complaints procedure all complaints are taken seriously and that she will receive a response in writing within ten working days. Lynn ensures she leaves the office's telephone number with Sarah should she have any other questions she wishes to discuss.

Evidencing AC3.2 to your assessor:

For AC3.2 you must evidence your knowledge of the main points of agreed procedures for handling complaints.

Assessment Methods:

Oral/Written Questioning or **Discussion** or a **Personal Statement** or **Reflection**.

- You can **tell** your assessor about the main points of agreed procedures for handling complaints.
- Or, you can **talk** to your assessor about the main points of agreed procedures for handling complaints.
- Or, you can write a **personal statement or reflection** about the main points of agreed procedures for handling complaints.

REMEMBER TO:

- Provide an **account** and explain the main points of agreed procedures for handling complaints.
- Include details about each stage of the process to follow.
- Provide details that relate to handling complaints about duty of care.
- Think about complaints relating to duty of care that have arisen or may arise in **your work setting** and the agreed procedures to follow for handling these.

What does AC1.1 mean?

- The lead word **define** means that you must **make clear** the **meanings** of each of the following types of abuse: physical abuse; sexual abuse; emotional/psychological abuse; financial abuse; institutional abuse; self-neglect; neglect by others.
- Your **definitions** must make clear what each of the seven types of abuse involves.
- For the key word **abuse** you can think about the danger and/or harm an individual may be in or at risk of having inflicted.

Read the following **Real Work Setting** scenario and think about how it relates to your work setting and role:

Real Work Setting

Name: Steve

Job role: Senior Support Worker to people who have diverse needs living independently

Steve works as a Senior Support Worker and provides support and supervision to three Support Workers. Steve's Senior responsibilities include: developing and reviewing person-centred plans; supporting individuals to maintain their own tenancies; providing day-to-day living support to individuals; leading team meetings.

Types of abuse: Steve has recently attended a safeguarding training update and is putting together a PowerPoint presentation of the different types of abuse that there are and what each one means and involves. He will show this at the next team meeting so that everyone is aware of what constitutes abuse and what is involved.

Evidencing AC1.1 to your assessor:

For AC1.1 you must evidence your knowledge of the meanings of the following types of abuse: physical abuse; sexual abuse; emotional/psychological abuse; financial abuse; institutional abuse; self-neglect; neglect by others.

Assessment Methods:
Oral/Written Questioning or **Discussion** or a **Spidergram**.

- You can **tell** your assessor about the meanings of the following types of abuse: physical abuse; sexual abuse; emotional/psychological abuse; financial abuse; institutional abuse; self-neglect; neglect by others.
- Or, you can **talk** to your assessor about the meanings of the following types of abuse: physical abuse; sexual abuse; emotional/psychological abuse; financial abuse; institutional abuse; self-neglect; neglect by others.
- Or, you can complete a **spidergram** showing the meanings of the following types of abuse: physical abuse; sexual abuse; emotional/psychological abuse; financial abuse; institutional abuse; self-neglect; neglect by others.

REMEMBER TO:
- Provide the **meanings** of each of the seven types of abuse.
- Include details about what each type of abuse involves.
- Provide details that **relate** specifically to each type of abuse.
- Think about different types of abuse that you have received training on in **your work setting** and the meanings of these.

Learning Outcome 1: Know how to recognise signs of abuse

Assessment Criterion 1.2: Identify the signs and/or symptoms associated with each type of abuse

What does AC1.2 mean?

○ The lead word **identify** means that you must **make clear** the signs and/or symptoms associated with each of the following types of abuse: physical abuse; sexual abuse; emotional/psychological abuse; financial abuse; institutional abuse; self-neglect; neglect by others.

○ Your **list** must make clear the signs and/or symptoms for each type of abuse.

○ For the key word **signs** you can think about the visible changes that may be seen and/or noticed in individuals who are being or have been abused.

○ For the key word **symptoms** you can think about how individuals who are being or have been abused may feel and how this may be expressed in a variety of ways.

○ For the key word **abuse** you can think about the danger and/or harm an individual may be in or at risk of having inflicted.

Read the following **Real Work Setting** scenario and think about how it relates to your work setting and role:

Real Work Setting

Name: Steve

Job role: Senior Support Worker to people who have diverse needs living independently

(See page 43 for a description of the role.)

Signs and/or symptoms of abuse: Steve has devised some activities for the team to undertake, including discussing the differences between a sign and a symptom of abuse and matching a list of signs and symptoms he has written down to each type of abuse. Steve will provide the team with an opportunity to share their findings with each other at the end of each activity. Steve hopes that this will be informative and help the team to understand how to recognise signs and symptoms of abuse in different individuals.

Evidencing AC1.2 to your assessor:

For AC1.2 you must evidence your knowledge of the signs and/or symptoms associated with the following types of abuse: physical abuse; sexual abuse; emotional/psychological abuse; financial abuse; institutional abuse; self-neglect; neglect by others.

Assessment Methods:

Oral/Written Questioning or **Discussion** or a **Spidergram**.

● You can **tell** your assessor about the signs and/or symptoms of the types of abuse.

● Or, you can **talk** to your assessor about the signs and/or symptoms of the types of abuse.

● Or, you can complete a **spidergram** showing the signs and/or symptoms of the types of abuse.

REMEMBER TO:

● Provide the **signs and/or symptoms** associated with each of the seven types of abuse.

● Include a **list** of the signs and/or symptoms for each type of abuse.

● Provide details that **relate** specifically to each type of abuse.

● Think about different types of abuse that you have received training on in **your work setting** and the signs and/or symptoms associated with each of these.

Learning Outcome 1: Know how to recognise signs of abuse

Assessment Criterion 1.3: Describe factors that may contribute to an individual being more vulnerable to abuse

What does AC1.3 mean?

- The lead word **describe** means that you must provide an **account** that **details** the factors that may contribute to an individual being more vulnerable to abuse.
- Your **account** must detail **different** factors that may contribute to an individual being more vulnerable to abuse.
- For the key word **factors** you can think about a particular situation or setting or the involvement of another individual.
- For the key word **vulnerable** you can think about how and why some individuals may be at higher risk of being abused.
- For the key word **abuse** you can think about the danger and/or harm an individual may be in or at risk of having inflicted.

Read the following **Real Work Setting** scenario and think about how it relates to your work setting and role:

Real Work Setting

Name: Steve

Job role: Senior Support Worker to people who have diverse needs living independently

(See page 43 for a description of the role.)

Individuals at risk of abuse: Steve actively promotes the ongoing assessment of individuals' needs and preferences, and has concerns over one individual in particular whose needs have changed. As a result of this individual's health she has become increasingly dependent on the team with respect to her physical needs. Steve is also concerned that this individual's tendency to become increasingly agitated is having an impact on her relationships with the Support Workers and others involved in her life.

Evidencing AC1.3 to your assessor:

For AC1.3 you must evidence your knowledge of the factors that may contribute to an individual being more vulnerable to abuse.

Assessment Methods:

Oral/Written Questioning or **Discussion** or a **Personal Statement** or **Reflection**.

- You can **tell** your assessor the factors that may contribute to an individual being more vulnerable to abuse.
- Or, you can **talk** to your assessor about the factors that may contribute to an individual being more vulnerable to abuse.
- Or, you can write a **personal statement or reflection** about your experience of the factors that may contribute to an individual being more vulnerable to abuse.

REMEMBER TO:

- Provide a detailed **account** of the factors that may contribute to an individual being more vulnerable to abuse.
- Include different **factors** to take into consideration.
- Think about examples of factors that may contribute to an individual in **your work setting** being more vulnerable to abuse.

Learning Outcome 2: Know how to respond to suspected or alleged abuse

Assessment Criterion 2.1: Explain the actions to take if there are suspicions that an individual is being abused

What does AC2.1 mean?

○ The lead word **explain** means that you must **make clear** the actions to take if you or others have suspicions that an individual is being abused.

○ Your **account** must make clear the **different** actions to take, as well as the **reasons why**.

○ The key words **actions to take** must include you taking responsibility for responding to allegations or suspicions of abuse that may implicate you, your line manager, a colleague, someone in the individual's personal network, and/or others.

○ For the key word **suspicions** you can think about the reasons that may lead you or others to believe that an individual is being abused.

Read the following **Real Work Setting** scenario and think about how it relates to your work setting and role:

Real Work Setting

Name: Bhuvan
Job role: Senior Personal Assistant for people who have learning disabilities
Bhuvan has been working as a Senior Personal Assistant for two months. His Senior responsibilities include: managing and providing support to a team of staff; leading shifts; updating care plans; administering medication; delivering personal care and support with carrying out domestic duties.
Suspected abuse: Bhuvan has noted that one of the individuals to whom the team provides support has become unusually and increasingly withdrawn over the last couple of weeks. He has most recently begun refusing to be supported by one of the Personal Assistants and become increasingly anxious when this Personal Assistant is on duty. Bhuvan has documented his concerns and has shared these in confidence with his manager.

Evidencing AC2.1 to your assessor:

For AC2.1 you must evidence your knowledge of the actions to take if there are suspicions that an individual is being abused.

Assessment Methods:

Oral/Written Questioning or **Discussion** or a **Personal Statement or Reflection**.

● You can **tell** your assessor the different actions to take, as well as the reasons why if there are suspicions that an individual is being abused.

● Or, you can **talk** to your assessor about the different actions to take, as well as the reasons why if there are suspicions that an individual is being abused.

● Or, you can write a **personal statement or reflection** about your experience of the different actions to take if there are suspicions an individual in **your work setting** is being abused, as well as the reasons why if there are suspicions that an individual is being abused.

REMEMBER TO:

● Provide an **account** of the actions to take if there are suspicions that an individual is being abused and explain why.

● Include **varied** reasons.

● Think about **your work setting** and why you must take action if there are suspicions that an individual is being abused.

Learning Outcome 2: Know how to respond to suspected or alleged abuse

Assessment Criterion 2.2: Explain the actions to take if an individual alleges that they are being abused

What does AC2.2 mean?

- The lead word **explain** means that you must **make clear** the actions to take if an individual alleges that they are being abused.
- Your **account** must make clear the **different actions** to take, as well as the reasons **why**.
- For the key word **alleges** you can think about the different ways an individual may disclose that they are being abused.

Read the following **Real Work Setting** scenario and think about how it relates to your work setting and role:

Real Work Setting

Name: Bhuvan

Job role: Senior Personal Assistant for people with learning disabilities

(See page 46 for a description of the role.)

Alleged abuse: Bhuvan attends a morning call with his colleague who is also a Senior Personal Assistant, and upon their arrival the individual who opens the door explains that he is too upset to speak to them both. He says his brother, who lives with him, shouted at him again this morning before leaving for work, and then he shuts the front door. Bhuvan and his colleague ring the doorbell again, and after waiting for a while hear the individual shout 'Leave me alone' through the letterbox. Bhuvan and his colleague leave and return to the office, document the incident and pass this on immediately and in confidence to the safeguarding officer.

Evidencing AC2.2 to your assessor:

For AC2.2 you must evidence your knowledge of the actions to take if an individual alleges that they are being abused.

Assessment Methods:

Oral/Written Questioning or **Discussion** or a **Personal Statement** or **Reflection**.

- You can **tell** your assessor the different actions to take, as well as the reasons why if an individual alleges that they are being abused.
- Or, you can **talk** to your assessor about the different actions to take, as well as the reasons why if an individual alleges that they are being abused.
- Or, you can write a **personal statement or reflection** about your experience of the different actions to take if an individual alleges they are being abused, as well as the reasons why if an individual alleges that they are being abused.

REMEMBER TO:

- Provide an **account** of the actions to take if an individual alleges that they are being abused and explain why.
- Include **varied** reasons.
- Think about **your work setting** and the actions you must take and why, if an individual alleges they are being abused.

Learning Outcome 2: Know how to respond to suspected or alleged abuse

Assessment Criterion 2.3: Identify ways to ensure that evidence of abuse is preserved

What does AC2.3 mean?

- The lead word **identify** means that you must **make clear** the different methods to ensure that evidence of abuse is preserved.
- Your **list** must make clear **different** ways to ensure that evidence of abuse is preserved.
- For the key word **evidence** you can think about how signs of abuse will need to be preserved in relation to both the individual and their environment.
- For the key word **abuse** you can think about the danger and/or harm an individual may be in and/or have inflicted.
- For the key word **preserved** you can think about the actions to take and not take when protecting evidence of abuse.

Read the following **Real Work Setting** scenario and think about how it relates to your work setting and role:

Real Work Setting

Name: Bhuvan

Job role: Senior Personal Assistant for people with learning disabilities

(See page 46 for a description of the role.)

Preserving evidence of abuse: Bhuvan is due to attend a safeguarding meeting in relation to one individual, who has made an allegation that her sister is taking money from her purse when she comes to visit her. Bhuvan has ensured that records have been kept of when this resident's sister has visited and when it is alleged that the money has gone missing from her purse. Bhuvan hopes that this will help with establishing what happened and what the risks are to this individual.

Evidencing AC2.3 to your assessor:

For AC2.3 you must evidence your knowledge of the different ways to ensure that evidence of abuse is preserved.

Assessment Methods:

Oral/Written Questioning or **Discussion** or a **Spidergram**.

- You can **tell** your assessor about the different ways to ensure that evidence of abuse is preserved.
- Or, you can **talk** to your assessor about the different ways to ensure that evidence of abuse is preserved.
- Or, you can complete a **spidergram** showing the different ways to ensure that evidence of abuse is preserved.

REMEMBER TO:

- Provide examples of the **different ways** to ensure that evidence of abuse is preserved.
- Ensure that the **examples** relate to different types of abuse.
- Think about the different ways to ensure that evidence of abuse is preserved in **your work setting**.

Learning Outcome 3: Understand the national and local context of safeguarding and protection from abuse

Assessment Criterion 3.1: Identify national policies and local systems that relate to safeguarding and protection from abuse

What does AC3.1 mean?

- The lead word **identify** means that you must **make clear** the different national policies and local systems that are in place and relate to safeguarding and protection from abuse.
- Your **list** must make clear **both** national policies and local systems that are in place.
- For the key words **national policies** you can think about the policies the government has in place in relation to safeguarding and protecting individuals from abuse.
- For the key words **local systems** you can think about the systems local authorities and organisations have in place in relation to safeguarding and protecting individuals from abuse, such as policies and procedures as well as multi-agency adult protection arrangements for a locality.
- For the key word **abuse** you can think about the danger and/or harm an individual may be in and/or have inflicted.

Read the following **Real Work Setting** scenario and think about how it relates to your work setting and role:

Real Work Setting

Name: Kathleen

Job role: Senior Support Worker to young adults who have learning disabilities

Kathleen works as a Senior Support Worker and her duties include: managing a small team of Support Workers; leading shifts; arranging activities; supporting individuals with their lifestyles and personal choices on a day-to-day basis.

National policies and local systems: Kathleen's induction involved reading through the safeguarding file. The information contained within this included the main pieces of legislation and policies that have been introduced in the UK to safeguard and protect individuals from abuse, as well as a list of all the relevant policies, procedures and professionals that are available in her workplace and in the local authority where she works.

Evidencing AC3.1 to your assessor:

For AC3.1 you must evidence your understanding of the different national policies and local systems that relate to safeguarding and protecting individuals from abuse.

Assessment Methods:

Oral/Written Questioning or Discussion or a Spidergram.

- You can **tell** your assessor about the different national policies and local systems that relate to safeguarding and protecting individuals from abuse.
- Or, you can **talk** to your assessor about the different national policies and local systems that relate to safeguarding and protecting individuals from abuse.
- Or, you can complete a **spidergram** showing the different national policies and local systems that relate to safeguarding and protecting individuals from abuse.

REMEMBER TO:

- Provide examples of **different** national policies and local systems.
- Ensure that the **examples** you provide relate to safeguarding and protecting individuals from abuse.
- Think about the different policies, procedures and systems available in **your work setting** and in the local authority in which you work.

Learning Outcome 3: Understand the national and local context of safeguarding and protection from abuse

Assessment Criterion 3.2: Explain the roles of different agencies in safeguarding and protecting individuals from abuse

What does AC3.2 mean?

- The lead word **explain** means that you must **make clear** the roles of different agencies in safeguarding and protecting individuals from abuse.
- Your **account** must make clear the roles of **different** agencies, as well as the reasons why they are involved.
- For the key word **agencies** you can think about the different organisations that work with the individual and/or are involved in their lives.

Read the following **Real Work Setting** scenario and think about how it relates to your work setting and role:

Real Work Setting

Name: Kathleen

Job role: Senior Support Worker to young adults who have learning disabilities

(See page 49 for a description of the role.)

Roles of different agencies: Kathleen and the safeguarding officer are working together to prepare a refresher safeguarding training session for the team. Together they have developed a list of numerous agencies that are involved in safeguarding and protecting individuals from abuse, including the local authority, social services, health care agencies, the Care Quality Commission, care organisations, voluntary agencies and the police. For each one they plan to ask the team to research what their role is, and how and why they are involved in safeguarding and protecting individuals from abuse.

Evidencing AC3.2 to your assessor:

For AC3.2 you must evidence your understanding of the roles of different agencies in safeguarding and protecting individuals from abuse.

Assessment Methods:

Oral/Written Questioning or **Discussion** or a **Personal Statement**.

- You can **tell** your assessor the roles of different agencies in safeguarding and protecting individuals from abuse, as well as the reasons why they are involved.
- Or, you can **talk** to your assessor about the roles of different agencies in safeguarding and protecting individuals from abuse, as well as the reasons why they are involved.
- Or, you can write a **personal statement** about the roles of different agencies in safeguarding and protecting individuals from abuse, as well as the reasons why they are involved.

REMEMBER TO:

- Provide an **account** of the roles of different agencies in safeguarding and protecting individuals from abuse and explain why they are involved.
- Include **varied** reasons.
- Think about **your work setting** and the different agencies that are involved in safeguarding and protecting individuals, including the reasons why they are involved.

Learning Outcome 3: Understand the national and local context of safeguarding and protection from abuse

Assessment Criterion 3.3: Identify reports into serious failures to protect individuals from abuse

What does AC3.3 mean?

- The lead word **identify** means that you must **make clear** the different reports into serious failures to protect individuals from abuse.
- Your **list** must make clear **different** reports that relate to serious failures to protect individuals from abuse.
- For the key word **reports** you can think about incidents of serious abuse that have been revealed and resulted in investigations and serious case reviews.

Read the following **Real Work Setting** scenario and think about how it relates to your work setting and role:

Real Work Setting
Name: Kathleen
Job role: Senior Support Worker to young adults who have learning disabilities
(See page 49 for a description of the role.)
Reports into serious failures to protect individuals from abuse: One of the activities Kathleen and the safeguarding officer have developed for the refresher safeguarding training session for the team includes asking the team to research examples from newspapers and the internet of different case reviews that have taken place into serious failures to protect individuals from abuse.

Evidencing AC3.3 to your assessor:

For AC3.3 you must evidence your understanding of different reports into serious failures to protect individuals from abuse.

Assessment Methods:

Oral/Written Questioning or Discussion or a Spidergram.

- You can **tell** your assessor about the different reports into serious failures to protect individuals from abuse.
- Or, you can **talk** to your assessor about the different reports into serious failures to protect individuals from abuse.
- Or, you can complete a **spidergram** showing the different reports into serious failures to protect individuals from abuse.

REMEMBER TO:

- Provide examples of **different** reports into serious failures to protect individuals from abuse.
- Ensure that the **examples** you provide relate to protecting individuals from abuse.
- Think about the different reports into serious failures to protect individuals from abuse that you may have discussed with others in **your work setting** and/or read or heard about in the media.

Learning Outcome 3: Understand the national and local context of safeguarding and protection from abuse

Assessment Criterion 3.4: Identify sources of information and advice about your role in safeguarding and protecting individuals from abuse

What does AC3.4 mean?

- The lead word **identify** means that you must **make clear** the different sources of both information and advice that are available.
- Your **list** must make clear **different** sources that relate to your role in safeguarding and protecting individuals from abuse.
- For the key word **sources** you can think about the places and people within and outside your workplace from which information and advice can be obtained.

Read the following **Real Work Setting** scenario and think about how it relates to your work setting and role:

Real Work Setting

Name: Kathleen

Job role: Senior Support Worker to young adults who have learning disabilities

(See page 49 for a description of the role.)

Sources of information and advice: As part of the refresher safeguarding training session for the team, Kathleen and the safeguarding officer plan to find out the team's knowledge about from whom and where they can access information and advice about their role within the workplace as well as other sources available externally. They then plan to draw up with the team a spidergram that reflects all their responses and to discuss the key sources that relate to their work setting and job roles.

Evidencing AC3.4 to your assessor:

For AC3.4 you must evidence your understanding of different sources of information and advice about your role in safeguarding and protecting individuals from abuse.

Assessment Methods:

Oral/Written Questioning or **Discussion** or **Spidergrams**.

- You can **tell** your assessor about the different sources of information and advice about your role in safeguarding and protecting individuals from abuse.
- Or, you can **talk** to your assessor about the different sources of information and advice about your role in safeguarding and protecting individuals from abuse.
- Or, you can complete two **spidergrams**: one showing the different sources of information, and another showing the different sources of advice about your role in safeguarding and protecting individuals from abuse.

REMEMBER TO:
- Provide examples of **different sources of both information and advice**.
- Ensure that the **examples** you provide relate to safeguarding and protecting individuals from abuse.
- Think about the different sources of information and advice about your role in safeguarding and protecting individuals from abuse that are available in **your work setting**.

Learning Outcome 4: Understand ways to reduce the likelihood of abuse

Assessment Criterion 4.1: Explain how the likelihood of abuse may be reduced by working with person-centred values, encouraging active participation and promoting choice and rights

What does AC4.1 mean?

⊙ The lead word **explain** means that you must **make clear** how working practices that use person-centred values, encourage active participation and promote choice and rights can reduce the likelihood of abuse.

⊙ Your **account** must make clear the **different** ways that each of these working practices can help to reduce the likelihood of abuse, as well as the reasons why.

⊙ For the key words **person-centred values** you can think about how you respect and support individuals' uniqueness.

⊙ For the key words **active participation** you can think about how you can support individuals to be fully involved in all aspects of their lives.

Read the following **Real Work Setting** scenario and think about how it relates to your work setting and role:

Real Work Setting

Name: Marion
Job role: Senior Personal Assistant to adults who have physical disabilities
Marion has been working as a Senior Personal Assistant for four years. Her Senior responsibilities include: assisting individuals to live independently in their own homes; supporting individuals to pursue their own interests; administering medication; working closely with colleagues and Service Managers.
Working with person-centred values: Marion ensures she treats each individual she works with as a unique person and with dignity and respect. Marion always encourages each individual to do as much for themselves as they can and asks how best she can support them in this.
Encouraging active participation: Marion likes to ensure that each individual is fully involved in how they wish to achieve their goals and enables each individual to make their own choices and decisions.
Promoting choice and rights: Marion likes to promote individuals' choices and rights by providing them with sufficient information about the options available and discussing with them which they would prefer.

Evidencing AC4.1 to your assessor:

For AC4.1 you must evidence your understanding of how the likelihood of abuse may be reduced by working with person-centred values, encouraging active participation, and promoting choice and rights.

Assessment Methods:

Oral/Written Questioning or Discussion or a Personal Statement or Reflection.

● You can **tell** your assessor about how the likelihood of abuse may be reduced by working with person-centred values, encouraging active participation, and promoting choice and rights.

● Or, you can **talk** to your assessor about how the likelihood of abuse may be reduced by working with person-centred values, encouraging active participation, and promoting choice and rights.

● Or, you can write a **personal statement or reflection** about your experience of how the likelihood of abuse may be reduced by working with person-centred values, encouraging active participation, and promoting choice and rights.

REMEMBER TO:

● Provide an **account** and explain how the likelihood of abuse may be reduced by working with person-centred values, encouraging active participation, and promoting choice and rights.

● Include **varied** reasons why the likelihood of abuse may be reduced.

● Include **details** about each of the three working approaches.

● Think about **your work setting** and how different approaches to working with individuals can reduce the likelihood of abuse.

Learning Outcome 4: Understand ways to reduce the likelihood of abuse

Assessment Criterion 4.2: Explain the importance of an accessible complaints procedure for reducing the likelihood of abuse

What does AC4.2 mean?

- The lead word **explain** means that you must **make clear** how an accessible complaints procedure can reduce the likelihood of abuse.
- Your **account** must make clear the **different** ways an accessible complaints procedure can help reduce the likelihood of abuse, as well as the reasons why.
- For the key word **accessible** you can think about how to ensure that a complaints procedure is open, easily understood and made available to all.

Read the following **Real Work Setting** scenario and think about how it relates to your work setting and role:

Real Work Setting

Name: Marion

Job role: Senior Personal Assistant to adults who have physical disabilities

(See page 53 for a description of the role.)

An accessible complaints procedure: Marion checks with each individual she works with that they have the service's complaints procedure in a format that they can understand and that they feel confident about what to do if they are unhappy about any aspect of the service. If any individual is not confident about when and/or how to follow the complaints process, Marion provides them with suitable information to enable them to do so.

Evidencing AC4.2 to your assessor:

For AC4.2 you must evidence your understanding of the importance of an accessible complaints procedure for reducing the likelihood of abuse.

Assessment Methods:

Oral/Written Questioning or **Discussion** or a **Personal Statement** or **Reflection**.

- You can **tell** your assessor the reasons why an accessible complaints procedure is important for reducing the likelihood of abuse.
- Or, you can **talk** to your assessor about the reasons why an accessible complaints procedure is important for reducing the likelihood of abuse.
- Or, you can write a **personal statement or reflection** about the reasons why an accessible complaints procedure is important for reducing the likelihood of abuse.

REMEMBER TO:

- Provide an **account** and explain why an accessible complaints procedure is important for reducing the likelihood of abuse.
- Include **varied** reasons.
- Include **details** about how the likelihood of abuse can be reduced.
- Think about **your work setting** and the importance of an accessible complaints procedure for reducing the likelihood of abuse.

Learning Outcome 5: Know how to recognise and report unsafe practices

Assessment Criterion 5.1: Describe unsafe practices that may affect the well-being of individuals

What does AC5.1 mean?

- The lead word **describe** means that you must provide an **account** that **details** the unsafe practices that may affect the well-being of individuals.
- Your **account** must detail **different** factors that may affect the well-being of individuals.
- For the key words **unsafe practices** you can think about poor working practices as well as resource and operational difficulties, such as insufficient staff or poorly maintained equipment.
- For the key word **well-being** you can think about an individual's physical, emotional and mental health.

Read the following **Real Work Setting** scenario and think about how it relates to your work setting and role:

Real Work Setting

Name: David

Job role: Senior Care Assistant to older people

David works as a Senior Residential Carer. His Senior responsibilities include: assisting in the supervision and appraisals of Care Assistants; assisting the manager in the administration of medication; contributing to the provision of quality care and support to individuals on a daily basis.

Unsafe practices: David has led the shifts over this weekend at the residential care home and has noted a number of unsafe working practices. These include Care Assistants not ensuring individuals' call bells in their rooms are within their reach, insufficient clean linen being available, and Care Assistants not following their allocated duties as set out at the beginning of the shift.

Evidencing AC5.1 to your assessor:

For AC5.1 you must evidence your knowledge of different unsafe practices that may affect the well-being of individuals.

Assessment Methods:

Oral/Written Questioning or Discussion or a Personal Statement or Reflection.

- You can **tell** your assessor about the different unsafe practices that may affect the well-being of individuals.
- Or, you can **talk** to your assessor about the different unsafe practices that may affect the well-being of individuals.
- Or, you can write a **personal statement or reflection** about your experience of the different unsafe practices that may affect the well-being of individuals in your work setting.

REMEMBER TO:

- Provide a detailed **account** of different unsafe practices that may affect the well-being of individuals.
- Include examples of different unsafe practices.
- Include how these examples can affect the well-being of individuals.
- Think about examples of unsafe practices that, if they occurred, may affect the well-being of individuals in **your work setting**.

Learning Outcome 5: Know how to recognise and report unsafe practices

Assessment Criterion 5.2: Explain the actions to take if unsafe practices have been identified

What does AC5.2 mean?

- The lead word **explain** means that you must **make clear** the actions to take if unsafe practices have been identified, as well as the reasons why.
- Your **account** must make clear the **different** actions to take, as well as the reasons why.
- For the key word **actions** you can think about the process you must follow if unsafe practices have been identified

Read the following **Real Work Setting** scenario and think about how it relates to your work setting and role:

Real Work Setting
Name: David
Job role: Senior Care Assistant to older people
(See page 55 for a description of the role.)
Actions taken: David has spoken with each relevant Care Assistant and brought to their attention why their working practices are unsafe. David has also explained to each Care Assistant that he will be reporting this to the Home Manager and raising these issues formally in their supervisions.

Evidencing AC5.2 to your assessor:

For AC5.2 you must evidence your understanding of the actions to take if unsafe practices have been identified.

Assessment Methods:

Oral/Written Questioning or **Discussion** or a **Personal Statement or Reflection**.

- You can **tell** your assessor the actions to take if unsafe practices have been identified, as well as the reasons why.
- Or, you can **talk** to your assessor the actions to take if unsafe practices have been identified, as well as the reasons why.
- Or, you can write a **personal statement or reflection** about your experience of the actions to take if unsafe practices have been identified, as well as the reasons why.

RREMEMBER TO:

- Provide an **account** of the actions to take if unsafe practices have been identified, and **explain why**.
- Include **varied** reasons.
- Include **details** about the process that must be followed when unsafe practices have been identified.
- Think about **your work setting** and the actions to take if unsafe practices have been identified.

Learning Outcome 5: Know how to recognise and report unsafe practices

Assessment Criterion 5.3: Describe the actions to take if suspected abuse or unsafe practices have been reported but nothing has been done in response

What does AC5.3 mean?

- The lead word **describe** means that you must provide an **account** that **details** the actions to take if suspected abuse or unsafe practices have been reported but nothing has been done in response, as well as the reasons why.
- Your **account** must detail the **different** actions to take, as well as the reasons why.
- For the key word **actions** you can think about the process you must follow if unsafe practices have been identified.

Read the following **Real Work Setting** scenario and think about how it relates to your work setting and role:

Real Work Setting

Name: David

Job role: Senior Care Assistant to older people

(See page 55 for a description of the role.)

Further actions if nothing has been done in response: David has referenced the home's complaints procedure and is aware of his rights to report his concerns to the home's owner and/or the Care Quality Commission if his manager or the owner does not respond satisfactorily to the concerns he has noted.

Evidencing AC5.3 to your assessor:

For AC5.3 you must evidence your knowledge of the actions to take if suspected abuse or unsafe practices have been reported but nothing has been done in response.

Assessment Methods:

Oral/Written Questioning or **Discussion** or a **Personal Statement** or **Reflection**.

- You can **tell** your assessor the actions to take if suspected abuse or unsafe practices have been reported but nothing has been done in response, as well as the reasons why.
- Or, you can **talk** to your assessor about the actions to take if suspected abuse or unsafe practices have been reported but nothing has been done in response, as well as the reasons why.
- Or, you can write a **personal statement or reflection** about your experience of the actions to take if suspected abuse or unsafe practices have been reported but nothing has been done in response, as well as the reasons why.

REMEMBER TO:

- Provide an **account** and detail the actions to take if suspected abuse or unsafe practices have been reported but nothing has been done in response, as well as the reasons why.
- Include **varied** reasons.
- Include **details** about the process that must be followed if suspected abuse or unsafe practices have been reported but nothing has been done in response.
- Think about **your work setting** and the actions to take if suspected abuse or unsafe practices have been reported but nothing has been done in response.

Learning Outcome 1: Understand working relationships in health and social care

Assessment Criterion 1.1: Explain how a working relationship is different from a personal relationship

What does AC1.1 mean?

- The lead word **explain** means that you must **make clear** the differences that exist between working and personal relationships.
- Your **account** must make clear how working and personal relationships are **different**.
- For the key words **working relationship** you can think about the different people you have contact with as part of your work role.
- For the key words **personal relationship** you can think about the different people you have contact with outside work.

Read the following **Real Work Setting** scenario and think about how it relates to your work setting and role:

Real Work Setting

Name: Alex

Job role: Senior Personal Assistant

Alex has been working as a Senior Personal Assistant for one year, providing support to adults with disabilities so that they can maintain their independence and live in their own homes. Alex leads a small team of Personal Assistants and provides guidance, support and regular supervisions. Alex also ensures he reviews all support packages in place with each individual so as to confirm all support being provided is fully meeting their needs and preferences.

Working and personal relationships: Alex will be inducting a recently recruited Personal Assistant who is new to the role and to this area of work, so he has prepared some induction material about Personal Assistants' roles and responsibilities, including the range of individuals Personal Assistants will work alongside as part of their roles and also the boundaries that must be adhered to when supporting individuals to socialise and participate in activities in the evenings and weekends.

Evidencing AC1.1 to your assessor:

For AC1.1 you must evidence your understanding of the differences between a working relationship and a personal relationship.

Assessment Methods:

Oral/Written Questioning or Discussion or a **Personal Statement**.

- You can **tell** your assessor the differences between a working and a personal relationship.
- Or, you can **talk** to your assessor about the differences between a working and a personal relationship.
- Or, you can write a **personal statement** about the differences between a working and a personal relationship.

REMEMBER TO:

- Provide an **account** and **explain** the differences between working and personal relationships.
- Include **varied** differences.
- Include **details** about what is meant by working and personal relationships.
- Think about **your work setting** and the working relationships you have.

Learning Outcome 1: Understand working relationships in health and social care

Assessment Criterion 1.2: Describe different working relationships in health and social care settings

What does AC1.2 mean?

- The lead word **describe** means that you must provide an **account** that **details** the different working relationships in health and social care settings.
- Your **account** must detail **different** working relationships that exist in health and social care settings.
- For the key words **working relationships** you can think about the different people you have contact with as part of your work role.

Read the following **Real Work Setting** scenario and think about how it relates to your work setting and role:

Real Work Setting

Name: Alex

Job role: Senior Personal Assistant

(See page 58 for a description of the role.)

Working relationships: As part of the Personal Assistant's induction Alex plans to ask the Personal Assistant to find out the roles of as many people as he can that he will be having contact with as part of his role, both within and outside the organisation.

Evidencing AC1.2 to your assessor:

For AC1.2 you must evidence your understanding of different working relationships in health and social care settings.

Assessment Methods:

Oral/Written Questioning or **Discussion** or a **Personal Statement** or **Reflection**.

- You can **tell** your assessor about different working relationships in health and social care settings.
- Or, you can **talk** to your assessor about different working relationships in health and social care settings.
- Or, you can write a **personal statement or reflection** about your experience of the different working relationships in **your work setting**.

REMEMBER TO:

- Provide a detailed **account** of different working relationships in health and social care settings.
- Include **examples** of different working relationships.
- Think about examples of working relationships in **your work setting**.

Learning Outcome 2: Be able to work in ways that are agreed with the employer

Assessment Criterion 2.1: Describe why it is important to adhere to the agreed scope of the job role

What does AC2.1 mean?

- ○ The lead word **describe** means that you must provide an **account** that **details** the reasons why it is important to carry out the duties and responsibilities of your job role as set out in your job description.
- ○ Your **account** must detail **different reasons why** it is important to adhere to the agreed scope of the job role.
- ○ For the key words **scope of the job role** you can think about the duties and responsibilities you are required to carry out as part of your job role.

Read the following **Real Work Setting** scenario and think about how it relates to your work setting and role:

Real Work Setting

Name: Beth

Job role: Senior Care Assistant for older people

Beth has been working as a Senior Care Assistant for twelve years. Her duties include: supervising a team of Care Assistants; providing cover in the absence of the team leader; updating care plans; leading residents' review meetings; assisting in the delivery of care and support to residents.

Adhering to the scope of the job role: Beth has agreed with the Home Manager that she will reduce her hours, as she wishes to spend more time at home with her family, and that she will support the recruitment of another part-time Senior Care Assistant. As part of this new member of staff's induction Beth will discuss the reasons why it is important to carry out the job's associated duties as per the job description, as well as the consequences of not doing so for all those involved.

Evidencing AC2.1 to your assessor:

For AC2.1 you must evidence your knowledge of why it is important to adhere to the agreed scope of the job role.

Assessment Methods:

Oral/Written Questioning or **Discussion** or a **Personal Statement** or **Reflection**.

- You can **tell** your assessor about different reasons it is important to adhere to the agreed scope of the job role.
- Or, you can **talk** to your assessor about different reasons it is important to adhere to the agreed scope of the job role.
- Or, you can write a **personal statement or reflection** about the different reasons it is important to adhere to the agreed scope of the job role.

REMEMBER TO:

- Provide a detailed **account** of why it is important to adhere to the agreed scope of the job role.
- Include examples of different reasons why it is important to adhere to the agreed scope of the job role.
- Think about the consequences of not adhering to the scope of the job role.
- Think about the importance of adhering to the scope of job roles in **your work setting**.

Learning Outcome 2: Be able to work in ways that are agreed with the employer

Assessment Criterion 2.2: Access full and up-to-date details of agreed ways of working

What does AC2.2 mean?

- The lead word **access** means that you must **be able to show** through **your work practices** how you can obtain full and up-to-date details of agreed ways of working.
- Your **observations** of your work practices must include you obtaining full and up-to-date details of agreed ways of working.
- For the key word **access** you can think about the different documents and records you obtain, read and complete as part of your job role.
- For the key words **agreed ways of working** you can think about your work setting's policies and procedures, as well as the specific guidelines that are in place for the individuals to whom you provide care and support.

Read the following **Real Work Setting** scenario and think about how it relates to your work setting and role:

Real Work Setting

Name: Beth

Job role: Senior Care Assistant for older people

(See page 60 for a description of the role.)

Accessing full and up-to-date details of agreed ways of working: Beth has agreed as part of the new staff member's induction to make available the home's policies and procedures as well as the current care plans in place for each of the residents.

Evidencing AC2.2 to your assessor:

For AC2.2 you must evidence your skills in accessing full and up-to-date details of agreed ways of working.

Assessment Methods:

Direct Observation of your work practices.

- You can **show** your assessor how you access full and up-to-date details of agreed ways of working.
- You can also use records that you have completed as part of your day-to-day activities in your current job role as a supporting piece of **work product evidence**.

REMEMBER TO:

- Make arrangements for **observation** of **your work practices**.
- Include evidence from your work practices of accessing agreed ways of working.
- Include evidence of how any documents and records you access are complete and up-to-date.
- Think about how you access agreed ways of working in your work setting.
- Think about different documents and records that are available to you in **your work setting**.

Learning Outcome 2: Be able to work in ways that are agreed with the employer

Assessment Criterion 2.3: Implement agreed ways of working

What does AC2.3 mean?

- ○ The lead word **implement** means that you must **be able to show** through **your work practices** how to put into practice agreed ways of working.
- ○ Your **observations** of your work practices must include you putting agreed ways of working into practice in your work setting.
- ○ For the key word **implement** you can think about how you put into practice agreed ways of working.
- ○ For the key words **agreed ways of working** you can think about your work setting's policies and procedures, as well as the specific guidelines that are in place for the individuals to whom you provide care and support.

Read the following **Real Work Setting** scenario and think about how it relates to your work setting and role:

Real Work Setting

Name: Beth

Job role: Senior Care Assistant for older people

(See page 60 for a description of the role.)

Implementing agreed ways of working: Beth has agreed to work alongside the part-time Senior Care Assistant as part of her induction into her work role. She thinks that it will be a good idea for this to involve both work shadowing and observations of her practice so as to ensure that the agreed ways of working in the home are being effectively put into practice.

Evidencing AC2.3 to your assessor:

For AC2.3 you must evidence your skills to implement agreed ways of working.

Assessment Methods:

Direct Observation of your work practices.

- You can **show** your assessor how you put into practice agreed ways of working.
- You can also use records that you have completed as part of your day-to-day activities in your current job role as a supporting piece of **work product evidence.**

REMEMBER TO:

- Make arrangements for **observation** of **your work practices**.
- Include evidence of how your work practices put agreed ways of working into practice.
- Include evidence of how any documents and records you access are complete and up to date.
- Think about how you put into practice agreed ways of working in your work setting.
- Think about **different documents and records** that you complete in **your work setting** as part of your job role.

Learning Outcome 3: Be able to work in partnership with others

Assessment Criterion 3.1: Explain why it is important to work in partnership with others

What does AC3.1 mean?

○ The lead word **explain** means that you must **make clear** the reasons why it is important to work in partnership with others.

○ Your **account** must make clear the **importance** of working in partnership with others.

○ For the key words **work in partnership** you can think about how and why you work together with other people to carry out your job role effectively.

○ For the key word **others** you can think about the people you work with, both within and outside your work setting. These may include colleagues, individuals who require care or support, their friends, families or advocates.

Read the following **Real Work Setting** scenario and think about how it relates to your work setting and role:

Real Work Setting

Name: Janet

Job role: Senior Support Worker

Janet has been working as a Senior Support Worker for six years and her Senior duties include: supporting people with alcohol-related difficulties in their own homes; providing coaching and mentoring to a team of three Support Workers; supporting the team to maintain and review individuals' support plans and provide high quality individualised support.

Working in partnership with others: Janet has arranged for a team meeting to take place this week. She plans to review with staff the arrangements in place for liaising with individuals' families and the other professionals involved in their lives, including how working alongside others can benefit the service provided as well as working relationships.

Evidencing AC3.1 to your assessor:

For AC3.1 you must evidence your understanding of the reasons why it is important to work in partnership with others.

Assessment Methods:

Oral/Written Questioning or **Discussion** or a **Personal Statement** or **Reflection**.

● You can **tell** your assessor about the reasons why it is important to work in partnership with others.

● Or, you can **talk** to your assessor about the reasons why it is important to work in partnership with others.

● Or, you can write a **personal statement or reflection** about your experience of the reasons why it is important to work in partnership with others.

REMEMBER TO:

● Provide an **account** and **explain** the reasons why it is important to work in partnership with others.

● Include **varied** examples of reasons why.

● Include **details** about the importance of working in partnership with others.

● Think about **your work setting** and the working relationships you have.

Learning Outcome 3: Be able to work in partnership with others

Assessment Criterion 3.2: Demonstrate ways of working that can help improve partnership working

What does AC3.2 mean?

- The lead word **demonstrate** means that you must **be able to show** through **your work practices** ways of working that can help improve working in partnership with others.
- Your **observations** of your work practices must include you putting into practice **different ways** of working to improve partnership working.
- For the key words **partnership working** you can think about how and why you work together with other people to carry out your job role effectively.

Read the following **Real Work Setting** scenario and think about how it relates to your work setting and role:

Real Work Setting

Name: Janet

Job role: Senior Support Worker

(See page 63 for a description of the role.)

Improving partnership working: As part of the team meeting Janet will be asking the team to think about ways of working that can help to improve how they work alongside each other, individuals, their families, friends and the other professionals involved in their lives.

Evidencing AC3.2 to your assessor:

For AC3.2 you must evidence your skills to work in ways that help improve partnership working.

Assessment Method:

Direct Observation of your work practices.

- You can **show** your assessor or an expert witness how you work in ways that help improve partnership working.

REMEMBER TO:

- Make arrangements for **observation** of **your work practices**.
- Include **evidence** of how your work practices can help improve partnership working.
- Include evidence of **different ways** of working that can help improve partnership working with others.
- Think about how ways of working that you use in **your work setting** can help improve partnership working.

Learning Outcome 3: Be able to work in partnership with others

Assessment Criterion 3.3: Identify skills and approaches for resolving conflicts

What does AC3.3 mean?

- The lead word **identify** means that you must **make clear** the skills and approaches needed for resolving conflicts.
- Your **list** must include **different** examples of skills and approaches.
- For the key word **skills** you can think about what you need to know and be able to do to resolve conflicts.
- For the key word **approaches** you can think about different ways of working that can be used to resolve conflicts.

Read the following **Real Work Setting** scenario and think about how it relates to your work setting and role:

Real Work Setting
Name: Janet
Job role: Senior Support Worker
(See page 63 for a description of the role.)
Identifying skills and approaches for resolving conflicts: Janet has arranged a meeting with two Support Workers, as a conflict has arisen around supporting one individual to access football training on Saturday mornings. One Support Worker is very keen to support the individual on a Saturday and ensures he always attends; the other Support Worker does not think that this individual is interested in football and so does not support him to do this activity. Neither Support Worker agrees with the other's decisions or working approaches.

Evidencing AC3.3 to your assessor:

For AC3.3 you must evidence your knowledge of skills and approaches that are needed for resolving conflicts.

Assessment Methods:

Oral/Written Questioning or **Discussion** or a **Spidergram**.

- You can **tell** your assessor the different skills and approaches that are needed for resolving conflicts.
- *Or*, you can **talk** to your assessor about the different skills and approaches that are needed for resolving conflicts.
- *Or*, you can complete a **spidergram** showing the different skills and approaches that are needed for resolving conflicts.

REMEMBER TO:

- **List** both skills and approaches that are needed for resolving conflicts.
- Include **different** examples of **both** skills and approaches in your list.
- Ensure they relate to resolving conflicts.
- Think about the skills and approaches that have been used in **your work setting** for resolving conflicts.

Learning Outcome 3: Be able to work in partnership with others

Assessment Criterion 3.4: Demonstrate how and when to access support and advice about partnership working and resolving conflicts

What does AC3.4 mean?

- The lead word **demonstrate** means that you must **be able to show** through **your work practices** how and when to access support and advice about partnership working and resolving conflicts.
- Your **observations** of your work practices must include you accessing support and advice about partnership working and resolving conflicts.
- For the key words **partnership working** you can think about the different working relationships you have with others.
- For the key word **conflicts** you can think about the disagreements that may arise in your work setting.

Read the following **Real Work Setting** scenario and think about how it relates to your work setting and role:

Real Work Setting

Name: Janet

Job role: Senior Support Worker

(See page 63 for a description of the role.)

Accessing support and advice: Before having the meeting Janet has discussed the situation with her manager and both have agreed on the various different ways that the two Support Workers can be guided to talk about and resolve the conflict over how they work with this individual, including how they can ensure they work more effectively together as a team. Janet agrees to meet up with her manager after the meeting to provide her with feedback in relation to a way forward.

Evidencing AC3.4 to your assessor:

For AC3.4 you must evidence your skills of how and when to access support and advice about partnership working and resolving conflicts.

Assessment Method:

Direct Observation of your work practices.

- You can **show** your assessor or an expert witness how and when to access support and advice about partnership working and resolving conflicts.

REMEMBER TO:

- Make arrangements for **observation** of **your work practices**.
- Include evidence of **how** you have accessed support and advice.
- Include evidence of **when** you have accessed support and advice.
- Think about sources of support and advice available to you **within and outside your work setting**.

Learning Outcome 1: Understand the application of person-centred approaches in health and social care

Assessment Criterion 1.1: Explain how and why person-centred values must influence all aspects of health and social care work

What does AC1.1 mean?

- The lead word **explain** means that you must **make clear** how and why person-centred values must influence all aspects of health and social care work.
- Your **account** must make clear **different ways how**, as well as **different reasons why**, person-centred values must influence all aspects of health and social care work.
- For the key words **person-centred values** you can think about how to carry out your job role in a way that respects the individuals you work with and supports them to lead their lives as they wish.

Read the following **Real Work Setting** scenario and think about how it relates to your work setting and role:

Real Work Setting

Name: Marcia

Job role: Senior Care Assistant for older people

Marcia's Senior responsibilities include supporting the team of Care Assistants to provide high quality support to residents with all aspects of their daily living, including administering medication, leading residents' review meetings, and developing and updating residents' care plans.

Person-centred values: A recently recruited Care Assistant will be shadowing Marcia on her shifts for one week, and Marcia plans to show through her working practices how she and the rest of the team are able to provide high quality care to the residents. She also plans to discuss with the Care Assistant the reasons why it is important for person-centred values to underpin all aspects of care provided.

Evidencing AC1.1 to your assessor:

For AC1.1 you must evidence your understanding of how and why person-centred values must influence all aspects of health and social care work.

Assessment Methods:

Oral/Written Questioning or **Discussion** or a **Personal Statement**.

- You can **tell** your assessor about how and why person-centred values must influence all aspects of health and social care work.
- *Or*, you can **talk** to your assessor about how and why person-centred values must influence all aspects of health and social care work.
- *Or*, you can write a **personal statement** about how and why person-centred values must influence all aspects of health and social care work.

REMEMBER TO:

- Provide an **account** and **explain** how and why person-centred values must influence all aspects of health and social care work.
- Include **varied** examples of how and the reasons why person-centred values must influence all aspects of health and social care work.
- Include **details** about what person-centred values are.
- Think about **your work setting** and how and why person-centred values must influence all aspects of health and social care work.

Learning Outcome 1: Understand the application of person-centred approaches in health and social care

Assessment Criterion 1.2: Evaluate the use of care plans in applying person-centred values

What does AC1.2 mean?

- The lead word **evaluate** means that you must **be able to show** how you assess to what extent care plans can be used in applying person-centred values.
- Your **evaluation** must include consideration of the role of using care plans in applying person-centred values.
- For the key words **care plans** you can think about how individuals' day-to-day care needs, support needs and preferences are met. Care plans may also be known by other names, such as support plans or individual plans.
- For the key words **person-centred values** you can think about how to carry out your job role in a way that respects the individuals you work with and supports them to lead their lives as they wish.

Read the following **Real Work Setting** scenario and think about how it relates to your work setting and role:

Real Work Setting
Name: Marcia
Job role: Senior Care Assistant for older people
(See page 67 for a description of the role.)
Using care plans: Marcia plans to review individuals' care plans with them and, together with their families and other people involved in their lives, to consider to what extent these have enabled them to live their lives as they would like, including their day-to-day activities and working towards their future wishes and goals.

Evidencing AC1.2 to your assessor:

For AC1.2 you must evidence your understanding of how to evaluate the use of care plans in applying person-centred values.

Assessment Methods:

Oral/Written Questioning or **Discussion** or a **Personal Statement.**

- You can **tell** your assessor about your evaluation of the use of care plans in applying person-centred values.
- Or, you can **talk** to your assessor about your evaluation of the use of care plans in applying person-centred values.
- Or, you can write a **personal statement** about your evaluation of the use of care plans in applying person-centred values.

REMEMBER TO:

- Provide an **account** and **explain** how care plans can be used in applying person-centred values.
- Include **varied** examples of how care plans can be used in applying person-centred values.
- Include **details** about how effective care plans are in applying person-centred values.
- Think about **your work setting** and whether care plans are used in applying person-centred values.

Learning Outcome 2: Be able to work in a person-centred way

Assessment Criterion 2.1: Work with an individual and others to find out the individual's history, preferences, wishes and needs

What does AC2.1 mean?

- The lead words **work with** mean that you must **be able to show** through **your work practices** how you work with an individual and others to find out the individual's history, preferences, wishes and needs.
- Your **observations** of your work practices must include you working with an individual and others to find out the individual's history, preferences, wishes and needs.
- For the key word **others** you can think about the different people involved in an individual's life. These may include your colleagues, individuals who require care or support, and the individual's friends, families or advocates.
- For the key word **history** you can think about the background and upbringing of the individual.
- For the key word **preferences** you can think about the day-to-day choices an individual makes.

Read the following **Real Work Setting** scenario and think about how it relates to your work setting and role:

Real Work Setting

Name: John

Job role: Senior Home Carer

John has been working as a Senior Home Carer for three years. His Senior responsibilities include coordinating and delivering individualised care to older people and people with disabilities in their own homes. John also reviews and updates individuals' care plans and supports individuals with day-to-day tasks.

Finding out an individual's history, preferences, wishes and needs: John will be visiting an individual at home for the first time to develop an individual plan of care and support. He plans to attend the visit with the two Support Workers who have been allocated to this individual. John has phoned the individual, who has explained that his sister and advocate will also be attending.

Evidencing AC2.1 to your assessor:

For AC2.1 you must evidence your skills to work with an individual and others to find out the individual's history, preferences, wishes and needs.

Assessment Methods:

Direct Observation of your work practices.

- You can **show** your assessor or an expert witness how you work with an individual and others to find out the individual's history, preferences, wishes and needs.
- You can use the information you have found out about an individual and documented in their care plan as a supporting piece of **work product evidence**.

REMEMBER TO:

- Make arrangements for **observation** of **your work practices**.
- Include evidence of how you work with an individual and others.
- Include evidence of what you have found out about the individual's history, preferences, wishes and needs.
- Think about sources of information available to you **within and outside your work setting**.

Learning Outcome 2: Be able to work in a person-centred way

Assessment Criterion 2.2: Demonstrate ways to put person-centred values into practice in a complex or sensitive situation

What does AC2.2 mean?

- The lead word **demonstrate** means that you must **be able to show** through **your work practices** how to put person-centred values into practice in a complex or sensitive situation.
- Your **observations** of your work practices must include you showing different ways you use to put person-centred values into practice in a complex or sensitive situation.
- For the key words **person-centred values** you can think about how to carry out your job role in a way that respects the individuals with whom you work and supports them to lead their lives as they wish.
- For the key word **complex** you can think about a situation that was difficult or confusing to deal with.
- For the key word **sensitive** you can think about a situation that needed to be dealt with carefully.
- **Complex or sensitive situations** may be distressing or traumatic, threatening or frightening, likely to have implications or consequences. They may be of a personal nature, or involve complex communication or cognitive needs.

Read the following **Real Work Setting** scenario and think about how it relates to your work setting and role:

Real Work Setting

Name: John
Job role: Senior Home Carer
(See page 69 for a description of the role.)
Putting person-centred values into practice: John has received a phone call from an individual's wife, who is concerned about her husband not wishing to accept that he is experiencing incontinence difficulties at night times. John listens to her concerns and suggests it may be useful in the first instance for her and her husband to access some information about different ways to manage incontinence and the aids and support that are available. John also suggests contacting the continence adviser or GP for further information.

Evidencing AC2.2 to your assessor:

For AC2.2 you must evidence your skills of different ways you put person-centred values into practice in a complex or sensitive situation.

Assessment Method:
Direct Observation of your work practices.

- You can **show** your assessor or an expert witness different ways you use to put person-centred values into practice in a complex or sensitive situation.

REMEMBER TO:
- Make arrangements for **observation** of **your work practices**.
- Include evidence of a complex or sensitive situation.
- Include evidence of the **different ways** you use to put person-centred values into practice.
- Think about a complex or sensitive situation that has occurred in **your work setting**.

Learning Outcome 2: Be able to work in a person-centred way

Assessment Criterion 2.3: Adapt actions and approaches in response to an individual's changing needs or preferences

What does AC2.3 mean?

- The lead word **adapt** means that you must **be able to show** through **your work practices** how to change **what** you do and **how** you do it in response to an individual's changing needs or preferences.
- Your **observations** of your work practices must include you showing how you can change and use **different** ways of working and approaches.
- For the key word **actions** you can think about the different ways you work.
- For the key word **approaches** you can think about the different ways you respond to changes in an individual.
- For the key word **preferences** you can think about the day-to-day choices an individual makes.

Read the following **Real Work Setting** scenario and think about how it relates to your work setting and role:

Real Work Setting

Name: John

Job role: Senior Home Carer

(See page 69 for a description of the role.)

Adapting actions and approaches: John has been supporting an individual to access the cinema tonight. The individual has decided that he no longer wishes to go the cinema and would prefer to visit a friend instead. Further to discussing this with the individual John has supported him to change his booking with the local cab company and informed them of the change in pick-up and return times, as well as the location being travelled to and picked up from. John has also agreed with the individual to escort him when travelling and to provide no further support.

Evidencing AC2.3 to your assessor:

For AC2.3 you must evidence your skills of adapting your actions and approaches in response to an individual's changing needs or preferences.

Assessment Method:

Direct Observation of your work practices.

- You can **show** your assessor or an expert witness how you adapt your actions and approaches in response to an individual's changing needs or preferences.

REMEMBER TO:

- Make arrangements for **observation** of **your work practices**.
- Include evidence of adapting both your actions and your approaches.
- Include evidence of the **different ways** you adapt your actions and approaches.
- Think about an individual in **your work setting** and how their needs or preferences have changed.

HSC036

AC 3.1

Learning Outcome 3: Be able to establish consent when providing care or support

Assessment Criterion 3.1: Analyse factors that influence the capacity of an individual to express consent

What does AC3.1 mean?

- The lead word **analyse** means that you must **examine in detail** different factors that influence the capacity of an individual to express consent.
- Your **account** must provide an analysis of **different** factors.
- For the key word **capacity** you can think about the ability of different individuals to make decisions.
- For the key word **consent** you can think about the ability of different individuals to show their agreement to carry out an activity or make a decision.

Read the following **Real Work Setting** scenario and think about how it relates to your work setting and role:

Real Work Setting

Name: Emma

Job role: Lead Volunteer in a self-advocacy group for adults who have physical and learning disabilities

Emma has worked as a Lead Volunteer for two years. Her Senior responsibilities include: assisting with training; supervising and supporting volunteer advocates; liaising with local services and support groups; supporting people to develop and use self-advocacy skills.

Factors that influence the capacity of an individual to express consent: Emma is supporting the group to put together a training session for two new volunteer advocates who have never before worked with people with physical and learning disabilities. As part of the preparations Emma is discussing with the group different situations they have experienced when they have found themselves unable to agree to an action or make a decision, and the reasons why this was the case.

Evidencing AC3.1 to your assessor:

For AC3.1 you must evidence your knowledge of factors that influence the capacity of an individual to express consent.

Assessment Methods:

Oral/Written Questioning or Discussion or a Personal Statement or Reflection.

- You can **tell** your assessor about factors that influence the capacity of an individual to express consent.
- Or, you can **talk** to your assessor about factors that influence the capacity of an individual to express consent.
- Or, you can write a **personal statement or reflection** about your experience of factors that influence the capacity of an individual to express consent in **your work setting**.

REMEMBER TO:
- Provide an **account** and an analysis of different factors that influence the capacity of an individual to express consent.
- Include details of what each factor is, as well as how and why it can affect the capacity of an individual to express consent.
- Think about how different factors that have affected the capacity of individuals in **your work setting** to express consent.

Learning Outcome 3: Be able to establish consent when providing care or support

Assessment Criterion 3.2: Establish consent for an activity or action

What does AC3.2 mean?

○ The lead word **establish** means that you must **be able to show** through **your work practices** how to agree consent with an individual for an activity or action.

○ Your **observations** of your work practices must include you showing how you can seek an individual's permission to do an activity or action.

○ For the key word **consent** you can think about the ways different individuals agree to an activity or action.

Read the following **Real Work Setting** scenario and think about how it relates to your work setting and role:

Real Work Setting

Name: Emma

Job role: Lead Volunteer in a self-advocacy group for adults who have physical and learning disabilities

(See page 72 for a description of the role.)

Establishing consent: Emma is reviewing with each group member their preferences for how to show their agreement to an activity or action. Emma has updated each individual's profile with this information so as to ensure that all volunteers can then be made aware of the process to follow for establishing consent with each individual.

Evidencing AC3.2 to your assessor:

For AC3.2 you must evidence your skills of how you establish consent for an activity or action.

Assessment Method:
Direct Observation of your work practices.

● You can **show** your assessor how you establish consent to an activity or action.

REMEMBER TO:
● Make arrangements for **observation** of **your work practices**.
● Include evidence of **how** you establish consent.
● Include evidence of **why** you establish consent in this way.
● Think about individuals in **your work setting** and how and why you establish consent in different ways when providing care or support.

Learning Outcome 3: Be able to establish consent when providing care or support

Assessment Criterion 3.3: Explain what steps to take if consent cannot readily be established

What does AC3.3 mean?

- The lead word **explain** means that you must **make clear** the steps that must be taken if consent cannot readily be established.
- Your **account** must make clear the process to follow if consent cannot readily be established.
- For the key word **consent** you can think about the action to take if an individual is not able to show their agreement to an activity or action.

Read the following **Real Work Setting** scenario and think about how it relates to your work setting and role:

Real Work Setting

Name: Emma

Job role: Lead Volunteer in a self-advocacy group for adults who have physical and learning disabilities

(See page 72 for a description of the role.)

When consent cannot be established: One of the members of the group finds it difficult at present to communicate her preferences to others in relation to the activities in which she would like to be involved. Emma is aware of the consent arrangements in place for this individual and decides that she will be seeking advice from her manager as well as from this individual's next of kin.

Evidencing AC3.3 to your assessor:

For AC3.3 you must evidence your understanding of the steps to take as well as the reasons why if consent cannot be readily established.

Assessment Methods:

Oral/Written Questioning or Discussion or a Personal Statement or Reflection.

- You can **tell** your assessor the steps to take if consent cannot readily be established, as well as the reasons why.
- Or, you can **talk** to your assessor about the steps to take if consent cannot readily be established, as well as the reasons why.
- Or, you can write a **personal statement or reflection** about your experience of the steps to take if consent cannot readily be established, as well as the reasons why.

REMEMBER TO:

- Provide an **account** and **explain** the steps to take as well as the reasons why if consent cannot readily be established.
- Include **details** about the process to follow if consent cannot readily be established.
- Think about **your work setting** and the steps to take as well as the reasons why if consent cannot be readily established.

Learning Outcome 4: Be able to implement and promote active participation

Assessment Criterion 4.1: Describe different ways of applying active participation to meet individual needs

What does AC4.1 mean?

- The lead word **describe** means that you must provide an **account** that **details** the different ways of applying active participation to meet individual needs.
- Your **account** must detail **different ways** of applying active participation to meet individual needs.
- For the key words **active participation** you can think about how you can ensure you support individuals to live their lives as they wish.

Read the following **Real Work Setting** scenario and think about how it relates to your work setting and role:

Real Work Setting

Name: Mark

Job role: Senior Personal Assistant to young adults who have autism

Mark has worked as a Senior Personal Assistant for one year. His Senior responsibilities include: supporting and leading a team of Personal Assistants; facilitating individuals' case reviews; liaising with families and external agencies; supporting a small caseload of individuals with practical day-to-day tasks, including arranging appointments and accessing the local community. As part of his role Mark works alongside one young man, John, and supports him to communicate in different ways so that he can make his own choices and decisions.

Applying active participation: Mark meets with John, together with his advocate, at the beginning of each week to discuss what activities John would like to do and what support he would he like in order to take part in his chosen activities.

Evidencing AC4.1 to your assessor:

For AC4.1 you must evidence your knowledge of the different ways of applying active participation to meet individual needs.

Assessment Methods:

Oral/Written Questioning or Discussion or a Personal Statement or Reflection.

- You can **tell** your assessor about the different ways of applying active participation to meet individual needs.
- Or, you can **talk** to your assessor about the different ways of applying active participation to meet individual needs.
- Or, You can write a **personal statement or reflection** about your experience of the different ways of applying active participation to meet individual needs.

REMEMBER TO:

- Provide a detailed **account** of the different ways of applying active participation to meet individual needs.
- Include **different ways** of applying active participation to meet individual needs.
- Think about examples of how you put into practice active participation in your work setting.
- Think about different individuals you work with in **your work setting**.

Learning Outcome 4: Be able to implement and promote active participation

Assessment Criterion 4.2: Work with an individual and others to agree how active participation will be implemented

What does AC4.2 mean?

- The lead words **work with** mean that you must **be able to show** through **your work practices** how to implement and promote active participation.
- Your **observation** of your work practices must include you showing **how** you work with an individual and others.
- For the key word **others** you can think about the different people you may work with who are involved in an individual's life.
- For the key words **active participation** you can think about how you can ensure that you support individuals to live their lives as they wish.

Read the following **Real Work Setting** scenario and think about how it relates to your work setting and role:

Real Work Setting

Name: Mark

Job role: Senior Personal Assistant to young adults who have autism

(See page 75 for a description of the role.)

Agreeing active participation: Mark uses both John's communication book and a series of short questions to check whether he is in agreement to go ahead with the activity planned for today. John's advocate and his sister reinforce what Mark is asking him about by showing John the pictures in his communication book about the activity he is doing today.

Evidencing AC4.2 to your assessor:

For AC4.2 you must evidence your skills of how you work with an individual and others to agree how active participation will be implemented.

Assessment Method:

Direct Observation of your work practices.

- You can **show** your assessor how you work with an individual and others to agree how active participation will be implemented.

REMEMBER TO:

- Make arrangements for **observation** of **your work practices**.
- Include evidence of how you work with an individual and others.
- Include evidence of how you agree how active participation will take place.
- Think about an individual in **your work setting** and how you work with the individual and others to agree how active participation will be implemented.

Learning Outcome 4: Be able to implement and promote active participation

Assessment Criterion 4.3: Demonstrate how active participation can address the holistic needs of an individual

What does AC4.3 mean?

- The lead word **demonstrate** means that you must **be able to show** through **your work practices** how active participation can address the holistic needs of an individual.
- Your **observations** of your work practices must include you showing **how** an individual's holistic needs are met through active participation.
- For the key words **active participation** you can think about how you can ensure that you support individuals to live their lives as they wish.
- For the key words **holistic needs** you can think about the unique needs of individuals.

Read the following **Real Work Setting** scenario and think about how it relates to your work setting and role:

Real Work Setting

Name: Mark

Job role: Senior Personal Assistant to young adults who have autism

(See page 75 for a description of the role.)

Addressing the holistic needs: John has chosen to go swimming this morning and would like to travel to the leisure centre on the bus on his own and meet Mark there. Mark agrees this with John and his advocate and together they agree that John will follow his travel plan for travelling on the bus on his own, which includes using his advocate to check that he has got on the correct bus and then to encourage him to show the bus driver where he would like to get off the bus.

Evidencing AC4.3 to your assessor:

For AC4.3 you must evidence your skills of how active participation can address the holistic needs of an individual.

Assessment Method:

Direct Observation of your work practices.

- You can **show** your assessor how active participation can address the holistic needs of an individual.

REMEMBER TO:

- Make arrangements for **observation of your work practices**.
- Include evidence of active participation.
- Include evidence of how you have addressed the holistic needs of an individual.
- Think about an individual in **your work setting** and how active participation can address their holistic needs.

Learning Outcome 4: Be able to implement and promote active participation

Assessment Criterion 4.4: Demonstrate ways to promote understanding and use of active participation

What does AC4.4 mean?

○ The lead word **demonstrate** means that you must **be able to show** through **your work practices** how to promote understanding and use of active participation.

○ Your **observations** of your work practices must include you showing **how** to promote understanding and use of active participation.

○ For the key words **active participation** you can think about how you can ensure that you support individuals to live their lives as they wish.

Read the following **Real Work Setting** scenario and think about how it relates to your work setting and role:

Real Work Setting

Name: Mark

Job role: Senior Personal Assistant to young adults who have autism

(See page 75 for a description of the role.)

Promoting understanding and use of active participation: Mark has agreed to meet with John, his advocate and his sister to review how his wish to go swimming and travel independently went. Together they discuss how John feels the journey on the bus went and whether he received the right amount of support to take part in the swimming activity he chose to do. It is agreed that next time John will wait for the right bus on his own without his advocate and will return back on the bus too on his own and then meet Mark back at John's flat.

Evidencing AC4.4 to your assessor:

For AC4.4 you must evidence your skills to promote understanding and use of active participation.

Assessment Method:

Direct Observation of your work practices.

● You can **show** your assessor different ways to promote understanding and use of active participation.

REMEMBER TO:

● Make arrangements for **observation** of **your work practices**.
● Include evidence of promoting understanding of active participation.
● Include evidence of using active participation.
● Think about an individual in **your work setting** and how you promote and use active participation in different ways.

Learning Outcome 5: Be able to support the individual's right to make choices

Assessment Criterion 5.1: Support an individual to make informed choices

What does AC5.1 mean?

○ The lead word **support** means that you must **be able to show** through **your work practices** how to assist an individual in making informed choices.
○ Your **observations** of your work practices must include you providing support to an individual to make informed choices.
○ For the key words **informed choices** you can think about how to support individuals to access and understand all available information before making choices in their lives.

Read the following **Real Work Setting** scenario and think about how it relates to your work setting and role:

Real Work Setting

Name: Charlotte
Job role: Senior Personal Assistant to adults who have physical disabilities
Charlotte has worked as a Senior Personal Assistant for one year. Her Senior responsibilities include: providing supervision to two Personal Assistants; leading on individuals' case reviews; liaising with families and external agencies; providing support to individuals with day-to-day living, including cooking, house work, arranging appointments, and accessing local services and facilities.
Making informed choices: Charlotte has arranged to meet with Jess, who has recently returned home from a stay in hospital after fracturing her hip. Charlotte has met with Jess and the intermediate care team to discuss the rehabilitation programme that she has completed. Jess is unsure whether she will be able to continue to manage to make her lunch on her own. Charlotte and Jess have discussed the support that can be made available to her at home, as well as the range of options that are available to Jess with respect to lunch, including the use of the microwave, having meals delivered and attending a local lunch club.

Evidencing AC5.1 to your assessor:

For AC5.1 you must evidence your skills to support an individual to make informed choices.

Assessment Method:
Direct Observation of your work practices.

● You can **show** your assessor how you support an individual to make informed choices.

REMEMBER TO:
● Make arrangements for **observation** of **your work practices**.
● Include evidence of providing support to an individual.
● Include evidence of how you support an individual to make informed choices.
● Think about how you support an individual in **your work setting** to make informed choices.

Learning Outcome 5: Be able to support the individual's right to make choices

Assessment Criterion 5.2: Use own role and authority to support the individual's right to make choices

What does AC5.2 mean?

○ The lead word **use** means that you must **be able to show** through **your work practices** how to use your own role and authority to support an individual's right to make choices.

○ Your **observations** of your work practices must include you supporting an individual's right to make choices within the scope of your role and authority.

○ For the key word **role** you can think about how supporting an individual's right to make choices forms part of your day-to-day work duties.

○ For the key word **authority** you can think about how supporting an individual's right to make choices forms part of your responsibilities at work.

Read the following **Real Work Setting** scenario and think about how it relates to your work setting and role:

Real Work Setting
Name: Charlotte
Job role: Senior Personal Assistant to adults who have physical disabilities
(See page 79 for a description of the role.)
Use of role and authority: Jess has contacted Charlotte and asked her whether she can talk through with her again the different options available to her in terms of continuing to make her lunch independently, as she very much enjoys cooking and does not want support with making her lunch. Jess and Charlotte agree to review the benefits and risks involved in Jess making lunch on her own without support. Charlotte encourages Jess to write these down so that she can review these again when making a decision about what she would like to do.

Evidencing AC5.2 to your assessor:

For AC5.2 you must evidence your skills in using your role and authority to support the individual's right to make choices.

Assessment Method:

Direct Observation of your work practices.

● You can **show** your assessor how you use your role and authority effectively to support the individual's right to make choices.

REMEMBER TO:

● Make arrangements for **observation** of **your work practices**.
● Include evidence of using both your role and your authority effectively.
● Include evidence of how you support the individual's right to make choices.
● Think about how you support an individual's right to make choices in **your work setting** by using your role and authority.

Learning Outcome 5: Be able to support the individual's right to make choices

Assessment Criterion 5.3: Manage risk in a way that maintains the individual's right to make choices

What does AC5.3 mean?

- The lead word **manage** means that you must **be able to show** through **your work practices** how to work with risk in a way that maintains the individual's right to make choices.
- Your **observations** of your work practices must include you managing risk in a way that maintains the individual's right to make choices.
- For the key word **manage** you can think about how to work in a way that identifies, controls and reduces risks whilst maintaining the individual's right to make choices.
- For the key word **risk** you can think about the potential that exists for danger and/or harm.

Read the following **Real Work Setting** scenario and think about how it relates to your work setting and role:

Real Work Setting
Name: Charlotte
Job role: Senior Personal Assistant to adults who have physical disabilities
(See page 79 for a description of the role.)
Managing risk: Jess has decided that she would like to try and make her lunch on her own with no support and has agreed with Charlotte that she will do this for the first week with her Personal Assistant present, in case support is required. Jess and Charlotte agree to review this together at the end of the first week.

Evidencing AC5.3 to your assessor:

For AC5.3 you must evidence your skills in managing risk in a way that maintains the individual's right to make choices.

Assessment Method:

Direct Observation of your work practices.

- You can **show** your assessor how you manage risk in a way that maintains the individual's right to make choices.

REMEMBER TO:

- Make arrangements for **observation** of **your work practices**.
- Include evidence of how to manage risk.
- Include evidence of how you maintain the individual's right to make choices.
- Think about how you manage risk in **your work setting** in a way that maintains the individual's right to make choices.

Learning Outcome 5: Be able to support the individual's right to make choices

Assessment Criterion 5.4: Describe how to support an individual to question or challenge decisions concerning them that are made by others

What does AC5.4 mean?

○ The lead word **describe** means that you must provide an **account** that **details** how to support an individual to question or challenge decisions concerning them that are made by others.

○ Your **account** must detail the support provided and be based on decisions concerning individuals that are made by others.

○ For the key word **others** you can think about the different people who are involved in individuals' lives.

Read the following **Real Work Setting** scenario and think about how it relates to your work setting and role:

Real Work Setting

Name: Charlotte

Job role: Senior Personal Assistant to adults who have physical disabilities

(See page 79 for a description of the role.)

Questioning or challenging decisions: Jess and Charlotte meet to review how Jess is managing to cook lunch for herself independently. Jess feels that she is able to continue to do so on her own and does not need a Personal Assistant to be present. Charlotte asks Jess whether any risks have been identified with her doing this; Jess explains that her Personal Assistant feels that it would not be safe for her to cook on her own as she did have a small slip in the kitchen. Jess feels that this is very harsh as anyone can have a slip. Charlotte asks Jess whether she would like to discuss how her first week has gone with her Personal Assistant present; Jess agrees this will be a good idea.

Evidencing AC5.4 to your assessor:

For AC5.4 you must evidence your knowledge of how to support an individual to question or challenge decisions concerning them that are made by others.

Assessment Methods:

Oral/Written Questioning or **Discussion** or a **Personal Statement** or **Reflection.**

- You can **tell** your assessor about how to support an individual to question or challenge decisions concerning them that are made by others.

- *Or,* you can **talk** to your assessor about how to support an individual to question or challenge decisions concerning them that are made by others.

- *Or,* you can write a **personal statement or reflection** about how to support an individual to question or challenge decisions concerning them that are made by others.

REMEMBER TO:

- Provide a detailed **account** of how to support an individual to question or challenge decisions concerning them that are made by others.
- Include **different ways** to support an individual.
- Think about **examples** of when an individual may question or challenge decisions concerning them.
- Include evidence of who made the decisions concerning them.
- Think about how to support an individual you work with in **your work setting** to challenge decisions concerning them that are made by others.

Learning Outcome 6: Be able to promote individuals' well-being

Assessment Criterion 6.1: Explain the links between identity, self-image and self-esteem

What does AC6.1 mean?

- The lead word **explain** means that you must **make clear** the links between identity, self-image and self-esteem.
- Your **account** must make clear what each of these terms means and how each one in turn is related to the others.
- For the key word **identity** you can think about the different characteristics that make each individual unique.
- For the key word **self-image** you can think about how individuals see themselves and how others can contribute to this image.
- For the key word **self-esteem** you can think about how individuals value themselves and how others can contribute to this.

Read the following **Real Work Setting** scenario and think about how it relates to your work setting and role:

Real Work Setting

Name: Linda

Job role: Senior Carer in a day service for older people

Linda has been working as a Senior Carer for ten months. Her Senior responsibilities: include managing and supervising Carers and volunteers; care planning; developing and evaluating programmes of activities; liaising with individuals' families and others involved in their lives. As part of her role Linda has to communicate with staff, volunteers, individuals, families and others; the way in which she communicates can affect these working relationships.

Identity, self-image and self-esteem: Linda has built up a strong team and believes that this is because she provides constructive feedback to staff and volunteers, and positive support to identify and address any developmental needs staff and/or volunteers may have. Linda would like to provide further training around those aspects that promote an individual's well-being, and she plans to provide the team with some information on how identity, self-image and self-esteem are linked and can impact on an individual's emotional, physical, cultural, religious, spiritual, political and social well-being.

Evidencing AC6.1 to your assessor:

For AC6.1 you must evidence your understanding of the links between identity, self-image and self-esteem.

Assessment Methods:

Oral/Written Questioning or **Discussion** or a **Personal Statement.**

- You can **tell** your assessor about the links that exist between identity, self-image and self-esteem.
- Or, you can **talk** to your assessor about the links that exist between identity, self-image and self-esteem.
- Or, you can write a **personal statement** about the links that exist between identity, self-image and self-esteem.

REMEMBER TO:

- Provide an **account** and **explain** what each term means, and how and why each concept is related to the others.
- Include **varied** examples of how each concept has an impact on the others.
- Include **details** about the links that exist and how these relate to promoting an individual's well-being.
- Think about **your work setting** and the links that exist between individuals' identity, self-image and self-esteem.

Learning Outcome 6: Be able to promote individuals' well-being

Assessment Criterion 6.2: Analyse factors that contribute to the well-being of individuals

What does AC6.2 mean?

- The lead word **analyse** means that you must **examine in detail** different factors that contribute to the well-being of individuals, in order to show your understanding of what these are and how these can affect individuals.
- Your **account** must provide an analysis of **different** factors that can affect **different** aspects of individuals' well-being.
- For the key word **well-being** you can think about how this involves emotional, physical, cultural, religious, spiritual, political and social aspects of individuals' lives.

Read the following **Real Work Setting** scenario and think about how it relates to your work setting and role:

Real Work Setting

Name: Linda

Job role: Senior Carer in a day service for older people

(See page 83 for a description of the role.)

Factors contributing to the well-being of individuals: During a training session with the team Linda leads discussions on the different factors that can affect the well-being of individuals, including getting the team to think about the effects of their working in a way that respects individuals for who they are, how clear reporting and good communications can affect individuals' well-being, as well as how the environment, and the attitudes and approaches of staff, can also have an impact.

Evidencing AC6.2 to your assessor:

For AC6.2 you must evidence your knowledge of the factors that contribute to the well-being of individuals.

Assessment Methods:

Oral/Written Questioning or **Discussion** or a **Personal Statement** or **Reflection**.

- You can **tell** your assessor about the factors that contribute to the well-being of individuals.
- Or, you can **talk** to your assessor about the factors that contribute to the well-being of individuals.
- Or, You can write a **personal statement or reflection** about your experience of the factors that contribute to the well-being of individuals in **your work setting**.

REMEMBER TO:

- Provide an **account** and an analysis of different factors that contribute to the well-being of individuals.
- Include **details** about what each factor is, and how and why each factor can contribute to individuals' well-being in the work setting.
- Include **varied** examples and link these to how they can contribute to individuals' well-being.
- Think about how **different factors** can contribute to **individuals' well-being** in **your work setting**.

Learning Outcome 6: Be able to promote individuals' well-being

Assessment Criterion 6.3: Support an individual in a way that promotes their sense of identity, self-image and self-esteem

What does AC6.3 mean?

- The lead word **support** means that you must **be able to show** through **your work practices** how to assist an individual in a way that promotes their sense of identity, self-image and self-esteem.
- Your **observations** of your work practices must include you providing support to an individual.
- For the key word **identity** you can take into account the different characteristics that make each individual unique when providing support.
- For the key word **self-image** you can think about how individuals see themselves, and how you and others can contribute to this image when providing support.
- For the key word **self-esteem** you can think about how individuals value themselves, and how you and others can contribute to this when providing support.

Read the following **Real Work Setting** scenario and think about how it relates to your work setting and role:

Real Work Setting

Name: Linda

Job role: Senior Carer in a day service for older people

(See page 83 for a description of the role.)

Supporting individuals and promoting their sense of identity, self-image and self-esteem: Linda shares with the team all feedback received from individuals and their relatives and others involved in their lives, so that the team is made aware of the many different ways that the support they provide on a day-to-day basis can promote individuals' sense of identity, self-image and self-esteem. Some of the staff tell Linda that they are surprised that their support has made such a difference for some individuals.

Evidencing AC6.3 to your assessor:

For AC6.3 you must evidence your skills to support an individual in a way that promotes their sense of identity, self-image and self-esteem.

Assessment Method:

Direct Observation of your work practices.

- You can **show** your assessor how you support an individual in a way that promotes their sense of identity, self-image and self-esteem.

REMEMBER TO:

- Make arrangements for **observation** of **your work practices**.
- Include evidence of you providing support to an individual.
- Include evidence of how you promoted an individual's sense of identity, self-image and self-esteem.
- Think about how you promoted an individual's sense of identity, self-image and self-esteem in **your work setting**.

Learning Outcome 6: Be able to promote individuals' well-being

Assessment Criterion 6.4: Demonstrate ways to contribute to an environment that promotes well-being

What does AC6.4 mean?

- ○ The lead word **demonstrate** means that you must **be able to show** through **your work practices** different ways to contribute to an environment that promotes well-being.
- ○ Your **observations** of your work practices must include you showing different ways to contribute to an environment that promotes well-being.
- ○ For the key word **environment** you can think about an individual's safety and physical surroundings, as well as the atmosphere and feel of an individual's environment.
- ○ For the key word **well-being** you can think about how this involves emotional, physical, cultural, religious, spiritual, political and social aspects of individuals' lives.

Read the following **Real Work Setting** scenario and think about how it relates to your work setting and role:

Real Work Setting

Name: Linda
Job role: Senior Carer in a day service for older people
(See page 83 for a description of the role.)
Contributing to an environment that promotes well-being: Linda asks the team at the end of the training session to think about all the different ways they contribute to making sure that every individual they work with feels safe, comfortable and relaxed in their environment. The team discusses all the ways they believe they do this and agrees on a list of ten ways that they believe are the most important.

Evidencing AC6.4 to your assessor:

For AC6.4 you must evidence your skills to show ways to contribute to an environment that promotes well-being.

Assessment Method:

Direct Observation of your work practices.

- You can **show** your assessor different ways to contribute to an environment that promotes well-being.

REMEMBER TO:

- Make arrangements for **observation** of **your work practices**.
- Include evidence of different ways to contribute to an environment that promotes well-being.
- Include evidence and examples of how you contribute to an environment that promotes well-being.
- Think about ways to contribute to an environment that promotes well-being in **your work setting**.

Learning Outcome 7: Understand the role of risk assessment in enabling a person-centred approach

Assessment Criterion 7.1: Compare different uses of risk assessment in health and social care

What does AC7.1 mean?

○ The lead word **compare** means that you must **make clear** the similarities and differences between the different uses of risk assessment in health and social care.

○ Your **account** must make clear **different** uses of risk assessment, as well as the **similarities and differences** in their uses.

○ For the key words **risk assessment** you can think about what may cause harm or injuries to people in your work setting and how to ensure that the risks identified are minimised and controlled.

Read the following **Real Work Setting** scenario and think about how it relates to your work setting and role:

Real Work Setting

Name: Alison

Job role: Relief Senior Carer to older people in a supported living scheme

Alison has been working as a Relief Senior Carer to older people for six years. Her Senior responsibilities include: leading the evening and weekend shifts; supervising and supporting Carers; leading with other Seniors on the review of individuals' care plans; monitoring and administering medication to individuals; liaising with families, external professionals and agencies as and when required. As part of her role Alison has to ensure effective communication with staff, individuals, families and others.

Uses of risk assessment: Alison delegates tasks to staff and completes the shift rota system for all the team. Anne believes that monitoring and supporting staff through supervision meetings, discussions, verbal and written feedback is crucial to the smooth running of the team. One of the areas Alison is reviewing at present is how effective the scheme's current risk assessments are in relation to two individuals with respect to their mobility, self-medication and outings to the local shops.

Evidencing AC7.1 to your assessor:

For AC7.1 you must evidence your understanding of the similarities and differences between the different uses of risk assessment in health and social care.

Assessment Methods:

Oral/Written Questioning or **Discussion** or a **Personal Statement**.

● You can **tell** your assessor about the different uses of risk assessment in health and social care, as well as the similarities and differences that exist between these.

● Or, you can **talk** to your assessor about the different uses of risk assessment in health and social care, as well as the similarities and differences that exist between these.

● Or, you can write a **personal statement** about the different uses of risk assessment in health and social care as well as the similarities and differences that exist between these.

REMEMBER TO:

● Provide an **account** and detail the similarities and differences between the different uses of risk assessment in health and social care.

● Include **varied** examples of different uses of risk assessment.

● Include **details** about how these are similar and different.

● Think about **your work setting** and how and when risk assessment is used.

Learning Outcome 7: Understand the role of risk assessment in enabling a person-centred approach

Assessment Criterion 7.2: Explain how risk taking and risk assessment relate to rights and responsibilities

What does AC7.2 mean?

- The lead word **explain** means that you must **make clear** how risk taking and risk assessment relate to rights and responsibilities.
- Your **account** must make clear what each of these terms means and how each one in turn relates to both rights and responsibilities.
- For the key words **risk taking** you can think about how promoting rights and responsibilities involves taking risks.
- For the key words **risk assessment** you can think about how ensuring risks identified are minimised and controlled relates to supporting and promoting individuals' rights and responsibilities.

Read the following **Real Work Setting** scenario and think about how it relates to your work setting and role:

Real Work Setting

Name: Alison

Job role: Relief Senior Carer to older people in a supported living scheme

(See page 87 for a description of the role.)

Risk taking and risk assessment: During supervisions with staff Alison reviews with each member of the team the care plan activities they have carried out with individuals. She includes how they have worked within the risk assessment guidelines in place and how effective these are in terms of to what extent they maintain individuals' safety without compromising their rights to take risks and make their own decisions when going out, self-medicating and using mobility aids.

Evidencing AC7.2 to your assessor:

For AC7.2 you must evidence your understanding of how risk taking and risk assessment relate to rights and responsibilities.

Assessment Methods:

Oral/Written Questioning or Discussion or a Personal Statement.

- You can **tell** your assessor how risk taking and risk assessment relate to rights and responsibilities.
- Or, you can **talk** to your assessor about how risk taking and risk assessment relate to rights and responsibilities.
- Or, you can write a **personal statement** about how risk taking and risk assessment relate to rights and responsibilities.

REMEMBER TO:

- Provide an **account** and **explain** what each term means, and how as well as the reasons why each term is related to rights and responsibilities.
- Include **varied** examples of how each term relates to both rights and responsibilities.
- Include **details** about the ways each term relates to both rights and responsibilities.
- Think about **your work setting** and how risk taking and risk assessment relate to rights and responsibilities.

Learning Outcome 7: Understand the role of risk assessment in enabling a person-centred approach

Assessment Criterion 7.3: Explain why risk assessments need to be regularly revised

What does AC7.3 mean?

- The lead word **explain** means that you must **make clear** why risk assessments need to be regularly revised.
- Your **account** must make clear the reasons **why**.
- For the key words **risk assessments** you can think about the purpose of risk assessments and the importance of their being regularly revised.

Read the following **Real Work Setting** scenario and think about how it relates to your work setting and role:

Real Work Setting

Name: Alison

Job role: Relief Senior Carer to older people in a supported living scheme

(See page 87 for a description of the role.)

Revision of risk assessments: During one staff member's supervision Alison discusses with the staff member the importance of ensuring that the risk assessments in place are always up to date and relevant to the individual and/or activity being risk assessed. Both talk through the consequences of not doing so for the individual, the service and the member of staff providing support to that individual.

Evidencing AC7.3 to your assessor:

For AC7.3 you must evidence your understanding of why risk assessments need to be regularly revised.

Assessment Methods:

Oral/Written Questioning or **Discussion** or a **Personal Statement**.

- You can **tell** your assessor why risk assessments need to be regularly revised.
- *Or*, you can **talk** to your assessor about why risk assessments need to be regularly revised.
- *Or*, you can write a **personal statement** about why risk assessments need to be regularly revised.

REMEMBER TO:

- Provide an **account** and **explain** the reasons why risk assessments need to be regularly revised.
- Include **varied** examples of reasons why.
- Include **details** about the consequences of not regularly revising risk assessments.
- Think about **your work setting** and the **reasons why** risk assessments that are in place need to be regularly revised.

Learning Outcome 1: Understand your responsibilities and the responsibilities of others relating to health and safety

Assessment Criterion 1.1: Identify legislation relating to health and safety in a health or social care work setting

What does AC1.1 mean?

- The lead word **identify** means that you must **make clear** health and safety legislation.
- Your **list** must include **different** examples of health and safety legislation.
- For the key word **legislation** you can think about the laws that are in place relating to health and safety in health and social care work settings.
- The key words **work setting** may include a specific location or various settings. This will depend on the context of the role.

Read the following **Real Work Setting** scenario and think about how it relates to your work setting and role:

Real Work Setting

Name: Louise

Job role: Senior Support Worker to people who have mental health needs

Louise has been working as a Senior Support Worker for seven years. Her Senior responsibilities include: leading shifts; providing group supervision to the team; liaising with individuals, health and social care professionals and individuals' families and/or advocates to review their current support plans. As part of her role Louise supports her team to provide person-centred support services.

Health and safety legislation: Louise is the health and safety officer in her workplace and one of her tasks this morning is to ensure the health and safety file is up to date. Louise begins by logging on to the Health and Safety Executive's (HSE) website to check if there have been changes or updates to the health and safety legislation in place in and relevant to her workplace so that she can then update the file with this information and show that she has reviewed its details.

Evidencing AC1.1 to your assessor:

For AC1.1 you must evidence your understanding of legislation relating to health and safety in a health or social care work setting.

Assessment Methods:

Oral/Written Questioning or Discussion or a Spidergram.

- You can **tell** your assessor the different health and safety legislation that exists.
- *Or*, you can **talk** to your assessor about the different health and safety legislation that exists.
- *Or*, you can complete a **spidergram** showing the different health and safety legislation that exists.

REMEMBER TO:

- **List** health and safety legislation.
- Include **different** examples of health and safety legislation.
- Ensure legislation relates to health and safety in a health or social care work setting.
- Think about the health and safety legislation in place in **your work setting**.

Learning Outcome 1: Understand your responsibilities and the responsibilities of others relating to health and safety

Assessment Criterion 1.2: Explain the main points of health and safety policies and procedures agreed with the employer

What does AC1.2 mean?

○ The lead word **explain** means that you must **make clear** the main points of health and safety policies and procedures that have been agreed with your employer.

○ Your **account** must make clear the key details included, as well as the reasons why these are the main points of health and safety policies and procedures.

○ For the key words **policies and procedures** you can think about how the setting where you work operates on a day-to-day basis in terms of health and safety.

Read the following **Real Work Setting** scenario and think about how it relates to your work setting and role:

Real Work Setting

Name: Louise

Job role: Senior Support Worker to people who have mental health needs

(See page 90 for a description of the role.)

Health and safety policies and procedures: Louise's next task as the health and safety officer is to induct a new Senior Support Worker and explain to her the various health and safety policies and procedures in place. Louise plans to begin by asking the new member of staff to read through the health and safety procedures that she has recently reviewed and then she will discuss these with her in more detail, including answering any questions she may have.

Evidencing AC1.2 to your assessor:

For AC1.2 you must evidence your understanding of the main points of health and safety policies and procedures agreed with your employer.

Assessment Methods:

Oral/Written Questioning or **Discussion** or a **Personal Statement**.

● You can **tell** your assessor about the main points of health and safety policies and procedures agreed with your employer.

● Or, you can **talk** to your assessor about the main points of health and safety policies and procedures agreed with your employer.

● Or, you can write a **personal statement** about the main points of health and safety policies and procedures agreed with your employer.

REMEMBER TO:

● Provide an **account** and **explain** the reasons why these are the main points of health and safety policies and procedures.

● Include **varied** examples of health and safety policies and procedures.

● Include **details** about their purpose and use, and ensure they relate to health and safety in a health or social care setting.

● Think about **your work setting** and the policies and procedures you have in place.

Learning Outcome 1: Understand your responsibilities and the responsibilities of others relating to health and safety

Assessment Criterion 1.3: Analyse the main health and safety responsibilities for yourself, the employer or manager, and others in the work setting

What does AC1.3 mean?

- ○ The lead word **analyse** means that you must **examine in detail** the different health and safety responsibilities for yourself, the employer or manager, and others in the work setting.
- ○ Your **account** must provide an analysis of **different** health and safety responsibilities for yourself, the employer or manager, and others in the work setting.
- ○ The key word **others** may include team members, other colleagues, those who use or commission their own health or social care services, as well as individuals' families, carers and advocates.
- ○ For the key word **responsibilities** you can think about **how and why** health and safety tasks are carried out in the work setting.

Read the following **Real Work Setting** scenario and think about how it relates to your work setting and role:

Real Work Setting
Name: Louise
Job role: Senior Support Worker to people who have mental health needs
(See page 90 for a description of the role.)
Health and safety responsibilities: As part of the team's annual health and safety training, all the participants have been asked to think about their job roles and what areas of health and safety they are responsible for, as well as the health and safety responsibilities of others who visit the work setting, including individuals' families, friends and advocates.

Evidencing AC1.3 to your assessor:

For AC1.3 you must evidence your knowledge of the main health and safety responsibilities for yourself, the employer or manager, and others in the work setting.

Assessment Methods:

Oral/Written Questioning or Discussion or a **Personal Statement or Reflection**.

- You can **tell** your assessor about the main health and safety responsibilities for yourself, your employer or manager, and others in the work setting.
- Or, you can **talk** to your assessor about the main health and safety responsibilities for yourself, your employer or manager, and others in the work setting.
- Or, you can write a **personal statement or reflection** about your experience of the main health and safety responsibilities for yourself, the employer or manager, and others in **your work setting**.

REMEMBER TO:
- Provide an **account** and an analysis of different health and safety responsibilities.
- Include **details** about what each responsibility is, who it is for and why.
- Include **varied** examples of health and safety responsibilities.
- Think about the health and safety responsibilities for yourself, the employer or manager, and others in **your work setting**.

Learning Outcome 1: Understand your responsibilities and the responsibilities of others relating to health and safety

Assessment Criterion 1.4: Identify specific tasks in the work setting that should not be carried out without special training

What does AC1.4 mean?

- The lead word **identify** means that you must **make clear** specific tasks that should not be carried out in the work setting without special training.
- Your **list** must include **different** examples of tasks.
- For the key word **tasks** you can think about the day-to-day work activities you carry out with individuals. Tasks for which special training may be required may include first aid, food handling and preparation, health care procedures, using equipment, or tasks involving medication.

Read the following **Real Work Setting** scenario and think about how it relates to your work setting and role:

Real Work Setting

Name: Louise

Job role: Senior Support Worker to people who have mental health needs

(See page 90 for a description of the role.)

Tasks that require special training: Louise and the Seniors have developed a short quiz for the team of Support Workers to complete at the end of their annual health and safety training, and this includes checking the team's knowledge of the work setting's procedures, including the tasks that they must not carry out at work without special training.

Evidencing AC1.4 to your assessor:

For AC1.4 you must evidence your understanding of specific tasks in the work setting that should not be carried out without special training.

Assessment Methods:

Oral/Written Questioning or **Discussion** or a **Spidergram**.

- You can **tell** your assessor the specific tasks in the workplace that should not be carried out without special training.
- *Or*, you can **talk** to your assessor about the specific tasks in the workplace that should not be carried out without special training.
- *Or*, you can complete a **spidergram** showing the specific tasks out in the workplace that should not be carried without special training.

REMEMBER TO:

- **List** specific tasks that should not be carried out without special training.
- Include **different** examples of tasks.
- Ensure they relate to the work setting.
- Think about the specific tasks that should not be carried out in **your work setting** without special training.

Learning Outcome 2: Be able to carry out your responsibilities for health and safety

Assessment Criterion 2.1: Use policies and procedures or other agreed ways of working that relate to health and safety

What does AC2.1 mean?

- The lead word **use** means that you must **be able to show** through **your work practices** how to put into practice your work setting's health and safety policies, procedures and guidelines.
- Your **observations** of your work practices must include you using health and safety policies, procedures or guidelines available in your work setting.
- For the key word **policies** you can think about the health and safety principles that are in place in your work setting.
- For the key word **procedures** you can think about how the health and safety principles that are in place in your work setting are carried out in practice.
- For the key words **agreed ways of working** you can think about your work setting's health and safety guidelines that are in place for the individuals to whom you provide care and support.

Read the following **Real Work Setting** scenario and think about how it relates to your work setting and role:

Real Work Setting

Name: Megan

Job role: Senior Support Worker for people who have mental health needs

Megan has been working as a Senior Support Worker for three years. Her job role involves providing direct supervision to a small team of Support Workers, holding regular team meetings and monitoring the team's training needs. Megan leads on implementing and reviewing individuals' support plans and reviews, as well as liaising with individuals' families and other relevant professionals.

Using health and safety policies, procedures or agreed ways of working: Megan considers her role as a Senior to be an important one and sees herself as a mentor to the team of Support Workers she manages. At this week's team meeting Megan plans to review the lone working and risk assessment procedures with the team so that they understand the purpose of these and to give them an opportunity to ask any questions they may have about these. Megan will then carry out observations of the team and assess their abilities to comply with these.

Evidencing AC2.1 to your assessor:

For AC2.1 you must evidence your skills in using policies and procedures or other agreed ways of working that relate to health and safety.

Assessment Method:
Direct Observation of your work practices.

- You can **show** your assessor how you use policies and procedures or other agreed ways of working that relate to health and safety.

REMEMBER TO:
- Make arrangements for **observation** of **your work practices**.
- Include evidence of using policies and procedures or agreed ways of working.
- Ensure these are related to health and safety.
- Think about how you use policies and procedures or other agreed ways of working that relate to health and safety in **your work setting**.

Learning Outcome 2: Be able to carry out your responsibilities for health and safety

Assessment Criterion 2.2: Support others to understand and follow safe practices

What does AC2.2 mean?

- ○ The lead word **support** means that you must **be able to show** through **your work practices** how to assist others in understanding and following safe practices.
- ○ Your **observations** of your work practices must include you providing assistance and guidance to others.
- ○ For the key word **others** you can think about how you provide support to your colleagues and individuals, as well as to visitors to your work setting, to ensure they understand and follow safe practices.

Read the following **Real Work Setting** scenario and think about how it relates to your work setting and role:

Real Work Setting

Name: Megan

Job role: Senior Support Worker for people who have mental health needs

(See page 94 for a description of the role.)

Supporting others to understand and follow safe practices: Megan frequently accompanies Support Workers on their calls to individuals so that she can check that they are working to the required standard and following the work setting's agreed ways of working. She also offers any support and advice she can, for example through discussing areas for improvement directly with Support Workers, referring them to read key points contained within the work setting's policies and procedures, and/or recommending further training.

Evidencing AC2.2 to your assessor:

For AC2.2 you must evidence your skills in supporting others to understand and follow safe practices.

Assessment Method:

Direct Observation of your work practices.

- You can **show** your assessor how you support others to understand and follow safe practices.

REMEMBER TO:

- Make arrangements for **observation** of **your work practices**.
- Include evidence of how you support different people.
- Ensure you provide evidence of how you support others to both understand and follow safe practices.
- Think about how you support others in **your work setting** to understand and follow safe practices.

Learning Outcome 2: Be able to carry out your responsibilities for health and safety

Assessment Criterion 2.3: Monitor and report potential health and safety risks

What does AC2.3 mean?

- The lead words **monitor and report** mean that you must **be able to show** through **your work practices** how to observe, check and provide verbal and written accounts of potential health and safety risks.
- Your **observations** of your work practices must include you **both** monitoring and reporting.
- For the key word **risks** you can think about the potential that exists for danger and/or harm to take place in your work setting.

Read the following **Real Work Setting** scenario and think about how it relates to your work setting and role:

Real Work Setting

Name: Megan

Job role: Senior Support Worker for people who have mental health needs

(See page 94 for a description of the role.)

Monitoring and reporting potential health and safety risks: Megan is carrying out a risk assessment in an individual's flat, as the Support Workers who work with him have reported to Megan that he is currently experiencing anxiety attacks when outside in the garden and insists on using the garden when the Support Workers visit him. Megan has agreed with the individual to visit him and review the risk assessment currently in place for outside his flat, as it is important that the work setting is a safe place for all the team and for him.

Evidencing AC2.3 to your assessor:

For AC2.3 you must evidence your skills in how you monitor and report potential health and safety risks.

Assessment Method:
Direct Observation of your work practices.

- You can **show** your assessor or an expert witness how you monitor and report potential health and safety risks.

REMEMBER TO:
- Make arrangements for **observation of your work practices**.
- Include evidence of how you both monitor and report.
- Ensure you provide evidence of different potential health and safety risks.
- Think about how you monitor and report potential health and safety risks in **your work setting**.

Learning Outcome 2: Be able to carry out your responsibilities for health and safety

Assessment Criterion 2.4: Use risk assessment in relation to health and safety

What does AC2.4 mean?

- The lead word **use** means that you must **be able to show** through **your work practices** how to put into practice health and safety risk assessment.
- Your **observations** of your work practices must include you using health and safety risk assessment.
- For the key words **risk assessment** you can think about how ensuring identified risks are minimised and controlled relates to supporting and promoting individuals' rights and responsibilities.

Read the following **Real Work Setting** scenario and think about how it relates to your work setting and role:

Real Work Setting

Name: Megan

Job role: Senior Support Worker for people who have mental health needs

(See page 94 for a description of the role.)

Using risk assessment: Megan is meeting with the team to discuss the support to be provided to an individual who is experiencing anxiety attacks when using his garden. It has been agreed with the individual to access the garden only with the support of his Community Mental Health Nurse, who visits him twice weekly; this arrangement will be reviewed in two weeks' time.

Evidencing AC2.4 to your assessor:

For AC2.4 you must evidence your skills in using risk assessment in relation to health and safety.

Assessment Methods:

Direct Observation of your work practices.

- You can **show** your assessor how you use risk assessment in relation to health and safety.
- You can also use the risk assessment you have completed as a supporting piece of **work product evidence**.

REMEMBER TO:

- Make arrangements for **observation** of **your work practices**.
- Include evidence of how you use risk assessment.
- Ensure you provide evidence of using risk assessment in relation to health and safety.
- Think about how you use health and safety risk assessment in **your work setting**.

Learning Outcome 2: Be able to carry out your responsibilities for health and safety

Assessment Criterion 2.5: Demonstrate ways to minimise potential risks and hazards

What does AC2.5 mean?

- The lead word **demonstrate** means that you must **be able to show** through **your work practices** how to use different methods to minimise potential risks and hazards.
- Your **observations** of your work practices must include you using different methods to minimise risks and hazards.
- For the key word **risks** you can think about the potential that exists for danger and/or harm to take place at work.
- For the key word **hazards** you can think about the actual dangers that exist for harm to take place at work.

Read the following **Real Work Setting** scenario and think about how it relates to your work setting and role:

Real Work Setting

Name: Megan

Job role: Senior Support Worker for people who have mental health needs

(See page 94 for a description of the role.)

Minimising potential risks and hazards: Megan is reviewing an individual's risk assessment and has agreed with her, her sister and the team of Support Workers how to work with her in order to minimise the risk of her falling. They agree to promote her use of her walking stick, encourage her to hold on to the hand rail when walking to her front door, and help her to tidy up the items in her hallway. This has been recorded in full in the individual's risk assessment.

Evidencing AC2.5 to your assessor:

For AC2.5 you must evidence your skills in using different methods to minimise risks and hazards.

Assessment Methods:

Direct Observation of your work practices.

- You can **show** your assessor the different methods you use to minimise potential risks and hazards.
- You can also use the risk assessment you have completed as a supporting piece of **work product evidence**.

REMEMBER TO:

- Make arrangements for **observation** of **your work practices**.
- Include evidence of the different methods you use.
- Ensure you provide evidence of how to minimise both potential risks and hazards.
- Think about how you use different methods to minimise potential risks and hazards in **your work setting**.

Learning Outcome 2: Be able to carry out your responsibilities for health and safety

Assessment Criterion 2.6: Access additional support or information relating to health and safety

What does AC2.6 mean?

- The lead word **access** means that you must **be able to show** through **your work practices** how to obtain additional support or information relating to health and safety.
- Your **observations** of your work practices must include you accessing additional support or information relating to health and safety.
- For the key words **additional support** you can think about the people to approach both within and outside your work setting for support relating to health and safety.
- For the key word **information** you can think about health and safety policies, procedures and guidelines available within your work setting, and useful websites and notices available from external organisations.

Read the following **Real Work Setting** scenario and think about how it relates to your work setting and role:

Real Work Setting

Name: Megan

Job role: Senior Support Worker for people who have mental health needs

(See page 94 for a description of the role.)

Accessing additional support or information: Megan has arranged a meeting with her manager as she is unsure about the new guidelines that have been put in place to support an individual who requires supervision when out shopping. Megan plans to discuss this with her manager so as to further her understanding of how these guidelines will work in practice and to establish how much supervision is required so that she can then explain this to the Support Workers who will be working with this individual.

Evidencing AC2.6 to your assessor:

For AC2.6 you must evidence your skills in accessing additional support or information relating to health and safety.

Assessment Methods:

Direct Observation of your work practices or an **Expert Witness Testimony**.

- You can **show** your assessor how you access additional support or information relating to health and safety.
- Or, your supervisor or manager can write an **expert witness testimony** of an occasion they observed you accessing additional support or information relating to health and safety.

REMEMBER TO:

- Make arrangements for **observation of your work practices**.
- Include evidence of you accessing either additional support or information.
- Ensure the evidence you provide relates to health and safety.
- Think about how you access additional support or information about health and safety in **your work setting**.

Learning Outcome 3: Understand procedures for responding to accidents and sudden illness

Assessment Criterion 3.1: Describe different types of accidents and sudden illness that may occur in your work setting

What does AC3.1 mean?

- The lead word **describe** means that you must provide an **account** that **details** the different types of accidents and sudden illness that may occur in your work setting.
- Your **account** must detail types of **both** accidents and sudden illness that may occur in your work setting.
- For the key word **accidents** you can think about the different hazards that exist in your work setting that may cause injury or harm.
- For the key words **sudden illness** you can think about the different types of unexpected medical conditions that may occur in individuals or others in your work setting.

Read the following **Real Work Setting** scenario and think about how it relates to your work setting and role:

Real Work Setting

Name: Tara
Job role: Senior Residential Carer to older people
Tara works as a Senior Residential Carer. Tara's Senior responsibilities include: ensuring the smooth running of shifts; supervising a team of Care Assistants; developing, reviewing and updating care plans in line with residents' individual and changing needs and preferences.
Accidents and sudden illness: Tara is leading the team meeting this week and plans to raise the Care Assistants' awareness of the different types of accidents and sudden illness that may arise whilst on shift, which may involve individuals, visitors and/or staff.

Evidencing AC3.1 to your assessor:

For AC3.1 you must evidence your understanding of the different types of accidents and sudden illness that may occur in your work setting.

Assessment Methods:

Oral/Written Questioning or Discussion or a Personal Statement or Reflection.

- You can **tell** your assessor about the different types of accidents and sudden illness that may occur in your work setting.
- Or, you can **talk** to your assessor about the different types of accidents and sudden illness that may occur in your work setting.
- Or, you can write a **personal statement or reflection** about your experience of the different types of accidents and sudden illness that may occur in **your work setting**.

REMEMBER TO:

- Provide a detailed **account** of the different types of accidents and sudden illness that may occur in your work setting.
- Include details of **different** types of accidents and sudden illness, including how they may occur.
- Think about **examples** of both accidents and sudden illness.
- Think about your experience of accidents and sudden illness that have occurred in **your work setting**.

Learning Outcome 3: Understand procedures for responding to accidents and sudden illness

Assessment Criterion 3.2: Explain procedures to be followed should an accident or sudden illness occur

What does AC3.2 mean?

- ○ The lead word **explain** means that you must **make clear** the procedures to be followed should an accident or sudden illness occur.
- ○ Your **account** must make clear the process to be followed for either an accident or a sudden illness.
- ○ For the key word **procedures** you can think about the steps you must take when an accident or sudden illness occurs.

Read the following **Real Work Setting** scenario and think about how it relates to your work setting and role:

Real Work Setting

Name: Tara

Job role: Senior Residential Carer to older people

(See page 100 for a description of the role.)

Procedures for an accident or sudden illness: Tara has also reviewed and updated the residential setting's procedures for the steps to be taken by Seniors and Care Assistants when an accident or sudden illness occurs. Tara plans to discuss these updates with the team to ensure they are aware of them.

Evidencing AC3.2 to your assessor:

For AC3.2 you must evidence your understanding of the procedures to be followed should an accident or sudden illness occur.

Assessment Methods:

Oral/Written Questioning or **Discussion** or a **Personal Statement** or **Reflection**.

- You can **tell** your assessor about the procedures to be followed should an accident or sudden illness occur.
- Or, you can **talk** to your assessor about the procedures to be followed should an accident or sudden illness occur.
- Or, you can write a **personal statement or reflection** about your experience of the procedures to be followed should an accident or sudden illness occur.

REMEMBER TO:

- Provide an **account** and **explain** the procedures to be followed.
- Include **details** about the procedures to be followed for either an accident or a sudden illness.
- Think about **your work setting** and the procedure you must follow when an accident or sudden illness occurs.

Learning Outcome 4: Be able to reduce the spread of infection

Assessment Criterion 4.1: Explain your role in supporting others to follow practices that reduce the spread of infection

What does AC4.1 mean?
- The lead word **explain** means that you must **make clear** your role in supporting others to follow practices that reduce the spread of infection.
- Your **account** must make clear what your role is and how you support others.
- For the key word **others** you can think about the support you provide to your colleagues, individuals and their families, friends and advocates.

Read the following **Real Work Setting** scenario and think about how it relates to your work setting and role:

Real Work Setting

Name: Betty
Job role: Senior Support Worker in a mental health unit
Betty has been working as a Senior Support Worker for six years. Her Senior responsibilities include: leading and supporting a team of Support Workers; working in partnership with the people who use the service, as well as with agencies and professionals; delivering person-centred support whilst offering a recovery-based approach.
Supporting others in reducing the spread of infection: Betty is leading the shift today and begins by washing her hands using the recommended hand-washing technique and putting on an apron and gloves to support one individual to get ready this morning. As part of her shift responsibilities Betty ensures her colleagues follow agreed work practices to reduce the spread of infection. She also advises her colleagues on how they can improve their practices to reduce the spread of infection and always refers them to the work setting's infection prevention and control procedures and the specific guidelines in place.

Evidencing AC4.1 to your assessor:

For AC4.1 you must evidence your knowledge of your role in supporting others to follow practices that reduce the spread of infection.

Assessment Methods:

Oral/Written Questioning or Discussion or a Personal Statement or Reflection.

- You can **tell** your assessor about your role in supporting others to follow practices that reduce the spread of infection.
- Or, you can **talk** to your assessor about your role in supporting others to follow practices that reduce the spread of infection.
- Or, you can write a **personal statement or reflection** about your experience of your role in supporting others to follow practices that reduce the spread of infection.

REMEMBER TO:
- Provide an **account** and **explain** your role in supporting others to follow practices that reduce the spread of infection.
- Include **details** about how you support others to follow practices that reduce the spread of infection and the reasons why.
- Include **examples** of how you support different people to follow practices that reduce the spread of infection.
- Think about **your work setting** and your role in supporting others to follow practices that reduce the spread of infection.

Learning Outcome 4: Be able to reduce the spread of infection

Assessment Criterion 4.2: Demonstrate the recommended method for hand washing

What does AC4.2 mean?

○ The lead word **demonstrate** means that you must **be able to show** through **your work practices** how to use the recommended method for hand washing.

○ Your **observations** of your work practices must include you using the recommended method.

○ For the key word **recommended** you can think about the approved guidelines in place for washing your hands.

Read the following **Real Work Setting** scenario and think about how it relates to your work setting and role:

Real Work Setting

Name: Betty

Job role: Senior Support Worker in a mental health unit

(See page 102 for a description of the role.)

Recommended method for hand washing: Betty is inducting a new Support Worker today and begins the shift by showing her the different steps to follow for washing her hands effectively. Betty begins by explaining to the new member of staff that it takes at least fifteen seconds to wash your hands, and shares with her how she sings 'Happy Birthday' twice through in her head to ensure she has spent enough time washing her hands. Betty then points to the diagram on the wall of the steps to follow when hand washing and shows her how to follow these steps.

Evidencing AC4.2 to your assessor:

For AC4.2 you must evidence your skills in demonstrating the recommended method for hand washing.

Assessment Method:

Direct Observation of your work practices.

● You can **show** your assessor how you wash your hands using the recommended method for hand washing.

REMEMBER TO:

● Make arrangements for **observation** of **your work practices**.

● Include evidence of you washing your hands.

● Ensure the evidence you provide complies with the recommended method for hand washing.

● Think about the recommended method for hand washing that you follow in **your work setting**.

Learning Outcome 4: Be able to reduce the spread of infection

Assessment Criterion 4.3: Demonstrate ways to ensure that your health and hygiene do not pose a risk to an individual or to others at work

What does AC4.3 mean?

- The lead word **demonstrate** means that you must **be able to show** through **your work practices** how to ensure that your health and hygiene do not pose a risk to an individual or to others at work.
- Your **observations** of your work practices must include you using **different ways** to ensure that your health and hygiene do not pose a risk to an individual or to others at work.
- For the key word **health** you can think about how your physical well-being can impact on others.
- For the key word **hygiene** you can think about how levels of cleanliness and health can impact on others.
- For the key word **risk** you can think about the dangers or harm that may be caused to an individual or to others at work.
- For the key word **others** you can think about your colleagues, professionals and visitors to the work setting.

Read the following **Real Work Setting** scenario and think about how it relates to your work setting and role:

Real Work Setting

Name: Betty

Job role: Senior Support Worker in a mental health unit

(See page 102 for a description of the role.)

Health and hygiene: Betty is fully aware of the work setting's infection prevention and control procedures and ensures she complies with these when carrying out her day-to-day responsibilities. Last week Betty phoned in to report that she was off sick as she had been vomiting the night before and agreed with her manager not to return to work until a couple of days later so as to ensure that she did not spread her infection to others.

Evidencing AC4.3 to your assessor:

For AC4.3 you must evidence your skills in demonstrating ways to ensure that your health and hygiene do not pose a risk to an individual or to others at work.

Assessment Method:

Direct Observation of your work practices.

- You can **show** your assessor different ways to ensure that your health and hygiene do not pose a risk to an individual or to others at work.

REMEMBER TO:

- Make arrangements for **observation of your work practices**.
- Include evidence of you using different ways to ensure that your health and hygiene do not pose a risk to an individual or to others at work.
- Ensure the evidence you provide is related to both your health and your hygiene.
- Think about the different ways to ensure that your health and hygiene do not pose a risk to an individual or to others in **your work setting**.

Learning Outcome 5: Be able to move and handle equipment and other objects safely

Assessment Criterion 5.1: Explain the main points of legislation that relates to moving and handling

What does AC5.1 mean?

- O The lead word **explain** means that you must **make clear** the details that are included in the main pieces of legislation relating to moving and handling.
- O Your **account** must make clear what the main pieces of legislation are and how they relate to moving and handling equipment and other objects.
- O For the key word **legislation** you can think about the laws that are in place relating to moving and handling in health and social care work settings.

Read the following **Real Work Setting** scenario and think about how it relates to your work setting and role:

Real Work Setting

Name: Joe

Job role: Senior Care Assistant for older people living in a residential care home

Joe works as a Senior Care Assistant and his duties include supporting and acting on behalf of the Home Manager, including administering medication and assisting residents with their day-to-day needs. These include facilitating care reviews and communications with others involved in their lives, namely families, friends, advocates and other professionals.

Moving and handling legislation: Joe's manager has asked him to provide the team with an update on relevant moving and handling legislation at next week's training session as he has recently completed a training update as part of his moving and handling trainer role in the home. Joe has developed a quiz for the team to complete that will test their knowledge of the current moving and handling legislation that exists and how this legislation relates to them and their day-to-day work activities.

Evidencing AC5.1 to your assessor:

For AC5.1 you must evidence your understanding of the main points of moving and handling legislation.

Assessment Methods:

Oral/Written Questioning or **Discussion** or a **Personal Statement**.

- You can **tell** your assessor about the main points of moving and handling legislation.
- Or, you can **talk** to your assessor about the main points of moving and handling legislation.
- Or, you can write a **personal statement** about the main points of moving and handling legislation.

REMEMBER TO:

- Provide an **account** and **explain** the main points of moving and handling legislation.
- Include **details** about the moving and handling legislation that exists and how it relates to your work setting and your job role.
- Include **examples** of different pieces of relevant moving and handling legislation.
- Think about how moving and handling legislation relates to **your work setting** and **your job role**.

Learning Outcome 5: Be able to move and handle equipment and other objects safely

Assessment Criterion 5.2: Explain principles for safe moving and handling

What does AC5.2 mean?

- O The lead word **explain** means that you must **make clear** the principles for safe moving and handling of equipment and other objects.
- O Your **account** must make clear the principles for safe moving and handling.
- O For the key word **principles** you can think about the different ways to make moving and handling safer.

Read the following **Real Work Setting** scenario and think about how it relates to your work setting and role:

Real Work Setting

Name: Joe

Job role: Senior Care Assistant for older people living in a residential care home

(See page 105 for a description of the role.)

Safe moving and handling principles: Joe plans to explore with the team in next week's training session how to ensure all moving and handling activities are safe, including the correct moving and handling procedures to follow and the correct use of moving and handling equipment provided at the home. Joe also plans to check with each team member their understanding of the home's moving and handling procedures.

Evidencing AC5.2 to your assessor:

For AC5.2 you must evidence your knowledge of the principles for safe moving and handling of equipment and other objects.

Assessment Methods:

Oral/Written Questioning or **Discussion** or a **Personal Statement**.

- You can **tell** your assessor about the principles for safe moving and handling.
- Or, you can **talk** to your assessor about the principles for safe moving and handling.
- Or, you can write a **personal statement** about the principles for safe moving and handling.

REMEMBER TO:

- Provide an **account** and **explain** the principles for safe moving and handling of equipment and other objects.
- Include **details** about the principles to follow for safe moving and handling.
- Include **examples** of different principles to follow.
- Think about the principles for safe moving and handling that are in place in **your work setting**.

Learning Outcome 5: Be able to move and handle equipment and other objects safely

Assessment Criterion 5.3: Move and handle equipment and other objects safely

What does AC5.3 mean?

- ⊙ The lead words **move and handle** mean that you must **be able to show** through **your work practices** how to use equipment safely and follow procedures for moving and handling both equipment and objects.
- ⊙ Your **observations** of your work practices must include you using equipment for moving and handling, and moving objects safely.
- ⊙ For the key words **move and handle** you can think about the procedures you follow in your work setting for the correct use of equipment and the safe moving of objects.
- ⊙ For the key word **equipment** you can think about the equipment you use in your work setting for moving and handling.
- ⊙ For the key word **objects** you can think about other items and loads you move in your work setting.

Read the following **Real Work Setting** scenario and think about how it relates to your work setting and role:

Real Work Setting

Name: Joe

Job role: Senior Care Assistant for older people living in a residential care home

(See page 105 for a description of the role.)

Safe moving and handling: As a follow-up to next week's training session Joe plans to observe all members of the team over the next 4–6 weeks when they move and handle equipment and objects, in order to assist the team to ensure their practices are safe and to provide them with another opportunity for advice and feedback.

Evidencing AC5.3 to your assessor:

For AC5.3 you must evidence your skills in moving and handling equipment and other objects safely.

Assessment Method:

Direct Observation of your work practices.

- You can **show** your assessor how you move and handle equipment and other objects safely.

REMEMBER TO:

- Make arrangements for **observation of your work practices**.
- Include evidence of you moving and handling equipment and other objects.
- Ensure the evidence you provide is related to moving and handling equipment and objects.
- Think about how you move and handle equipment and other objects safely in **your work setting**.

Learning Outcome 6: Be able to handle hazardous substances and materials

Assessment Criterion 6.1: Describe types of hazardous substances that may be found in the work setting

What does AC6.1 mean?

- ○ The lead word **describe** means that you must provide an **account** that **details** the different types of hazardous substances that exist in your work setting.
- ○ Your **account** must detail the **different** types of hazardous substances that exist.
- ○ For the key word **types** you can think about the different reasons substances are classed as hazardous.
- ○ For the key word **hazardous** you can think about the different forms that a substance may take.

Read the following **Real Work Setting** scenario and think about how it relates to your work setting and role:

Real Work Setting

Name: Dennis

Job Role: Senior Support Worker for adults with mental health needs

Dennis has been working as a Senior Support Worker for one year. His Senior responsibilities include: assisting in the development of recovery plans for individuals so that they can move on to independent living; liaising with agencies and services on behalf of individuals; leading shifts at weekends and managing a small team of Support Workers.

Hazardous substances: Dennis will be assisting the health and safety officer in his work setting to provide the team with an up-to-date information handout about the different types of hazardous substances that exist in the work setting and that they need to be aware of when carrying out their job roles.

Evidencing AC6.1 to your assessor:

For AC6.1 you must evidence your knowledge of the different types of hazardous substances that may be found in the work setting.

Assessment Methods:

Oral/Written Questioning or **Discussion** or a **Personal Statement.**

- You can **tell** your assessor the different types of hazardous substances that exist in your work setting.
- Or, you can **talk** to your assessor about the different types of hazardous substances that exist in your work setting.
- Or, you can write a **personal statement** about the different types of hazardous substances that exist in your work setting.

REMEMBER TO:

- Provide a detailed **account** of the different types of hazardous substances that may be found in the work setting.
- Include **details** of different types of hazardous substances that exist in your work setting.
- Think about **examples** of different types of hazardous substances.
- Think about different types of hazardous substances that exist in **your work setting**.

Learning Outcome 6: Be able to handle hazardous substances and materials

Assessment Criterion 6.2: Demonstrate safe practices for storing hazardous substances, using hazardous substances and disposing of hazardous substances and materials

What does AC6.2 mean?

- The lead word **demonstrate** means that you must **be able to show** through **your work practices** how to store, use and dispose of hazardous substances and materials safely.
- Your **observations** of your work practices must include you storing, using and disposing of hazardous substances and materials safely.
- For the key word **storing** you can think about the procedures to follow in your work setting for ensuring hazardous substances are kept secure.
- For the key word **using** you can think about the procedures to follow in your work setting for ensuring the safe application of hazardous substances.
- For the key word **disposing** you can think about the procedures to follow in your work setting for ensuring the safe removal of hazardous substances and materials.
- For the key word **hazardous** you can think about the different substances and materials that are found in your work setting that can cause ill health.

Read the following **Real Work Setting** scenario and think about how it relates to your work setting and role:

Real Work Setting

Name: Dennis
Job Role: Senior Support Worker for adults with mental health needs
(See page 108 for a description of the role.)
Following safe practices: Dennis is being observed by his assessor this morning and has prepared for his observation by ensuring that he will be able to show his assessor how he stores, uses and disposes of a variety of hazardous substances and materials as part of his day-to-day work activities.

Evidencing AC6.2 to your assessor:

For AC6.2 you must evidence your skills in following safe practices for storing, using and disposing of hazardous substances and materials.

Assessment Method:
Direct Observation of your work practices.

- You can **show** your assessor how you follow safe practices for storing, using and disposing of hazardous substances and materials.

REMEMBER TO:
- Make arrangements for **observation** of your **work practices**.
- Include evidence of you storing, using and disposing of different hazardous substances and materials.
- Ensure the evidence you provide is related to hazardous substances and materials.
- Think about how you store, use and dispose of hazardous substances and materials safely in **your work setting**.

Learning Outcome 7: Be able to promote fire safety in the work setting

Assessment Criterion 7.1: Describe practices that prevent fires from starting and spreading

What does AC7.1 mean?

- The lead word **describe** means that you must provide an **account** that **details** the different ways to prevent fires starting and spreading.
- Your **account** must detail the different ways to prevent fires starting and spreading.
- For the key word **practices** you can think about your work setting's fire safety procedures.

Read the following **Real Work Setting** scenario and think about how it relates to your work setting and role:

Real Work Setting
Name: Simone
Job Role: Senior Support Worker
Simone has been working as a Senior Support Worker for six years. Her Senior responsibilities include: inducting, supporting and monitoring Support Workers; updating and developing care and staff records, including support plans, risk assessments, staff rotas and supervision records.
Fire safety work practices: Simone is completing her fire safety checks this morning, which will include testing the smoke alarms, ensuring that the fire doors are all working correctly and that all fire exit routes continue to be well maintained and kept clear. Simone will also review the fire risk assessments currently in place for individuals and the building.

Evidencing AC7.1 to your assessor:

For AC7.1 you must evidence your knowledge of the practices that prevent fires starting and spreading.

Assessment Methods:

Oral/Written Questioning or Discussion or a Personal Statement.

- You can **tell** your assessor the different ways to prevent fires starting and spreading in your work setting.
- Or, you can **talk** to your assessor about the different ways to prevent fires starting and spreading in your work setting.
- Or, you can write a **personal statement** about the different ways to prevent fires starting and spreading in your work setting.

REMEMBER TO:

- Provide a detailed **account** of the practices that prevent fires starting and spreading.
- Include **details** of different work practices you use to prevent fires starting and spreading.
- Include examples of **different ways** to prevent fires starting and spreading.
- Think about different ways of working that exist in **your work setting** to prevent fires starting and spreading.

Learning Outcome 7: Be able to promote fire safety in the work setting

Assessment Criterion 7.2: Demonstrate measures that prevent fires from starting

What does AC7.2 mean?

- The lead word **demonstrate** means that you must **be able to show** through **your work practices** how to prevent fires starting.
- Your **observations** of your work practices must include you working in ways to prevent fires starting.
- For the key word **measures** you can think about the fire safety procedures you follow as well as the actions you take that prevent fires starting.

Read the following **Real Work Setting** scenario and think about how it relates to your work setting and role:

Real Work Setting

Name: Simone

Job Role: Senior Support Worker

(See page 110 for a description of the role.)

Fire prevention procedures: Simone is meeting with individuals today for a house meeting and will be making available at today's meeting the poster that has been designed to help raise awareness about how fires start and how they can be prevented. Some of the items Simone wishes to discuss with individuals in particular include the no-smoking house policy and ensuring that all appliances are turned off when left unattended.

Evidencing AC7.2 to your assessor:

For AC7.2 you must evidence your skills in working in ways that prevent fires starting.

Assessment method:

Direct Observation of your work practices.

- You can **show** your assessor how you work in ways that prevent fires starting.

REMEMBER TO:

- Make arrangements for **observation** of **your work practices**.
- Include evidence of you planning and taking actions that prevent fires starting.
- Ensure the evidence you provide is related to fire prevention.
- Think about the procedures in place in **your work setting** that prevent fires starting.

Learning Outcome 7: Be able to promote fire safety in the work setting

Assessment Criterion 7.3: Explain emergency procedures to be followed in the event of a fire in the work setting

What does AC7.3 mean?

- The lead word **explain** means that you must **make clear** the emergency procedures to be followed in the event of a fire in your work setting.
- Your **account** must make clear how and why these emergency procedures must be followed.
- For the key words **emergency procedures** you can think about the actions that must be taken in the event of a fire in your work setting.

Read the following **Real Work Setting** scenario and think about how it relates to your work setting and role:

Real Work Setting

Name: Simone

Job Role: Senior Support Worker

(See page 110 for a description of the role.)

Fire emergency procedures: Simone is supporting a group of individuals today to provide a short presentation to others about the actions that must be taken in the event of a fire, including the 'Dos and Don'ts'. Simone has also arranged for the manager to attend so that he can discuss with the group the importance of taking these actions quickly and correctly.

Evidencing AC7.3 to your assessor:

For AC7.3 you must evidence your understanding of the emergency procedures to follow in the event of a fire in your work setting.

Assessment Methods:

Oral/Written Questioning or Discussion or a Personal Statement.

- You can **tell** your assessor about the emergency procedures to follow in the event of a fire in your work setting.
- Or, you can **talk** to your assessor about the emergency procedures to follow in the event of a fire in your work setting.
- Or, you can write a **personal statement** about the emergency procedures to follow in the event of a fire in your work setting.

REMEMBER TO:
- Provide an **account** and **explain** the emergency procedures to follow in the event of a fire in your work setting.
- Include **details** about the actions that must be taken and why.
- Include **examples** of the actions to take.
- Think about the emergency procedures that are in place in **your work setting** in the event of a fire.

Learning Outcome 7: Be able to promote fire safety in the work setting

Assessment Criterion 7.4: Ensure that clear evacuation routes are maintained at all times

What does AC7.4 mean?

- The lead word **ensure** means that you must **be able to show** through **your work practices** how to maintain clear fire evacuation routes at all times.
- Your **observations** of your work practices must include you working in ways to maintain clear fire evacuation routes at all times.
- For the key words **evacuation routes** you can think about the fire escape routes that exist in your work setting.

Read the following **Real Work Setting** scenario and think about how it relates to your work setting and role:

Real Work Setting

Name: Simone

Job Role: Senior Support Worker

(See page 110 for a description of the role.)

Maintaining evacuation routes: Simone is inducting a new Senior Support Worker today and as part of her induction will be showing her round the work setting, including how to complete the fire safety checks. Simone begins by showing the new Support Worker the fire escape routes and the checks to be made to ensure these are in good working order and are being kept clear, and the reasons why it is important to do so.

Evidencing AC7.4 to your assessor:

For AC7.4 you must evidence your skills in working in ways that ensure clear fire evacuation routes are maintained at all times.

Assessment Method:

Direct Observation of your work practices.

- You can **show** your assessor how you work in ways that ensure clear fire evacuation routes are maintained at all times.

REMEMBER TO:

- Make arrangements for **observation** of **your work practices**.
- Include evidence of you ensuring that clear fire evacuation routes are maintained at all times.
- Ensure the evidence you provide is related to fire safety.
- Think about the procedures in place in **your work setting** to ensure that clear fire evacuation routes are maintained at all times.

Learning Outcome 8: Be able to implement security measures in the work setting

Assessment Criterion 8.1: Demonstrate use of agreed procedures for checking the identity of anyone requesting access to the premises and/or information

What does AC8.1 mean?

- ○ The lead word **demonstrate** means that you must **be able to show** through **your work practices** how to check the identity of anyone requesting access to the premises and/or information.
- ○ Your **observations** of your work practices must include you checking the identity of people requesting access to the premises and/or information.
- ○ For the key words **agreed procedures** you can think about your work setting's procedures for checking a person's identity and for sharing information with others.

Read the following **Real Work Setting** scenario and think about how it relates to your work setting and role:

Real Work Setting

Name: Saheed
Job Role: Senior Residential Care Worker for adults who have complex needs
Saheed has been working as a Senior Residential Care Worker for ten years. His Senior responsibilities include: supervising a team of Care Workers; managing the rotas; developing care plans; working closely with the manager, other professionals and individuals' families, friends and advocates.
Checking visitors' identity: Saheed is holding a staff meeting today to inform staff of the building works that will soon be commencing and to remind staff to be extra vigilant in maintaining everyone's safety and security during the works. Saheed plans to take along with him a copy of the procedures to be followed if someone requests access to the premises and/or to information.

Evidencing AC8.1 to your assessor:

For AC8.1 you must evidence your skills in following your work setting's procedures for checking the identity of anyone requesting access to the premises and/or information.

Assessment Method:	**REMEMBER TO:**
Direct Observation of your work practices. • You can **show** your assessor or an expert witness how you comply with your work setting's procedures for checking the identity of anyone requesting access to the premises and/or information.	• Make arrangements for **observation** of **your work practices**. • Include evidence of you checking a person's identity. • Ensure the evidence you provide is related to both access to the premises and a request for information. • Think about the procedures in place in **your work setting** for checking the identity of anyone requesting access to the premises and/or information.

Learning Outcome 8: Be able to implement security measures in the work setting

Assessment Criterion 8.2: Demonstrate use of measures to protect own security and the security of others in the work setting

What does AC8.2 mean?

- ○ The lead word **demonstrate** means that you must **be able to show** through **your work practices** how to protect your security and that of others.
- ○ Your **observations** of your work practices must include you working in ways that protect your security and that of others.
- ○ For the key word **measures** you can think about your work setting's procedures for protecting your security and that of others.

Read the following **Real Work Setting** scenario and think about how it relates to your work setting and role:

Real Work Setting

Name: Saheed

Job Role: Senior Residential Care Worker for adults who have complex needs

(See page 114 for a description of the role.)

Security procedures: Saheed is meeting with his manager today and will be conducting a review of the effectiveness of the service's current security procedures. Areas that will be looked at and discussed include the building, the safety equipment in place, the staff who work there and the individuals who live there.

Evidencing AC8.2 to your assessor:

For AC8.2 you must evidence your skills in following your work setting's procedures for protecting your security and the security of others.

Assessment Method:

Direct Observation of your work practices.

- You can **show** your assessor how you follow your work setting's procedures for protecting your security and the security of others.

REMEMBER TO:

- ● Make arrangements for **observation** of **your work practices**.
- ● Include evidence of you protecting both your security and the security of others.
- ● Ensure the evidence you provide is related to security.
- ● Think about the procedures in place in **your work setting** for protecting both your security and that of others.

Learning Outcome 8: Be able to implement security measures in the work setting

Assessment Criterion 8.3: Explain the importance of ensuring that others are aware of your whereabouts

What does AC8.3 mean?
- The lead word **explain** means that you must **make clear** the reasons why it is important to ensure that others are aware of your whereabouts when you are working.
- Your **account** must make clear why it is important to ensure that others are aware of your whereabouts when you are working.
- For the key word **whereabouts** you can think about why it is important to let others know where you are working, with whom, and the times you arrive and leave the work setting.

Read the following **Real Work Setting** scenario and think about how it relates to your work setting and role:

Real Work Setting

Name: Saheed

Job Role: Senior Residential Care Worker for adults who have complex needs

(See page 114 for a description of the role.)

Security procedures: Saheed's review of the effectiveness of the service's current security procedures has identified that staff are not always accurately recording the times they arrive at and leave the work setting with different individuals during the day. Saheed plans to raise this with each staff member during their supervisions and to provide each staff member the opportunity to discuss with him the importance of ensuring that others are aware of their whereabouts at all times.

Evidencing AC8.3 to your assessor:

For AC8.3 you must evidence your understanding of the importance of ensuring that others are aware of your whereabouts.

Assessment Methods:

Oral/Written Questioning or **Discussion** or a **Personal Statement.**

- You can **tell** your assessor about the reasons why it is important to ensure that others are aware of your whereabouts when you are working.
- Or, you can **talk** to your assessor about the reasons why it is important to ensure that others are aware of your whereabouts when you are working.
- Or, you can write a **personal statement** about the reasons why it is important to ensure that others are aware of your whereabouts when you are working.

REMEMBER TO:
- Provide an **account** and **explain** the importance of ensuring that others are aware of your whereabouts when you are working.
- Include **details** about the reasons why.
- Include **examples** of the consequences of not doing so.
- Think about the importance of ensuring that others in **your work setting** are aware of your whereabouts.

Learning Outcome 9: Know how to manage stress

Assessment Criterion 9.1: Describe common signs and indicators of stress

What does AC9.1 mean?

- The lead word **describe** means that you must provide an **account** that **details** the common signs and indicators of stress.
- Your **account** must detail the **different** signs and indicators of stress.
- For the key word **signs** you can think about the visible changes that may be seen and/or noticed in anyone who is stressed.
- For the key word **indicators** you can think about how anyone who is stressed may feel and how this may be expressed in a variety of ways.

Read the following **Real Work Setting** scenario and think about how it relates to your work setting and role:

Real Work Setting

Name: Karma

Job Role: Senior Carer in a dementia care service

Karma has been working as a Senior Carer for six months. Her Senior responsibilities include: mentoring and supervising a team of Support Workers; maintaining full care records; reviewing individuals' packages of care; ordering and administering medication.

Signs and indicators of stress: Karma is leading the staff meeting on Thursday this week and plans to discuss with the team her recent experience of participating in a stress management course. Karma plans to introduce the topic of stress to the team through a variety of different activities, including sharing her own personal experience of stress at work, inviting other staff members to do the same, and then agreeing on a list of different signs and indicators of stress that may occur in different people.

Evidencing AC9.1 to your assessor:

For AC9.1 you must evidence your knowledge of the common signs and indicators of stress.

Assessment Methods:

Oral/Written Questioning or Discussion or a Personal Statement.

- You can **tell** your assessor about the common signs and indicators of stress.
- Or, you can **talk** to your assessor about the common signs and indicators of stress.
- Or, you can write a **personal statement** about the common signs and indicators of stress.

REMEMBER TO:

- Provide a detailed **account** of the common signs and indicators of stress.
- Include details of **different** common signs and indicators of stress.
- Include examples of different signs and indicators of stress.
- Think about different signs and indicators of stress that you've experienced or identified in others in **your work setting**.

Learning Outcome 9: Know how to manage stress

Assessment Criterion 9.2: Describe signs that indicate own stress

What does AC9.2 mean?

○ The lead word **describe** means that you must provide an **account** that **details** the signs that indicate that you are stressed.
○ Your **account** must detail the **different** signs of your own stress.
○ For the key word **signs** you can think about the visible changes that may be seen and/or noticed in you when you are stressed.
○ For the key word **indicate** you can think about you may feel when you are stressed and how this may be expressed in a variety of ways.

Read the following **Real Work Setting** scenario and think about how it relates to your work setting and role:

Real Work Setting
Name: Karma
Job Role: Senior Carer in a dementia care service
(See page 117 for a description of the role.)
Signs of own stress: Karma reflects with her manager on the learning she gained from the stress management course she attended. Karma shares with her manager how she gained a greater insight into the signs indicating that she is stressed, and how she noted that these were different depending on whether she was at work or at home with her family.

Evidencing AC9.2 to your assessor:

For AC9.2 you must evidence your knowledge of the signs that indicate you are stressed.

Assessment Methods:

Oral/Written Questioning or Discussion or a Personal Statement.

- You can **tell** your assessor the signs that indicate you are stressed.
- Or, you can **talk** to your assessor about the signs that indicate you are stressed.
- Or, you can write a **personal statement** about the signs that indicate you are stressed.

REMEMBER TO:

- Provide a detailed **account** of the signs that indicate you are stressed.
- Include details of **different** signs that indicate you are stressed.
- Include examples of different signs.
- Ensure these signs relate to **your own stress**.
- Think about different signs of stress that you've experienced or others have noted in you.

Learning Outcome 9: Know how to manage stress

Assessment Criterion 9.3: Analyse factors that tend to trigger own stress

What does AC9.3 mean?

- ○ The lead word **analyse** means that you must **examine in detail** the different factors that tend to trigger stress in you.
- ○ Your **account** must provide an analysis of **different factors** that tend to trigger your stress.
- ○ For the key word **trigger** you can think about the reasons that cause you to get stressed.

Read the following **Real Work Setting** scenario and think about how it relates to your work setting and role:

Real Work Setting

Name: Karma

Job Role: Senior Carer in a dementia care service

(See page 117 for a description of the role.)

Triggers of stress: Karma's manager suggests that it would be useful if she could share the different causes of her stress, both at work and at home, with the rest of the team in the planned meeting, and then invite the rest of the team to share their experiences.

Evidencing AC9.3 to your assessor:

For AC9.3 you must evidence your knowledge of the factors that tend to trigger your stress.

Assessment Methods:

Oral/Written Questioning or Discussion or a Personal Statement or Reflection.

- You can **tell** your assessor about the factors that tend to trigger your stress.
- Or, you can **talk** to your assessor about the factors that tend to trigger your stress.
- Or, you can write a **personal statement or reflection** about your experience of the factors that tend to trigger your stress.

REMEMBER TO:

- Provide an **account** and an **analysis** of different factors that tend to trigger your stress.
- Include details about **what** each factor is, and **how and why** it acts as a trigger of your own stress.
- Include **varied** examples of factors that trigger your stress.
- Think about the triggers of your stress both **within and outside your work setting**.

Learning Outcome 9: Know how to manage stress

Assessment Criterion 9.4: Compare strategies for managing stress

What does AC9.4 mean?

- ○ The lead word **compare** means that you must **consider in detail** the similarities and differences between different ways for managing stress.
- ○ Your **account** must provide a comparison of **different** strategies for managing stress.
- ○ For the key word **strategies** you can think about the different methods for managing stress that exist and how effective they are.

Read the following **Real Work Setting** scenario and think about how it relates to your work setting and role:

Real Work Setting

Name: Karma

Job Role: Senior Carer in a dementia care service

(See page 117 for a description of the role.)

Managing stress: Karma discusses with her manager the final activity she plans to undertake with the team, which involves sharing ideas for different ways of managing stress and the reasons why the team thinks these strategies help with reducing stress levels. Karma has also devised a questionnaire for each team member to complete after the meeting to provide them with greater insight into the different ways of managing stress that exist, and the benefits of using these in different ways and in different situations.

Evidencing AC9.4 to your assessor:

For AC9.4 you must evidence your knowledge of how strategies for managing stress compare.

Assessment Methods:

Oral/Written Questioning or Discussion or a Personal Statement or Reflection.

- You can **tell** your assessor about the similarities and differences between different strategies for managing stress.
- Or, you can **talk** to your assessor about the similarities and differences between different strategies for managing stress.
- Or, you can write a **personal statement or reflection** about your experience of the similarities and differences between different strategies for managing stress.

REMEMBER TO:

- Provide an **account** and a **comparison** of different strategies for managing stress.
- Include details about what each strategy is, its main features, and its similarities and differences to others.
- Include **varied** examples of strategies for managing stress.
- Think about strategies for managing stress both **within and outside your work setting**.

Learning Outcome 1: Understand requirements for handling information in health and social care settings

Assessment Criterion 1.1: Identify legislation and codes of practice that relate to handling information in health and social care settings

What does AC1.1 mean?

- The lead word **identify** means that you must **make clear** legislation and codes of practice relating to handling information in health and social care settings.
- Your **list** must include **different** examples of **both** legislation and codes of practice.
- For the key word **legislation** you can think about the laws that are in place relating to handling information in health and social care settings.
- For the key words **codes of practice** you can think about the guidelines and regulations that are in place relating to handling information in health and social care settings.
- For the key words **handling information** you can think about how and when you and others share information verbally, in writing and electronically.

Read the following **Real Work Setting** scenario and think about how it relates to your work setting and role:

Real Work Setting

Name: Sophie

Job Role: Senior Support Worker for adults with mental health needs

Sophie has been working as a Senior Support Worker for four years. Her Senior responsibilities include: leading a team of Support Workers; developing and reviewing individuals' support plans; enhancing individuals' life skills for independent living.

Legislation and codes of practice: Sophie has been asked by her manager to review the service's procedures and guidelines relating to handling information. As part of this process Sophie plans to reinforce the ways of working in terms of handling information that have been set down in writing for this service with the current team, and to provide any advice and guidance she can.

Evidencing AC1.1 to your assessor:

For AC1.1 you must evidence your understanding of legislation and codes of practice relating to handling information in health and social care.

Assessment Methods:

Oral/Written Questioning or **Discussion** or a **Spidergram**.

- You can **tell** your assessor the different legislation and codes of practice that exist relating to handling information.
- Or, You can **talk** to your assessor about the different legislation and codes of practice that exist relating to handling information.
- Or, you can complete a **spidergram** showing the different legislation and codes of practice that exist relating to handling information.

REMEMBER TO:

- **List** legislation and codes of practice relating to handling information.
- Include **different** examples of **both** legislation and codes of practice.
- Ensure they relate to handling information in a health or social care work setting.
- Think about the legislation and codes of practice in place in **your work setting**.

Learning Outcome 1: Understand requirements for handling information in health and social care settings

Assessment Criterion 1.2: Summarise the main points of legal requirements and codes of practice for handling information in health and social care settings

What does AC1.2 mean?

- The lead word **summarise** means that you must provide brief details of the **main points** of legal requirements and codes of practice for handling information in health and social care settings.
- Your summary must include **details** with examples of the main features of both legislation and codes of practice for handling information in health and social care settings.
- For the key words **legal requirements** you can think about the laws that are in place relating to handling information in health and social care settings.
- For the key words **codes of practice** you can think about the guidelines and regulations that are in place relating to handling information in health and social care settings.
- For the key words **handling information** you can think about how and when you and others share information verbally, in writing and electronically.

Read the following **Real Work Setting** scenario and think about how it relates to your work setting and role:

Real Work Setting

Name: Sophie

Job Role: Senior Support Worker for adults with mental health needs

(See page 121 for a description of the role.)

Legal requirements and codes of practice: Following on from the meeting Sophie held with the team in relation to their practices when handling information, she has agreed to book another training session with the two newest members of the team. They both indicated that they required further training and support to fully understand how to share information in ways that comply with the service's guidelines.

Evidencing AC1.2 to your assessor:

For AC1.2 you must evidence your understanding of the main points of legal requirements and codes of practice for handling information in health and social care settings.

Assessment Methods:

Oral/Written Questioning or **Discussion** or a **Personal Statement**.

- You can **tell** your assessor about the main points of legal requirements and codes of practice for handling information in health and social care settings.
- Or, you can **talk** to your assessor about the main points of legal requirements and codes of practice for handling information in health and social care settings.
- Or, you can write a **personal statement** about the main points of legal requirements and codes of practice for handling information in health and social care settings.

REMEMBER TO:

- Provide **brief details** of the legal requirements and codes of practice relating to handling information.
- Include **different** examples of **both** legal requirements and codes of practice.
- Ensure they relate to handling information in a health or social care work setting.
- Think about the legal requirements and codes of practice in place in **your work setting**.

Learning Outcome 2: Be able to implement good practice in handling information

Assessment Criterion 2.1: Describe features of manual and electronic information storage systems that help ensure security

What does AC2.1 mean?

- ○ The lead word **describe** means that you must provide an **account** that **details** the features of manual and electronic information storage systems that help ensure security.
- ○ Your **account** must detail the **different** features of both manual and electronic information storage systems.
- ○ For the key word **features** you can think about the main characteristics of both manual and electronic information storage systems.
- ○ For the key words **manual information storage systems** you can think about how hard copies of information are stored and kept secure.
- ○ For the key words **electronic information storage systems** you can think about how electronic copies of information are stored and kept secure.
- ○ For the key word **security** you can think about how to prevent information being accessed by those who are not authorised to do so.

Read the following **Real Work Setting** scenario and think about how it relates to your work setting and role:

Real Work Setting

Name: Jerry
Job Role: Senior Waking Night Support Worker
Jerry has been working as a Senior Waking Night Support Worker for nine months. His Senior responsibilities include: organising staff rotas; supervising a small team of Night Support Workers; undertaking health and safety responsibilities; maintaining accurate and complete records; maintaining and reviewing individuals' support plans; providing individuals with support to lead fulfilling lives.
Features of manual and electronic information storage systems: Jerry is being observed working tonight by his assessor. He has agreed to complete a discussion with his assessor that will focus on the secure handling of information. To prepare for this Jerry has spent some time considering how manual and electronic information and records are kept secure in his work setting.

Evidencing AC2.1 to your assessor:

For AC2.1 you must evidence your knowledge of the features of manual and electronic information storage systems that help ensure security.

Assessment Methods:

Oral/Written Questioning or Discussion or a Personal Statement.

- You can **tell** your assessor the features of manual and electronic information storage systems that help ensure security.
- Or, you can **talk** to your assessor about the features of manual and electronic information storage systems that help ensure security.
- Or, you can write a **personal statement** about the features of manual and electronic information storage systems that help ensure security.

REMEMBER TO:

- Provide a detailed **account** of the features of manual and electronic information storage systems that help ensure security.
- Include details of **different** features of **manual** and **electronic** information storage systems.
- Include examples of **both** manual and electronic information storage systems.
- Ensure you detail how these systems keep information secure.
- Think about the different manual and electronic information storage systems that help ensure security in **your work setting**.

Learning Outcome 2: Be able to implement good practice in handling information

Assessment Criterion 2.2: Demonstrate practices that ensure security when storing and accessing information

What does AC2.2 mean?

○ The lead word **demonstrate** means that you must **be able to show** through **your work practices** how to ensure security when storing and accessing information.

○ Your **observations** of your work practices must include you working in ways that ensure security when storing and accessing information.

○ For the key word **security** you can think about your work setting's procedures for how you and others must ensure security when storing and accessing information.

Read the following **Real Work Setting** scenario and think about how it relates to your work setting and role:

Real Work Setting

Name: Jerry

Job Role: Senior Waking Night Support Worker

(See page 123 for a description of the role.)

Storing and accessing information: To support Jerry's discussion with his assessor Jerry has agreed to be observed tonight storing and accessing information in a secure and confidential manner. Every night at the end of his shift, Jerry is responsible for securely storing a range of different records, such as the night reports completed by all staff, individuals' support plans and the setting's risk assessments. As part of his Senior role Jerry also meets with the evening staff at the end of their shift. He requests that they hand over to him and the rest of the night team information about the needs of each individual, as well as any current issues or tasks that need to be addressed by the team.

Evidencing AC2.2 to your assessor:

For AC2.2 you must evidence your skills in following your work setting's procedures for practising in ways that ensure security when storing and accessing information.

Assessment Method:

Direct Observation of your work practices.

● You can **show** your assessor how you follow your work setting's procedures for ensuring security when storing and accessing information.

REMEMBER TO:

● Make arrangements for **observation** of **your work practices**.

● Include evidence of you ensuring security when both storing and accessing information.

● Ensure the evidence you provide is related to the security of information.

● Think about the procedures in place in **your work setting** for ensuring security when storing and accessing information.

Learning Outcome 2: Be able to implement good practice in handling information

Assessment Criterion 2.3: Maintain records that are up to date, complete, accurate and legible

What does AC2.3 mean?

- ○ The lead word **maintain** means that you must **be able to show** through **your work practices** how to ensure records completed are up to date, complete, accurate and legible.
- ○ Your **observations** of your work practices must include you working in ways that ensure records completed are up to date, complete, accurate and legible.
- ○ For the key word **records** you can think about your work setting's procedures for how you and others must ensure manual and electronic records are up to date, complete, accurate and legible.

Read the following **Real Work Setting** scenario and think about how it relates to your work setting and role:

Real Work Setting

Name: Jerry

Job Role: Senior Waking Night Support Worker

(See page 123 for a description of the role.)

Maintaining records: Jerry's assessor has completed his observation and provides him with feedback on the tasks he observed him carry out, how these were carried out by him and their relation to evidencing the skills required around record keeping. Jerry is pleased with his feedback and the assessor's observation confirms that he is maintaining records well and effectively as part of his Senior role and is ensuring that he is also supporting other members of the team to do the same.

Evidencing AC2.3 to your assessor:

For AC2.3 you must evidence your skills in following your work setting's procedures for maintaining records that are up to date, complete, accurate and legible.

Assessment Method:

Direct Observation of your work practices.

- You can **show** your assessor how you follow your work setting's procedures for ensuring that you maintain records that are up to date, complete, accurate and legible.

REMEMBER TO:

- Make arrangements for **observation** of **your work practices**.
- Include evidence of you maintaining records.
- Ensure the evidence you provide is related to maintaining records that are up to date, complete, accurate and legible.
- Think about the procedures in place in **your work setting** for maintaining records.

Learning Outcome 3: Be able to support others to handle information

Assessment Criterion 3.1: Support others to understand the need for secure handling of information

What does AC3.1 mean?

○ The lead word **support** means that you must **be able to show** through **your work practices** how to assist others to ensure they understand the need for secure handling of information.

○ Your **observations** of your work practices must include you working in ways that support others to understand the need for secure handling of information.

○ For the key word **others** you can think about people you work with in your work setting, such as individuals, colleagues, other professionals and visitors, including individuals' families, friends and advocates.

Read the following **Real Work Setting** scenario and think about how it relates to your work setting and role:

Real Work Setting

Name: May
Job Role: Senior Carer for older people
May has been working as a Senior Carer for fifteen years. May's Senior responsibilities include: ensuring the team of Carers delivers a high standard of care to the residents in the home; inducting, training and supervising Carers; leading on the development of all activities and support provided to residents to ensure these consistently meet individuals' needs and wishes.
Supporting others in handling information securely: May is supporting another Senior to induct three new Carers, and has discussed with the Senior how best to support the three new recruited Carers to understand the importance of handling all information securely. Both agree that they will provide a short briefing to all three Carers as part of their inductions. They explain that during the observations completed of them during their first three months in post they will also support them to understand how to follow the home's procedures for the effective secure handling of information, and help them to understand the reasons for doing this as well as the consequences of not doing so.

Evidencing AC3.1 to your assessor:

For AC3.1 you must evidence your skills in following your work setting's procedures for supporting others to understand the need for secure handling of information.

Assessment Method:

Direct Observation of your work practices.

● You can **show** your assessor how you follow your work setting's procedures for supporting others to understand the need for secure handling of information.

REMEMBER TO:

● Make arrangements for **observation** of **your work practices**.
● Include evidence of you supporting others.
● Ensure the evidence you provide is related to the secure handling of information.
● Think about the procedures in place in **your work setting** for supporting others to understand the need for secure handling of information.

Learning Outcome 3: Be able to support others to handle information

Assessment Criterion 3.2: Support others to understand and contribute to records

What does AC3.2 mean?

- The lead word **support** means that you must **be able to show** through **your work practices** how to assist others to ensure they understand how to contribute to records.
- Your **observations** of your work practices must include you working in ways that provide support to others in relation to contributing to records.
- For the key word **others** you can think about other people you work with in your work setting who contribute to records, such as other members of the team.
- For the key word **contribute** you can think about how other members of the team are involved in participating in records as part of their day-to-day work responsibilities.

Read the following **Real Work Setting** scenario and think about how it relates to your work setting and role:

Real Work Setting
Name: May
Job Role: Senior Carer for older people
(See page 126 for a description of the role.)
Supporting others in understanding and completing records: May has arranged for the three newly recruited Carers to shadow her for two shifts this week, a morning shift and an evening shift. This is so that they can learn more about how they can contribute to records, including sharing information with others verbally, completing written records accurately and ensuring security is maintained.

Evidencing AC3.2 to your assessor:

For AC3.2 you must evidence your skills in following your work setting's procedures for supporting others to understand and contribute to records.

Assessment Method:

Direct Observation of your work practices.

- You can **show** your assessor how you follow your work setting's procedures for supporting others to understand and contribute to records.

REMEMBER TO:

- Make arrangements for **observation** of **your work practices**.
- Include evidence of you supporting others.
- Ensure the evidence you provide is related to understanding and contributing to records.
- Think about the procedures in place in **your work setting** for supporting others to understand and contribute to records.

Learning Outcome 1: Know the main forms of mental ill health

Assessment Criterion 1.1: Describe the main types of mental ill health according to the psychiatric (DSM/ICD) classification system: mood disorders, personality disorders, anxiety disorders, psychotic disorders, substance-related disorders, eating disorders and cognitive disorders

What does AC1.1 mean?

○ The lead word **describe** means that you must provide an **account** that **details** the main types of mental ill health according to the psychiatric (DSM/ICD) classification system.

○ Your **account** must detail **different** types of mental ill health and include details of the following disorder types: mood, personality, anxiety, psychotic, substance-related, eating and cognitive.

○ For the key words **psychiatric (DSM/ICD) classification system** you can think about the standards that mental health professionals, such as psychiatrists, use to make formal diagnoses and categorise psychiatric disorders.

Read the following **Real Work Setting** scenario and think about how it relates to your work setting and role:

Real Work Setting

Name: Barry

Job role: Senior Mental Health Support Worker in a Mental Health Project

Barry has been working as a Senior Mental Health Support Worker for five years. His Senior responsibilities include: assessment; support planning; inducting and mentoring Support Workers; leading inter-agency meetings; developing and maintaining links with other professionals and agencies.

Main types of mental ill health: Barry is mentoring two Support Workers as both have recently started working for the Project and are new to working in the mental health field. One of the Support Workers has asked Barry whether he can explain to him the psychiatric (DSM/ICD) classification system, as he is unsure what this is. Barry explains to the Support Worker that DSM and ICD refer to two sets of standards that are used by mental health professionals to diagnose symptoms of psychiatric disorders so as to ensure some consistency between professionals when providing diagnoses.

Evidencing AC1.1 to your assessor:

For AC1.1 you must evidence your knowledge of the main types of mental ill health according to the psychiatric (DSM/ICD) classification system: mood disorders, personality disorders, anxiety disorders, psychotic disorders, substance-related disorders, eating disorders and cognitive disorders.

Assessment Methods:

Oral/Written Questioning or **Discussion** or a **Personal Statement.**

● You can **tell** your assessor about the main types of mental ill health.

● Or, you can **talk** to your assessor about the main types of mental ill health.

● Or, you can write a **personal statement** about the main types of mental ill health.

REMEMBER TO:

● Provide a detailed **account** of the main types of mental ill health according to the psychiatric (DSM/ICD) classification system.

● Include details of all the types of mental ill health disorders according to the psychiatric (DSM/ICD) classification system.

● Ensure you detail the meaning of each of these disorders, including associated signs and symptoms.

● Think about **your work setting** and the types of mental ill health individuals and people you work with may experience.

Learning Outcome 1: Know the main forms of mental ill health

Assessment Criterion 1.2: Explain the key strengths and limitations of the psychiatric classification system

What does AC1.2 mean?

- The lead word **explain** means that you must **make clear** the key strengths and limitations of the psychiatric classification system.
- Your **account** must make clear **both** the strengths and the limitations of the psychiatric classification system.
- For the key word **strengths** you can think about the advantages of classifying mental health disorders using the psychiatric classification system.
- For the key word **limitations** you can think about the disadvantages of classifying mental health disorders using the psychiatric classification system.
- For the key words **psychiatric classification system** you can think about the DSM and ICD standards that mental health professionals, such as psychiatrists, use to make formal diagnoses and categorise psychiatric disorders.

Read the following **Real Work Setting** scenario and think about how it relates to your work setting and role:

Real Work Setting

Name: Barry

Job role: Senior Mental Health Support Worker in a Mental Health Project

(See page 128 for a description of the role.)

Strengths and limitations of the psychiatric classification system: Barry meets with the two Support Workers and suggests some useful websites for them to undertake some research about the psychiatric classification system used by mental health professionals. Barry has suggested to both Support Workers that they put together a short presentation about the main strengths and limitations of the psychiatric classification system for the individuals and professionals involved, and then present this at the team meeting in two weeks' time.

Evidencing AC1.2 to your assessor:

For AC1.2 you must evidence your knowledge of the key strengths and limitations of the psychiatric classification system.

Assessment Methods:

Oral/Written Questioning or **Discussion** or a **Personal Statement**.

- You can **tell** your assessor about the key strengths and limitations of the psychiatric classification system.
- Or, you can **talk** to your assessor about the key strengths and limitations of the psychiatric classification system.
- Or, you can write a **personal statement** about the key strengths and limitations of the psychiatric classification system.

REMEMBER TO:

- Provide an **account** and explain the **key strengths and limitations**.
- Include **details** about both the strengths and the limitations of the psychiatric classification system.
- Think about the strengths and limitations of the psychiatric classification system for **your work setting**.

Learning Outcome 1: Know the main forms of mental ill health

Assessment Criterion 1.3: Explain two alternative frameworks for understanding mental distress

What does AC1.3 mean?

- ○ The lead word **explain** means that you must **make clear** two alternative frameworks for understanding mental distress.
- ○ Your **account** must make clear **details** of two alternative frameworks.
- ○ For the key words **alternative frameworks** you can think about concepts and ideas that can help you understand what mental distress is and what it involves.
- ○ For the key words **mental distress** you can think about the range of symptoms experienced by people with mental ill health.

Read the following **Real Work Setting** scenario and think about how it relates to your work setting and role:

Real Work Setting

Name: Barry

Job role: Senior Mental Health Support Worker in a Mental Health Project

(See page 128 for a description of the role.)

Alternative frameworks for understanding mental distress: Barry meets with the two Support Workers and begins by sharing with them that he read this morning an article in the newspaper, which stated that mental illness is the single largest cause of disability in the UK, and that at least one in four people will experience a mental health problem at some point in their life and that one in six adults has a mental health problem at any one time. Barry then suggests when researching alternative frameworks for understanding mental distress that both Support Workers might find it useful to begin by reading through the Department of Health's mental health outcomes strategy 'No Health Without Mental Health' and its accompanying framework.

Evidencing AC1.3 to your assessor:

For AC1.3 you must evidence your knowledge of two alternative frameworks for understanding mental distress.

Assessment Methods:

Oral/Written Questioning or **Discussion** or a **Personal Statement or Reflection.**

- ● You can **tell** your assessor about two alternative frameworks for understanding mental distress.
- ● Or, you can **talk** to your assessor about two alternative frameworks for understanding mental distress.
- ● Or, you can write a **personal statement or reflection** about your experience of two alternative frameworks for understanding mental distress.

REMEMBER TO:

- ● Provide an **account** and explain two alternative frameworks.
- ● Include **details** about how both alternative frameworks can be used to understand mental distress.
- ● Think about how alternative frameworks for understanding mental distress can be used in **your work setting**.

Learning Outcome 1: Know the main forms of mental ill health

Assessment Criterion 1.4: Explain how mental ill health may be indicated through an individual's emotions, thinking and behaviour

What does AC1.4 mean?

○ The lead word **explain** means that you must **make clear** how mental ill health may be indicated through an individual's emotions, thinking and behaviour.

○ Your **account** must make clear **how** mental ill health may be indicated.

○ For the key word **emotions** you can think about how mental ill health may affect an individual's feelings and mood.

○ For the key word **thinking** you can think about how mental ill health may affect an individual's thoughts and thought processes.

○ For the key word **behaviour** you can think about how mental ill health may affect the way an individual responds and acts towards him/herself and others.

Read the following **Real Work Setting** scenario and think about how it relates to your work setting and role:

Real Work Setting

Name: Barry

Job role: Senior Mental Health Support Worker in a Mental Health Project

(See page 128 for a description of the role.)

Mental ill health indicators: Barry has asked both the Support Workers to think about one individual they are either currently supporting in the Project or have supported in a past job role, and to complete a detailed case study of how mental ill health can present, including details of the observable changes in the individual's emotions, thinking and behaviour and the reasons why and how these changes may occur.

Evidencing AC1.4 to your assessor:

For AC1.4 you must evidence your knowledge of how mental ill health may be indicated through an individual's emotions, thinking and behaviour.

Assessment Methods:

Oral/Written Questioning or **Discussion** or a **Personal Statement or Reflection**.

● You can **tell** your assessor about how mental ill health may be indicated through an individual's emotions, thinking and behaviour.

● Or, you can **talk** to your assessor about how mental ill health may be indicated through an individual's emotions, thinking and behaviour.

● Or, you can write a **personal statement or reflection** about your experience of how mental ill health may be indicated through an individual's emotions, thinking and behaviour.

REMEMBER TO:

● Provide an **account** about how mental ill health may be indicated through an individual's emotions, thinking and behaviour.

● Include **details** about the indicators of mental ill health in terms of an individual's emotions, thinking and behaviour.

● Think about **your work setting** and how mental ill health may be indicated through an individual's emotions, thinking and behaviour.

Learning Outcome 2: Know the impact of mental ill health on individuals and others in their social network

Assessment Criterion 2.1: Explain how individuals experience discrimination due to misinformation, assumptions and stereotypes about mental ill health

What does AC2.1 mean?

- The lead word **explain** means that you must **make clear** how individuals experience discrimination due to misinformation, assumptions and stereotypes about mental ill health.
- Your **account** must make clear **details** of how individuals experience discrimination.
- For the key word **discrimination** you can think about the unfair treatment experienced by individuals with mental ill health.
- For the key word **misinformation** you can think about inaccurate or deliberately misleading information that exists about mental ill health.
- For the key word **assumptions** you can think about untrue beliefs that exist about mental ill health.
- For the key word **stereotypes** you can think about how individuals with mental ill health may be labelled by others.

Read the following **Real Work Setting** scenario and think about how it relates to your work setting and role:

Real Work Setting

Name: Ana-Maria

Job role: Senior Mental Health Support Worker for adults who have mental health needs

Ana-Maria has been working as a Senior Mental Health Support Worker for two years. Her Senior responsibilities include: coordinating the 24-hour service; supervising and mentoring staff; promoting the recovery-based model; providing direct support to enable individuals to lead fulfilling lives.

Experiencing discrimination: Ana-Maria has recently attended a mental health awareness conference and found it interesting to hear directly from individuals about the impact of mental ill health on their lives. Ana-Maria was shocked to hear of some individuals' experiences of discrimination and the reasons why it occurs, and how there are still a lot of myths, stereotypes and assumptions being made about mental ill health, in particular about what it is and its potential effects on how individuals live their lives.

Evidencing AC2.1 to your assessor:

For AC2.1 you must evidence your knowledge of how individuals experience discrimination due to misinformation, assumptions and stereotypes about mental ill health.

Assessment Methods:

Oral/Written Questioning or **Discussion** or a **Personal Statement or Reflection**.

- You can **tell** your assessor about how individuals experience discrimination due to misinformation, assumptions and stereotypes about mental ill health.
- Or, you can **talk** to your assessor about how individuals experience discrimination due to misinformation, assumptions and stereotypes about mental ill health.
- Or, you can write a **personal statement or reflection** about your experience of how individuals experience discrimination due to misinformation, assumptions and stereotypes about mental ill health.

REMEMBER TO:

- Provide an **account** of how individuals experience discrimination about mental ill health.
- Include **details** about the different experiences of discrimination for different individuals.
- Ensure you evidence how discrimination arises due to misinformation, assumptions and stereotypes about mental ill health.
- Think about **your work setting** and how individuals experience discrimination due to misinformation, assumptions and stereotypes about mental ill health.

Learning Outcome 2: Know the impact of mental ill health on individuals and others in their social network

Assessment Criterion 2.2: Explain how mental ill health may impact on the individual, including:
a) psychologically and emotionally; b) practically and financially; c) the impact on using services; d) social exclusion; e) positive impacts

What does AC2.2 mean?

- The lead word **explain** means that you must **make clear** the impact that mental ill health may have on an individual.
- Your **account** must make clear **details** about its effects on an individual psychologically, emotionally, practically, financially, socially, positively, and in terms of their using services.
- For the key words **psychologically and emotionally** you can think about how mental ill health may affect how an individual thinks and feels about him/herself and others.
- For the key words **practically and financially** you can think about how mental ill health may affect an individual's finances and daily tasks.
- For the key words **using services** you can think about how mental ill health may affect the services an individual uses.
- For the key words **social exclusion** you can think about how mental ill health may affect an individual's relationships with others.

Read the following **Real Work Setting** scenario and think about how it relates to your work setting and role:

Real Work Setting

Name: Ana-Maria

Job role: Senior Mental Health Support Worker for adults who have mental health needs

(See page 132 for a description of the role.)

Mental ill health and its impacts: Ana-Maria is meeting with the team to discuss how mental ill health is impacting both negatively and positively on individuals' lives and the assistance that is required to support individuals through their experiences and to promote their well-being.

Evidencing AC2.2 to your assessor:

For AC2.2 you must evidence your knowledge of how mental ill health may have an impact on an individual.

Assessment Methods:
Oral/Written Questioning or **Discussion** or a **Personal Statement or Reflection**.

- You can **tell** your assessor about how mental ill health may have an impact on an individual.
- Or, you can **talk** to your assessor about how mental ill health may have an impact on an individual.
- Or, you can write a **personal statement or reflection** about your experience of how mental ill health may have an impact on an individual.

REMEMBER TO:
- Provide an **account** of how mental ill health may have an impact on an individual.
- Include **details** about the different **impacts** mental ill health may have on an individual.
- Think about **your work setting** and how mental ill health impacts on different individuals.

AC 2.3

Learning Outcome 2: Know the impact of mental ill health on individuals and others in their social network

Assessment Criterion 2.3: Explain how mental ill health may have an impact on those in the individual's familial, social or work network, including: a) psychologically and emotionally; b) practically and financially; c) the impact on using services; d) social exclusion; e) positive impacts

What does AC2.3 mean?

- The lead word **explain** means that you must **make clear** the impact mental ill health may have on those in an individual's familial, social or work circles.
- Your **account** must make clear **details** about the effects on others.
- For the key words **psychologically and emotionally** you can think about how mental ill health may affect how people think and feel about themselves and the individual.
- For the key words **practically and financially** you can think about how mental ill health may affect people's finances and daily tasks.
- For the key words **using services** you can think about how mental ill health may affect the services people use.
- For the key words **social exclusion** you can think about how mental ill health may affect people's relationships with the individual and others.

Read the following **Real Work Setting** scenario and think about how it relates to your work setting and role:

Real Work Setting

Name: Ana-Maria

Job role: Senior Mental Health Support Worker for adults who have mental health needs

(See page 132 for a description of the role.)

Mental ill health and its impacts on others: Ana-Maria asks the team to reflect on how mental ill health also impacts both negatively and positively on the people involved in individuals' lives.

Evidencing AC2.3 to your assessor:

For AC2.3 you must evidence your knowledge of how mental ill health may have an impact on those people in an individual's familial, social or work circles.

Assessment Methods:

Oral/Written Questioning or **Discussion** or a **Personal Statement** or **Reflection**.

- You can **tell** your assessor about how mental ill health may have an impact on those in an individual's familial, social or work circles.
- *Or,* you can **talk** to your assessor about how mental ill health may have an impact on those in an individual's familial, social or work circles.
- *Or,* you can write a **personal statement or reflection** about your experience of how mental ill health may impact on those in an individual's familial, social or work circles.

REMEMBER TO:

- Provide an **account** of how mental ill health may have an impact on those in an individual's familial, social or work circles.
- Include **details** about the different **impacts** mental ill health may have on those in an individual's familial, social or work circles.
- Think about **your work setting** and how mental ill health impacts on different people.

Learning Outcome 2: Know the impact of mental ill health on individuals and others in their social network

Assessment Criterion 2.4: Explain the benefits of early intervention in promoting an individual's mental health and well-being

What does AC2.4 mean?
- The lead word **explain** means that you must **make clear** the benefits of early intervention in promoting an individual's mental health and well-being.
- Your **account** must make clear **details** about the benefits of early intervention.
- For the key word **benefits** you can think about how early intervention can benefit an individual psychologically, emotionally, practically, financially and socially.
- For the key words **early intervention** you can think about the specialised services in place to provide early treatment and support for people experiencing mental ill health.

Read the following **Real Work Setting** scenario and think about how it relates to your work setting and role:

Real Work Setting

Name: Ana-Maria

Job role: Senior Mental Health Support Worker for adults who have mental health needs

(See page 132 for a description of the role.)

Early intervention and its benefits: Ana-Maria reviews with the team the range of specialised services individuals can access for advice, information, treatment and support, including therapies and medication. Ana-Maria then reflects with the team on how useful these early intervention services have been in terms of enabling individuals to go back to college and employment and to ensure they are receiving the correct benefits.

Evidencing AC2.4 to your assessor:

For AC2.4 you must evidence your knowledge of the benefits of early intervention in promoting an individual's mental health and well-being.

Assessment Methods:
Oral/Written Questioning or **Discussion** or a **Personal Statement** or **Reflection**.

- You can **tell** your assessor about the benefits of early intervention in promoting an individual's mental health and well-being.
- Or, you can **talk** to your assessor about the benefits of early intervention in promoting an individual's mental health and well-being.
- Or, you can write a **personal statement or reflection** about your experience of the benefits of early intervention in promoting an individual's mental health and well-being.

REMEMBER TO:
- Provide an **account** of the benefits of early intervention in promoting an individual's mental health and well-being.
- Include **details** about the different **benefits** of early intervention.
- Ensure you detail how early intervention promotes an individual's mental health and well-being.
- Think about **your work setting** and the role early intervention plays in promoting individuals' mental health and well-being.

Learning Outcome 1: Understand the neurology of dementia

Assessment Criterion 1.1: Describe a range of causes of dementia syndrome

What does AC1.1 mean?

○ The lead word **describe** means that you must provide an **account** that **details** the different causes of dementia syndrome.

○ Your **account** must detail a range of causes of dementia syndrome.

○ For the key words **dementia syndrome** you can think about the different types of dementia that exist as well as the different causes of these, such as the result of specific diseases like Alzheimer's or as a result of damage to the brain as a result of a stroke or other conditions. Dementia syndrome is caused by a combination of conditions and is sometimes called a mixed dementia.

Read the following **Real Work Setting** scenario and think about how it relates to your work setting and role:

Real Work Setting

Name: Joanne

Job role: Senior Residential Worker for adults who have dementia

Joanne has been working as a Senior Residential Worker for four months. Her Senior responsibilities include: leading a team of Residential Workers to meet the physical, social, emotional and spiritual developmental needs of older people with dementia; coordinating person-centred planning for all individuals and ensuring the care and support provided fully meets their needs; assisting with, supervising and attending individuals' reviews; liaising with individuals' Social Workers, GPs, District Nurses, family, friends and advocates; maintaining accurate and complete records and reports.

Causes of dementia syndrome: As part of Joanne's induction to her work setting and role, she recently attended a training session on dementia. The session began by defining the term dementia as meaning a deterioration in the brain's functions that impairs an individual's ability to do everyday tasks; this may mean a decline in memory or thinking skills. The training day then provided information on the causes of dementia, including: Alzheimer's disease; a deprivation of oxygen to the brain, i.e. a stroke; other conditions that cause changes in the way the brain functions, such as dementia with Lewy bodies; damage to different parts of the brain, such as frontotemporal dementia.

Evidencing AC1.1 to your assessor:

For AC1.1 you must evidence your understanding of a range of causes of dementia syndrome.

Assessment Methods:

Oral/Written Questioning or **Discussion** or a **Personal Statement or Reflection**.

● You can **tell** your assessor about a range of causes of dementia syndrome.

● Or, you can **talk** to your assessor about a range of causes of dementia syndrome.

● Or, you can write a **personal statement or reflection** about your experience of a range of causes of dementia syndrome.

REMEMBER TO:

● Provide a detailed **account** of a range of causes of dementia syndrome.

● Include **details** about a range of causes of dementia syndrome.

● Include **varied** examples of causes of dementia syndrome.

● Think about **your work setting** and the range of causes of dementia syndrome.

Learning Outcome 1: Understand the neurology of dementia

Assessment Criterion 1.2: Describe the types of memory impairment commonly experienced by individuals with dementia

What does AC1.2 mean?

- The lead word **describe** means that you must provide an **account** that **details** the types of memory impairment commonly experienced by individuals with dementia.
- Your **account** must detail **different** types of memory impairment that are commonly experienced.
- For the key words **memory impairment** you can think about how dementia can affect the storing, retaining and recalling of information in the brain and can cause difficulties for the individual with dementia.

Read the following **Real Work Setting** scenario and think about how it relates to your work setting and role:

Real Work Setting

Name: Joanne

Job role: Senior Residential Worker for adults who have dementia

(See page 136 for a description of the role.)

Types of memory impairment: Joanne will be sharing with the team some of the key information points from the training session she attended on dementia. Joanne plans to ask the team to consider the different memory difficulties experienced by two individuals with dementia to whom they provide support. For the first individual Joanne would like the team to consider the memory difficulties she is experiencing regarding her short-term memory and the impact this has on her ability to have conversations with others. For the second individual Joanne would like the team to consider the memory difficulties he is experiencing regarding his long-term memory, including how this has affected his ability to remember places he has visited, people he knows and daily life skills he has learnt.

Evidencing AC1.2 to your assessor:

For AC1.2 you must evidence your understanding of the types of memory impairment commonly experienced by individuals with dementia.

Assessment Methods:

Oral/Written Questioning or **Discussion** or a **Personal Statement** or **Reflection**.

- You can **tell** your assessor about the types of memory impairment commonly experienced by individuals who have dementia.
- Or, you can **talk** to your assessor about the types of memory impairment commonly experienced by individuals who have dementia.
- Or, you can write a **personal statement or reflection** about your experience of the types of memory impairment commonly experienced by individuals who have dementia.

REMEMBER TO:

- Provide a detailed **account** of the types of memory impairment commonly experienced by individuals with dementia.
- Include **details** about different types of memory impairment.
- Include **varied** examples of memory impairment commonly experienced by individuals who have dementia.
- Think about **your work setting** and the types of memory impairment commonly experienced by individuals with dementia.

Learning Outcome 1: Understand the neurology of dementia

Assessment Criterion 1.3: Explain the way that individuals process information, with reference to the abilities and limitations of individuals with dementia

What does AC1.3 mean?

- The lead word **explain** means that you must **make clear** the way that individuals process information, with reference to the abilities and limitations of individuals with dementia.
- Your **account** must make clear **details** of how individuals process information.
- For the key words **process information** you can think about how the left and right hemispheres of the brain are responsible for interpreting the information individuals see, hear and sense around them.
- For the key word **abilities and limitations** you can think about how individuals with dementia will have difficulties with their memory, the language and words they use, their skills, their perceptions of what is real and what is false, interpreting information and understanding what they see, hear and sense.

Read the following **Real Work Setting** scenario and think about how it relates to your work setting and role:

Real Work Setting

Name: Joanne

Job role: Senior Residential Worker for adults who have dementia

(See page 136 for a description of the role.)

Processing information: Joanne carries out some research about how the brain works to process information so that she can use this to explain to the team how an individual with dementia experiences difficulties in processing information.

Evidencing AC1.3 to your assessor:

For AC1.3 you must evidence your understanding of the way that individuals process information with reference to the abilities and limitations of individuals with dementia.

Assessment Methods:

Oral/Written Questioning or Discussion or a Personal Statement or Reflection.

- You can **tell** your assessor about the way that individuals process information, with reference to the abilities and limitations of individuals with dementia.
- Or, you can **talk** to your assessor about the way that individuals process information, with reference to the abilities and limitations of individuals with dementia.
- Or, you can write a **personal statement or reflection** about your experience of the way that individuals process information, with reference to the abilities and limitations of individuals with dementia.

REMEMBER TO:

- Provide an **account** of the way that individuals process information, with reference to the abilities and limitations of individuals with dementia.
- Include **details** and **examples** of the way that individuals process information, with reference to the abilities and limitations of individuals with dementia.
- Think about **your work setting** and the way that individuals process information, with reference to the abilities and limitations of individuals with dementia.

Learning Outcome 1: Understand the neurology of dementia

Assessment Criterion 1.4: Explain how other factors can cause changes in an individual's condition that may not be attributable to dementia

What does AC1.4 mean?

- The lead word **explain** means that you must **make clear** how other factors that may not be attributable to dementia can cause changes in an individual's condition.
- Your **account** must make clear details of how other factors can cause changes in an individual's condition.
- For the key words **other factors** you can think about how depression, anxiety, stress, injuries to the brain and some medications may cause changes in an individual's physical and emotional condition.

Read the following **Real Work Setting** scenario and think about how it relates to your work setting and role:

Real Work Setting

Name: Joanne

Job role: Senior Residential Worker for adults who have dementia

(See page 136 for a description of the role.)

Effects of other factors on an individual's condition: Joanne's team has raised a concern about one of the individuals they provide care and support to, as they have all noticed that this individual does not seem her usual self. Her sleep pattern seems disturbed at night, she is showing a lack of enthusiasm in the mornings to get up, and a lack of appetite. Joanna decides that the best course of action is for the individual to visit her GP as there may be reasons other than dementia why these changes are occurring.

Evidencing AC1.4 to your assessor:

For AC1.4 you must evidence your understanding of how other factors can cause changes in an individual's condition that may not be attributable to dementia.

Assessment Methods:

Oral/Written Questioning or **Discussion** or a **Personal Statement or Reflection**.

- You can **tell** your assessor about how other factors can cause changes in an individual's condition that may not be attributable to dementia.
- Or, you can **talk** to your assessor about how other factors can cause changes in an individual's condition that may not be attributable to dementia.
- Or, you can write a **personal statement or reflection** about your experience of how other factors can cause changes in an individual's condition that may not be attributable to dementia.

REMEMBER TO:

- Provide an **account** of how other factors can cause changes in an individual's condition that may not be attributable to dementia.
- Include **details** and examples of **other factors** that can cause changes in an individual's condition.
- Think about **your work setting** and how other factors can cause changes in an individual's condition.

Learning Outcome 1: Understand the neurology of dementia

Assessment Criterion 1.5: Explain why the abilities and needs of an individual with dementia may fluctuate

What does AC1.5 mean?

- The lead word **explain** means that you must **make clear** the reasons why the abilities and needs of an individual with dementia may fluctuate.
- Your **account** must make clear details of the reasons **why**.
- For the key words **abilities and needs** you can think about the reasons why what an individual with dementia is able to do and what their needs are may change from hour to hour, from day to day or from one activity to another.

Read the following **Real Work Setting** scenario and think about how it relates to your work setting and role:

Real Work Setting

Name: Joanne

Job role: Senior Residential Worker for adults who have dementia

(See page 136 for a description of the role.)

Reasons for fluctuating abilities and needs: An individual who has dementia is sharing with Joanna her reflective diary of what she did and how she was feeling on each day of her week-long holiday away with her husband. Joanne notes that the individual experienced some stressful days and other days where she seemed content and calm. This individual's stressful days seemed to be linked to when her husband took her on an outing to a new place for the morning or afternoon; the individual confirmed to Joanna that she liked her routine of being at home during the day and going out in the evening with her husband.

Evidencing AC1.5 to your assessor:

For AC1.5 you must evidence your understanding of why the abilities and needs of an individual with dementia may fluctuate.

Assessment Methods:

Oral/Written Questioning or **Discussion** or a **Personal Statement or Reflection.**

- You can **tell** your assessor about why the abilities and needs of an individual with dementia may fluctuate.
- *Or*, you can **talk** to your assessor about why the abilities and needs of an individual with dementia may fluctuate.
- *Or*, you can write a **personal statement or reflection** about your experience of why the abilities and needs of an individual with dementia may fluctuate.

REMEMBER TO:

- Provide an **account** and explain **why** the abilities and needs of an individual with dementia may fluctuate.
- Include **details** and examples of the reasons why the abilities and needs of an individual with dementia may fluctuate.
- Think about **your work setting** and why the abilities and needs of an individual with dementia may fluctuate.

Learning Outcome 2: Understand the impact of recognition and diagnosis of dementia

Assessment Criterion 2.1: Describe the impact of early diagnosis and follow-up diagnosis

What does AC2.1 mean?

○ The lead word **describe** means that you must provide an **account** that **details** the impact of early diagnosis and follow-up diagnosis.

○ Your **account** must **detail the impact of both** early diagnosis and follow-up diagnosis.

○ For the key words **early diagnosis** you can think about both the positive and negative effects of an early diagnosis of dementia for the individual and for their family, friends and others who are involved in their lives.

○ For the key words **follow-up diagnosis** you can think about the impact that this will have on an individual and their family, friends and others who are involved in their lives.

Read the following **Real Work Setting** scenario and think about how it relates to your work setting and role:

Real Work Setting

Name: Ahmed

Job role: Senior Support Worker for an individual who has dementia living at home

Ahmed has been working as a Senior Support Worker for one month. His Senior responsibilities include: providing support and supervision to a small team of Support Workers; developing and reviewing the individual's care plan; ensuring the implementation of the individual's care plan is consistent across the team and reflects person-centred approaches and thinking; recording and reporting as required.

Impact of early diagnosis and follow-up diagnosis: Ahmed has lately begun working with an individual who has been recently diagnosed with dementia. Receiving an early diagnosis of dementia allowed the individual and his family to think through how dementia may affect their lives and to make the decision to bring a package of support into the individual's home. Some of the shifts Ahmed works are spent with the individual and his wife, talking through the possible ways the individual's dementia may impact on both their lives and what changes they may need to make to prepare for this.

Evidencing AC2.1 to your assessor:

For AC2.1 you must evidence your understanding of the impact of early diagnosis and follow-up diagnosis.

Assessment Methods:

Oral/Written Questioning or Discussion or a Personal Statement or Reflection.

● You can **tell** your assessor about the impact of early diagnosis and follow-up diagnosis of dementia.

● Or, you can **talk** to your assessor about the impact of early diagnosis and follow-up diagnosis of dementia.

● Or, you can write a **personal statement or reflection** about your experience of the impact of early diagnosis and follow-up diagnosis of dementia.

REMEMBER TO:

● Provide a detailed **account** of the impact of early diagnosis and follow-up diagnosis of dementia.

● Include **details** about **both** early and follow-up diagnosis.

● Include **varied** examples of both early and follow-up diagnosis.

● Think about **your work setting** and the impact of early diagnosis and follow-up diagnosis of dementia.

Learning Outcome 2: Understand the impact of recognition and diagnosis of dementia

Assessment Criterion 2.2: Explain the importance of recording possible signs or symptoms of dementia in an individual in line with agreed ways of working

What does AC2.2 mean?

- The lead word **explain** means that you must **make clear** the importance of recording possible signs or symptoms of dementia in an individual in line with agreed ways of working.
- Your **account** must **detail** the reasons why it is important to record possible signs or symptoms of dementia in an individual in line with agreed ways of working.
- For the key words **signs or symptoms** you can think about the changes that an individual with dementia may experience and show in terms of their memory, understanding and behaviour.
- For the key words **agreed ways of working** you can think about the process you must follow when recording possible signs or symptoms of dementia in an individual.

Read the following **Real Work Setting** scenario and think about how it relates to your work setting and role:

Real Work Setting

Name: Ahmed

Job role: Senior Support Worker for an individual who has dementia living at home

(See page 141 for a description of the role.)

Recording possible signs or symptoms of dementia: Ahmed, along with his team, continues to record the dates and times when and activities where the individual with dementia needed promoting to remember, became confused or frustrated, so that they can continue to build up a profile of his needs and well-being and plan for the future.

Evidencing AC2.2 to your assessor:

For AC2.2 you must evidence your understanding of the importance of recording possible signs or symptoms of dementia in an individual in line with agreed ways of working.

Assessment Methods:

Oral/Written Questioning or **Discussion** or a **Personal Statement** or **Reflection.**

- You can **tell** your assessor about the importance of recording possible signs or symptoms of dementia in an individual.
- Or, you can **talk** to your assessor about the importance of recording possible signs or symptoms of dementia in an individual.
- Or, you can write a **personal statement or reflection** about your experience of the importance of recording possible signs or symptoms of dementia in an individual.

REMEMBER TO:

- Provide an **account** and explain the importance of recording possible signs or symptoms of dementia in an individual.
- Include **details** and examples of reasons why it is important to record possible signs or symptoms of dementia in an individual.
- Ensure the evidence you provide is in line with **agreed ways of working**.
- Think about **your work setting** and the possible signs or symptoms of dementia in an individual.

Learning Outcome 2: Understand the impact of recognition and diagnosis of dementia

Assessment Criterion 2.3: Explain the process of reporting possible signs of dementia within agreed ways of working

What does AC2.3 mean?

- ○ The lead word **explain** means that you must **make clear** the process of reporting possible signs of dementia within agreed ways of working.
- ○ Your **account** must **detail** the process of reporting possible signs of dementia.
- ○ For the key words **process of reporting** you can think about the procedures that you must follow in your work setting to report both verbally and in writing any possible signs of dementia.
- ○ For the key words **agreed ways of working** you can think about the actions you are required to take in your job role when reporting possible signs of dementia.

Read the following **Real Work Setting** scenario and think about how it relates to your work setting and role:

Real Work Setting

Name: Ahmed

Job role: Senior Support Worker for an individual who has dementia living at home

(See page 141 for a description of the role.)

Reporting possible signs or symptoms of dementia: Ahmed has noted that the wife of the individual he and his team provide support to may also be showing possible signs of dementia. Ahmed has expressed his concerns confidentially to his line manager, detailing clearly his observations of the individual's wife and the actions he has taken in those situations. Ahmed has also produced a written report containing the facts of what he has observed.

Evidencing AC2.3 to your assessor:

For AC2.3 you must evidence your understanding of the process of reporting possible signs of dementia within agreed ways of working.

Assessment Methods:

Oral/Written Questioning or **Discussion** or a **Personal Statement** or **Reflection**.

- You can **tell** your assessor about the process of reporting possible signs of dementia within agreed ways of working.
- Or, you can **talk** to your assessor about the process of reporting possible signs of dementia within agreed ways of working.
- Or, you can write a **personal statement or reflection** about your experience of the process of reporting possible signs of dementia within agreed ways of working.

REMEMBER TO:

- Provide an **account** and **explain** the process of reporting possible signs of dementia.
- Include **details** and examples of how to report verbally and in writing possible signs of dementia.
- Ensure the evidence you provide is in line with **agreed ways of working**.
- Think about **your work setting** and the process of reporting possible signs of dementia.

Learning Outcome 2: Understand the impact of recognition and diagnosis of dementia

Assessment Criterion 2.4: Describe the possible impact of receiving a diagnosis of dementia on the individual and the individual's family and friends

What does AC2.4 mean?

- The lead word **describe** means that you must provide an **account** that **details** the possible impact of receiving a diagnosis of dementia on the individual and the individual's family and friends.
- Your **account** must **detail** the possible impact of receiving a diagnosis of dementia.
- For the key words **diagnosis of dementia** you can think about both the positive and negative effects of having a diagnosis of dementia for the individual and the individual's family and friends.

Read the following **Real Work Setting** scenario and think about how it relates to your work setting and role:

Real Work Setting

Name: Ahmed
Job role: Senior Support Worker for an individual who has dementia living at home
(See page 141 for a description of the role.)
Possible impact of receiving a diagnosis of dementia: Ahmed has received a telephone call from the individual with dementia he and his team currently support. He is feeling confused and worried about his wife, who thinks that she may have dementia. The individual explains to Ahmed that since meeting with the GP she feels very frightened and fearful of the future for both of them.

Evidencing AC2.4 to your assessor:

For AC2.4 you must evidence your understanding of the possible impact of receiving a diagnosis of dementia on the individual and the individual's family and friends.

Assessment Methods:

Oral/Written Questioning or **Discussion** or a **Personal Statement** or **Reflection.**

- You can **tell** your assessor about the possible impact of receiving a diagnosis of dementia on the individual and the individual's family and friends.
- Or, you can **talk** to your assessor about the possible impact of receiving a diagnosis of dementia on the individual and the individual's family and friends.
- Or, you can write a **personal statement or reflection** about your experience of the possible impact of receiving a diagnosis of dementia on the individual and the individual's family and friends.

REMEMBER TO:

- Provide a detailed **account** of the possible impact of receiving a diagnosis of dementia on the individual and the individual's family and friends.
- Include **details** about the possible impact of receiving a diagnosis of dementia.
- Include **varied** examples of how this can impact on both the individual and their family and friends.
- Think about **your work setting** and the possible impact of receiving a diagnosis of dementia on the individual and their family and friends.

Learning Outcome 3: Understand how dementia care must be underpinned by a person-centred approach

Assessment Criterion 3.1: Compare a person-centred and a non-person-centred approach to dementia care

What does AC3.1 mean?

- ○ The lead word **compare** means that you must **detail** the similarities and differences that exist between a person-centred and a non-person-centred approach to dementia care.
- ○ Your **account** must detail the **similarities and differences** between the approaches.
- ○ For the key words **person-centred approach** you can think about how this way of working involves seeing individuals with dementia first and foremost as unique people, each with their own unique background, beliefs, needs, wishes and preferences.
- ○ For the key words **non-person-centred approach** you can think about how this way of working involves *not* seeing individuals with dementia first and foremost as unique people with their own background, beliefs, needs, wishes and preferences, and instead placing the dementia rather than the individual at the centre of the care provided.

Read the following **Real Work Setting** scenario and think about how it relates to your work setting and role:

Real Work Setting

Name: Beryl

Job role: Senior Support Worker for young adults who have dementia

Beryl has been working as a Senior Support Worker for two years. Her Senior responsibilities include: providing emotional and practical support to individuals who have dementia; liaising with professionals on the care package agreed with the individual; training and guiding new members of staff.

Person-centred and non-person-centred approaches to dementia care: Beryl has put together some training for the team of Support Workers, focusing on a person-centred approach to dementia care. Beryl begins the training session by asking each team member to think about what person-centred and non-person-centred approaches to dementia care mean and then to discuss in two groups examples of ways of working using both approaches.

Evidencing AC3.1 to your assessor:

For AC3.1 you must evidence your understanding of a person-centred and a non-person-centred approach to dementia care.

Assessment Methods:

Oral/Written Questioning or **Discussion** or a **Personal Statement** or **Reflection**.

- You can **tell** your assessor about the similarities and differences between a person-centred and a non-person-centred approach to dementia care.
- *Or,* you can **talk** to your assessor about the similarities and differences between a person-centred and a non-person-centred approach to dementia care.
- *Or,* you can write a **personal statement or reflection** about your experience of the similarities and differences between a person-centred and a non-person-centred approach to dementia care.

REMEMBER TO:

- Provide a detailed **account** of the similarities and differences between a person-centred and a non-person-centred approach to dementia care.
- Include **details** about the similarities and differences between a person-centred and a non-person-centred approach to dementia care.
- Think about **your work setting** and the similarities and differences between a person-centred and a non-person-centred approach to dementia care.

Learning Outcome 3: Understand how dementia care must be underpinned by a person-centred approach

Assessment Criterion 3.2: Describe a range of different techniques that can be used to meet the fluctuating abilities and needs of the individual with dementia

What does AC3.2 mean?

- The lead word **describe** means that you must provide an **account** that **details** a range of different techniques that can be used to meet the fluctuating abilities and needs of the individual with dementia.
- Your **account** must detail a range of different techniques.
- For the key words **different techniques** you can think about how to complete a life story profile of an individual so you and others can understand about the individual's background and past, ensure all relevant information about the individual is kept up to date and reflects the individual's current needs and preferences and how these are met, promote the individual's rights and develop positive responses to an individual's changing abilities and needs.

Read the following **Real Work Setting** scenario and think about how it relates to your work setting and role:

Real Work Setting

Name: Beryl

Job role: Senior Support Worker for young adults who have dementia

(See page 145 for a description of the role.)

Meeting the fluctuating abilities and needs of an individual with dementia: Beryl is meeting with the team to discuss and agree different ways that can be used to meet the fluctuating abilities and needs of Harry, an individual with dementia.

Evidencing AC3.2 to your assessor:

For AC3.2 you must evidence your understanding of a range of different techniques that can be used to meet the fluctuating abilities and needs of the individual with dementia.

Assessment Methods:

Oral/Written Questioning or Discussion or a **Personal Statement or Reflection**.

- You can **tell** your assessor about a range of different techniques that can be used to meet the fluctuating abilities and needs of the individual who has dementia.
- Or, you can **talk** to your assessor about a range of different techniques that can be used to meet the fluctuating abilities and needs of the individual who has dementia.
- Or, you can write a **personal statement or reflection** about your experience of a range of different techniques that can be used to meet the fluctuating abilities and needs of the individual who has dementia.

REMEMBER TO:

- Provide a detailed **account** of a range of different techniques.
- Include **details** about a range of different techniques that can be used to meet the fluctuating abilities and needs of the individual with dementia.
- Think about **your work setting** and a range of different techniques that can be used to meet the fluctuating abilities and needs of the individual with dementia.

Learning Outcome 3: Understand how dementia care must be underpinned by a person-centred approach

Assessment Criterion 3.3: Describe how myths and stereotypes related to dementia may affect the individual and their carers

What does AC3.3 mean?

- ○ The lead word **describe** means that you must provide an **account** that **details** how myths and stereotypes related to dementia may affect the individual and their carers, who may be a partner, family, friends or neighbours.
- ○ Your **account** must **detail** different myths and stereotypes related to dementia.
- ○ For the key words **myths and stereotypes** you can think about how individuals with dementia may be perceived unfairly as helpless, challenging, out of control, or a burden to others.

Read the following **Real Work Setting** scenario and think about how it relates to your work setting and role:

Real Work Setting

Name: Beryl

Job role: Senior Support Worker for young adults who have dementia

(See page 145 for a description of the role.)

Myths and stereotypes: During the team meeting a Support Worker raises her concerns over Harry's next door neighbour, who has on several occasions made inappropriate remarks to her and Harry when he sees her visiting Harry's flat. The team member explains to Beryl that she has told the neighbour that his remarks are unnecessary and upsetting but he has continued to say that Harry is unstable and should not be living on his own as he has dementia. Beryl thanks the team member for sharing this information and confirms that this is discrimination and must not be tolerated. Beryl suggests that the team writes a letter to Harry's neighbour outlining the situation and asking him to refrain from making such comments, and that they include some information leaflets with the letter about what dementia is and what it is not.

Evidencing AC3.3 to your assessor:

For AC3.3 you must evidence your understanding of how myths and stereotypes related to dementia may affect the individual and their carers.

Assessment Methods:

Oral/Written Questioning or **Discussion** or a **Personal Statement** or **Reflection**.

- You can **tell** your assessor about how myths and stereotypes related to dementia may affect the individual and their carers.
- Or, you can **talk** to your assessor about how myths and stereotypes related to dementia may affect the individual and their carers.
- Or, you can write a **personal statement or reflection** about your experience of how myths and stereotypes related to dementia may affect the individual and their carers.

REMEMBER TO:

- Provide a detailed **account** of how myths and stereotypes related to dementia may affect the individual and their carers.
- Include **details** about myths and stereotypes related to dementia.
- Ensure your evidence includes how these affect the individual and their carers.
- Think about **your work setting** and how myths and stereotypes related to dementia may affect the individual and their carers.

Learning Outcome 3: Understand how dementia care must be underpinned by a person-centred approach

Assessment Criterion 3.4: Describe ways in which individuals and carers can be supported to overcome their fears

What does AC3.4 mean?

○ The lead word **describe** means that you must provide an **account** that **details** ways in which individuals and carers can be supported to overcome their fears.

○ Your **account** must detail **different** ways in which individuals and carers can be supported to overcome their fears.

○ For the key word **supported** you can think about how individuals and those involved in their lives, such as family, friends and advocates, can be supported through making available information and advice, access to specialist services including therapy, support groups and additional care and support from others.

Read the following **Real Work Setting** scenario and think about how it relates to your work setting and role:

Real Work Setting

Name: Beryl

Job role: Senior Support Worker for young adults who have dementia

(See page 145 for a description of the role.)

Support for individuals and carers: The team is reviewing the support they have in place for individuals who have dementia, their families and friends, and the staff who provide care and support to them. At present the service obtains information from the Alzheimer's Society to give out to individuals and others involved in their lives, and also provides access to a support group that is held in the evenings for both individuals and those who care for and support them. Individuals' support plans and time spent with them is also used to support them, as is helping their families to understand more about dementia and the different ways to manage their lives positively.

Evidencing AC3.4 to your assessor:

For AC3.4 you must evidence your understanding of ways in which individuals and carers can be supported to overcome their fears.

Assessment Methods:

Oral/Written Questioning or **Discussion** or a **Personal Statement** or **Reflection**.

● You can **tell** your assessor about ways in which individuals and carers can be supported to overcome their fears.

● Or, you can **talk** to your assessor about ways in which individuals and carers can be supported to overcome their fears.

● Or, you can write a **personal statement or reflection** about your experience of ways in which individuals and carers can be supported to overcome their fears.

REMEMBER TO:

● Provide a detailed **account** of different ways in which individuals and carers can be supported to overcome their fears.

● Include **details** about different ways of supporting individuals and carers.

● Ensure your evidence relates to supporting individuals' carers in overcoming their fears.

● Think about **your work setting** and ways in which individuals and carers can be supported to overcome their fears.

Learning Outcome 1: Understand the meaning of personalisation in social care

Assessment Criterion 1.1: Define the term 'personalisation' as it applies in social care

What does AC1.1 mean?
- The lead word **define** means that you must **make clear** the meaning of the term personalisation.
- Your **account** must make clear the **meaning** of the term personalisation as it applies in social care.
- For the key word **personalisation** you can think about your role and how you can ensure that the care and support you provide to individuals meets their needs, enabling them to make their own informed decisions and choices and to access their local communities and services.

Read the following **Real Work Setting** scenario and think about how it relates to your work setting and role:

Real Work Setting

Name: Marta
Job role: Senior Care Worker in a day service for adults who have physical disabilities
Marta has been working as a Senior Care Worker for one year. Her Senior responsibilities include: supporting and mentoring a small team of Care Workers; supporting individuals to manage their monies; ensuring they are in receipt of the correct benefits; liaising with professionals and others to ensure the service complies with relevant standards and requirements.
Personalisation: Marta and her team work closely together to ensure that all assessments completed at the day service are led by individuals, in partnership with the team and other relevant professionals. Marta meets regularly with each individual to review their support plans, and also explains to each individual the available finances in place and the different ways to manage this financial support; in this way each individual can make informed decisions about the support they need to achieve their goals.

Evidencing AC1.1 to your assessor:

For AC1.1 you must evidence your understanding of what is meant by personalisation as it applies in social care.

Assessment Methods:

Oral/Written Questioning or **Discussion** or a **Personal Statement.**

- You can **tell** your assessor about the meaning of personalisation as it applies in social care.
- Or, you can **talk** to your assessor about the meaning of personalisation as it applies in social care.
- Or, you can write a **personal statement** about the meaning of personalisation as it applies in social care.

REMEMBER TO:
- Provide a **definition** of the term personalisation.
- Include different **examples** to show your understanding of this term.
- Ensure your definition relates to social care.
- Think about the meaning of personalisation in **your work setting** and with the individuals with whom you work.

Learning Outcome 1: Understand the meaning of personalisation in social care

Assessment Criterion 1.2: Explain how personalisation can benefit individuals

What does AC1.2 mean?

- The lead word **explain** means that you must **make clear** the benefits of personalisation for individuals.
- Your **account** must make clear **how** personalisation can benefit individuals.
- For the key word **personalisation** you can think about your role and how you can ensure that the care and support you provide to individuals meets their needs, enabling them to make their own informed decisions and choices and to access their local communities and services.
- For the key word **benefit** you can think about the difference personalisation can make to the services being provided and to individuals' lives and goals.

Read the following **Real Work Setting** scenario and think about how it relates to your work setting and role:

Real Work Setting

Name: Marta

Job role: Senior Care Worker in a day service for adults who have physical disabilities

(See page 149 for a description of the role.)

Personalisation and its benefits: Marta and a Care Worker are preparing for Simon's support plan review at the end of the month. In preparation for this, Simon has decided that he would like to make a short film about his life to show to his parents and sister. Simon would like his film to show the following: how he manages his finances through the weekly support provided by one of the Care Workers; his friends at the allotment; the table tennis club he attends twice a week; the new aids he has bought for his kitchen that now enable him to cook for himself.

Evidencing AC1.2 to your assessor:

For AC1.2 you must evidence your understanding of how personalisation can benefit individuals.

Assessment Methods:

Oral/Written Questioning or **Discussion** or a **Personal Statement** or **Reflection**.

- You can **tell** your assessor about how personalisation can benefit individuals.
- Or, you can **talk** to your assessor about how personalisation can benefit individuals.
- Or, you can write a **personal statement or reflection** about your experience of how personalisation can benefit individuals.

REMEMBER TO:

- Provide an **account** and **explain** how personalisation can benefit individuals.
- Include **details** about the benefits of personalisation.
- Include examples of different individuals.
- Include examples of different benefits.
- Think about the benefits of personalisation for individuals in **your work setting**.

Learning Outcome 1: Understand the meaning of personalisation in social care

Assessment Criterion 1.3: Explain the relationship between rights, choice and personalisation

What does AC1.3 mean?

- The lead word **explain** means that you must **make clear** the relationship that exists between rights, choice and personalisation.
- Your **account** must make clear how rights, choice and personalisation are linked.
- For the key word **rights** you can think about what moral and legal entitlements individuals have in relation to their lives and their local communities.
- For the key word **choice** you can think about what individuals need in order to make informed decisions in line with their needs and preferences.
- For the key word **personalisation** you can think about your role and how you can ensure that the care and support you provide to individuals meets their needs, enabling them to make their own informed decisions and choices and to access their local communities and services.

Read the following **Real Work Setting** scenario and think about how it relates to your work setting and role:

Real Work Setting

Name: Marta

Job role: Senior Care Worker in a day service for adults who have physical disabilities

(See page 149 for a description of the role.)

Rights, choice and personalisation: Marta is welcoming an individual who is thinking about whether he wishes to access the day service. Marta has arranged for him to meet with some of the Care Workers and the individuals who use the service during his visit so that they can tell him more about it and what they do there. Marta also plans to give a brief overview of the service to the individual and reinforce how the service is very much led by the individuals who use it, and that all the activities and services provided are also chosen and reviewed by the individuals who request and use them.

Evidencing AC1.3 to your assessor:

For AC1.3 you must evidence your understanding of the relationship between rights, choice and personalisation.

Assessment Methods:

Oral/Written Questioning or **Discussion** or a **Personal Statement** or **Reflection**.

- You can **tell** your assessor about the relationship between rights, choice and personalisation.
- Or, you can **talk** to your assessor about the relationship between rights, choice and personalisation.
- Or, you can write a **personal statement or reflection** about your experience of the relationship between rights, choice and personalisation.

REMEMBER TO:

- Provide an **account** and **explain** the relationship between rights, choice and personalisation.
- Include **details** about **how** and **why** rights, choice and personalisation are linked.
- Include examples of different rights.
- Include examples of different choices.
- Think about the links that exist between rights, choice and personalisation for individuals in **your work setting**.

Learning Outcome 1: Understand the meaning of personalisation in social care

Assessment Criterion 1.4: Identify legislation and other national policy documents that promote personalisation

What does AC1.4 mean?

- The lead word **identify** means that you must **make clear** legislation and national policies that promote personalisation.
- Your **list** must include **different** examples of **both** legislation and national policies.
- For the key word **legislation** you can think about the laws that are in place relating to personalisation.
- For the key words **national policy documents** you can think about the publications that have been published relating to personalisation.
- For the key word **personalisation** you can think about the role legislation and national policy documents play in ensuring that the care and support you provide to individuals meets their needs, enabling them to make their own informed decisions and choices and to access their local communities and services.

Read the following **Real Work Setting** scenario and think about how it relates to your work setting and role:

Real Work Setting

Name: Marta

Job role: Senior Care Worker in a day service for adults who have physical disabilities

(See page 149 for a description of the role.)

Legislation, national policy documents and personalisation: Marta is reviewing the service's information pack, which provides an overview of the service, how it is managed and what it offers. Marta also wants to ensure that the information handouts that it contains are up to date in relation to legislation and policy documents that have been published on personalisation.

Evidencing AC1.4 to your assessor:

For AC1.4 you must evidence your understanding of legislation and national policy documents that promote personalisation.

Assessment Methods:

Oral/Written Questioning or **Discussion** or a **Spidergram**.

- You can **tell** your assessor about the different legislation and national policy documents that promote personalisation.
- Or, you can **talk** to your assessor about the different legislation and national policy documents that promote personalisation.
- Or, you can complete a **spidergram** showing the different legislation and national policy documents that promote personalisation.

REMEMBER TO:

- **List** legislation and national policy documents that promote personalisation.
- Include **different** examples of **both** legislation and national policy documents that promote personalisation.
- Ensure they relate to personalisation in health or social care.
- Think about the legislation and national policy documents that promote personalisation that are relevant to **your work setting**.

Learning Outcome 2: Understand systems that support personalisation

Assessment Criterion 2.1: List local and national systems that are designed to support personalisation

What does AC2.1 mean?

- The lead word **list** means that you must **identify** local and national systems that are designed to support personalisation.
- Your list must include **different** examples of **both** local and national systems.
- For the key words **local systems** you can think about the local services and providers available to meet individuals' health, education, housing and social needs.
- For the key words **national systems** you can think about the government-led services and information available to meet individuals' health, education, housing and social needs.
- For the key word **personalisation** you can think about the role local and national systems play in ensuring that the care and support you provide to individuals meets their needs, enabling them to make their own informed decisions and choices and to access their local communities and services.

Read the following **Real Work Setting** scenario and think about how it relates to your work setting and role:

Real Work Setting

Name: Keith

Job role: Senior Live-in Carer to a young man who has a visual impairment

Keith has been working as a Senior Live-in Carer for eight months. Keith supervises and supports a team of four Live-in Carers who provide Craig with day-to-day care, and support with housework, shopping and using public transport. Keith is also responsible for arranging regular review meetings and for developing and reviewing a personalised care plan.

Local and national systems that support personalisation: Keith and his team work closely with a number of professionals and services that together support personalisation, enabling Craig to live independently in a flat and to access his local community. Craig is in contact with the Community Transport Team in his local area and also meets regularly with his Housing Officer. Craig finds his regular meetings with Keith very useful as they can discuss how best to manage any risks whilst also updating his knowledge about current government guidance promoting personalisation.

Evidencing AC2.1 to your assessor:

For AC2.1 you must evidence your understanding of the local and national systems that are designed to support personalisation.

Assessment Methods:

Oral/Written Questioning or **Discussion** or a **Spidergram**.

- You can **tell** your assessor about the different local and national systems that are designed to support personalisation.
- Or, you can **talk** to your assessor about the different local and national systems that are designed to support personalisation.
- Or, you can complete a **spidergram** showing the different local and national systems that are designed to support personalisation.

REMEMBER TO:

- **List** local and national systems that are designed to support personalisation.
- Include **different** examples of **both** local and national systems.
- Ensure they relate to supporting personalisation in health or social care.
- Think about the local and national systems that are designed to support personalisation that are relevant to **your work setting**.

Learning Outcome 2: Understand systems that support personalisation

Assessment Criterion 2.2: Describe the impact that personalisation has on the process of commissioning social care

What does AC2.2 mean?

- The lead word **describe** means that you must provide an **account** that **details** how personalisation impacts on the process of commissioning social care.
- Your **account** must detail **how** personalisation affects the process of commissioning social care.
- For the key word **impact** you can think about the changes that have occurred in health and social care services as a result of personalisation.
- For the key word **personalisation** you can think about the role personalisation plays in ensuring that the care and support services provided to individuals meet their needs, enabling them to make their own informed decisions and choices and to access their local communities.
- For the key words **commissioning social care** you can think about how the monies available for health and social care services must focus on improving their quality, the fair allocation of resources and ensuring the services provided are effective.

Read the following **Real Work Setting** scenario and think about how it relates to your work setting and role:

Real Work Setting

Name: Keith

Job role: Senior Live-in Carer to a young man who has a visual impairment

(See page 153 for a description of the role.)

Impact of personalisation: Keith and Craig discuss how the support in place is working. From Craig's point of view he thinks it is working well as he feels he is very much able to do what he enjoys and wants to do. From Keith's point of view he feels that the changes in Craig have been very positive. In terms of managing the team, Keith does find it a challenge at times to ensure that support is available when Craig needs it.

Evidencing AC2.2 to your assessor:

For AC2.2 you must evidence your understanding of the impact that personalisation has on the process of commissioning social care.

Assessment Methods:
Oral/Written Questioning or **Discussion** or a **Personal Statement or Reflection**.

- You can **tell** your assessor the impact that personalisation has on the process of commissioning social care.
- Or, you can **talk** to your assessor about the impact that personalisation has on the process of commissioning social care.
- Or, you can write a **personal statement or reflection** about your experience of the impact that personalisation has on the process of commissioning social care.

REMEMBER TO:
- Provide a detailed **account** of the impact that personalisation has on the process of commissioning social care.
- Include details of **different ways** that personalisation impacts.
- Ensure you detail **how** this affects the process of commissioning social care.
- Think about **your work setting** and the impact personalisation has on the process of commissioning social care.

Learning Outcome 2: Understand systems that support personalisation

Assessment Criterion 2.3: Explain how direct payments and individual budgets support personalisation

What does AC2.3 mean?

- The lead word **explain** means that you must **make clear** how direct payments and individual budgets support personalisation.
- Your **account** must make clear **how both** direct payments and individual budgets support personalisation.
- For the key words **direct payments** you can think about how personalisation can be supported by individuals making their own choices over which services to buy and for how long.
- For the key words **individual budgets** you can think about how personalisation can be supported by individuals making their own choices over how much to spend on their ongoing care and support.
- For the key word **personalisation** you can think about the role direct payments and individual budgets play in ensuring the care and support you provide to individuals meets their needs, enabling them to make their own informed decisions and choices and to access their local communities and services.

Read the following **Real Work Setting** scenario and think about how it relates to your work setting and role:

Real Work Setting

Name: Keith

Job role: Senior Live-in Carer to a young man who has a visual impairment

(See page 153 for a description of the role.)

Direct payments and individual budgets: Keith and Craig are reviewing Craig's outgoings over the last month, including all the costs associated with the Live-in Carers he employs. Craig and Keith begin by reviewing the statement Craig has received about his individual budget, which details the monies spent and the remaining balance. Craig and Keith also decide to review other new social activities that have become available in the local area and their associated costs.

Evidencing AC2.3 to your assessor:

For AC2.3 you must evidence your understanding of how direct payments and individual budgets support personalisation.

Assessment Methods:

Oral/Written Questioning or **Discussion** or a **Personal Statement** or **Reflection**.

- You can **tell** your assessor about how direct payments and individual budgets support personalisation.
- Or, you can **talk** to your assessor about how direct payments and individual budgets support personalisation.
- Or, you can write a **personal statement or reflection** about how direct payments and individual budgets support personalisation.

REMEMBER TO:
- Provide an **account** about how direct payments and individual budgets support personalisation.
- Include **details** about **how both** direct payments and individual budgets support personalisation.
- Think about **your work setting** and how direct payments and individual budgets can support personalisation.

Learning Outcome 3: Understand how personalisation affects the way support is provided

Assessment Criterion 3.1: Explain how person-centred thinking, person-centred planning and person-centred approaches support personalisation

What does AC3.1 mean?

- ○ The lead word **explain** means that you must **make clear** how person-centred thinking, planning and approaches support personalisation.
- ○ Your **account** must make clear **how** all three concepts support personalisation.
- ○ For the key words **person-centred thinking** you can think about what personalisation means and how putting individuals at the focus of the service benefits them.
- ○ For the key words **person-centred planning** you can think about how to ensure that the services and support that are planned fit the individual.
- ○ For the key words **person-centred approaches** you can think about how to ensure that individuals have choice and control over the way they live their lives.
- ○ For the key word **personalisation** you can think about how person-centred thinking, planning and approaches put individuals at the focus of the service.

Read the following **Real Work Setting** scenario and think about how it relates to your work setting and role:

Real Work Setting

Name: Fatema

Job role: Senior Mental Health Worker in a drop-in service for adults who have mental health needs

Fatema has been working as a Senior Mental Health Worker for four years. Her Senior responsibilities include: supervising two Mental Health Workers; providing support and guidance to staff; contributing to staff training; organising and leading staff meetings.

Person-centred thinking, planning and approaches: Fatema has been asked by her manager to put together and deliver a training session for the team on the recovery approach in mental health and how it links to personalisation. This means ensuring individuals retain a sense of who they are and use services and support to access the opportunities available, and also ensuring that individuals work towards their hopes and dreams.

Evidencing AC3.1 to your assessor:

For AC3.1 you must evidence your understanding of how person-centred thinking, planning and approaches support personalisation.

Assessment Methods:

Oral/Written Questioning or **Discussion** or a **Personal Statement** or **Reflection.**

- You can **tell** your assessor about how person-centred thinking, planning and approaches support personalisation.
- *Or,* you can **talk** to your assessor about how these concepts support personalisation.
- *Or,* you can write a **personal statement or reflection** about your experience of how these concepts support personalisation.

REMEMBER TO:

- Provide an **account** of how person-centred thinking, person-centred planning and person-centred approaches support personalisation.
- Include **details** about **how** these approaches support personalisation.
- Think about **how** these concepts support personalisation in **your work setting**.

Learning Outcome 3: Understand how personalisation affects the way support is provided

Assessment Criterion 3.2: Describe how personalisation affects the balance of power between individuals and those providing support

What does AC3.2 mean?

○ The lead word **describe** means that you must provide an **account** that **details** how personalisation affects the balance of power between individuals and those providing support.

○ Your **account** must detail **how** the balance of power between individuals and those providing support is affected.

○ For the key word **personalisation** you can think about the role personalisation plays in ensuring that the care and support services provided to individuals meet their needs, enabling them to make their own informed decisions and choices and to access their local communities.

○ For the key words **balance of power** you can think about how personalisation ensures that the individual remains at the focus and in control of the care and support provided.

Read the following **Real Work Setting** scenario and think about how it relates to your work setting and role:

Real Work Setting

Name: Fatema

Job role: Senior Mental Health Worker in a drop-in service for adults who have mental health needs

(See page 156 for a description of the role.)

Balance of power: Fatema plans to share some accounts provided by individuals who use the service, which detail in their own words what the service means to them and how it has impacted on them as individuals to be able to have a say and control over the drop-in service, including how it operates on a day-to-day basis.

Evidencing AC3.2 to your assessor:

For AC3.2 you must evidence your knowledge of how personalisation affects the balance of power between individuals and those providing support.

Assessment Methods:

Oral/Written Questioning or Discussion or a Personal Statement or Reflection.

● You can **tell** your assessor how personalisation affects the balance of power between individuals and those providing support.

● Or, you can **talk** to your assessor about how personalisation affects the balance of power between individuals and those providing support.

● Or, you can write a **personal statement or reflection** about your experience of how personalisation affects the balance of power between individuals and those providing support.

REMEMBER TO:

● Provide a detailed **account** of how personalisation affects the balance of power between individuals and those providing support.

● Include details of **different ways** that personalisation affects the balance of power.

● Ensure you detail **how** the balance of power between individuals and those providing support is affected.

● Think about **your work setting** and how personalisation affects the balance of power between individuals and those providing support.

Learning Outcome 3: Understand how personalisation affects the way support is provided

Assessment Criterion 3.3: Give examples of how personalisation may affect the way an individual is supported from day to day

What does AC3.3 mean?

- ○ The lead words **give examples** mean that you must provide an **account** that **details** how personalisation may affect the way an individual is supported from day to day.
- ○ Your **account** must detail **examples** of different ways that personalisation may affect the way an individual is supported from day to day.
- ○ For the key word **personalisation** you can think about the role personalisation plays in ensuring that the care and support services provided to individuals meet their needs, enabling them to make their own informed decisions and choices and to access their local communities.

Read the following **Real Work Setting** scenario and think about how it relates to your work setting and role:

Real Work Setting

Name: Fatema

Job role: Senior Mental Health Worker in a drop-in service for adults who have mental health needs

(See page 156 for a description of the role.)

How personalisation affects support provided: Fatema plans to organise a role-play with one of the individuals who has been using the drop-in service over the last six months, in order to show the team what working in a way that supports personalisation means and how to ensure this is consistently applied every day across all members of the team and all individuals.

Evidencing AC3.3 to your assessor:

For AC3.3 you must evidence your knowledge of how personalisation may affect the way an individual is supported from day to day.

Assessment Methods:

Oral/Written Questioning or **Discussion** or a **Personal Statement** or **Reflection**.

- You can **tell** your assessor about examples of how personalisation may affect the way an individual is supported from day to day.
- Or, you can **talk** to your assessor about examples of how personalisation may affect the way an individual is supported from day to day.
- Or, you can write a **personal statement or reflection** about your experience of examples of how personalisation may affect the way an individual is supported from day to day.

REMEMBER TO:

- Provide a detailed **account** of how personalisation may affect the way an individual is supported from day to day.
- Include details of different **examples** of ways that personalisation can affect the way an individual is supported from day to day.
- Ensure you detail **how** an individual is supported and can be affected.
- Think about **your work setting** and how personalisation may affect the way an individual is supported from day to day.

Learning Outcome 4: Understand how to implement personalisation

Assessment Criterion 4.1: Analyse the skills, attitudes and approaches needed by those providing support or brokering services in order to implement personalisation

What does AC4.1 mean?

- The lead word **analyse** means that you must **examine in detail** the different skills, attitudes and approaches needed by those providing support or brokering services in order to implement personalisation.
- Your **account** must provide an analysis of the **different** skills, attitudes and approaches that are required.
- For the key word **skills** you can think about what expertise is required to support individuals to live their lives fully and in line with their needs, wishes and hopes.
- For the key word **attitudes** you can think about the ways of thinking that are required to support individuals to live their lives fully and in line with their needs, wishes and hopes.
- For the key word **approaches** you can think about the ways of working required in different situations to support individuals to live their lives fully and in line with their needs, wishes and hopes.

Read the following **Real Work Setting** scenario and think about how it relates to your work setting and role:

Real Work Setting

Name: Hope
Job role: Senior Carer in a residential care home for older people
Hope has been working as a Senior Carer for three years. Her Senior responsibilities include: leading shifts; allocating duties to staff on shift; supervising staff; ordering and administering medication; maintaining care records; supporting individuals with daily activities.
Skills, attitudes and approaches: Hope will be assisting the manager to recruit more staff for the home. They both agree that there are a number of essential skills, attitudes and approaches that those recruited must have. For the Senior's post these include experience of supervising staff and providing support to staff on shift, being able to problem-solve and being flexible. For the Carers' posts these include experience of supporting older people to have choice and control in their lives, being able to listen to how individuals want to live their lives and knowing how to help them to achieve it.

Evidencing AC4.1 to your assessor:

For AC4.1 you must evidence your knowledge of the skills, attitudes and approaches needed by those providing support or brokering services in order to implement personalisation.

Assessment Methods:

Oral/Written Questioning or **Discussion** or a **Personal Statement** or **Reflection**.

- You can **tell** your assessor about the skills, attitudes and approaches needed by those providing support or brokering services in order to implement personalisation.
- Or, you can **talk** to your assessor about the skills, attitudes and approaches needed by those providing support or brokering services in order to implement personalisation.
- Or, you can write a **personal statement or reflection** about your experience of the skills, attitudes and approaches needed by those providing support or brokering services in order to implement personalisation.

REMEMBER TO:

- Provide an **account** and an **analysis** of different skills, attitudes and approaches needed.
- Ensure **examples** relate to those providing support or brokering services in order to implement personalisation.
- Think about the **skills, attitudes and approaches** needed in **your work setting**.

Learning Outcome 4: Understand how to implement personalisation

Assessment Criterion 4.2: Identify potential barriers to personalisation

What does AC4.2 mean?

- ○ The lead word **identify** means that you must **make clear** potential barriers to personalisation.
- ○ Your **list** must include **different** examples of potential barriers to personalisation.
- ○ For the key word **barriers** you can think about what may prevent personalisation, in terms of staff, monies and/or services available.
- ○ For the key word **personalisation** you can think about the barriers that may arise in ensuring that the care and support you provide to individuals meets their needs, enabling them to make their own informed decisions and choices and to access their local communities and services.

Read the following **Real Work Setting** scenario and think about how it relates to your work setting and role:

Real Work Setting

Name: Hope

Job role: Senior Carer in a residential care home for older people

(See page 159 for a description of the role.)

Potential barriers to personalisation: Hope is meeting with her manager for her supervision next week and in preparation has drawn up a list of areas she wishes to discuss with her, all of which could result in potential barriers to personalisation if they are not addressed. The areas are: ensuring all staff who did not attend the last training update on person-centred planning attend one of the training sessions planned for this month; ensuring information relevant to all individuals is updated regularly and accurately in their care plans; ensuring another coffee morning is arranged for individuals' families and friends, as requested by individuals at their last house meeting.

Evidencing AC4.2 to your assessor:

For AC4.2 you must evidence your understanding of the potential barriers to personalisation.

Assessment Methods:

Oral/Written Questioning or **Discussion** or a **Spidergram**.

- You can **tell** your assessor about the potential barriers to personalisation.
- Or, you can **talk** to your assessor about the potential barriers to personalisation.
- Or, you can complete a **spidergram** showing the potential barriers to personalisation.

REMEMBER TO:

- **List** potential barriers to personalisation.
- Include different **examples** of potential barriers to personalisation.
- Think about the potential barriers to personalisation in **your work setting**.

Learning Outcome 4: Understand how to implement personalisation

Assessment Criterion 4.3: Describe ways to overcome barriers to participation in day-to-day work

What does AC4.3 mean?

- The lead word **describe** means that you must provide an **account** that **details** ways to overcome barriers to participation in day-to-day work.
- Your **account** must detail how to use **different ways** to overcome barriers.
- For the key word **overcome** you can think about how to work in different ways to address any barriers to participation that you may come across.
- For the key word **barriers** you can think about what may prevent you and others from participation in day-to-day work.
- For the key word **participation** you can think about what may prevent individuals and others getting involved and making contributions.

Read the following **Real Work Setting** scenario and think about how it relates to your work setting and role:

Real Work Setting

Name: Hope

Job role: Senior Carer in a residential care home for older people

(See page 159 for a description of the role.)

Overcoming barriers to personalisation: Hope has recently attended a training update on person-centred planning, in which one of the activities involved her and other participants sharing different methods, tools and ways of working that helped with overcoming barriers to personalisation. Hope found it interesting to learn more about these and also noted that some of the methods she used could also be used in different ways across a variety of different situations. Hope plans to share this learning at the Senior team meeting next month.

Evidencing AC4.3 to your assessor:

For AC4.3 you must evidence your knowledge of ways to overcome barriers to participation in day-to-day work.

Assessment Methods:

Oral/Written Questioning or **Discussion** or a **Personal Statement** or **Reflection**.

- You can **tell** your assessor about ways to overcome barriers to participation in day-to-day work.
- Or, you can **talk** to your assessor about ways to overcome barriers to participation in day-to-day work.
- Or, you can write a **personal statement or reflection** about your experience of ways to overcome barriers to participation in day-to-day work.

REMEMBER TO:

- Provide a detailed **account** of ways to overcome barriers to participation in day-to-day work.
- Include **details** of different ways to overcome barriers to participation.
- Ensure you detail **how** to overcome barriers.
- Think about different ways to overcome barriers to participation in day-to-day work in **your work setting**.

Learning Outcome 4: Understand how to implement personalisation

Assessment Criterion 4.4: Describe types of support that individuals or their families might need in order to maximise the benefits of a personalised service

What does AC4.4 mean?

○ The lead word **describe** means that you must provide an **account** that **details** the types of support individuals or their families might need in order to maximise the benefits of a personalised service.

○ Your **account** must detail **different** types of support that individuals or their families might need.

○ For the key words **types of support** you can think about the emotional, social and practical support that may be required.

○ For the key words **personalised service** you can think about what is required to ensure that the service being provided supports individuals to live their lives fully and in line with their needs, wishes and hopes.

Read the following **Real Work Setting** scenario and think about how it relates to your work setting and role:

Real Work Setting

Name: Hope

Job role: Senior Carer in a residential care home for older people

(See page 159 for a description of the role.)

Types of support: Hope ensures that she spends time talking through with each member of her team the support that may be required by individuals or their families at different times, and also ensures she makes the team aware of any issues that have arisen with respect to how individuals feel about the service being provided. She also talks to the team of individuals' strengths, wishes and hopes and advice provided to them, as well as the methods used to address any difficulties that have arisen.

Evidencing AC4.4 to your assessor:

For AC4.4 you must evidence your knowledge of the types of support that individuals or their families might need in order to maximise the benefits of a personalised service.

Assessment Methods:

Oral/Written Questioning or **Discussion** or a **Personal Statement or Reflection.**

● You can **tell** your assessor about the types of support that individuals or their families might need in order to maximise the benefits of a personalised service.

● *Or*, you can **talk** to your assessor about the types of support that individuals or their families might need in order to maximise the benefits of a personalised service.

● *Or*, you can write a **personal statement or reflection** about your experience of the types of support that individuals or their families might need in order to maximise the benefits of a personalised service.

REMEMBER TO:

● Provide a detailed **account** of the types of support that individuals or their families might need in order to maximise the benefits of a personalised service.

● Include **details** of different types of support that individuals or their families might need.

● Ensure you detail **how** to maximise the benefits of a personalised service.

● Think about **your work setting** and the different types of support that individuals or their families might need.

What does AC1.1 mean?

- ○ The lead word **identify** means that you must **make clear** current legislation, guidelines, policies and protocols relevant to administration of medication.
- ○ Your **list** must make clear current legislation, guidelines, policies and protocols.
- ○ For the key word **legislation** you can think about the relevant laws in place that relate to administering medication.
- ○ For the key word **guidelines** you can think about relevant guidance in place, such as that from the Nursing and Midwifery Council's Standards.
- ○ For the key words **policies and protocols** you can think about the medication policies and procedures available in your work setting.

Read the following **Real Work Setting** scenario and think about how it relates to your work setting and role:

Real Work Setting

Name: Joshua

Job Role: Senior Personal Assistant for an adult who has physical disabilities

Joshua has been working as a Senior Personal Assistant for two years. His Senior responsibilities include: providing support to five Personal Assistants; organising the rotas to ensure staff cover over days, evenings and weekends; supporting the individual, Nathan, to manage his team of Personal Assistants; providing training and guidance on an ongoing basis.

Identifying current legislation, guidelines, policies and procedures: As part of the induction for a newly recruited Personal Assistant who will be working with Nathan, Joshua is supporting Nathan to decide what needs to be included in the induction. One of the areas of responsibility that the Personal Assistant will have will be administering medication, so Nathan suggests that this must be included. Joshua agrees and asks Nathan to think about providing some information that can be given to the Personal Assistant about the legal requirements that govern the administration of medication, and offers to show him an information handout he has developed that he can use.

Evidencing AC1.1 to your assessor:

For AC1.1 you must evidence your knowledge of current legislation, guidelines, policies and protocols relevant to administration of medication.

Assessment Methods:

- ● You can **tell** your assessor about current legislation, guidelines, policies and protocols relevant to administration of medication.
- ● *Or*, you can **talk** to your assessor about current legislation, guidelines, policies and protocols relevant to administration of medication.
- ● *Or*, you can complete a **spidergram** showing current legislation, guidelines, policies and protocols relevant to administration of medication.

REMEMBER TO:

- ● Include a **list** of current legislation, guidelines, policies and protocols.
- ● Ensure the list relates to the administration of medication.
- ● Think about **your work setting** and current legislation, guidelines, policies and protocols relevant to administration of medication.

Learning Outcome 2: Know about common types of medication and their use

Assessment Criterion 2.1: Describe common types of medication, including their effects and potential side effects

What does AC2.1 mean?

- ○ The lead word **describe** means that you must provide an **account** that **details** common types of medication, including their effects and potential side effects.
- ○ Your **account** must detail common types of medication.
- ○ For the key words **types of medication** you can think about how the Medicines Act 1968 classifies medication into different groups.
- ○ For the key word **effects** you can think about the different purposes of medications, how they are used and how they work.
- ○ For the key words **potential side effects** you can think about the ways that medications may impact both positively and negatively on an individual's physical, mental or emotional well-being.

Read the following **Real Work Setting** scenario and think about how it relates to your work setting and role:

Real Work Setting

Name: Theresa

Job Role: Senior Home Carer for older people

Theresa has been working as a Senior Home Carer for three years. Her Senior responsibilities include: providing care and support to individuals living in a range of settings; providing supervision and support to a team of Home Carers; organising staff rotas; developing, implementing, updating and reviewing individuals' care plans; liaising with individuals' families, friends and other professionals involved in their lives.

Common types of medication: Theresa is a Registered Nurse and has been asked by her line manager if she can provide an update to two Carers about the common types of medication that exist, including their effects and potential side effects. Theresa has recently attended a medication training update and plans to use some of the information detailed in the handouts she was given. She begins by thinking about how the common types of medication fall under four main groups: analgesics; antibiotics; antidepressants; anticoagulants. Theresa thinks about the common types of medication and notes how these are also the ones used by the individuals to whom the Carers provide support.

Evidencing AC2.1 to your assessor:

For AC2.1 you must evidence your knowledge of common types of medication, including their effects and potential side effects.

Assessment Methods:
Oral/Written Questioning or Discussion or Personal Statement or Reflection.

- You can **tell** your assessor about common types of medication, including their effects and potential side effects.
- Or, you can **talk** to your assessor about common types of medication, including their effects and potential side effects.
- Or, you can complete a **personal statement or reflection** about your experience of common types of medication, including their effects and potential side effects.

REMEMBER TO:
- Provide an **account** that details common types of medication.
- Ensure your evidence includes both their effects and their potential side effects.
- Think about **your work setting** and common types of medication, including their effects and potential side effects.

Learning Outcome 2: Know about common types of medication and their use

Assessment Criterion 2.2: Identify medication that demands specific physiological measurements to be made

What does AC2.2 mean?

- The lead word **identify** means that you must **make clear** the medications that require specific physiological measurements to be made.
- Your **list** must make clear **different** medications that require specific physiological measurements to be made.
- For the key words **specific physiological measurements** you can think about the requirements of some medications to make checks of how well the body is working before and after the medication is administered or used.

Read the following **Real Work Setting** scenario and think about how it relates to your work setting and role:

Real Work Setting

Name: Theresa

Job Role: Senior Home Carer for older people

(See page 164 for a description of the role.)

Specific physiological measurements: Theresa has also included in her training update details of individuals the two Carers will provide care and support to, who will require checks to be made both before and after they use their medication. Marjorie requires her blood glucose levels to be checked before administering her medication; Sally needs her blood pressure to be checked after administering the medication she uses to lower her blood pressure; Stan requires his pulse to be taken before administering his heart medication. Theresa also shows both Carers where this information is recorded for each individual and how they must do this in line with the work setting's agreed ways of working, and explains to them that all three individuals are supported by two Carers at all times and so they will have an opportunity to observe these important checks being done.

Evidencing AC2.2 to your assessor:

For AC2.2 you must evidence your knowledge of the medication that requires specific physiological measurements be made.

Assessment Methods:

Oral/Written Questioning or **Discussion** or a **Spidergram**.

- You can **tell** your assessor about the medication that requires specific physiological measurements be made.
- Or, you can **talk** to your assessor about the medication that requires specific physiological measurements be made.
- Or, you can complete a **spidergram** showing the medication that requires specific physiological measurements be made.

REMEMBER TO:

- **List** examples of different medications.
- Ensure that your list is for medications that require specific physiological measurements.
- Think about **your work setting** and the medication that requires specific physiological measurements to be made.

Learning Outcome 2: Know about common types of medication and their use

Assessment Criterion 2.3: Describe the common adverse reactions to medication, how each can be recognised and the appropriate action(s) required

What does AC2.3 mean?

- The lead word **describe** means that you must provide an **account** that **details** the common adverse reactions to medication, how each can be recognised and the appropriate action(s) required.
- Your **account** must detail **different** common adverse reactions to medication.
- For the key words **adverse reactions** you can think about the negative side effects that a medication may have on an individual's physical, mental or emotional well-being.
- For the key words **appropriate action(s) required** you can think about the actions to take in line with your work setting's agreed ways of working and your job role and responsibilities.

Read the following **Real Work Setting** scenario and think about how it relates to your work setting and role:

Real Work Setting

Name: Theresa

Job Role: Senior Home Carer for older people

(See page 164 for a description of the role.)

Common adverse reactions to medication: Theresa is reading through her work setting's medication policies and procedures this morning, as she plans to discuss these with the team at their next team meeting. She will also make the team aware of the additional guidelines that all individuals have in their medication files, which must also be taken into account. One of the areas that Theresa plans to focus on is raising the team's awareness of the common adverse reactions to medication, how these may present differently in each individual and the action that must be taken when they occur.

Evidencing AC2.3 to your assessor:

For AC2.3 you must evidence your knowledge of the common adverse reactions to medication, how each can be recognised and the appropriate action(s) required.

Assessment Methods:

Oral/Written Questioning or **Discussion** or a **Personal Statement or Reflection**.

- You can **tell** your assessor about the common adverse reactions to medication, how each can be recognised and the appropriate action(s) required.
- Or, you can **talk** to your assessor about the common adverse reactions to medication, how each can be recognised and the appropriate action(s) required.
- Or, you can write a **personal statement or reflection** about your experience of the common adverse reactions to medication, how each can be recognised and the appropriate action(s) required.

REMEMBER TO:

- Provide a detailed **account** of the common adverse reactions to medication.
- Include **details** about common adverse reactions to medication.
- Ensure your evidence includes how to recognise each reaction and the actions that must be taken.
- Think about **your work setting** and the common adverse reactions to medication, how each can be recognised and the appropriate action(s) required.

Learning Outcome 2: Know about common types of medication and their use

Assessment Criterion 2.4: Explain the different routes of medicine administration

What does AC2.4 mean?

○ The lead word **explain** means that you must **make clear** the different routes of medicine administration.

○ Your **account** must **detail** different routes.

○ For the key word **routes** you can think about how medication can be administered in different ways, such as via inhalation or instillation, orally, transdermally, topically, intravenously, rectally, vaginally, subcutaneously or intramuscularly.

Read the following **Real Work Setting** scenario and think about how it relates to your work setting and role:

Real Work Setting

Name: Theresa

Job Role: Senior Home Carer for older people

(See page 164 for a description of the role.)

Routes of medicine administration: Theresa shows her line manager an information handout that she developed as part of an induction programme for a group of Carers, which explains the different routes of medicine administration. She asks her line manager whether she thinks the team may benefit from reading through this to refresh their knowledge of the different routes of medication administration, including what each route involves and any specific requirements for administering medicines for each route. Theresa's line manager thinks the handout is a very useful resource for the team, but asks Theresa to think about finding out first from each team member their current knowledge in this area by completing either a quiz or a short questionnaire with each of them. She can then provide them with the information handout after they have had an opportunity to share and discuss their responses.

Evidencing AC2.4 to your assessor:

For AC2.4 you must evidence your knowledge of the different routes of medicine administration.

Assessment Methods:

Oral/Written Questioning or Discussion or a Personal Statement or Reflection.

● You can **tell** your assessor about the different routes of medicine administration.

● Or, you can **talk** to your assessor about the different routes of medicine administration.

● Or, you can write a **personal statement or reflection** about your experience of the different routes of medicine administration.

REMEMBER TO:

● Provide an **account** and **explain** the different routes of medicine administration.

● Include **details** about what each route involves.

● Provide **examples** of medications that can be administered by each of the different routes.

● Include details of any special requirements that must be followed.

● Think about **your work setting** and the different routes of medicine administration used with individuals.

Learning Outcome 3: Understand procedures and techniques for the administration of medication

Assessment Criterion 3.1: Explain the types, purpose and function of materials and equipment needed for the administration of medication via the different routes

What does AC3.1 mean?

- ○ The lead word **explain** means that you must **make clear** the types, purpose and function of materials and equipment needed for the administration of medication via the different routes.
- ○ Your **account** must **detail** different routes of medication administration.
- ○ For the key words **materials and equipment** you can think about the range of items that can help in the administration of medication, such as gloves, inhalers, nebulisers, medication cups and spoons. Think about what they are, why they are used and how.
- ○ For the key word **routes** you can think about how medication can be administered in different ways, such as via inhalation or instillation, orally, transdermally, topically, intravenously, rectally, vaginally, subcutaneously or intramuscularly, and the materials and equipment needed for each.

Read the following **Real Work Setting** scenario and think about how it relates to your work setting and role:

Real Work Setting

Name: Jack	

Job Role: Senior Home Carer for young adults

Jack has been working as a Senior Home Carer for one year. His Senior responsibilities include: providing and reviewing care and support packages in place for individuals; providing supervision, training and support to a team of Home Carers; updating individuals' care plans; liaising with individuals' families, friends and other professionals involved in their lives.

Materials and equipment needed for medicine administration: Jack reflects on the training needs of his team and decides to develop further the team's knowledge around the types, purpose and function of materials and equipment needed for the administration of medication via the different routes. To do this he is going to ask the team to complete a group activity that involves carrying out some research and a group discussion, and then putting together their own information handbook on materials and equipment.

Evidencing AC3.1 to your assessor:

For AC3.1 you must evidence your knowledge of the types, purpose and function of materials and equipment needed for the administration of medication via the different routes.

Assessment Methods:

Oral/Written Questioning or **Discussion** or a **Personal Statement or Reflection.**

- You can **tell** your assessor about the types, purpose and function of materials and equipment needed for the administration of medication via the different routes.
- Or, you can **talk** to your assessor about the types, purpose and function of materials and equipment needed for the administration of medication via the different routes.
- Or, you can write a **personal statement or reflection** about your experience of the types, purpose and function of materials and equipment needed for the administration of medication via the different routes.

REMEMBER TO:

- Provide an **account** and **explain** the different materials and equipment needed.
- Include **details** about what these are, why they are used and how.
- Provide **examples** of both materials and equipment.
- Think about **your work setting** and the types, purpose and function of materials and equipment needed for the administration of medication via the different routes.

Learning Outcome 3: Understand procedures and techniques for the administration of medication

Assessment Criterion 3.2: Identify the required information from prescriptions and medication administration charts

What does AC3.2 mean?

○ The lead word **identify** means that you must **make clear** the information that is required from prescriptions and medication charts.
○ Your **list** must include the information that is required.
○ For the key words **prescriptions and medication administration charts** you can think about the information that is required about both the individual and the medication in order to be able to administer the medication.

Read the following **Real Work Setting** scenario and think about how it relates to your work setting and role:

Real Work Setting
Name: Jack
Job Role: Senior Home Carer for young adults
(See page 168 for a description of the role.)
Information required from prescriptions and medication administration charts: Following a recent medicines audit of the service, Jack and his manager are working closely with the team to ensure they follow the correct procedures and techniques for the administration of medication. As part of this process Jack plans to reinforce with the team at their next team meeting that they must check the information on individuals' prescriptions and medication administration charts before administering medication. This includes the individual's details, the medication that has been prescribed for them and any other details that may be of importance to the administration of medication.

Evidencing AC3.2 to your assessor:

For AC3.2 you must evidence your understanding of the required information from prescriptions and medication administration charts.

Assessment Methods:

Oral/Written Questioning or **Discussion** or a **Spidergram**.

● You can **tell** your assessor about the required information from prescriptions and medication administration charts.
● Or, you can **talk** to your assessor about the required information from prescriptions and medication administration charts.
● Or, you can complete a **spidergram** showing the required information from prescriptions and medication administration charts.

REMEMBER TO:

● List **different** items of information.
● Include **examples** of information items.
● Ensure that your list includes the **details** required from prescriptions and medication administration charts.
● Think about **your work setting** and the required information from prescriptions and medication administration charts.

Learning Outcome 4: Prepare for the administration of medication

Assessment Criterion 4.1: Apply standard precautions for infection control

What does AC4.1 mean?

- The lead word **apply** means that you must **be able to show** through **your work practices** how to put into practice standard precautions for infection control.
- Your **observations** of your work practices must include you putting into practice standard precautions for infection control.
- For the key words **standard precautions** you can think about the different procedures that exist to protect you, individuals and others from the spread of infection.
- For the key words **infection control** you can think about the policies and procedures used in your work setting to minimise the risk of spreading infection.

Read the following **Real Work Setting** scenario and think about how it relates to your work setting and role:

Real Work Setting

Name: Natalie

Job Role: Senior Residential Carer for older adults who have dementia

Natalie has been working as a Senior Residential Carer for five years. Her Senior responsibilities include: assisting the deputy manager in providing day-to-day care and support to individuals; conducting supervisions with Carers, including mentoring and inducting new Carers; developing, implementing and reviewing individuals' care plans; attending individuals' care planning and review meetings; developing good working relationships with individuals, their families, friends and other professionals who are involved in their lives.

Applying standard precautions for infection control: Natalie is inducting a new Carer today, and as part of her induction Natalie has arranged for her to observe her administer medication to individuals. Before Natalie enters the medication room she washes her hands thoroughly using the approved hand-washing technique and points out to the Carer the poster on the wall above the sink that explains this technique. Natalie also asks the Carer to note how she washes her hands in the sink in the medication room rather than anywhere else, for the purposes of infection control. Natalie then unlocks the medication cupboard and begins to prepare the materials and equipment she will need for this morning. Natalie wears disposable gloves whilst doing this and shows the Carer the sink where all the equipment was washed by her yesterday evening; again Natalie asks the Carer to note how only this sink is used to wash the medication equipment, again for the purposes of infection control.

Evidencing AC4.1 to your assessor:

For AC4.1 you must evidence your skills in applying standard precautions for infection control.

Assessment Method:
Direct Observation of your work practices.

- You can **show** your assessor how you apply standard precautions for infection control.

REMEMBER TO:

- Make arrangements for **observation** of **your work practices**.
- Include evidence of you applying different standard precautions.
- Ensure the evidence you include relates to infection control.
- Think about **your work setting** and how to apply standard precautions for infection control.

Learning Outcome 4: Prepare for the administration of medication

Assessment Criterion 4.2: Explain the appropriate timing of medication, e.g. check that the individual has not taken any medication recently

What does AC4.2 mean?
- The lead word **explain** means that you must **make clear** the appropriate timing of medication.
- Your **account** must **detail** why the appropriate timing of medication is necessary and how to ensure this.
- For the key words **appropriate timing** you can think about the reasons why it is necessary to administer medication at the correct time as prescribed, including how much time should be left between administering one dose and the next, and how to ensure that this is done.

Read the following **Real Work Setting** scenario and think about how it relates to your work setting and role:

Real Work Setting

Name: Natalie

Job Role: Senior Residential Carer for older adults who have dementia

(See page 170 for a description of the role.)

Appropriate timing of medication: Natalie continues to prepare the medications she will be administering this morning and for the first individual she reads through his medication administration record (MAR) and checks what medication he will be using this morning, the name and dose. Natalie also checks his MAR for when the last dose was administered and checks that the timing of administering his medication this morning is correct and suitable for the requirements of his prescription and agreed procedure.

Evidencing AC4.2 to your assessor:

For AC4.2 you must evidence your knowledge of the appropriate timing of medication, e.g. check that the individual has not taken any medication recently.

Assessment Methods:

Oral/Written Questioning or Discussion or a Personal Statement or Reflection.

- You can **tell** your assessor about the appropriate timing of medication, e.g. check that the individual has not taken any medication recently.
- Or, you can **talk** to your assessor about the appropriate timing of medication, e.g. check that the individual has not taken any medication recently.
- Or, you can write a **personal statement or reflection** about your experience of the appropriate timing of medication, e.g. check that the individual has not taken any medication recently.

REMEMBER TO:
- Provide an **account** and explain the appropriate timing of medication.
- Include **details** about what is involved in administering medication at the correct times.
- Provide **examples** of how to do this and reasons why.
- Think about **your work setting** and the appropriate timing of medication, e.g. check that the individual has not taken any medication recently.

Learning Outcome 4: Prepare for the administration of medication

Assessment Criterion 4.3: Obtain the individual's consent and offer information, support and reassurance throughout in a manner that encourages their cooperation and is appropriate to their needs and concerns

What does AC4.3 mean?

- The lead word **obtain** means that you must **be able to show** through **your work practices** how to gain the individual's consent and offer information, support and reassurance throughout in a manner that encourages their cooperation and is appropriate to their needs and concerns.
- Your **observations** of your work practices must include you gaining the individual's consent and offering information, support and reassurance throughout.
- For the key word **consent** you can think about the different ways to seek an individual's agreement for you to administer their medication.
- For the key words **needs and concerns** you can think about how the ways in which you provide information, support and reassurance will vary depending on an individual's communication needs and concerns.

Read the following **Real Work Setting** scenario and think about how it relates to your work setting and role:

Real Work Setting

Name: Natalie

Job Role: Senior Residential Carer for older adults who have dementia

(See page 170 for a description of the role.)

Obtaining consent, offering information, support and reassurance: Natalie shows the Carer with her how she approaches Reginald. Natalie shows Reginald his medication in the medicines pot, Reginald smiles and puts his hand out. Natalie explains to him what each tablet is and what it is for and checks whether he wants any water. Reginald shows Natalie the water jug and then pours himself out a glass. Natalie sits down next to Reginald until he has finished taking his medication and then thanks him.

Evidencing AC4.3 to your assessor:

For AC4.3 you must evidence your skills in obtaining the individual's consent and offering information, support and reassurance throughout in a manner that encourages their cooperation and is appropriate to their needs and concerns.

Assessment Method:

Direct Observation of your work practices.

- You can **show** your assessor how you obtain the individual's consent and offer information, support and reassurance throughout in a manner that encourages their cooperation and is appropriate to their needs and concerns.

REMEMBER TO:
- Make arrangements for **observation** of **your work practices**.
- Include evidence of you obtaining consent and offering information, support and reassurance.
- Think about **your work setting** and how to obtain the individual's consent and offer information, support and reassurance throughout in a manner that encourages their cooperation and is appropriate to their needs and concerns.

Learning Outcome 4: Prepare for the administration of medication

Assessment Criterion 4.4: Select, check and prepare correctly the medication according to the medication administration record or medication information leaflet

What does AC4.4 mean?

○ The lead words **select, check and prepare** mean that you must **be able to show** through **your work practices** how to prepare medication for administration correctly and according to the medication administration record or medication information leaflet.

○ Your **observations** of your work practices must include you selecting, checking and preparing the medication correctly.

○ For the key words **select, check and prepare** you can think about the procedures you must follow in your work setting to ensure that you administer the correct medication to individuals, including the checks you must carry out and any special instructions that must be followed.

Read the following **Real Work Setting** scenario and think about how it relates to your work setting and role:

Real Work Setting

Name: Natalie

Job Role: Senior Residential Carer for older adults who have dementia

(See page 170 for a description of the role.)

Selecting, checking and preparing: Natalie then returns to the medication cupboard, unlocks it, washes her hands, changes her gloves and prepares the medication for the second individual, Ruth. Natalie reads through Ruth's medication profile and medication administration record and then cross checks that her details match to those on the medication container. She then checks the name of the medication, the last dose given and the time now for administering it to her, as well as details about how it is to be taken, i.e. with food. Natalie places the tablets on a spoon using a non-touch technique and locks the cupboard.

Evidencing AC4.4 to your assessor:

For AC4.4 you must evidence your skills in correctly selecting, checking and preparing the medication according to the medication administration record or medication information leaflet.

Assessment Method:

Direct Observation of your work practices.

● You can **show** your assessor how you select, check and prepare correctly the medication according to the medication administration record or medication information leaflet.

REMEMBER TO:

● Make arrangements for **observation** of **your work practices**.
● Include **evidence** of you selecting, checking and preparing correctly medication.
● Ensure the evidence you provide is in line with the medication administration record or medication information leaflet.
● Think about **your work setting** and how to select, check and prepare medication correctly according to the medication administration record or medication information leaflet.

Learning Outcome 5: Administer and monitor individuals' medication

Assessment Criterion 5.1: Select the route for the administration of medication, according to the individual's plan of care and the drug to be administered, and prepare the site if necessary

What does AC5.1 mean?

- The lead word **select** means that you must **be able to show** through **your work practices** how to choose the route for administration of medication, according to the individual's plan of care and the drug to be administered, and to prepare the site if necessary.
- Your **observations** of your work practices must include you selecting the route for the administration of medication.
- For the key word **select** you can think about the procedures you must follow in your work setting to ensure that you choose the route for administration of medication, according to the individual's plan of care and the drug to be administered, and prepare the site if necessary.
- For the key word **route** you can think about how medication can be administered in different ways, such as via inhalation or instillation, orally, transdermally, topically, intravenously, rectally, vaginally, subcutaneously or intramuscularly, and the preparations required for each of these.

Read the following **Real Work Setting** scenario and think about how it relates to your work setting and role:

Real Work Setting

Name: Thomas

Job Role: Senior Carer for adults who have mental health needs

Thomas has been working as a Senior Carer for seven years. His Senior responsibilities include: administering medication to individuals; assisting the manager with admissions; inducting new staff; reviewing individuals' care plans; completing and maintaining accurate records.

Selecting the route for administration of medication: Thomas is administering medication this evening and is checking the individual's plan of care to select the route for the administration of medication; the individual takes his medication orally by swallowing tablets and via the optic route by drops into the ear. After checking the individual's medication administration record against the monitored dose system in order to ensure that the details of the individual and the details of the medication match and are correct, using a non-touch technique and wearing gloves Thomas pops the tablet out of the blister pack and into a medication cup. Thomas then unlocks the medicines fridge, checks that the temperature of the fridge is correct and then cross checks the information recorded on the bottle of this individual's ear drops against his medication administration record.

Evidencing AC5.1 to your assessor:

For AC5.1 you must evidence your skills in selecting the route for the administration of medication, according to the individual's plan of care and the drug to be administered, and preparing the site if necessary.

Assessment Method:
Direct Observation of your work practices.

- You can **show** your assessor how you select the route for the administration of medication, according to the individual's plan of care and the drug to be administered, and prepare the site if necessary.

REMEMBER TO:
- Make arrangements for **observation of your work practices**.
- Include **evidence** of you selecting the route for the administration of medication, and preparing the site if necessary.
- Ensure the evidence you provide is in line with the individual's plan of care and the drug to be administered.
- Think about **your work setting** and how to select the route for the administration of medication, according to the individual's plan of care and the drug to be administered, and to prepare the site if necessary.

Learning Outcome 5: Administer and monitor individuals' medication

Assessment Criterion 5.2: Safely administer the medication in line with legislation and local policies, in a way that minimises pain, discomfort and trauma to the individual

What does AC5.2 mean?

- The lead words **safely administer** mean that you must **be able to show** through **your work practices** how to administer medication using safe practices and in line with legislation and local policies, in a way that minimises pain, discomfort and trauma to the individual.
- Your **observations** of your work practices must include you safely administering medication in line with legislation and local policies.
- For the key word **legislation** you can think about relevant laws in place that relate to the safe administration of medication.
- For the key words **local policies** you can think about the policies, procedures and ways of working available in your work setting for the safe administration of medication.

Read the following **Real Work Setting** scenario and think about how it relates to your work setting and role:

Real Work Setting

Name: Thomas

Job Role: Senior Carer for adults who have mental health needs

(See page 174 for a description of the role.)

Safely administer medication: After Thomas administers the individual's tablets he then explains to him that he has some ear drops to administer and waits for the individual to tell him that he is ready for these. When he confirms that he is, Thomas asks him to lean his head to one side and explains that he will now insert the top of the applicator into his outer ear to apply two drops and that he will not experience any discomfort or pain. Once finished, Thomas explains to the individual that his medication has all now been administered and that he has cooperated very well throughout the process. The individual confirms that he is feeling well and does not mind having his ear drops.

Evidencing AC5.2 to your assessor:

For AC5.2 you must evidence your skills in safely administering the medication in line with legislation and local policies, in a way that minimises pain, discomfort and trauma to the individual.

Assessment Method:

Direct Observation of your work practices.

- You can **show** your assessor how you safely administer medication in line with legislation and local policies, in a way that minimises pain, discomfort and trauma to the individual.

REMEMBER TO:

- Make arrangements for **observation** of **your work practices**.
- Include evidence of you safely administering medication in line with legislation and local policies.
- Ensure the evidence you provide shows how you do this in a way that minimises pain, discomfort and trauma to the individual.
- Think about **your work setting** and how to safely administer medication in line with legislation and local policies, in a way that minimises pain, discomfort and trauma to the individual.

Learning Outcome 5: Administer and monitor individuals' medication

Assessment Criterion 5.3: Describe how to report any immediate problems with the administration of medication

What does AC5.3 mean?

- The lead word **describe** means that you must provide an **account** that **details** how to report any immediate problems with the administration of medication.
- Your **account** must detail **how** to report any immediate problems.
- For the key word **report** you can think about how to provide a verbal and/or written account to an appointed person in your work setting about any immediate problems with the administration of medication.
- For the key word **problems** you can think about difficulties that may arise with the administration of medication, such as when medication is missing or has been dropped or spilt, when an individual refuses to take medication, and when there are difficulties in administering medication in its prescribed form, adverse reactions, or anomalies in medication administration records or in directions for use.

Read the following **Real Work Setting** scenario and think about how it relates to your work setting and role:

Real Work Setting

Name: Thomas

Job Role: Senior Carer for adults who have mental health needs

(See page 174 for a description of the role.)

Reporting any immediate problems: When Thomas administers Frank's medication Frank refuses, saying that he is feeling too unwell to take it. Thomas puts the medication cup down and sits next to Frank and asks him to tell him about how he is feeling. Frank explains that since taking his medication in the morning he has felt a little faint and dizzy; he thinks it might be due to his medication and so does not want to take any more. Thomas reassures Frank and explains to him that he is going to inform his manager about what he has told him and will also record it on his medication administration record and his support plan. Thomas reports this with immediate effect to his manager, who contacts Frank's GP.

Evidencing AC5.3 to your assessor:

For AC5.3 you must evidence your knowledge of how to report any immediate problems with the administration of medication.

Assessment Methods:

Oral/Written Questioning or Discussion or a Personal Statement or Reflection.

- You can **tell** your assessor about how to report any immediate problems with the administration of medication.
- Or, you can **talk** to your assessor about how to report any immediate problems with the administration of medication.
- Or, you can write a **personal statement or reflection** about your experience of how to report any immediate problems with the administration of medication.

REMEMBER TO:

- Provide a **detailed** account of how to report any immediate problems with the administration of medication.
- Include **details** about how to report any immediate problems with the administration of medication.
- Ensure your evidence includes details of the reporting procedures you must follow.
- Think about **your work setting** and how to report any immediate problems with the administration of medication.

Learning Outcome 5: Administer and monitor individuals' medication

Assessment Criterion 5.4: Monitor the individual's condition throughout, recognise any adverse effects and take the appropriate action without delay

What does AC5.4 mean?

○ The lead word **monitor** means that you must **be able to show** through **your work practices** how to observe and check the individual's condition throughout, recognise any adverse effects and take the appropriate action without delay.

○ Your **observations** of your work practices must include you monitoring the individual's condition throughout.

○ For the key word **condition** you can think about how to observe and check any changes in the individual's physical, mental or emotional condition.

○ For the key words **appropriate action** you can think about the procedure you must follow in your work setting if you recognise any adverse effects in the individual.

Read the following **Real Work Setting** scenario and think about how it relates to your work setting and role:

Real Work Setting

Name: Thomas

Job Role: Senior Carer for adults who have mental health needs

(See page 174 for a description of the role.)

Monitoring the individual's condition: Thomas returns to Frank and sits down beside him again and explains to him that he has recorded what he has told him about how he is feeling and has also reported it to the manager, who is phoning Frank's GP to inform him. Thomas asks Frank how he is feeling; Frank says he's feeling much the same and so Thomas agrees with Frank for him to rest in his room for now and ensures his call alarm is within his reach, asking him to press it should he feel any worse or want anything. Thomas also agrees with Frank that he will come back to monitor his condition every fifteen minutes and as soon as the manager has heard back from his GP he will also come and inform him about the advice he has provided. Thomas ensures that all this information is recorded in full, including the fifteen-minute observation checks.

Evidencing AC5.4 to your assessor:

For AC5.4 you must evidence your skills in monitoring the individual's condition throughout, recognising any adverse effects and taking the appropriate action without delay.

Assessment Method:

Direct Observation of your work practices.

● You can **show** your assessor or an expert witness how to monitor the individual's condition throughout, recognise any adverse effects and take the appropriate action without delay.

REMEMBER TO:

● Make arrangements for **observation** of **your work practices**.

● Include evidence of you monitoring the individual's condition throughout.

● Ensure the evidence you provide includes recognising any adverse effects and taking the appropriate action without delay.

● Think about **your work setting** and how to monitor the individual's condition throughout, recognise any adverse effects and take the appropriate action without delay.

Learning Outcome 5: Administer and monitor individuals' medication

Assessment Criterion 5.5: Explain why it may be necessary to confirm that the individual actually takes the medication and does not pass the medication to others

What does AC5.5 mean?

- The lead word **explain** means that you must make clear the reasons why it may be necessary to confirm that the individual actually takes the medication and does not pass the medication to others.
- Your **account** must **detail** the reasons why this may be necessary.
- For the key word **confirm** you can think about the procedures you must follow in your work setting to ensure that the individual actually takes the medication and does not pass the medication to others.

Read the following **Real Work Setting** scenario and think about how it relates to your work setting and role:

Real Work Setting

Name: Thomas

Job Role: Senior Carer for adults who have mental health needs

(See page 174 for a description of the role.)

Confirming that the individual actually takes the medication: At the team meeting Thomas is holding this week with his manager he raises the concerns he has about Senior Carers following the correct procedures when they are administering medication to individuals, as he noticed that there was a tablet on the small coffee table in the lounge yesterday afternoon when he arrived on duty. Thomas talks the team through the dangers of not observing individuals actually take their medication, including how they may pass their prescribed medication on to other individuals. Thomas's manager explains that he will be monitoring this closely.

Evidencing AC5.5 to your assessor:

For AC5.5 you must evidence your knowledge of why it may be necessary to confirm that the individual actually takes the medication and does not pass the medication to others.

Assessment Methods:

Oral/Written Questioning or **Discussion** or a **Personal Statement** or **Reflection**.

- You can **tell** your assessor about why it may be necessary to confirm that the individual actually takes the medication and does not pass the medication to others.
- Or, you can **talk** to your assessor about why it may be necessary to confirm that the individual actually takes the medication and does not pass the medication to others.
- Or, you can write a **personal statement or reflection** about why it may be necessary to confirm that the individual actually takes the medication and does not pass the medication to others.

REMEMBER TO:

- Provide an **account** and explain why it may be necessary to confirm that the individual actually takes the medication and does not pass the medication to others.
- Include **details** about why this may be necessary.
- Provide **examples** of how to do this and the reasons why.
- Think about **your work setting** and why it may be necessary to confirm that the individual actually takes the medication and does not pass the medication to others.

Learning Outcome 5: Administer and monitor individuals' medication

Assessment Criterion 5.6: Maintain the security of medication and related records throughout the process and return them to the correct place for storage

What does AC5.6 mean?

- ○ The lead word **maintain** means that you must **be able to show** through **your work practices** how to keep medication and related records secure throughout the process and return them to the correct place for storage.
- ○ Your **observations** of your work practices must include you maintaining the security of medication and related records throughout the process.
- ○ For the key words **security of medication** you can think about the different ways of ensuring medication is kept secure whilst you administer it, such as not leaving the medication cupboard or medicines fridge unlocked, the keys for both being held only by authorised staff, and storing medication administration records, medication plans and profiles safely and securely in a designated area after use.
- ○ For the key words **correct place for storage** you can think about the different ways of storing different types of medication and where the medication administration records are stored in your work setting.

Read the following **Real Work Setting** scenario and think about how it relates to your work setting and role:

Real Work Setting

| **Name:** Thomas |
| **Job Role:** Senior Carer for adults who have mental health needs |
| (See page 174 for a description of the role.) |
| **Maintaining the security of medication and related records throughout the process:** Thomas is being visited by his assessor today, who observes him take many precautions for the security of medication and related records whilst he is administering medication to individuals. These include Thomas locking the medication cupboard every time he leaves it unattended, not leaving the medication file and individuals' plans out, ensuring these are also put away in the medication cupboard after he has finished using them, and ensuring the medicines fridge is locked when it is left unattended. |

Evidencing AC5.6 to your assessor:

For AC5.6 you must evidence your skills in maintaining the security of medication and related records throughout the process and returning them to the correct place for storage.

Assessment Method:

Direct Observation of your work practices.

- You can **show** your assessor how you maintain the security of medication and related records throughout the process and return them to the correct place for storage.

REMEMBER TO:

- Make arrangements for **observation of your work practices**.
- Include evidence of you maintaining the security of medication and related records throughout the process.
- Include evidence of you returning medication and related records to the correct place for storage.
- Think about **your work setting** and how to maintain the security of medication and related records throughout the process and return them to the correct place for storage.

Learning Outcome 5: Administer and monitor individuals' medication

Assessment Criterion 5.7: Describe how to dispose of out-of-date and part-used medications in accordance with legal and organisational requirements

What does AC5.7 mean?

○ The lead word **describe** means that you must provide an **account** that **details** how to dispose of out-of-date and part-used medications in accordance with legal and organisational requirements.

○ Your **account** must detail **how** to dispose of out-of-date and part-used medications.

○ For the key words **out-of-date and part-used medications** you can think about how if a medication is not effective for an individual or if the individual requests it in a different form or if an individual refuses to take their medication, that this may result in out-of-date and part-used medications.

○ For the key words **legal and organisational requirements** you can think about the standards, regulations and work setting procedures in place that set out how to dispose of out-of-date and part-used medications.

Read the following **Real Work Setting** scenario and think about how it relates to your work setting and role:

Real Work Setting

Name: Thomas

Job Role: Senior Carer for adults who have mental health needs

(See page 174 for a description of the role.)

Disposal of out-of-date and part-used medications: Thomas's assessor asks him to reflect on the situation he encountered with Frank, where his GP advised him to discontinue the medication he had prescribed in case it was causing him adverse effects, and to write an account of how Thomas disposed of Frank's part-used medication in line with his work setting's disposal procedure and legal requirements. Thomas's assessor asks him also to include in his account the procedure he follows for disposal of out-of-date medication.

Evidencing AC5.7 to your assessor:

For AC5.7 you must evidence your knowledge of how to dispose of out-of-date and part-used medications in accordance with legal and organisational requirements.

Assessment Methods:

Oral/Written Questioning or **Discussion** or a **Personal Statement** or **Reflection**.

● You can **tell** your assessor about how to dispose of out-of-date and part-used medications in accordance with legal and organisational requirements.

● Or, you can **talk** to your assessor about how to dispose of out-of-date and part-used medications in accordance with legal and organisational requirements.

● Or, you can write a **personal statement or reflection** about your experience of how to dispose of out-of-date and part-used medications in accordance with legal and organisational requirements.

REMEMBER TO:

● Provide a **detailed** account of how to dispose of out-of-date and part-used medications in accordance with legal and organisational requirements.

● Include **details** about how to dispose of out-of-date and part-used medications.

● Ensure your evidence includes details of how to do this in line with legal and organisational requirements.

● Think about **your work setting** and how to dispose of out-of-date and part-used medications in accordance with legal and organisational requirements.

HSC3003 Provide support to maintain and develop skills for everyday life

Learning Outcome 1: Understand the context of supporting skills for everyday life

Assessment Criterion 1.1: Compare methods for developing and maintaining skills for everyday life

What does AC1.1 mean?

- The lead word **compare** means that you must **consider in detail** the similarities and differences between the different methods for developing and maintaining skills for everyday life.
- Your **account** must provide a comparison of **different methods** for developing and maintaining skills for everyday life.
- For the key word **developing** you can think about the different ways to introduce new skills and improve existing skills for everyday life.
- For the key word **maintaining** you can think about the different ways to use existing skills for everyday life.
- For the key words **everyday life** you can think about the skills required to enable individuals to live their lives fully and in the ways they want to.

Read the following **Real Work Setting** scenario and think about how it relates to your work setting and role:

Real Work Setting

Name: Penny

Job role: Senior Personal Assistant for adults with epilepsy

Penny has been working as a Senior Personal Assistant for one year. Her Senior responsibilities include training and supporting a team of Personal Assistants to support individuals to complete personal care tasks and housework tasks, to manage their bills, prepare and cook meals, do their shopping and attend social events.

Developing and maintaining skills for everyday life: Penny is preparing for her monthly meeting with the team of Personal Assistants and would like to provide an update to the team on the different ways they can work with different individuals so that they have full control over their lives. Penny plans to begin by asking each team member the different ways they currently do this with the individuals they are supporting.

Evidencing AC1.1 to your assessor:

For AC1.1 you must evidence your understanding of the different methods for developing and maintaining skills for everyday life.

Assessment Methods:

Oral/Written Questioning or Discussion or a Personal Statement or Reflection.

- You can **tell** your assessor about the similarities and differences between different methods for developing and maintaining skills for everyday life.
- Or, you can **talk** to your assessor about the similarities and differences between different methods for developing and maintaining skills for everyday life.
- Or, you can write a **personal statement or reflection** about your experience of the similarities and differences between different methods for developing and maintaining skills for everyday life.

REMEMBER TO:

- Provide an **account** and a **comparison** of different methods for developing and maintaining skills for everyday life.
- Include **details** about what each method is, its main features, and its similarities and differences to others.
- Include **varied** examples of methods for developing and maintaining skills for everyday life.
- Think about the individuals in **your work setting** and the different methods for developing and maintaining their skills for everyday life.

Learning Outcome 1: Understand the context of supporting skills for everyday life

Assessment Criterion 1.2: Analyse reasons why individuals may need support to maintain, regain or develop skills for everyday life

What does AC1.2 mean?

- The lead word **analyse** means that you must **examine in detail** the reasons why individuals may need support to maintain, regain or develop skills for everyday life.
- Your **account** must provide an analysis of the **different** reasons individuals may need support to maintain, regain or develop skills for everyday life.
- For the key word **maintain** you can think about the different ways skills for everyday life are used.
- For the key word **regain** you can think about the different ways in which new ways for using skills for everyday life are learned.
- For the key word **develop** you can think about the different ways to introduce new skills and improve existing skills for everyday life.

Read the following **Real Work Setting** scenario and think about how it relates to your work setting and role:

Real Work Setting

Name: Penny

Job role: Senior Personal Assistant for adults with epilepsy

(See page 181 for a description of the role.)

Reasons for support: Penny has also developed two case studies of two different individuals who used to access support from the team of Personal Assistants. She will use these at the monthly meeting in order to encourage the team to think about individuals' personal situations, their experiences and the reasons why they may need support at different times in their lives with maintaining, regaining or developing skills.

Evidencing AC1.2 to your assessor:

For AC1.2 you must evidence your understanding of the reasons why individuals may need support to maintain, regain or develop skills for everyday life.

Assessment Methods:

Oral/Written Questioning or **Discussion** or a **Personal Statement** or **Reflection**.

- You can **tell** your assessor about the reasons individuals may need support to maintain, regain or develop skills for everyday life.
- Or, you can **talk** to your assessor about the reasons individuals may need support to maintain, regain or develop skills for everyday life.
- Or, you can write a **personal statement or reflection** about your experience of the reasons individuals may need support to maintain, regain or develop skills for everyday life.

REMEMBER TO:

- Provide an **account** and an **analysis** of different reasons individuals may need support to maintain, regain or develop skills for everyday life.
- Ensure **examples** relate to maintaining, regaining or developing skills for everyday life.
- Think about the individuals in **your work setting** and the reasons they may need support to maintain, regain or develop skills for everyday life.

Learning Outcome 1: Understand the context of supporting skills for everyday life

Assessment Criterion 1.3: Explain how maintaining, regaining or developing skills can benefit individuals

What does AC1.3 mean?

- The lead word **explain** means that you must **make clear** the benefits for individuals of maintaining, regaining or developing skills.
- Your **account** must make clear **details** about the benefits for individuals.
- For the key word **maintaining** you can think about the benefits for individuals of using skills for everyday life.
- For the key word **regaining** you can think about the benefits for individuals of learning new ways to use skills for everyday life.
- For the key word **developing** you can think about the benefits for individuals of introducing new skills and improving existing skills for everyday life.

Read the following **Real Work Setting** scenario and think about how it relates to your work setting and role:

Real Work Setting

Name: Penny

Job role: Senior Personal Assistant for adults with epilepsy

(See page 181 for a description of the role.)

Benefits for individuals: Penny will also be sharing with the team at the monthly meeting her experiences of the range of benefits that maintaining, regaining or developing skills can bring for individuals, in terms of their physical, emotional and social well-being, their access to services and their participation in their communities. Penny plans then to invite each member of the team to share one benefit of maintaining, regaining or developing skills for one individual with whom they are currently working.

Evidencing AC1.3 to your assessor:

For AC1.3 you must evidence your understanding of how maintaining, regaining or developing skills can benefit individuals.

Assessment Methods:

Oral/Written Questioning or **Discussion** or a **Personal Statement** or **Reflection**.

- You can **tell** your assessor about how maintaining, regaining or developing skills can benefit individuals.
- Or, you can **talk** to your assessor about how maintaining, regaining or developing skills can benefit individuals.
- Or, you can write a **personal statement or reflection** about your experience of how maintaining, regaining or developing skills can benefit individuals.

REMEMBER TO:

- Provide an **account** of how maintaining, regaining or developing skills can benefit individuals.
- Include **details** about the different benefits for individuals of maintaining, regaining or developing skills.
- Think about **your work setting** and how maintaining, regaining or developing skills can benefit individuals.

Learning Outcome 2: Be able to support individuals to plan for maintaining and developing skills for everyday life

Assessment Criterion 2.1: Work with an individual and others to identify skills for everyday life that need to be supported

What does AC2.1 mean?

- The lead words **work with** mean that you must **be able to show** through **your work practices** how to support an individual and others to identify skills for everyday life that need to be supported.
- Your **observations** of your work practices must include you working with an individual and others to identify skills for everyday life that need to be supported.
- For the key word **others** you can think about other people involved in individuals' lives, such as their families, friends and advocates, as well as your team members, colleagues, manager and other external professionals or specialists, such as GPs, Social Workers, Speech Therapists, nurses, Occupational Therapists and Physiotherapists.
- For the key words **skills for everyday life** you can think about the skills required to enable individuals to live their lives fully and in the ways they want to.

Read the following **Real Work Setting** scenario and think about how it relates to your work setting and role:

Real Work Setting

Name: Christian

Job role: Senior Carer for older people living in the community

Christian has been working as a Senior Carer for five years. Christian's Senior responsibilities include: supporting individuals to remain living in their own homes; providing support with personal care, including meeting complex care needs such as PEG feeds and insulin injections, medication, housework, laundry and shopping.

Identifying skills for everyday life: Joan sustained a shoulder and hip injury when she fell down an escalator in the shopping centre and she has spent four weeks in hospital. Joan has been assessed by the reablement team and has been discharged this morning from hospital. Christian visits Joan at home and, together with her and her daughter, reviews the support plan in place to address some of the difficulties that Joan is experiencing with everyday skills, in order to ensure that Joan maintains her independence.

Evidencing AC2.1 to your assessor:

For AC2.1 you must evidence your skills in working with an individual and others to identify skills for everyday life that need to be supported.

Assessment Method:	REMEMBER TO:
Direct Observation of your work practices. • You can **show** your assessor how you work with an individual and others to identify skills for everyday life that need to be supported.	• Make arrangements for **observation** of **your work practices**. • Include evidence of you working with an individual and others. • Ensure the evidence you provide includes identifying skills for everyday life that need to be supported. • Think about **your work setting** and how you work with an individual and others to identify skills for everyday life that need to be supported.

Learning Outcome 2: Be able to support individuals to plan for maintaining and developing skills for everyday life

Assessment Criterion 2.2: Agree with the individual a plan for developing or maintaining the skills identified

What does AC2.2 mean?

- The lead word **agree** means that you must **be able to show** through **your work practices** how to establish with an individual a plan of which the individual approves for developing or maintaining the skills identified.
- Your **observations** of your work practices must include you agreeing with the individual a plan for developing or maintaining the skills identified.
- The **plan** may include short-, medium- and long-term goals, as well as the type and level of support needed to achieve these goals, the roles and responsibilities of those involved, the ways to address any risks involved in your role, and the ways to monitor your progress with your plan.
- For the key word **developing** you can think about how to agree with an individual a plan of support for introducing new skills and improving existing skills identified.
- For the key word **maintaining** you can think about how to agree with an individual a plan of support for using skills identified.

Read the following **Real Work Setting** scenario and think about how it relates to your work setting and role:

Real Work Setting

Name: Christian

Job role: Senior Carer for older people living in the community

(See page 184 for a description of the role.)

Agreeing a plan: Christian talks through with Joan all the different daily living activities and asks her how she manages with these, including what activities she can manage well, with what activities she has difficulties, and with what activities she would like support. Christian then records in Joan's support plan the activities with which she would like support, the type of support she requires, when it is to be provided and by whom. Whilst doing so Christian answers all of Joan's questions about how the support will be provided and provides guidance to her daughter about other professionals and services that they may find useful to access. Christian summarises at the end of the visit all the areas that have been agreed and checks with Joan that she agrees to these before asking her to sign her support plan.

Evidencing AC2.2 to your assessor:

For AC2.2 you must evidence your skills in agreeing with an individual a plan for developing or maintaining the skills identified.

Assessment Method:	REMEMBER TO:
Direct Observation of your work practices. • You can **show** your assessor how you agree with an individual a plan for developing or maintaining the skills identified.	• Make arrangements for **observation** of **your work practices**. • Include evidence of you agreeing a plan with an individual. • Ensure the evidence you provide includes developing or maintaining skills for everyday life. • Think about **your work setting** and how you work with an individual and others to identify skills for everyday life that need to be supported.

Learning Outcome 2: Be able to support individuals to plan for maintaining and developing skills for everyday life

Assessment Criterion 2.3: Analyse possible sources of conflict that may arise when planning, and ways to resolve them

What does AC2.3 mean?

- The lead word **analyse** means that you must **examine in detail** the possible sources of conflict that may arise when planning, and ways to resolve them.
- Your **account** must provide an analysis of the **different** possible sources of conflict that may arise when planning, as well as **different** ways to resolve them.
- For the key words **sources of conflict** you can think about why differences of opinion may arise when planning support, in relation to the individual's personality and outlook on their life, their relationship with others involved in their lives and the types of services and support available.

Read the following **Real Work Setting** scenario and think about how it relates to your work setting and role:

Real Work Setting

Name: Christian

Job role: Senior Carer for older people living in the community

(See page 184 for a description of the role.)

Sources of conflict: Christian has received a phone call from Joan's daughter because both are a little anxious about Joan continuing to be just escorted to the supermarket by the Carer. Both feel that although Joan is able to do her food shopping on her own she would benefit from her Support Worker being with her whilst doing her shopping, as this would reduce her anxiety over being on her own in the community. Christian explains that he will meet with his manager to discuss possible support that may be available to meet Joan's needs.

Evidencing AC2.3 to your assessor:

For AC2.3 you must evidence your knowledge of the possible sources of conflict that may arise when planning and ways to resolve them.

Assessment Methods:

Oral/Written Questioning or **Discussion** or a **Personal Statement or Reflection**.

- You can **tell** your assessor about the possible sources of conflict that may arise when planning, and ways to resolve them.
- Or, you can **talk** to your assessor about the possible sources of conflict that may arise when planning, and ways to resolve them.
- Or, you can write a **personal statement or reflection** about the possible sources of conflict that may arise when planning, and ways to resolve them.

REMEMBER TO:

- Provide an **account** and an **analysis** of different sources of conflict that may arise when planning, and ways to resolve them.
- Ensure examples relate to **both** sources of conflict when planning and methods of resolving them.
- Think about **your work setting** and the sources of conflict that may arise when planning support with individuals, and the ways to resolve them.

Learning Outcome 2: Be able to support individuals to plan for maintaining and developing skills for everyday life

Assessment Criterion 2.4: Support the individual to understand the plan and any processes, procedures or equipment needed to implement or monitor it

What does AC2.4 mean?

- The lead word **support** means that you must **be able to show** through **your work practices** how to assist an individual in understanding the support plan and any processes, procedures or equipment needed to implement or monitor it.
- Your **observations** of your work practices must include you assisting an individual to understand their plan of support.
- For the key word **processes** you can think about the steps that are required either to put an individual's plan into practice or to monitor it.
- For the key word **procedures** you can think about the different ways and approaches that could be used either to put an individual's plan into practice or to monitor it.
- For the key word **equipment** you can think about the resources that are required either to put an individual's plan into practice or to monitor it.

Read the following **Real Work Setting** scenario and think about how it relates to your work setting and role:

Real Work Setting

Name: Christian

Job role: Senior Carer for older people living in the community

(See page 184 for a description of the role.)

Understanding the plan of support: Christian is meeting with Joan this morning to explain the additional support with shopping that Carers will provide. Christian suggests that Joan be accompanied by a Carer whilst in the supermarket for one month. Christian agrees with Joan that during this time her aim will be to work towards feeling more confident and less anxious when in the supermarket on her own. Both agree that over this period the Carer will try to gradually reduce her support so that Joan is able to manage the food shopping on her own, and that they will review the plan in two weeks' time.

Evidencing AC2.4 to your assessor:

For AC2.4 you must evidence your skills in supporting the individual to understand the plan and any processes, procedures or equipment needed to implement or monitor it.

Assessment Method:

Direct Observation of your work practices.

- You can **show** your assessor how you support an individual to understand their plan and any processes, procedures or equipment needed to implement or monitor it.

REMEMBER TO:

- Make arrangements for **observation** of **your work practices**.
- Include evidence of you supporting an individual to understand their plan.
- Ensure the evidence you provide includes understanding any processes, procedures or equipment needed to implement or monitor the plan.
- Think about **your work setting** and how you support individuals to understand their plan and any processes, procedures or equipment needed to implement or monitor it.

Learning Outcome 3: Be able to support individuals to retain, regain or develop skills for everyday life

Assessment Criterion 3.1: Provide agreed support to develop or maintain skills in a way that promotes active participation

What does AC3.1 mean?

- O The lead words **provide agreed support** mean that you must **be able to show** through **your work practices** how to assist an individual to develop or maintain skills in a way that promotes active participation.
- O Your **observations** of your work practices must include you assisting an individual to develop or maintain skills.
- O For the key word **develop** you can think about how to support an individual with new skills and improve existing skills for everyday life.
- O For the key word **maintain** you can think about how to support an individual using skills for everyday life.
- O For the key words **active participation** you can think about how you can ensure that you support individuals to develop or maintain skills to live their lives as they wish.

Read the following **Real Work Setting** scenario and think about how it relates to your work setting and role:

Real Work Setting

Name: Ollie

Job role: Senior Support Worker for people who have learning disabilities

Ollie has been recently appointed as a Senior Support Worker. Ollie's Senior responsibilities include: overseeing a team of Support Workers to provide support to individuals living in both residential and community settings; arranging and conducting supervisions and appraisals with Support Workers; implementing and reviewing support plans; maintaining records; ordering, receiving, storing and administering medication for individuals.

Providing agreed support: Ollie has attended a training session as part of his induction to provide him with an overview of the work setting's principles and ways of working. These ensure that all support provided to individuals develops or maintains skills in a way that promotes active participation. It is important that Ollie understands and puts into practice the work setting's ethos and approaches used so that he can be a positive role model to others in his team.

Evidencing AC3.1 to your assessor:

For AC3.1 you must evidence your skills in providing agreed support to an individual to develop or maintain skills in a way that promotes active participation.

Assessment Method:

Direct Observation of your work practices.

- You can **show** your assessor how you provide agreed support to an individual to develop or maintain skills in a way that promotes active participation.

REMEMBER TO:

- Make arrangements for **observation** of **your work practices**.
- Include evidence of you providing agreed support to an individual to develop or maintain skills.
- Ensure the evidence you provide includes providing agreed support in a way that promotes active participation.
- Think about **your work setting** and how you provide agreed support to an individual to develop or maintain skills in a way that promotes active participation.

Learning Outcome 3: Be able to support individuals to retain, regain or develop skills for everyday life

Assessment Criterion 3.2: Give positive and constructive feedback to the individual during activities to develop or maintain their skills

What does AC3.2 mean?

○ The lead words **give positive and constructive feedback** mean that you must **be able to show** through **your work practices** how to give positive and constructive feedback to an individual during activities.

○ Your **observations** of your work practices must include you giving positive and constructive feedback to an individual to develop or maintain their skills.

○ For the key word **develop** you can think about how to support an individual with new skills or using existing skills for everyday life.

○ For the key word **maintain** you can think about how to support an individual in using skills for everyday life.

Read the following **Real Work Setting** scenario and think about how it relates to your work setting and role:

Real Work Setting

Name: Ollie

Job role: Senior Support Worker for people who have learning disabilities

(See page 188 for a description of the role.)

Giving feedback: Ollie is supporting Sam to wash his clothes this morning. Ollie begins by praising Sam for remembering to load the washing machine the night before and on selecting the right programme to wash his clothes. Before he switches the washing machine on Ollie asks Sam to think about what else he needs to wash his clothes, and then observes him adding washing powder and conditioner, and suggests that he may find this easier if he stands a little closer to the washing machine. Sam moves a little closer to the washing machine and smiles and nods his head in agreement.

Evidencing AC3.2 to your assessor:

For AC3.2 you must evidence your skills in giving positive and constructive feedback to the individual during activities to develop or maintain their skills.

Assessment Method:

Direct Observation of your work practices.

● You can **show** your assessor how you give positive and constructive feedback to an individual during activities to develop or maintain their skills.

REMEMBER TO:

● Make arrangements for **observation** of **your work practices**.

● Include evidence of you giving positive and constructive feedback to an individual.

● Ensure the evidence you provide includes providing feedback during activities to develop or maintain their skills.

● Think about **your work setting** and how you give positive and constructive feedback to the individual during activities to develop or maintain their skills.

AC 3.3

Learning Outcome 3: Be able to support individuals to retain, regain or develop skills for everyday life

Assessment Criterion 3.3: Describe actions to take if an individual becomes distressed or unable to continue

What does AC3.3 mean?

- ○ The lead word **describe** means that you must provide an **account** that **details** the actions to take if an individual becomes distressed or unable to continue activities.
- ○ Your **account** must detail the actions to take.
- ○ For the key word **distressed** you can think about the reasons an individual may become distressed during activities and the actions to take.
- ○ For the key words **unable to continue** you can think about the reasons an individual may be unable to continue with activities and the actions to take.

Read the following **Real Work Setting** scenario and think about how it relates to your work setting and role:

Real Work Setting

Name: Ollie

Job role: Senior Support Worker for people who have learning disabilities

(See page 188 for a description of the role.)

Actions to take: Ollie and his colleague Fran are supporting Leanne to pack her suitcase, as she will be visiting her parents this weekend. During this activity Leanne gets very upset and runs out of her room. Ollie and Fran stop the activity and check on Leanne, who is sitting on the floor in the lounge. Leanne is given some time to relax and calm down and then both talk through with her what she found upsetting. A written report is made of the incident.

Evidencing AC3.3 to your assessor:

For AC3.3 you must evidence your knowledge of the actions to take if an individual becomes distressed or unable to continue.

Assessment Methods:

Oral/Written Questioning or **Discussion** or a **Personal Statement or Reflection** or a **Witness Testimony**.

- You can **tell** your assessor about the actions to take if an individual becomes distressed or unable to continue with activities.
- Or, you can **talk** to your assessor about the actions to take if an individual becomes distressed or unable to continue with activities.
- Or, you can write a **personal statement or reflection** about your experience of the actions to take if an individual becomes distressed or unable to continue with activities.
- Or, you can obtain a **witness testimony** from your supervisor or manager about an occasion you took action when an individual became distressed or was unable to continue with activities.

REMEMBER TO:

- Provide a detailed **account** of the actions to take if an individual becomes distressed or unable to continue with activities.
- Include details of all the actions to take.
- Ensure you include evidence of an individual who became distressed or was unable to continue with activities.
- Think about **your work setting** and the actions to take if an individual becomes distressed or unable to continue with activities.

Learning Outcome 4: Be able to evaluate support for developing or maintaining skills for everyday life

Assessment Criterion 4.1: Work with an individual and others to agree criteria and processes for evaluating support

What does AC4.1 mean?

- The lead words **work with** mean that you must **be able to show** through **your work practices** how to assist an individual and others to agree criteria and processes for evaluating support.
- Your **observations** of your work practices must include you assisting an individual and others.
- For the key word **criteria** you can think about how you can assist an individual and others to agree the standards against which to measure the effectiveness of the support provided.
- For the key word **processes** you can think about how you can assist an individual and others to agree the steps needed to measure the effectiveness of the support provided.
- For the key word **evaluating** you can think about how to assist an individual and others to assess the support provided.

Read the following **Real Work Setting** scenario and think about how it relates to your work setting and role:

Real Work Setting

Name: Rebecca

Job role: Senior Mental Health Support Worker for adults who have mental health needs

Rebecca's Senior responsibilities include: providing support to a team of Peer Support Workers and Peer Mentors; recruiting and training Peer Support Workers and Peer Mentors; encouraging individuals to live independently; supporting individuals to be actively involved in developing and evaluating the service.

Agreeing how to evaluate support: Rebecca is meeting with the Peer Support team to review how the service is working and to agree on the procedures and systems to use to evaluate the service as a whole. Rebecca also wishes to review the processes in place that underpin peer support and to establish with the team their views on how effective these are. Once Rebecca has met with the team she plans to discuss with the individuals who use the service their ideas and views on how best to evaluate the support provided, including the methods to use to establish the quality of the peer support and service being provided.

Evidencing AC4.1 to your assessor:

For AC4.1 you must evidence your skills in working with an individual and others to agree criteria and processes for evaluating support.

Assessment Method:
Direct Observation of your work practices.
- You can **show** your assessor or an expert witness how to work with an individual and others to agree criteria and processes for evaluating support.

REMEMBER TO:
- Make arrangements for **observation** of **your work practices**.
- Include evidence of you working with an individual and others.
- Ensure the evidence you provide includes agreeing criteria and processes for evaluating support.
- Think about **your work setting** and how you work with individuals and others to agree criteria and processes for evaluating support.

Learning Outcome 4: Be able to evaluate support for developing or maintaining skills for everyday life

Assessment Criterion 4.2: Carry out agreed role to evaluate progress towards goals and the effectiveness of methods used

What does AC4.2 mean?

- The lead words **carry out** mean that you must **be able to show** through **your work practices** how to fulfil your role to evaluate progress towards goals and the effectiveness of methods used.
- Your **observations** of your work practices must include you evaluating progress towards goals and the effectiveness of methods used.
- For the key words **agreed role** you can think about your duties and responsibilities for evaluating progress towards goals and the effectiveness of methods used.
- For the key word **evaluate** you can think about how you can assess the progress being made towards agreed goals and the effectiveness of methods used.
- For the key word **effectiveness** you can think about how valid the methods being used for evaluating support are.

Read the following **Real Work Setting** scenario and think about how it relates to your work setting and role:

Real Work Setting

Name: Rebecca

Job role: Senior Mental Health Support Worker for adults who have mental health needs

(See page 191 for a description of the role.)

Carrying out agreed role: Rebecca has organised a joint meeting between the Peer Support team and the individuals who use the service to evaluate together the progress made towards agreed roles, as well as the effectiveness of the methods used to do this. Rebecca has also sent out individual questionnaires to every individual so as to provide them with an opportunity to be actively involved in evaluating their current support and in developing any future support required. Rebecca plans to collate all information shared and use this to continue to build on the achievements of the Peer Support team.

Evidencing AC4.2 to your assessor:

For AC4.2 you must evidence your skills in carrying out your agreed role to evaluate progress towards goals and the effectiveness of methods used.

Assessment Method:

Direct Observation of your work practices.

- You can **show** your assessor or an expert witness how to carry out your agreed role to evaluate progress towards goals and the effectiveness of methods used.

REMEMBER TO:

- Make arrangements for **observation of your work practices**.
- Include evidence of you carrying out your agreed role.
- Ensure the evidence you provide includes evaluating progress towards goals and the effectiveness of methods used.
- Think about **your work setting** and how you evaluate progress towards goals and the effectiveness of methods used.

Learning Outcome 4: Be able to evaluate support for developing or maintaining skills for everyday life

Assessment Criterion 4.3: Agree revisions to the plan

What does AC4.3 mean?

- The lead word **agree** means that you must **be able to show** through **your work practices** how to establish with an individual revisions to the plan of support for developing or maintaining skills for everyday life.
- Your **observations** of your work practices must include you agreeing on how to make revisions to a plan of support.
- For the key word **revisions** you can think about the changes to plans of support that may sometimes be necessary, and why these changes may be needed.

Read the following **Real Work Setting** scenario and think about how it relates to your work setting and role:

Real Work Setting

Name: Rebecca

Job role: Senior Mental Health Support Worker for adults who have mental health needs

(See page 191 for a description of the role.)

Agreeing revisions to an individual's plan: Rebecca is meeting today with Jan, one of the individuals who receives regular support from the Peer Support team. Rebecca begins by explaining that the purpose of today's meeting is to talk through the positive changes that Jan is making with her recovery programme and to agree the revisions to the support plan in place to reflect this. Rebecca asks Jan how she is finding getting the bus to work on her own in the mornings; Jan explains that she is enjoying being able to do this independently and wants to continue to do so. Rebecca agrees with Jan that this seems to be working well and explains to her that her Peer Support Worker has also reported that he is pleased with the progress Jan has made with achieving this goal. Rebecca and Jan revise the support plan to indicate that Jan is to continue to travel independently to work in the mornings. Rebecca and Jan also agree that no further support or monitoring is needed from the Peer Support team. Rebecca encourages Jan to think about what she has achieved, how she feels and how this is already making a difference to her everyday life.

Evidencing AC4.3 to your assessor:

For AC4.3 you must evidence your skills in agreeing revisions to an individual's plan of support.

Assessment Method:

Direct Observation of your work practices.

- You can **show** your assessor or an expert witness how to agree revisions to an individual's plan of support.

REMEMBER TO:

- Make arrangements for **observation** of **your work practices**.
- Include evidence of you agreeing revisions.
- Ensure the evidence you provide includes deciding on revisions to an individual's plan of support.
- Think about **your work setting** and how you agree revisions to individuals' plans of support.

Learning Outcome 4: Be able to evaluate support for developing or maintaining skills for everyday life

Assessment Criterion 4.4: Record and report in line with agreed ways of working

What does AC4.4 mean?

- The lead words **record and report** mean that you must **be able to show** through **your work practices** how to document and share information about evaluating support in line with agreed ways of working.
- Your **observations** of your work practices must include you recording and reporting in line with agreed ways of working.
- For the key words **agreed ways of working** you can think about your work setting's policies and procedures, as well as the specific guidelines that are in place for recording and reporting the evaluation of support for developing or maintaining skills for everyday life.

Read the following **Real Work Setting** scenario and think about how it relates to your work setting and role:

Real Work Setting

Name: Rebecca

Job role: Senior Mental Health Support Worker for adults who have mental health needs

(See page 191 for a description of the role.)

Recording and reporting: Rebecca and Jan agree to amend Jan's plan of support and record that Jan has achieved her goal of getting the bus to work on her own, with no support from the Peer Support team, and that no further monitoring in this area of her plan of support is required. Rebecca and Jan both read through the change made and sign and date to indicate their agreement to this. Rebecca then explains to Jan that she will also inform the team of this change and ask each of them to read through her revised plan of support and then sign and date it to indicate that they have done so. Jan states that she is very happy with her achievement and will also tell her Support Workers and her family when she sees them that she no longer requires support in this area.

Evidencing AC4.4 to your assessor:

For AC4.4 you must evidence your skills in recording and reporting in line with agreed ways of working.

Assessment Method:

Direct Observation of your work practices.

- You can **show** your assessor or an expert witness how to record and report in line with agreed ways of working.

REMEMBER TO:

- Make arrangements for **observation** of **your work practices**.
- Include evidence of you both recording and reporting.
- Ensure the evidence you provide includes you recording and reporting in line with agreed ways of working.
- Think about **your work setting** and how you record and report in line with agreed ways of working.

HSC3013 Support individuals to access and use services and facilities

Learning Outcome 1: Understand factors that influence individuals' access to services and facilities

Assessment Criterion 1.1: Describe how accessing a range of services and facilities can be beneficial to an individual's well-being

What does AC1.1 mean?

- ○ The lead word **describe** means that you must provide an **account** that **details** how accessing a range of services and facilities can benefit an individual's well-being.
- ○ Your **account** must detail **different** types of services and facilities and the benefits of these to an individual's well-being.
- ○ The key words **services and facilities** may include services provided within an individual's home, services to enable an individual to meet their social care needs, and community facilities such as the GP, dentist, hairdresser, shops, leisure centre, restaurants and parks.
- ○ For the key word **beneficial** you can think about the positive impact accessing a range of services and facilities can have on an individual psychologically, emotionally, practically, financially and socially.
- ○ For the key word **well-being** you can think about the benefits to the emotional, physical, cultural, religious, spiritual, political and social aspects of individuals' lives.

Read the following **Real Work Setting** scenario and think about how it relates to your work setting and role:

Real Work Setting

Name: Gillian

Job role: Senior Support Worker to people who have multiple sensory impairments

Gillian has been working as a Senior Support Worker for eight years. Her Senior responsibilities include: enabling individuals to live as independently as possible and access community, work and leisure opportunities; supporting a team of Support Workers to provide high quality support using total communication with all individuals; leading service review meetings; implementing and reviewing individuals' care plans; maintaining accurate records.

Accessing a range of services and facilities: Gillian is meeting with the team to review individuals' care plans so as to enable the team to contribute to the plans prior to her meetings with each individual. Gillian begins by asking the team to think about positive changes they have noted in individuals' well-being as result of empowering them to access different services and facilities.

Evidencing AC1.1 to your assessor:

For AC1.1 you must evidence your understanding of how accessing a range of services and facilities can be beneficial to an individual's well-being.

Assessment Methods:

Oral/Written Questioning or Discussion or a Personal Statement or Reflection.

- You can **tell** your assessor about how accessing a range of services and facilities can be beneficial to an individual's well-being.
- Or, you can **talk** to your assessor about how accessing a range of services and facilities can be beneficial to an individual's well-being.
- Or, you can write a **personal statement or reflection** about your experience of how accessing a range of services and facilities can be beneficial to an individual's well-being.

REMEMBER TO:

- Provide a detailed **account** of how accessing a range of services and facilities can be beneficial.
- Include **details** of a range of services and facilities.
- Ensure you detail the benefits to an individual's well-being.
- Ensure your evidence includes details of different aspects of an individual's well-being that are affected.
- Think about **your work setting** and how accessing a range of services and facilities can be beneficial to individuals' well-being.

Learning Outcome 1: Understand factors that influence individuals' access to services and facilities

Assessment Criterion 1.2: Identify barriers that individuals may encounter in accessing services and facilities

What does AC1.2 mean?

○ The lead word **identify** means that you must **make clear** the barriers that individuals may encounter in accessing services and facilities.
○ Your **list** must make clear the barriers that individuals may encounter in accessing services and facilities.
○ For the key word **barriers** you can think about the different factors that may prevent individuals from accessing services and facilities.

Read the following **Real Work Setting** scenario and think about how it relates to your work setting and role:

Real Work Setting

Name: Gillian

Job role: Senior Support Worker for people who have multiple sensory impairments

(See page 195 for a description of the role.)

Barriers: At the team meeting, one of the Support Workers raises a concern she has with an individual she is supporting at present who has sustained loss of both vision and hearing. She is finding it difficult to continue to meet with her friends at the bowling club and at restaurants she used to visit regularly with them. The Support Worker goes on to explain that as a result of this individual's loss of both her sight and hearing her personal confidence is low; she feels she is unable to travel to these places on her own and would be unable to take an active part in conversations even if she could travel there.

Evidencing AC1.2 to your assessor:

For AC1.2 you must evidence your understanding of the barriers that individuals may encounter in accessing services and facilities.

Assessment Methods:
Oral/Written Questioning or **Discussion** or a **Spidergram**
● You can **tell** your assessor about the barriers that individuals may encounter in accessing services and facilities.
● Or, you can **talk** to your assessor about the barriers that individuals may encounter in accessing services and facilities.
● Or, you can complete a **spidergram** showing the barriers that individuals may encounter in accessing services and facilities.

REMEMBER TO:
● Provide a **list** of the different **barriers** that individuals may encounter.
● Provide details that **relate** specifically to barriers that may stop individuals accessing services and facilities.
● Think about different barriers that individuals in **your work setting** have experienced when accessing services and facilities.

Learning Outcome 1: Understand factors that influence individuals' access to services and facilities

Assessment Criterion 1.3: Describe ways of overcoming barriers to accessing services and facilities

What does AC1.3 mean?

- ○ The lead word **describe** means that you must provide an **account** that **details** methods of overcoming barriers to accessing services and facilities.
- ○ Your **account** must detail **different** ways of overcoming barriers to accessing services and facilities.
- ○ For the key word **overcoming** you can think about the different ways to deal with the barriers that exist when individuals access services and facilities.

Read the following **Real Work Setting** scenario and think about how it relates to your work setting and role:

Real Work Setting

Name: Gillian

Job role: Senior Support Worker for people who have multiple sensory impairments

(See page 195 for a description of the role.)

Overcoming barriers: Gillian asks the team for their ideas on how an individual who has experienced a loss of both her sight and hearing can be supported to access the bowling club and restaurants she used to visit regularly with her friends. One team member suggests that the Support Worker could refer this on to a Senior Support Worker, who could then meet with the individual and reassess her needs. Another team member suggests finding out more about the individual's friends and whether anyone is available to support her to access these places. Gillian suggests that the individual needs to be empowered to access the support she requires to access the places she wants to go to and to continue the friendships she has.

Evidencing AC1.3 to your assessor:

For AC1.3 you must evidence your understanding of ways to overcome barriers to accessing services and facilities.

Assessment Methods:

Oral/Written Questioning or **Discussion** or a **Personal Statement** or **Reflection**.

- You can **tell** your assessor about different ways to overcome barriers to accessing services and facilities.
- Or, you can **talk** to your assessor about different ways to overcome barriers to accessing services and facilities.
- Or, you can write a **personal statement or reflection** about your experience of different ways to overcome barriers to accessing services and facilities.

REMEMBER TO:

- Provide a detailed **account** of different ways to overcome barriers to accessing services and facilities.
- Ensure you detail how to overcome barriers to accessing services and facilities.
- Ensure your evidence includes details of **different ways** to overcome barriers.
- Think about **your work setting** and the different ways to overcome barriers when individuals are accessing services and facilities.

Learning Outcome 1: Understand factors that influence individuals' access to services and facilities

Assessment Criterion 1.4: Explain why it is important to support individuals to challenge information about services that may present a barrier to participation

What does AC1.4 mean?

- The lead word **explain** means that you must **make clear the reasons why** it is important to support individuals to challenge information about services that may present a barrier to participation.
- Your **account** must make clear the **details** of the reasons why.
- For the key word **challenge** you can think about how to support an individual to question services that they may be prevented from using.
- For the key word **information** you can think about how services may exclude individuals from using them. Information that is misleading, inaccurate, discriminatory or inaccessible may also need to be challenged.
- For the key word **barrier** you can think about the different factors that may prevent individuals from using services.

Read the following **Real Work Setting** scenario and think about how it relates to your work setting and role:

Real Work Setting

Name: Gillian

Job role: Senior Support Worker for people who have multiple sensory impairments

(See page 195 for a description of the role.)

Challenge information about services: Gillian is meeting with an individual, Jonathan, to support him to contact the outpatients department of his local hospital. He would like to find out whether the room in which he will be meeting with his consultant will be fitted with a hearing loop as the letter he has received does not state whether one will be provided.

Evidencing AC1.4 to your assessor:

For AC1.4 you must evidence your understanding of why it is important to support individuals to challenge information about services that may present a barrier to participation.

Assessment Methods:

Oral/Written Questioning or **Discussion** or a **Personal Statement or Reflection**.

- You can **tell** your assessor about why it is important to support individuals to challenge information about services.
- Or, you can **talk** to your assessor about why it is important to support individuals to challenge information about services.
- Or, you can write a **personal statement or reflection** about your experience of why it is important to support individuals to challenge information about services.

REMEMBER TO:

- Provide an **account** of why it is important to support individuals to challenge information about services.
- Include **details** about the different reasons why it is important to support individuals to challenge information about services that may present a barrier to participation.
- Think about **your work setting** and why it is important to support individuals to challenge information about services that may present a barrier to participation.

Learning Outcome 2: Be able to support individuals to select services and facilities

Assessment Criterion 2.1: Work with an individual to identify a range of services and facilities likely to meet their assessed needs

What does AC2.1 mean?

○ The lead words **work with** mean that you must **be able to show** through **your work practices** how to assist an individual to identify a range of services and facilities likely to meet their assessed needs.

○ Your **observations** of your work practices must include you working with an individual to identify a range of services and facilities.

○ For the key word **identify** you can think about how to work with an individual to find out about the services and facilities that will best meet their needs.

○ For the key words **assessed needs** you can think about the support and services required to meet the unique requirements of individuals.

Read the following **Real Work Setting** scenario and think about how it relates to your work setting and role:

Real Work Setting

Name: Sandra

Job role: Senior Care Assistant for older people

Sandra has been working as a Senior Care Assistant for six months. Her Senior responsibilities include: supervising four Care Assistants; implementing and reviewing individuals' care plans; liaising with individuals' families, friends and other professionals involved in their lives; administering medication; maintaining records.

Identifying a range of services and facilities: Sandra is holding a meeting with Reg and his daughter for a review of Reg's care plan. Reg explains that he would like to take up a new hobby and is thinking about enrolling in a painting class in the evenings at the local college. Sandra talks through with Reg the different services and facilities that are available that he can use to achieve this. Sandra suggests that Reg and his daughter access their websites, which contain more information, and then meet with her again to decide which services and facilities best meet his needs.

Evidencing AC2.1 to your assessor:

For AC2.1 you must evidence your skills in working with an individual to identify a range of services and facilities likely to meet their assessed needs.

Assessment Method:	REMEMBER TO:
Direct Observation of your work practices. ● You can **show** your assessor or an expert witness how to work with an individual to identify a range of services and facilities likely to meet their assessed needs.	● Make arrangements for **observation** of **your work practices**. ● Include evidence of you working with an individual. ● Ensure the evidence you include relates to identifying a range of services and facilities that will meet individuals' assessed needs. ● Think about **your work setting** and how you work with individuals to identify a range of services and facilities likely to meet their assessed needs.

Learning Outcome 2: Be able to support individuals to select services and facilities

Assessment Criterion 2.2: Agree with an individual their preferred options for accessing services and facilities

What does AC2.2 mean?

- The lead word **agree** means that you must **be able to show** through **your work practices** how to establish with an individual their preferred options for accessing services and facilities.
- Your **observations** of your work practices must include you agreeing with an individual their preferred options for accessing services and facilities.
- For the key words **preferred options** you can think about the factors that make some services and facilities more suitable for an individual's needs.

Read the following **Real Work Setting** scenario and think about how it relates to your work setting and role:

Real Work Setting

Name: Sandra
Job role: Senior Care Assistant for older people
(See page 199 for a description of the role.)
Preferred options for services and facilities: Sandra and Reg are meeting this morning to discuss where Reg has decided he would like to enrol in a painting class. Reg explains that he has looked at the options available for painting classes in the evening with his daughter, and he particularly likes the classes offered by a voluntary organisation that is situated not too far away from his home and is also on the local bus route. Reg feels that if this isn't possible then he wouldn't mind going to the painting classes offered at his local college, although these are held on Wednesday afternoons only. Sandra talks through with Reg what is most important to him when deciding to enrol in painting classes, including the location of classes, times classes are held, content of the classes, whom the classes are provided by and whom they are aimed at.

Evidencing AC2.2 to your assessor:

For AC2.2 you must evidence your skills in agreeing with an individual their preferred options for accessing services and facilities.

Assessment Method:

Direct Observation of your work practices.

- You can **show** your assessor how you agree with an individual their preferred options for accessing services and facilities.

REMEMBER TO:

- Make arrangements for **observation** of **your work practices**.
- Include evidence of you **agreeing** their preferred options with an individual.
- Ensure the evidence you include relates to accessing services and facilities.
- Think about **your work setting** and how you agree with individuals their preferred options for accessing services and facilities.

Learning Outcome 2: Be able to support individuals to select services and facilities

Assessment Criterion 2.3: Work with an individual to select services and facilities that meet their assessed needs and preferences

What does AC2.3 mean?

- The lead words **work with** mean that you must **be able to show** through **your work practices** how to assist an individual to select services and facilities that meet their assessed needs and preferences.
- Your **observations** of your work practices must include you working with an individual to select services and facilities.
- For the key words **assessed needs** you can think about the support and services required to meet the unique requirements of individuals.

Read the following **Real Work Setting** scenario and think about how it relates to your work setting and role:

Real Work Setting

Name: Sandra

Job role: Senior Care Assistant for older people

(See page 199 for a description of the role.)

Selecting services and facilities: During Sandra and Reg's meeting, Reg's daughter arrives and Sandra explains to her how they have just discussed together Reg's preferences for enrolling in a painting class, in order of importance. Reg explains that he would not like to have to travel very far, he would prefer to be able to travel on his own on the bus, he would like to enrol in an evening class rather than attend a class during the day, and that he would like to meet lots of different people. Sandra adds that the painting classes held by the local voluntary organisation seem to meet both Reg's preferences and his needs in terms of taking up a new hobby, socialising with others and maintaining his independence when travelling.

Evidencing AC2.3 to your assessor:

For AC2.3 you must evidence your skills in working with an individual to select services and facilities that meet their assessed needs and preferences.

Assessment Method:	REMEMBER TO:
Direct Observation of your work practices. • You can **show** your assessor how you work with an individual to select services and facilities that meet their assessed needs and preferences.	• Make arrangements for **observation** of **your work practices**. • Include evidence of you working with an individual. • Ensure the evidence you include relates to selecting services and facilities that meet an individual's assessed needs and preferences. • Think about **your work setting** and how you work with individuals to select services and facilities that meet their assessed needs and preferences.

Learning Outcome 3: Be able to support individuals to access and use services and facilities

Assessment Criterion 3.1: Identify with an individual the resources, support and assistance required to access and use selected services and facilities

What does AC3.1 mean?

- O The lead word **identify** means that you must **make clear** through **your work practices** how to establish with an individual the resources, support and assistance required to access and use selected services and facilities.
- O Your **observations** of your work practices must include you identifying with an individual the resources, support and assistance required.
- O For the key word **resources** you can think about the finances, personnel and information required to access and use selected services and facilities.

Read the following **Real Work Setting** scenario and think about how it relates to your work setting and role:

Real Work Setting

Name: Stuart

Job role: Senior Support Worker for people who have learning disabilities

Stuart has been working as a Senior Support Worker for three years. His Senior responsibilities include: assessing and reviewing individuals' needs; participating in the care planning process; sharing in day to-day activities with individuals; developing good working relationships with individuals' families, carers and other professionals involved in their lives.

Identifying resources, support and assistance required: Stuart is meeting today with Craig to review his care plan. Craig's parents and advocate have also been invited by Craig to be present. Craig has decided that he would like to go away this summer without his parents. He met with his advocate last week and together they have drawn up a list of four friends with whom he would like to go away. Craig and Stuart have also been researching at their weekly meetings the different places Craig and his friends might like to go, the support he will need to arrange to go away on his own with his friends, as well as the costs.

Evidencing AC3.1 to your assessor:

For AC3.1 you must evidence your skills in identifying with an individual the resources, support and assistance required to access and use selected services and facilities.

Assessment Method:

Direct Observation of your work practices.

- You can **show** your assessor how you identify with an individual the resources, support and assistance required to access and use selected services and facilities.

REMEMBER TO:

- Make arrangements for **observation** of **your work practices**.
- Include evidence of you **identifying** with an individual the resources, support and assistance required.
- Ensure the evidence you include relates to both accessing and using selected services and facilities.
- Think about **your work setting** and how you identify with individuals the resources, support and assistance required to access and use selected services and facilities.

Learning Outcome 3: Be able to support individuals to access and use services and facilities

Assessment Criterion 3.2: Carry out agreed responsibilities to enable the individual to access and use services and facilities

What does AC3.2 mean?

○ The lead words **carry out** mean that you must **be able to show** through **your work practices** how to follow through agreed responsibilities to enable the individual to access and use services and facilities.

○ Your **observations** of your work practices must include you following through agreed responsibilities.

○ For the key words **agreed responsibilities** you can think about how carrying out your job role duties enables individuals to access and use selected services and facilities.

Read the following **Real Work Setting** scenario and think about how it relates to your work setting and role:

Real Work Setting

Name: Stuart

Job role: Senior Support Worker for people who have learning disabilities

(See page 202 for a description of the role.)

Carrying out agreed responsibilities: Stuart has agreed to take the lead in enabling Craig to go on holiday with his friends. Craig's parents have discussed the associated costs of the holiday with Craig and together they have drawn up a plan to help Craig budget for this. Stuart has enabled Craig to select three different preferred types of holidays from the research that they have carried out together. Stuart has also enabled Craig to arrange a meeting with his four friends to discuss together the three holiday options, along with their associated costs and the services and facilities available at each.

Evidencing AC3.2 to your assessor:

For AC3.2 you must evidence your skills in carrying out agreed responsibilities to enable the individual to access and use selected services and facilities.

Assessment Method:

Direct Observation of your work practices.

● You can **show** your assessor how you carry out agreed responsibilities to enable an individual to access and use selected services and facilities.

REMEMBER TO:

● Make arrangements for **observation** of **your work practices**.
● Include evidence of you carrying out agreed responsibilities.
● Include evidence of you enabling an individual.
● Ensure the evidence you include relates to both accessing and using selected services and facilities.
● Think about **your work setting** and how your job role links to enabling individuals to access and use selected services and facilities.

Learning Outcome 3: Be able to support individuals to access and use services and facilities

Assessment Criterion 3.3: Explain how to ensure individuals' rights and preferences are promoted when accessing and using services and facilities

What does AC3.3 mean?

- The lead word **explain** means that you must **make clear how** as well as **the reasons why** it is important to ensure individuals' rights and preferences are promoted when accessing and using services and facilities.
- Your **account** must make clear **details** of how as well as the reasons why.
- For the key word **rights** you can think about what moral and legal entitlements individuals have when accessing and using services and facilities.
- For the key word **preferences** you can think about what aspects of accessing and using services and facilities are important to different individuals.

Read the following **Real Work Setting** scenario and think about how it relates to your work setting and role:

Real Work Setting

Name: Stuart

Job role: Senior Support Worker for people who have learning disabilities

(See page 202 for a description of the role.)

Ensuring individuals' rights and preferences are promoted: Stuart is meeting with the team of three Support Workers who will support Craig and his friends. He will share with them information about Craig's and his friends' individual needs and preferences in relation to the holiday. This is so that they can all provide consistent and high quality support during the holiday that promotes individuals' rights and preferences at all times.

Evidencing AC3.3 to your assessor:

For AC3.3 you must evidence your understanding of how to ensure individuals' rights and preferences are promoted when accessing and using services and facilities.

Assessment Methods:

Oral/Written Questioning or **Discussion** or a **Personal Statement** or **Reflection**.

- You can **tell** your assessor about how to ensure individuals' rights and preferences are promoted when accessing and using services and facilities.
- Or, you can **talk** to your assessor about how to ensure individuals' rights and preferences are promoted when accessing and using services and facilities.
- Or, you can write a **personal statement or reflection** about your experience of how to ensure individuals' rights and preferences are promoted when accessing and using services and facilities.

REMEMBER TO:

- Provide an **account** about how to ensure individuals' rights and preferences are promoted when accessing and using services and facilities.
- Include **details** about the actions to take, and the different reasons why it is important to ensure individuals' rights and preferences are promoted.
- Ensure your evidence relates to both accessing and using services and facilities.
- Think about **your work setting** and why it is important to ensure individuals' rights and preferences are promoted when accessing and using services and facilities.

Learning Outcome 4: Be able to support individuals to review their access to and use of services and facilities

Assessment Criterion 4.1: Work with an individual to evaluate whether services or facilities have met their assessed needs and preferences

What does AC4.1 mean?

- The lead words **work with** mean that you must **be able to show** through **your work practices** how to assist an individual to evaluate whether services or facilities have met their assessed needs and preferences.
- Your **observations** of your work practices must include you working with an individual to evaluate services or facilities.
- For the key words **assessed needs and preferences** you can think about the support and services required to meet the unique requirements and wishes of an individual.

Read the following **Real Work Setting** scenario and think about how it relates to your work setting and role:

Real Work Setting

Name: Katie

Job role: Senior Personal Assistant to a young disabled woman

Katie has been working as a Senior Personal Assistant for three months. Her Senior responsibilities include: working with and supporting two Personal Assistants; providing support with daily living, accessing community facilities and travelling to and from work.

Evaluating services or facilities: Katie is reviewing Sharon's support package with her. As part of this process Katie has asked Sharon to think about whether the support she is receiving from the team is meeting her needs and preferences. In particular she asks her to think about whether the support times available are flexible enough and whether the approaches used by the team enable her to maintain her independence and live her life as she wants to. Katie has also asked Sharon for her views on the community services and facilities she accesses on a regular basis, in relation to whether they meet her needs and preferences.

Evidencing AC4.1 to your assessor:

For AC4.1 you must evidence your skills in working with an individual to evaluate whether services or facilities have met their assessed needs and preferences.

Assessment Method:

Direct Observation of your work practices.

- You can **show** your assessor how you work with an individual to evaluate whether services or facilities have met their assessed needs and preferences.

REMEMBER TO:

- Make arrangements for **observation of your work practices**.
- Include evidence of you working with an individual.
- Include evidence of you evaluating services or facilities.
- Ensure the evidence you include relates to meeting the individual's assessed needs and preferences.
- Think about **your work setting** and how you work with individuals to evaluate whether services or facilities have met their assessed needs and preferences.

Learning Outcome 4: Be able to support individuals to review their access to and use of services and facilities

Assessment Criterion 4.2: Support an individual to provide feedback on their experience of accessing and using services or facilities

What does AC4.2 mean?

○ The lead word **support** means that you must **be able to show** through **your work practices** how to assist an individual in providing feedback on their experience of accessing and using services and facilities.

○ Your **observations** of your work practices must include you assisting an individual to provide feedback.

○ For the key words **provide feedback** you can think about how you can support individuals to make known their views and opinions on their experience of accessing and using services and facilities.

Read the following **Real Work Setting** scenario and think about how it relates to your work setting and role:

Real Work Setting

Name: Katie
Job role: Senior Personal Assistant to a young disabled woman
(See page 205 for a description of the role.)
Providing feedback: Katie listens to Sharon explain that there are some community services and facilities she uses that do meet her needs and preferences and others that don't. Sharon shares with Katie her positive experiences of going to the hairdressers, the local shops and the supermarket in town. Sharon then shares with Katie the difficulties she has had recently in accessing her local drama group as the group has moved temporarily to another building, which has no lift. Using her local gym at the times that are suitable for her has also been difficult to arrange; she has been working longer hours and therefore wishes to change her times from evenings to weekends but requires someone to accompany her both to and from the gym.

Evidencing AC4.2 to your assessor:

For AC4.2 you must evidence your skills in supporting an individual to provide feedback on their experience of accessing and using services and facilities.

Assessment Method:
Direct Observation of your work practices.

● You can **show** your assessor how you support an individual to provide feedback on their experience of accessing and using services and facilities.

REMEMBER TO:
● Make arrangements for **observation** of **your work practices**.
● Include evidence of you supporting an individual to provide feedback.
● Ensure the evidence you include relates to an individual's experience of accessing and using services and facilities.
● Think about **your work setting** and how you support individuals to provide feedback on their experience of accessing and using services and facilities.

Learning Outcome 4: Be able to support individuals to review their access to and use of services and facilities

Assessment Criterion 4.3: Work with an individual to evaluate the support provided for accessing and using services or facilities

What does AC4.3 mean?

○ The lead words **work with** mean that you must **be able to show** through **your work practices** how to assist an individual to evaluate the support provided for accessing and using services or facilities.

○ Your **observations** of your work practices must include you working with an individual to evaluate the support provided.

○ For the key word **evaluate** you can think about how to assist individuals to assess the effectiveness of support provided for accessing and using services or facilities.

Read the following **Real Work Setting** scenario and think about how it relates to your work setting and role:

Real Work Setting

Name: Katie

Job role: Senior Personal Assistant to a young disabled woman

(See page 205 for a description of the role.)

Evaluating support: Sharon explains that she feels that the team understands her well, that they are all reliable and have excellent timekeeping skills. In addition Sharon feeds back that the team also respects her, her environment and her wishes to remain independent. In terms of the support provided for accessing community facilities and services, Sharon has found this to be positive and non-judgemental. At times Sharon does feel that there needs to be more flexibility over when support is available, particularly when her requirements change unexpectedly. She also feels that she would like a clearer agreement with the team over the support that is provided when using different services and facilities.

Evidencing AC4.3 to your assessor:

For AC4.3 you must evidence your skills in working with an individual to evaluate the support provided for accessing and using services or facilities.

Assessment Method:

Direct Observation of your work practices.

● You can **show** your assessor how you work with an individual to evaluate the support provided for accessing and using services or facilities.

REMEMBER TO:
● Make arrangements for **observation** of your **work practices**.
● Include evidence of you working with an individual.
● Include evidence of you evaluating the support provided.
● Ensure the evidence you include relates to accessing and using services or facilities.
● Think about **your work setting** and how you work with individuals to evaluate the support provided for accessing and using services or facilities.

Learning Outcome 4: Be able to support individuals to review their access to and use of services and facilities

Assessment Criterion 4.4: Identify and agree any changes needed to improve the experience and outcomes of accessing and using services or facilities

What does AC4.4 mean?

○ The lead words **identify and agree** mean that you must **be able to show** through **your work practices** how to establish and decide with an individual any changes needed to improve the experience and outcomes of accessing and using services or facilities.

○ Your **observations** of your work practices must include you identifying and agreeing with an individual any changes needed.

○ For the key word **experience** you can think about how to improve the personal participation of an individual in accessing and using services and facilities.

○ For the key word **outcomes** you can think about how to improve the effects on an individual of accessing and using services and facilities.

Read the following **Real Work Setting** scenario and think about how it relates to your work setting and role:

Real Work Setting
Name: Katie
Job role: Senior Personal Assistant to a young disabled woman
(See page 205 for a description of the role.)
Identify and agree changes: Katie thanks Sharon for all her open and detailed feedback. Both decide to make a list of all the changes needed to improve Sharon's experience and outcomes of accessing and using services. In drawing up the list of changes Katie guides Sharon to think about whether she would like these changes to be made immediately or gradually over time, as well as the impact of doing so on her life.

Evidencing AC4.4 to your assessor:

For AC4.4 you must evidence your skills in identifying and agreeing any changes needed to improve the experience and outcomes of accessing and using services or facilities.

Assessment Method:

Direct Observation of your work practices.

● You can **show** your assessor how you identify and agree any changes needed to improve the experience and outcomes of accessing and using services or facilities.

REMEMBER TO:

● Make arrangements for **observation** of **your work practices**.

● Include evidence of you identifying and agreeing any changes.

● Ensure the evidence you include relates to improving both the experience and the outcomes of accessing and using services or facilities.

● Think about **your work setting** and how you identify and agree any changes needed to improve the experience and outcomes of accessing and using services or facilities.

Learning Outcome 1: Understand the principles of person-centred assessment and care planning

Assessment Criterion 1.1: Explain the importance of a holistic approach to assessment and planning of care or support

What does AC1.1 mean?
- The lead word **explain** means that you must **make clear** the reasons why it is important to have a holistic approach to assessment and planning of care or support.
- Your **account** must make clear the **details** of the importance of a holistic approach.
- For the key word **holistic** you can think about how to ensure that assessment and planning of care or support takes into account all of an individual's unique needs and preferences.
- For the key words **assessment and planning** you can think about how assessments will take place and plans of care or support will change throughout an individual's life to reflect the individual's current needs and preferences.

Read the following **Real Work Setting** scenario and think about how it relates to your work setting and role:

Real Work Setting

Name: Sonia

Job Role: Senior Care Assistant for older people

Sonia has been working as a Senior Care Assistant for ten years. Her Senior responsibilities include: providing support to a team of Care Assistants; encouraging individuals to lead fulfilling lives; monitoring and reporting individuals' needs and any changes that occur; administering medication and maintaining accurate records and reports.

The principles of person-centred assessment and care planning: Sonia is preparing to complete an individual's care assessment next week and has arranged for a newly recruited Senior Care Assistant to observe the preparations for this. Sonia begins by explaining to the Senior the home's commitment to ensuring that the completion of all assessments and care plans involves the individual and their family or advocate in order to obtain a full understanding of the whole individual and to encourage the individual's physical, emotional, mental and spiritual well-being.

Evidencing AC1.1 to your assessor:

For AC1.1 you must evidence your understanding of the importance of a holistic approach to assessment and planning of care or support.

Assessment Methods:

Oral/Written Questioning or **Discussion** or a **Personal Statement or Reflection**.

- You can **tell** your assessor about the importance of a holistic approach to assessment and planning of care or support.
- Or, you can **talk** to your assessor about the importance of a holistic approach to assessment and planning of care or support.
- Or, you can write a **personal statement or reflection** about your experience of the importance of a holistic approach to assessment and planning of care or support.

REMEMBER TO:
- Provide an **account** and explain the importance of a holistic approach to assessment and planning of care or support.
- Include **details** about the reasons why a holistic approach is important.
- Ensure your evidence relates to assessment and planning of care or support.
- Think about **your work setting** and the importance of a holistic approach to assessment and planning of care or support.

Learning Outcome 1: Understand the principles of person-centred assessment and care planning

Assessment Criterion 1.2: Describe ways of supporting the individual to lead the assessment and planning process

What does AC1.2 mean?

- The lead word **describe** means that you must provide an **account** that **details** methods of supporting the individual to lead the assessment and planning process.
- Your **account** must detail **different** ways of supporting the individual to lead the assessment and planning process.
- For the key word **supporting** you can think about the different ways to assist an individual to lead the assessment and planning process.
- For the key words **assessment and planning process** you can think about the different stages that are involved in assessing an individual and planning their care and support.

Read the following **Real Work Setting** scenario and think about how it relates to your work setting and role:

Real Work Setting
Name: Sonia
Job Role: Senior Care Assistant for older people
(See page 209 for a description of the role.)
Supporting an individual to lead the assessment and planning process: Sonia explains to the newly recruited Senior that she will have an opportunity today to see how to support an individual to lead the assessment and planning process. Sonia then goes on to say that as each individual is unique, the ways used to support them to actively lead the assessment and planning process will also be unique and personal to each individual, and will depend on their strengths, needs, abilities and preferences. The newly recruited Senior agrees with Sonia and explains to her that she also finds this is true when working with different individuals.

Evidencing AC1.2 to your assessor:

For AC1.2 you must evidence your understanding of different ways of supporting an individual to lead the assessment and planning process.

Assessment Methods:

Oral/Written Questioning or **Discussion** or a **Personal Statement** or **Reflection**.

- You can **tell** your assessor about the different ways of supporting an individual to lead the assessment and planning process.
- Or, you can **talk** to your assessor about the different ways of supporting an individual to lead the assessment and planning process.
- Or, you can write a **personal statement or reflection** about your experience of the different ways of supporting an individual to lead the assessment and planning process.

REMEMBER TO:

- Provide a detailed **account** of different ways to support an individual to lead the assessment and planning process.
- Ensure you detail **how** to support an individual.
- Ensure your evidence includes details of **different ways** to support an individual to lead the assessment and planning process.
- Think about **your work setting** and the different ways to support an individual to lead the assessment and planning process.

Learning Outcome 1: Understand the principles of person-centred assessment and care planning

Assessment Criterion 1.3: Describe ways the assessment and planning process or documentation can be adapted to maximise an individual's ownership and control of it

What does AC1.3 mean?

- ○ The lead word **describe** means that you must provide an **account** that **details** methods of adapting the assessment and planning process or documentation to maximise an individual's ownership and control of it.
- ○ Your **account** must detail **different** ways of adapting the assessment and planning process or documentation.
- ○ For the key words **assessment and planning process** you can think about the different stages and documentation that are involved in assessing an individual and planning their care and support.
- ○ For the key word **maximise** you can think about the different ways of ensuring individuals can understand and use the documentation and can lead the assessment and planning process.

Read the following **Real Work Setting** scenario and think about how it relates to your work setting and role:

Real Work Setting

Name: Sonia

Job Role: Senior Care Assistant for older people

(See page 209 for a description of the role.)

Adapting the assessment and planning process or documentation: Sonia shows the newly recruited Senior a video clip that was put together by an individual prior to her care assessment, as due to her fluctuating health needs she could not guarantee that she would be able to express what she wanted to say on the day of her care assessment.

Evidencing AC1.3 to your assessor:

For AC1.3 you must evidence your understanding of different ways the assessment and planning process or documentation can be adapted to maximise an individual's ownership and control of it.

Assessment Methods:

Oral/Written Questioning or Discussion or a Personal Statement or Reflection.

- You can **tell** your assessor about the different ways the assessment and planning process or documentation can be adapted to maximise an individual's ownership and control of it.
- Or, you can **talk** to your assessor about the different ways the assessment and planning process or documentation can be adapted to maximise an individual's ownership and control of it.
- Or, you can write a **personal statement or reflection** about the different ways the assessment and planning process or documentation can be adapted to maximise an individual's ownership and control of it.

REMEMBER TO:

- Provide a detailed **account** of the different ways the assessment and planning process or documentation can be adapted to maximise an individual's ownership and control of it.
- Ensure you detail how to adapt the assessment and planning process or documentation.
- Ensure your evidence includes details of maximising an individual's ownership and control.
- Think about **your work setting** and the different ways of adapting the assessment and planning process or documentation.

Learning Outcome 2: Be able to facilitate person-centred assessment

Assessment Criterion 2.1: Establish with the individual a partnership approach to the assessment process

What does AC2.1 mean?

- ○ The lead word **establish** means that you must **be able to show** through **your work practices** how to agree and build on using a partnership approach to the assessment process with an individual.
- ○ Your **observations** of your work practices must include you agreeing and using a partnership approach.
- ○ For the key words **partnership approach** you can think about how to share roles, responsibilities, ideas and decisions with an individual in the assessment process.
- ○ For the key words **assessment process** you can think about the different stages that are involved in assessing an individual.

Read the following **Real Work Setting** scenario and think about how it relates to your work setting and role:

Real Work Setting

Name: Marcus

Job Role: Senior Support Worker for people who have learning disabilities and complex needs

Marcus has been working as a Senior Support Worker for four years. His Senior responsibilities include: assisting the Service Manager in coordinating a person-centred service; leading a team of Support Workers to provide person-centred care and support to three individuals with learning disabilities and complex needs; monitoring and reviewing individuals' needs and support plans on a daily basis.

A partnership approach to the assessment process: As part of the person-centred service provided, Marcus ensures that he meets with each individual on a one-to-one basis every week. They discuss and review the individual's changing needs, including the completion of any additional assessments that are required to ensure that the support being provided addresses in full what each individual wants and needs. Marcus thinks that in order to succeed in doing this it is important that all Support Workers develop a partnership approach to the assessment process, in which they see each individual as an equal partner when making decisions about the support that is required and how it is provided on a day-to-day basis.

Evidencing AC2.1 to your assessor:

For AC2.1 you must evidence your skills in how to establish with the individual a partnership approach to the assessment process.

Assessment Method:

Direct Observation of your work practices.

- You can **show** your assessor how you establish with an individual a partnership approach to the assessment process.

REMEMBER TO:

- Make arrangements for **observation** of **your work practices**.
- Include evidence of you working with an individual.
- Include evidence of you establishing with an individual a partnership approach.
- Ensure the evidence you include relates to the assessment process.
- Think about **your work setting** and how you work with individuals to establish a partnership approach to the assessment process.

Learning Outcome 2: Be able to facilitate person-centred assessment

Assessment Criterion 2.2: Establish with the individual how the assessment process should be carried out and who else should be involved in the process

What does AC2.2 mean?

○ The lead word **establish** means that you must **be able to show** through **your work practices** how to agree with an individual how the assessment process should be carried out and who else should be involved in the process.

○ Your **observations** of your work practices must include you agreeing with an individual the assessment process and who should be involved in it.

○ For the key words **assessment process** you can think about how to agree with an individual the different stages that are involved in assessment and whom to involve in the process.

Read the following **Real Work Setting** scenario and think about how it relates to your work setting and role:

Real Work Setting

Name: Marcus

Job Role: Senior Support Worker for people who have learning disabilities and complex needs

(See page 212 for a description of the role.)

Establishing how to carry out the assessment process and who should be involved: Marcus is meeting with Craig, a Support Worker on the team, to discuss how best to involve Steve in the assessment process and how to support him to decide how this should be carried out and whom to involve. Marcus begins by talking through with Craig all those involved in Steve's support network and suggests that perhaps this can be one way of enabling Steve to think about whom he would like to be involved in his assessment. Marcus then suggests that Craig and Steve discuss whether there is anything Steve would like to change or improve about the way his last assessment was completed.

Evidencing AC2.2 to your assessor:

For AC2.2 you must evidence your skills in how to establish with the individual how the assessment process should be carried out and who else should be involved in the process.

Assessment Method:

Direct Observation of your work practices.

● You can **show** your assessor how you establish with an individual how the assessment process should be carried out and who else should be involved in the process.

REMEMBER TO:

● Make arrangements for **observation** of **your work practices**.

● Include evidence of you agreeing with an individual how the assessment process should be carried out and who should be involved in the assessment process.

● Think about **your work setting** and how you agree with an individual how the assessment process should be carried out and who else should be involved in the process.

Learning Outcome 2: Be able to facilitate person-centred assessment

Assessment Criterion 2.3: Agree with the individual and others the intended outcomes of the assessment process and care plan

What does AC2.3 mean?

- The lead word **agree** means that you must **be able to show** through **your work practices** how to establish with an individual and others (carers, friends and relatives, professionals and others important to the individual's well-being) the intended outcomes of the assessment process and care plan.
- Your **observations** of your work practices must include you establishing with an individual and others the intended outcomes of the assessment process and care plan.
- For the key words **intended outcomes** you can think about how to agree with an individual and others how the individual would like the assessment process and care plan to meet their needs, wishes and preferences.
- For the key words **assessment process** you can think about how to agree with an individual and others the intended outcomes of the assessment process and care plan.
- For the key words **care plan** you can think about how individuals' day-to-day care and support needs and preferences are met. Care plans may also be known by other names, such as support plans or individual plans.

Read the following **Real Work Setting** scenario and think about how it relates to your work setting and role:

Real Work Setting

Name: Marcus

Job Role: Senior Support Worker for people who have learning disabilities and complex needs

(See page 212 for a description of the role.)

Agreeing the intended outcomes of the assessment process: Marcus is meeting with Adrian, one of the individuals to whom he provides support, as well as his key worker and his father, to discuss Adrian's needs and plans for the next three months. This is so that the team can ensure they provide the necessary support to meet Adrian's needs and enable him to carry out his plans on a day-to-day basis. Marcus has arranged for Adrian to lead the discussions and then for the others to contribute their ideas and thoughts.

Evidencing AC2.3 to your assessor:

For AC2.3 you must evidence your skills in how to agree with an individual and others the intended outcomes of the assessment process and care plan.

Assessment Method:
Direct Observation of your work practices.

- You can **show** your assessor how you agree with an individual and others the intended outcomes of the assessment process and care plan.

REMEMBER TO:
- Make arrangements for **observation** of **your work practices**.
- Include evidence of you agreeing with an individual and others the intended outcomes of the assessment process and care plan.
- Think about **your work setting** and how you agree with an individual and others the intended outcomes of the assessment process and care plan.

Learning Outcome 2: Be able to facilitate person-centred assessment

Assessment Criterion 2.4: Ensure that assessment takes account of the individual's strengths and aspirations as well as needs

What does AC2.4 mean?

○ The lead word **ensure** means that you must **be able to show** through **your work practices** how to make sure that assessment takes account of an individual's strengths and aspirations as well as their needs.

○ Your **observations** of your work practices must include you making sure that the assessment takes into consideration an individual's strengths, aspirations and needs.

○ For the key word **assessment** you can think about how to ensure that this focuses on and is led by the individual's unique strengths, aspirations and needs.

Read the following **Real Work Setting** scenario and think about how it relates to your work setting and role:

Real Work Setting

Name: Marcus

Job Role: Senior Support Worker for people who have learning disabilities and complex needs

(See page 212 for a description of the role.)

Assessment and an individual's strengths, aspirations and needs: Marcus begins the meeting by asking Adrian, one of the individuals he provides support to, the aspects of his life that he feels he manages well and enjoys. Marcus then asks Adrian whether he's had time to think about what his hopes and dreams are for the immediate and long-term future, and what he feels he needs from the team to help him to progress and achieve these goals. Finally, Marcus talks through with Adrian the aspects of his life with which he receives support from the team and whether he feels this help is sufficient, is provided in a way with which he feels comfortable, and meets his requirements.

Evidencing AC2.4 to your assessor:

For AC2.4 you must evidence your skills in ensuring that assessment takes account of an individual's strengths, aspirations and needs.

Assessment Method:

Direct Observation of your work practices.

● You can **show** your assessor how you ensure that assessment takes account of the individual's strengths and aspirations as well as their needs.

REMEMBER TO:

● Make arrangements for **observation** of **your work practices**.
● Include evidence of you ensuring that assessment takes account of the individual's strengths and aspirations as well as their needs.
● Include evidence of the individual's strengths, aspirations and needs.
● Think about **your work setting** and how you ensure that assessment takes account of the individual's strengths and aspirations as well as their needs.

Learning Outcome 2: Be able to facilitate person-centred assessment

Assessment Criterion 2.5: Work with the individual and others to identify support requirements and preferences

What does AC2.5 mean?

- The lead words **work with** mean that you must **be able to show** through **your work practices** how to assist an individual and others to identify support requirements and preferences.
- Your **observations** of your work practices must include you working with an individual and others.
- For the key words **support requirements** you can think about how to assist an individual and others to establish the individual's support requirements, including what support is provided, how, when and why.
- For the key word **preferences** you can think about how to assist an individual and others to establish what an individual's likes are and what is important to the individual.

Read the following **Real Work Setting** scenario and think about how it relates to your work setting and role:

Real Work Setting

Name: Marcus

Job Role: Senior Support Worker for people who have learning disabilities and complex needs

(See page 212 for a description of the role.)

Identifying an individual's support requirements and preferences: Marcus has collected a lot of information from Adrian about his needs, preferences and strengths and how he would like the team to support him in fulfilling these. To build up an even stronger assessment of Adrian that focuses on him as a unique individual, Marcus agrees with Adrian for his key worker to share the aspects of Adrian's life he's been supporting him with, including the positive skills and approaches Adrian has learnt and the areas with which he requires further support. Adrian's father has also been invited to share his ideas with everyone as he has a very close relationship with Adrian and approaches daily tasks and activities with him in different ways.

Evidencing AC2.5 to your assessor:

For AC2.5 you must evidence your skills in working with an individual and others to identify their support requirements and preferences.

Assessment Method:

Direct Observation of your work practices.

- You can **show** your assessor how you work with an individual and others to identify their support requirements and preferences.

REMEMBER TO:

- Make arrangements for **observation** of **your work practices**.
- Include evidence of you working with an individual and others.
- Include evidence of **identifying** an individual's support requirements and preferences.
- Think about **your work setting** and how you work with an individual and others to identify their support requirements and preferences.

Learning Outcome 3: Be able to contribute to the planning of care or support

Assessment Criterion 3.1: Take account of factors that may influence the type and level of care or support to be provided

What does AC3.1 mean?

- The lead words **take account of** mean that you must **be able to show** through **your work practices** how to take into consideration factors that may influence the type and level of care or support to be provided.
- Your **observations** of your work practices must include you taking into consideration different factors.
- For the key word **factors** you can think about how an individual's strengths, aspirations, beliefs, values and preferences, and the risks and services available, may affect the type and level of care or support that is provided.
- For the key words **type and level of care or support** you can think about the different types and levels of support that are available for individuals.

Read the following **Real Work Setting** scenario and think about how it relates to your work setting and role:

Real Work Setting

Name: Sharon

Job Role: Senior Carer to young adults who have physical disabilities

Sharon has been working as a Senior Carer for one year. Her Senior responsibilities include: providing support and leadership to the care team; supervising the care team; deputising for the Care Manager; carrying out needs assessments; leading on care planning and risk assessments; maintaining all records accurately.

Factors that influence the type and level of care or support: Sharon is meeting with the care team today to discuss four individuals' care plans and risk assessments that require reviewing. For each individual Sharon ensures that the discussion focuses on what the team knows about the individual through the profile they have built up over time, as well as what has changed in each individual's life, so as to ensure that the support that is being provided continues to benefit each individual and their whole person.

Evidencing AC3.1 to your assessor:

For AC3.1 you must evidence your skills in taking account of factors that may influence the type and level of care or support to be provided.

Assessment Method:

Direct Observation of your work practices.

- You can **show** your assessor how you take account of factors that may influence the type and level of care or support to be provided.

REMEMBER TO:

- Make arrangements for **observation** of **your work practices**.
- Include evidence of different factors that may influence the type and level of care or support to be provided.
- Include evidence of you taking into account different factors when contributing to the planning of an individual's care or support.
- Think about **your work setting** and how you take account of factors that may influence the type and level of care or support to be provided.

Learning Outcome 3: Be able to contribute to the planning of care or support

Assessment Criterion 3.2: Work with the individual and others to explore options and resources for the delivery of the plan

What does AC3.2 mean?

○ The lead words **work with** mean that you must **be able to show** through **your work practices** how to collaborate with an individual and others to explore options and resources for the delivery of the plan.

○ Your **observations** of your work practices must include you working with an individual and others, exploring the options and resources available for the plan of care and support to be delivered.

○ For the key word **options** you can think about the different ways that the plan of care or support can be delivered.

○ For the key word **resources** you can think about the services, facilities, finances, people and support networks available. These may include both formal and informal support. These may include, for example, care or support services, community facilities, and an individual's personal networks.

Read the following **Real Work Setting** scenario and think about how it relates to your work setting and role:

Real Work Setting

Name: Sharon

Job Role: Senior Carer to young adults who have physical disabilities

(See page 217 for a description of the role.)

Exploring options and resources: Sharon is meeting with Tara and her partner to explore the range of options and resources that are available to enable Tara to continue to live independently in her flat. Tara's partner offers to support Tara with what she can, but she is also wary of not taking over and wants to make sure that Tara feels that she can be independent in their relationship. Sharon asks Tara about what support she thinks she may require during the day whilst her partner is out at work; Tara explains that she would like support with the food shopping, housework and cooking, and would like to learn the skills required to do these tasks independently herself.

Evidencing AC3.2 to your assessor:

For AC3.2 you must evidence your skills in working with an individual and others to explore options and resources for the delivery of the plan.

Assessment Method:

Direct Observation of your work practices.

● You can **show** your assessor how you work with the individual and others to explore options and resources for the delivery of the plan.

REMEMBER TO:

● Make arrangements for **observation** of **your work practices**.
● Include evidence of exploring different options and resources with an individual and others.
● Ensure the evidence relates to the delivery of an individual's plan of care or support.
● Think about **your work setting** and how you work with individuals and others to explore options and resources for the delivery of the care or support plan.

Learning Outcome 3: Be able to contribute to the planning of care or support

Assessment Criterion 3.3: Contribute to agreement on how component parts of a plan will be delivered and by whom

What does AC3.3 mean?

- The lead words **contribute to** mean that you must **be able to show** through **your work practices** how to agree with an individual and others how component parts of a plan will be delivered and by whom.
- Your **observations** of your work practices must include you agreeing on how component parts of a plan will be delivered and by whom.
- For the key words **component parts** you can think about the different aspects of a care or support plan.

Read the following **Real Work Setting** scenario and think about how it relates to your work setting and role:

Real Work Setting

Name: Sharon
Job Role: Senior Carer to young adults who have physical disabilities
(See page 217 for a description of the role.)

Agreeing on how component parts of a plan will be delivered and by whom: Sharon is meeting again with Tara and her partner to decide how to enable Tara to continue to live independently in her flat. After much discussion, Tara and her partner decide that they can manage on their own in terms of support with personal care tasks, as Tara's partner is more than willing to support her with these tasks on a daily basis. Sharon agrees that they can carry this out themselves and would like to review how this is working out in practice in one week's time. Sharon agrees to support Tara with registering for online supermarket shopping, as well as with finding out more information about the support available from her local advocacy group to enable her to complete her daily housework and cooking tasks.

Evidencing AC3.3 to your assessor:

For AC3.3 you must evidence your skills in contributing to agreement on how component parts of a plan will be delivered and by whom.

Assessment Method:

Direct Observation of your work practices.

- You can **show** your assessor how you contribute to agreement on how component parts of a plan will be delivered and by whom.

REMEMBER TO:

- Make arrangements for **observation** of **your work practices**.
- Include evidence of you contributing to how component parts of a plan of care or support will be delivered and by whom.
- Ensure the evidence relates to how and by whom an individual's plan of care or support will be delivered.
- Think about **your work setting** and how you contribute to agreement on how component parts of a plan will be delivered and by whom.

Learning Outcome 3: Be able to contribute to the planning of care or support

Assessment Criterion 3.4: Record the plan in a suitable format

What does AC3.4 mean?

- ○ The lead word **record** means that you must **be able to show** through **your work practices** how to make a record of the plan of care or support.
- ○ Your **observations** of your work practices must include you recording the plan in a suitable format.
- ○ For the key words **suitable format** you can think about the different ways that are available to make a record of an individual's plan of care or support, to ensure the individual knows what it contains and understands the care or support that has been agreed.

Read the following **Real Work Setting** scenario and think about how it relates to your work setting and role:

Real Work Setting
Name: Sharon
Job Role: Senior Carer to young adults who have physical disabilities
(See page 217 for a description of the role.)
Recording the plan in a suitable format: Sharon shows Tara the support planning documentation she will now complete to document the areas of support that have been agreed, how these will be provided, by whom and when. Tara's partner suggests this information could also be added to the pictorial plan that Tara uses, as she finds key words and photographs of the people she will be meeting with useful in terms of reminding her what is happening and when. Tara agrees and adds that she finds the visual aid very useful as this helps her to remember the people she will be meeting with every day and why.

Evidencing AC3.4 to your assessor:

For AC3.4 you must evidence your skills in recording the plan of care or support in a suitable format.

Assessment Method:
Direct Observation of your work practices.
○ You can **show** your assessor how you record the plan of care or support in a suitable format.

REMEMBER TO:
- Make arrangements for **observation** of **your work practices**.
- Include evidence of recording the plan of care or support.
- Include evidence of recording the plan in a suitable format that meets the individual's needs and preferences.
- Think about **your work setting** and how individuals' plans of care and support are recorded in suitable formats.

Learning Outcome 4: Be able to support the implementation of care plans

Assessment Criterion 4.1: Carry out assigned aspects of a care plan

What does AC4.1 mean?

○ The lead words **carry out** mean that you must **be able to show** through **your work practices** how to put the agreed aspects of a care plan into practice.

○ Your **observations** of your work practices must include you carrying out agreed aspects of a care plan.

○ For the key words **assigned aspects** you can think about the duties and responsibilities you must carry out to ensure an individual's care plan is carried out.

Read the following **Real Work Setting** scenario and think about how it relates to your work setting and role:

Real Work Setting

Name: Michelle

Job Role: Senior Live-in Carer to an individual who has dementia

Michelle has been working as a Senior Live-in Carer for two years. Her Senior responsibilities include: supporting a team of Carers to provide assistance with carrying out household and personal care tasks, and with preparing meals, shopping, managing bills and going out. Michelle also monitors and reviews the individual's plan of care and liaises with a team of health professionals and the individual's support network of family and friends.

Carrying out assigned aspects of a care plan: Michelle is very keen to show that she is a good role model to the rest of the Carers in the team and always makes sure that she carries out her own job role and responsibilities well, professionally and in a timely manner. Yesterday, for example, it was Michelle's responsibility to ensure that Mo, the individual with dementia whom the team supports, attended her appointment at the hairdressers and dropped in her repeat prescriptions at the GP's surgery. Michelle ensured that she prompted Mo several times in the morning to remind her of where she would be going so that she did not feel anxious about going out and visiting the hairdressers and the GP's surgery. The regular prompting worked well and helped to prepare Mo for the day ahead, which she enjoyed and was able to show successful completion of both activities. At the end of her shift Michelle shared this information with the Carer on duty and recorded it in Mo's daily plan of care.

Evidencing AC4.1 to your assessor:

For AC4.1 you must evidence your skills in carrying out assigned aspects of a care plan.

Assessment Method:

Direct Observation of your work practices.

● You can **show** your assessor how you carry out assigned aspects of a care plan.

REMEMBER TO:

● Make arrangements for **observation** of **your work practices**.
● Include evidence of you carrying out aspects of an individual's care plan.
● Ensure the evidence relates to aspects of an individual's care plan that have been allocated to you.
● Think about **your work setting** and how you carry out assigned aspects of an individual's care plan.

Learning Outcome 4: Be able to support the implementation of care plans

Assessment Criterion 4.2: Support others to carry out aspects of a care plan for which they are responsible

What does AC4.2 mean?

- The lead words **support others** mean that you must **be able to show** others through **your work practices** how to carry out aspects of a care plan for which they are responsible.
- Your **observations** of your work practices must include you supporting others to carry out aspects of a care plan.
- For the key word **others** you can think about the different people to whom you may be responsible for providing support, to ensure that they carry out the aspects of an individual's care plan for which they are responsible.

Read the following **Real Work Setting** scenario and think about how it relates to your work setting and role:

Real Work Setting

Name: Michelle

Job Role: Senior Live-in Carer to an individual who has dementia

(See page 221 for a description of the role.)

Supporting others to carry out aspects of an individual's care plan: Michelle is working with Kate, one of the Live-in Carers in the team, today to assist her to support Mo, the individual with dementia whom the team supports, in arranging a weekend break. Michelle begins by supporting Kate with thinking through how she is going to engage Mo and maintain her interest in completing this task. Michelle then shows Kate the possible different visual aids she can use with Mo, including the photographs in her living room of the family away on holiday and the brochures that have been recently delivered to Mo's home. Michelle then suggests that once Kate has found out Mo's preferences for where she would like to go that she shows her what is available there and within her budget.

Evidencing AC4.2 to your assessor:

For AC4.2 you must evidence your skills in supporting others to carry out aspects of a care plan for which they are responsible.

Assessment Method:

Direct Observation of your work practices.

- You can **show** your assessor how you support others to carry out aspects of a care plan for which they are responsible.

REMEMBER TO:

- Make arrangements for **observation** of **your work practices**.
- Include evidence of you supporting others.
- Ensure the evidence relates to supporting others with carrying out aspects of a care plan for which they are responsible.
- Think about **your work setting** and how you support others to carry out aspects of a care plan for which they are responsible.

Learning Outcome 4: Be able to support the implementation of care plans

Assessment Criterion 4.3: Adjust the plan in response to changing needs or circumstances

What does AC4.3 mean?

○ The lead word **adjust** means that you must **be able to show** through **your work practices** how to alter a care or support plan in response to an individual's changing needs or circumstances.

○ Your **observations** of your work practices must include you altering an individual's care or support plan to meet changing needs or circumstances.

○ For the key words **changing needs** you can think about how an individual's physical, emotional and social needs may change.

○ For the key word **circumstances** you can think about how an individual's well-being, support network, housing, employment and finances may change.

Read the following **Real Work Setting** scenario and think about how it relates to your work setting and role:

Real Work Setting

Name: Michelle

Job Role: Senior Live-in Carer to an individual who has dementia

(See page 221 for a description of the role.)

Adjusting a care or support plan in response to changing needs or circumstances: Michelle is meeting with Mo today to review her care plan, as due to a recent fall she has been experiencing difficulties with her balance when moving around. Usually, Mo would be supported by one Live-in Carer, but due to her unsteadiness on her feet it is becoming quite difficult for just one Carer to provide her with the assistance she requires with activities that involve her walking or standing for longer periods of time, such as cooking, hanging out the washing and walking to the shops. After discussing this Mo, her daughter, her best friend and Michelle agree to alter her care plan and identify that two Live-in Carers must provide the required support for these high-risk tasks.

Evidencing AC4.3 to your assessor:

For AC4.3 you must evidence your skills in adjusting the plan in response to changing needs or circumstances.

Assessment Method:

Direct Observation of your work practices.

● You can **show** your assessor or an expert witness how to adjust an individual's care or support plan in response to changing needs or circumstances.

REMEMBER TO:

● Make arrangements for **observation** of your work practices.
● Include evidence of you adjusting an individual's care or support plan.
● Ensure the evidence relates to an individual's changing needs or circumstances.
● Think about **your work setting** and how you adjust an individual's plan of care or support in response to changing needs or circumstances.

Learning Outcome 5: Be able to monitor a care plan

Assessment Criterion 5.1: Agree methods for monitoring the way a care plan is delivered

What does AC5.1 mean?

- ○ The lead word **agree** means that you must **be able to show** through **your work practices** how to establish methods for monitoring the way a care plan is delivered.
- ○ Your **observations** of your work practices must include you agreeing methods for monitoring the way a care plan is delivered.
- ○ For the key word **monitoring** you can think about how to agree on the different ways to observe and check the progress of an individual's care plan.

Read the following **Real Work Setting** scenario and think about how it relates to your work setting and role:

Real Work Setting

Name: Sejal

Job Role: Senior Support Worker to adults who have mental health needs

Sejal has been working as a Senior Support Worker for three years. Her Senior responsibilities include: planning, implementing and monitoring the provision of quality support; supporting individuals to engage in a range of activities; providing guidance and support to a team of Support Workers; carrying out supervisions and appraisals with Support Workers; identifying the team's training needs; ensuring a safe and secure environment for individuals, staff and visitors.

Agreeing how to monitor how a care plan is delivered: At this week's staff meeting Sejal discusses with the team one of the individuals who is new to the service. She shares with them her ideas and the individual's ideas for how the care plan that has been developed should be monitored over the next four weeks. Sejal explains that this will include hourly observation checks during the daytime only and a one-to-one meeting between her and the individual at 4 p.m. on Fridays. One of the Support Workers asks Sejal for her advice over whether the team should also encourage the individual on a daily basis to talk about her plan of care and how she feels it is being implemented. Sejal asks the rest of the team for their input and all think that this is a good idea, so long as the individual is willing to engage in providing feedback every day. The team agrees to monitor the situation closely and record their findings.

Evidencing AC5.1 to your assessor:

For AC5.1 you must evidence your skills in agreeing methods for monitoring the way a care plan is delivered.

Assessment Method:

Direct Observation of your work practices.

- You can **show** your assessor how you agree methods for monitoring the way a care plan is delivered.

REMEMBER TO:
- Make arrangements for **observation of your work practices**.
- Include evidence of you agreeing methods for monitoring the way a care plan is delivered.
- Ensure the evidence relates to monitoring how an individual's care plan is delivered.
- Think about **your work setting** and how you agree methods for monitoring the way a care plan is delivered.

Learning Outcome 5: Be able to monitor a care plan

Assessment Criterion 5.2: Collate monitoring information from agreed sources

What does AC5.2 mean?

- ○ The lead word **collate** means that you must **be able to show** through **your work practices** how to gather monitoring information from agreed sources.
- ○ Your **observations** of your work practices must include you collating monitoring information from agreed sources.
- ○ For the key words **monitoring information** you can think about the different ways to gather monitoring information, what information is required and why.
- ○ For the key words **agreed sources** you can think about from whom and from where you may gather monitoring information to collate.

Read the following **Real Work Setting** scenario and think about how it relates to your work setting and role:

Real Work Setting

Name: Sejal
Job Role: Senior Support Worker to adults who have mental health needs
(See page 224 for a description of the role.)
Collating monitoring information from agreed sources: In preparation for an individual's care review, Sejal is collating monitoring information from a range of sources agreed with the individual prior to him using the service. The agreed sources of information include: the individual; the team of Support Workers who work with the individual on a daily basis; the approved mental health practitioner who has assessed the individual and has been leading on the planning and implementation of his care plan; the individual's key worker, who has worked closely with the individual in completing specific care plan activities. Sejal is collating this information over a period of time as the individual's well-being has changed several times in the time he has been using the service. Sejal plans to collate the monitoring information by meeting in person with individuals, and requesting and reading through reports and records that have been completed.

Evidencing AC5.2 to your assessor:

For AC5.2 you must evidence your skills in collating monitoring information from agreed sources.

Assessment Method:	**REMEMBER TO:**
Direct Observation of your work practices. • You can **show** your assessor how you collate monitoring information from agreed sources.	• Make arrangements for **observation** of **your work practices**. • Include evidence of you collating monitoring information. • Ensure the monitoring information you collate is from agreed sources. • Ensure the monitoring information relates to the individual's care plan. • Think about **your work setting** and how you collate monitoring information from agreed sources for an individual's plan of care.

Learning Outcome 5: Be able to monitor a care plan

Assessment Criterion 5.3: Record changes that affect the delivery of an individual's care plan

What does AC5.3 mean?

○ The lead word **record** means that you must **be able to show** through **your work practices** how to document any changes that occur and affect the delivery of an individual's care plan.

○ Your **observations** of your work practices must include you recording changes.

○ For the key word **changes** you can think about the different changes that may occur in an individual's well-being and circumstances, and how these will then impact on the way the individual's care plan is delivered.

Read the following **Real Work Setting** scenario and think about how it relates to your work setting and role:

Real Work Setting

Name: Sejal

Job Role: Senior Support Worker to adults who have mental health needs

(See page 224 for a description of the role.)

Recording changes: One of the individuals Sejal and her team of Support Workers are currently supporting in the mental health unit has received news of a bereavement of a close relative. Since receiving this news it has been noted by Sejal and the team that the individual appears to be quite tearful in the mornings and no longer enjoys participating in activities with others. Recently it was also reported to Sejal that this individual refused to have a shower in the morning; this again is unusual for this individual as she always used to enjoy having an early morning shower. Sejal and the team have discussed these observations and Sejal has documented them all in full and informed the approved mental health practitioner of the team's observations.

Evidencing AC5.3 to your assessor:

For AC5.3 you must evidence your skills in recording changes that affect the delivery of an individual's care plan.

Assessment Method:
Direct Observation of your work practices.

● You can **show** your assessor how you record changes that affect the delivery of an individual's care plan.

REMEMBER TO:
● Make arrangements for **observation** of **your work practices**.
● Include evidence of you recording changes.
● Ensure the evidence you provide relates to how these changes have affected how an individual's care plan is delivered.
● Think about **your work setting** and how you record changes that affect the delivery of an individual's care plan.

Learning Outcome 6: Be able to facilitate a review of care plans and their implementation

Assessment Criterion 6.1: Seek agreement with the individual and others about who should be involved in the review process and the criteria by which to judge the effectiveness of the care plan

What does AC6.1 mean?

- The lead words **seek agreement** mean that you must **be able to show** through **your work practices** how to establish with the individual and others who should be involved in the review process, as well as the criteria by which to judge how effective the care plan is.
- Your **observations** of your work practices must include you seeking agreement with the individual and others.
- For the key words **review process** you can think about why an individual's care plan may need to be reviewed and who should be involved in doing this.
- For the key word **criteria** you can think about how to establish with an individual and others how best to measure the effectiveness of the care plan being delivered.

Read the following **Real Work Setting** scenario and think about how it relates to your work setting and role:

Real Work Setting

Name: Lia

Job Role: Senior Residential Care Worker with older people

Lia has been working as a Senior Residential Care Worker for four years. Her Senior responsibilities include: supporting a team of Care Workers to provide a high quality care service that enhances individuals' quality of life and promotes independence; ensuring care plans and risk assessments are adhered to; maintaining accurate records.

Seeking agreement about the review process and how effective the care plan is: Lia is meeting with Jeremy, his brother and his key worker to ask them whom Jeremy would like to involve in the review of his care plan and what they think is important when measuring how effective his care plan is.

Evidencing AC6.1 to your assessor:

For AC6.1 you must evidence your skills in seeking agreement with the individual and others about who should be involved in the review process and the criteria by which to judge the effectiveness of the care plan.

Assessment Method:

Direct Observation of your work practices.

- You can **show** your assessor how you seek agreement with the individual and others about who should be involved in the review process and the criteria by which to judge the effectiveness of the care plan.

REMEMBER TO:
- Make arrangements for **observation of your work practices**.
- Include evidence of you seeking agreement with the individual and others.
- Ensure the evidence includes who should be involved in the review process, as well as the **criteria** by which to judge the effectiveness of the care plan.
- Think about **your work setting** and how you seek agreement with an individual and others about who should be involved in the review process, as well as the criteria by which to judge the effectiveness of the care plan.

Learning Outcome 6: Be able to facilitate a review of care plans and their implementation

Assessment Criterion 6.2: Seek feedback from the individual and others about how the plan is working

What does AC6.2 mean?

○ The lead words **seek feedback** mean that you must **be able to show** through **your work practices** how to ascertain from the individual and others the areas of the care plan that are working well and those that require improvement.

○ Your **observations** of your work practices must include you seeking feedback from the individual and others.

○ For the key word **feedback** you can think about how the views and suggestions of an individual and others can provide information on the care plan's strengths and areas for improvement.

Read the following **Real Work Setting** scenario and think about how it relates to your work setting and role:

Real Work Setting

Name: Lia

Job Role: Senior Residential Care Worker with older people

(See page 227 for a description of the role.)

Seeking feedback about how the plan is working: Lia has arranged a meeting with Ruth to discuss how she is settling into the home and how she has found the care and support she has received over the last three months. Lia is meeting on her own with Ruth, as she hopes this will encourage Ruth to say what she thinks and feels rather than what she thinks others may want her to say. Lia plans to telephone Ruth's niece later on this week to discuss her view of how the plan of care agreed has been working. Finally, Lia plans to ask the team of Carers at their next meeting for their views on what is working well and what requires further improvements with respect to Ruth's plan of care.

Evidencing AC6.2 to your assessor:

For AC6.2 you must evidence your skills in seeking feedback from the individual and others about how the plan is working.

Assessment Method:

Direct Observation of your work practices.

● You can **show** your assessor how you seek feedback from the individual and others about how the plan is working.

REMEMBER TO:

● Make arrangements for **observation** of **your work practices**.
● Include evidence of you seeking feedback from an individual and others.
● Ensure the evidence relates to how the care plan is working in practice.
● Think about **your work setting** and how you seek feedback from an individual and others about how the plan is working.

Learning Outcome 6: Be able to facilitate a review of care plans and their implementation

Assessment Criterion 6.3: Use feedback and monitoring or other information to evaluate whether the plan has achieved its objectives

What does AC6.3 mean?

- The lead words **use feedback** mean that you must **be able to show** through **your work practices** how to apply the feedback, monitoring and other information obtained to evaluate whether the care plan has achieved its objectives.
- Your **observations** of your work practices must include you using feedback and monitoring or other information.
- For the key word **feedback** you can think about how the views and suggestions of an individual and others can provide information about the care plan's strengths and areas for improvement and whether its agreed purpose has been met.
- For the key word **evaluate** you can think about how to assess whether the care plan that has been put in place meets its agreed purpose and the individual's goals.

Read the following **Real Work Setting** scenario and think about how it relates to your work setting and role:

Real Work Setting

Name: Lia

Job Role: Senior Residential Care Worker with older people

(See page 227 for a description of the role.)

Using feedback, monitoring or other information: Lia will be meeting with Ruth next week to update her care plan. In preparation for this she has already met with Ruth, spoken to her niece and conducted a meeting with the team of Residential Care Workers. Lia has found doing so to be very useful because it has become evident that, apart from two areas of Ruth's current plan of care, the support being provided is raising her quality of life and promoting her independence. The two areas that require improvement involve more encouragement from the team to enable Ruth to contact her close friends, and more key worker time at the weekends to enable Ruth to sort through her correspondence.

Evidencing AC6.3 to your assessor:

For AC6.3 you must evidence your skills in using feedback and monitoring or other information to evaluate whether the plan has achieved its objectives.

Assessment Method:
Direct Observation of your work practices.

- You can **show** your assessor how you use feedback and monitoring or other information to evaluate whether the plan has achieved its objectives.

REMEMBER TO:
- Make arrangements for **observation** of **your work practices**.
- Include evidence of you using feedback and monitoring or other information.
- Ensure the evidence relates to evaluating whether the care plan has achieved its objectives.
- Think about **your work setting** and how you use feedback and monitoring or other information to evaluate whether an individual's care plan has achieved its objectives.

Learning Outcome 6: Be able to facilitate a review of care plans and their implementation

Assessment Criterion 6.4: Work with the individual and others to agree any revisions to the plan

What does AC6.4 mean?

○ The lead words **work with** mean that you must **be able to show** through **your work practices** how you **support** the individual and others to agree any revisions to the plan.

○ Your **observations** of your work practices must include you working with the individual and others to agree any revisions to the care plan.

○ For the key word **revisions** you can think about why an individual's care plan may need to be revised and how you work alongside individuals and others to agree any necessary amendments.

Read the following **Real Work Setting** scenario and think about how it relates to your work setting and role:

Real Work Setting
Name: Lia
Job Role: Senior Residential Care Worker with older people
(See page 227 for a description of the role.)
Agreeing revisions to an individual's care plan: Lia meets with Ruth and her niece as planned and together they agree to update Ruth's care plan to reflect the two areas of support that need to addressed: more encouragement from the team to enable Ruth to contact her close friends, and more key worker time at the weekends to enable Ruth to sort through her correspondence. All agree that Ruth and her niece will draw up a list of Ruth's close friends and include their contact numbers and addresses so that the team can ask Ruth whether she wishes to contact any of them. Lia has also set aside an additional hour at the weekends for Ruth to spend time with her key worker reading through the letters and emails she receives.

Evidencing AC6.4 to your assessor:

For AC6.4 you must evidence your skills in working with the individual and others to agree any revisions to the plan.

Assessment Method:	REMEMBER TO:
Direct Observation of your work practices. ● You can **show** your assessor how you work with the individual and others to agree any revisions to the plan.	● Make arrangements for **observation** of **your work practices**. ● Include evidence of you working with an individual and others. ● Ensure the evidence includes you agreeing revisions to an individual's care plan by working with an individual and others. ● Think about **your work setting** and how you work with the individual and others to agree any revisions to the plan.

Learning Outcome 6: Be able to facilitate a review of care plans and their implementation

Assessment Criterion 6.5: Document the review process and revisions as required

What does AC6.5 mean?

- The lead word **document** means that you must **be able to show** through **your work practices** how to record the review process and revisions as required.
- Your **observations** of your work practices must include you documenting the review process and revisions as required.
- For the key words **review process** you can think about how reviewing an individual's care plan is documented.
- For the key word **revisions** you can think about how any amendments to an individual's care plan are documented.

Read the following **Real Work Setting** scenario and think about how it relates to your work setting and role:

Real Work Setting

Name: Lia

Job Role: Senior Residential Care Worker with older people

(See page 227 for a description of the role.)

Documenting the review process and revisions made: Lia accurately and fully completes the care plan review documentation as required and reads this out to Ruth as she is documenting the information agreed, in order to ensure she understands and agrees to this. Lia then asks Ruth's niece to read through the care review form, including the changes made to Ruth's care plan. Once both have read and indicated their agreement with the information recorded, Lia asks Ruth and her niece to sign and date to indicate their agreement that these are a true representation of what has been agreed today. Finally, Lia also signs and dates the records as the reviewing Senior Residential Care Worker.

Evidencing AC6.5 to your assessor:

For AC6.5 you must evidence your skills in documenting the review process and revisions as required.

Assessment Method:

Direct Observation of your work practices.

- You can **show** your assessor how you document the review process and revisions as required.

REMEMBER TO:
- Make arrangements for **observation** of **your work practices**.
- Include evidence of you documenting the review process.
- Include evidence of you documenting any revisions that are made to the individual's care plan.
- Think about **your work setting** and how you document the review process and revisions as required.

Learning Outcome 1: Understand the principles of supporting individuals to live at home

Assessment Criterion 1.1: Describe how being supported to live at home can benefit an individual

What does AC1.1 mean?

- The lead word **describe** means that you must provide an **account** that **details** how being supported to live at home can benefit an individual.
- Your **account** must detail the **different** benefits to an individual.
- For the key word **supported** you can think about the different types of support individuals may require, such as practical assistance with household tasks, managing bills or shopping, as well as emotional support and companionship to live at home.
- For the key word **benefit** you can think about how being supported to live at home can have a positive impact on an individual's physical, emotional, social and financial well-being.

Read the following **Real Work Setting** scenario and think about how it relates to your work setting and role:

Real Work Setting

Name: Seeny

Job role: Senior Personal Assistant to a young man who has autism

Seeny has been working as a Senior Personal Assistant for two and a half years. His Senior responsibilities include: supporting the individual to manage a team of Personal Assistants; providing assistance three times a week with supporting the individual to get up and dressed in the morning; supporting the individual to organise transport to and from work.

Benefits of being supported to live at home: Seeny has developed a good working relationship with Charles, the young man he supports. Since Charles has employed his own Personal Assistants Seeny has seen many positive changes in him with respect to his motivation, his verbal and non-verbal interpersonal skills, and his outlook on his life and future. This in turn has meant that he has been a lot more committed to arriving for work on time and has felt a lot more confident in himself both at work and when he goes out.

Evidencing AC1.1 to your assessor:

For AC1.1 you must evidence your understanding of how being supported to live at home can benefit an individual.

Assessment Methods:
Oral/Written Questioning or **Discussion** or a **Personal Statement or Reflection.**

- You can **tell** your assessor about how being supported to live at home can benefit an individual.
- *Or*, you can **talk** to your assessor about how being supported to live at home can benefit an individual.
- *Or*, you can write a **personal statement or reflection** about your experience of how being supported to live at home can benefit an individual.

REMEMBER TO:
- Provide a detailed **account** of how being supported to live at home can benefit an individual.
- Ensure you include evidence of **how** being supported to live at home can benefit an individual.
- Include examples of the different benefits to an individual.
- Think about **your work setting** and how being supported to live at home can benefit an individual.

Learning Outcome 1: Understand the principles of supporting individuals to live at home

Assessment Criterion 1.2: Compare the roles of people and agencies that may be needed to support an individual to live at home

What does AC1.2 mean?

○ The lead word **compare** means that you must provide an **account** that **details** the similarities and differences that exist between the roles of various people and agencies that may be needed to support an individual to live at home.

○ Your **account** must detail **similarities and differences** that exist between the roles of various people and agencies.

○ For the key word **roles** you can think about the different duties, responsibilities, support and services that are provided by both people and agencies to support an individual to live at home.

○ For the key word **people** you can think about how partners, family, friends, Senior Care Workers, Senior Personal Assistants, Reablement Officers, Physiotherapists and Occupational Therapists can be sources of informal and formal support for an individual to live at home.

Read the following **Real Work Setting** scenario and think about how it relates to your work setting and role:

Real Work Setting

Name: Seeny

Job role: Senior Personal Assistant to a young man who has autism

(See page 232 for a description of the role.)

The roles of people and agencies: Seeny has received a phone call from Charles's sister, asking for more information about the role of the Reablement Officer who will soon be visiting Charles at home.

Evidencing AC1.2 to your assessor:

For AC1.2 you must evidence your understanding of the similarities and differences that exist between the roles of various people and agencies that may be needed to support an individual to live at home.

Assessment Methods:

Oral/Written Questioning or **Discussion** or a **Personal Statement or Reflection.**

● You can **tell** your assessor about the similarities and differences that exist between the roles of people and agencies.

● *Or*, you can **talk** to your assessor about the similarities and differences that exist between the roles of various people and agencies.

● *Or*, you can write a **personal statement or reflection** about your experience of the similarities and differences that exist between the roles of various people and agencies.

REMEMBER TO:

● Provide a detailed **account** of the similarities and differences between the roles of various people and agencies.

● Include a **comparison** of the roles of different people and agencies that may be needed to support an individual to live at home.

● Think about **your work setting** and the similarities and differences that exist between the roles of various people and agencies that may be needed to support an individual to live at home.

Learning Outcome 1: Understand the principles of supporting individuals to live at home

Assessment Criterion 1.3: Explain the importance of providing information about benefits, allowances and financial planning that could support individuals to live at home

What does AC1.3 mean?
- The lead word **explain** means that you must **make clear** the importance of providing information to individuals about benefits, allowances and financial planning.
- Your **account** must make clear the importance of providing this information to support individuals to live at home.
- For the key word **benefits** you can think about the different government payments that individuals may be entitled to receive.
- For the key word **allowances** you can think about the different payments that may be made to individuals to meet their needs or expenses.
- For the key words **financial planning** you can think about the support required for individuals to manage their finances to achieve their goals in life.

Read the following **Real Work Setting** scenario and think about how it relates to your work setting and role:

Real Work Setting

Name: Seeny

Job role: Senior Personal Assistant to a young man who has autism

(See page 232 for a description of the role.)

The importance of information about benefits, allowances and financial planning: Seeny is supporting Charles to write a job description for another Personal Assistant to assist him with managing his money. They discuss the essential requirement that the person has the ability to provide up-to-date information about benefits, allowances and financial planning.

Evidencing AC1.3 to your assessor:

For AC1.3 you must evidence your understanding of the importance of providing information about benefits, allowances and financial planning that could support individuals to live at home.

Assessment Methods:
Oral/Written Questioning or **Discussion** or a **Personal Statement or Reflection**.
- You can **tell** your assessor about the importance of providing information about benefits, allowances and financial planning that could support individuals to live at home.
- Or, you can **talk** to your assessor about the importance of providing information about benefits, allowances and financial planning that could support individuals to live at home.
- Or, you can write a **personal statement or reflection** about your experience of the importance of providing information about benefits, allowances and financial planning that could support individuals to live at home.

REMEMBER TO:
- Provide an **account** and explain the **importance** of providing information about benefits, allowances and financial planning.
- Include **details** about the reasons why it is important to provide information about benefits, allowances and financial planning that could support individuals to live at home.
- Think about **your work setting** and the importance of providing information about benefits, allowances and financial planning that could support individuals to live at home.

Learning Outcome 1: Understand the principles of supporting individuals to live at home

Assessment Criterion 1.4: Explain how risk management contributes to supporting individuals to live at home

What does AC1.4 mean?

- The lead word **explain** means that you must **make clear** how risk management contributes to supporting individuals to live at home.
- Your **account** must make clear the contribution that risk management makes.
- For the key words **risk management** you can think about how to support an individual to identify, control and minimise risks that may occur when living at home.

Read the following **Real Work Setting** scenario and think about how it relates to your work setting and role:

Real Work Setting

Name: Seeny
Job role: Senior Personal Assistant to a young man who has autism
(See page 232 for a description of the role.)
How risk management contributes: Seeny discusses with Charles how, when he interviews for the new Personal Assistant, he will need to think about the qualities and skills this person must have. They discuss the importance of ensuring that the Personal Assistant understands that this is Charles's home and that his environment as well as his possessions must be respected at all times. Both agree that it will also be important for the Personal Assistant to respect Charles's privacy and dignity, as well as his right to take risks and to be supported to understand how to manage these well so that he can continue to enjoy his flat and living his life independently.

Evidencing AC1.4 to your assessor:

For AC1.4 you must evidence your understanding of how risk management contributes to supporting individuals to live at home.

Assessment Methods:

Oral/Written Questioning or **Discussion** or a **Personal Statement** or **Reflection**.

- You can **tell** your assessor about how risk management contributes to supporting individuals to live at home.
- Or, you can **talk** to your assessor about how risk management contributes to supporting individuals to live at home.
- Or, you can write a **personal statement or reflection** about your experience of how risk management contributes to supporting individuals to live at home.

REMEMBER TO:

- Provide an **account** of how risk management contributes to supporting individuals to live at home.
- Include **details** and **examples** about how risk management contributes to supporting individuals to live at home.
- Think about **your work setting** and how risk management contributes to supporting individuals to live at home.

Learning Outcome 2: Be able to contribute to planning support for living at home

Assessment Criterion 2.1: Identify with an individual the strengths, skills and existing networks they have that could support them to live at home

What does AC2.1 mean?

- The lead word **identify** means that you must **make clear** through **your work practices** how to establish with an individual their strengths, skills and existing networks that could support them to live at home.
- Your **observations** of your work practices must include you identifying with an individual their strengths, skills and existing networks.
- For the key word **strengths** you can think about how an individual's personal qualities could support them to live at home.
- For the key word **skills** you can think about how an individual's abilities and expertise could support them to live at home.
- For the key words **existing networks** you can think about how an individual's circles of family, friends, professionals and agencies could support them to live at home.

Read the following **Real Work Setting** scenario and think about how it relates to your work setting and role:

Real Work Setting

Name: Andrea

Job role: Senior Reablement Officer for individuals living in their own homes

Andrea has been working as a Senior Reablement Officer for six months. Her Senior responsibilities include: ensuring the delivery of a person-centred service as part of a reablement; planning, designing and implementing individuals' reablement plans; leading the review process; supervising, advising and guiding a team of Reablement Officers.

Identifying an individual's strengths, skills and existing networks: Andrea is meeting with Sean for the first time and together they plan to build up a profile of Sean's current circumstances, including his personal qualities and abilities to live at home as well as the support being provided by the individuals and agencies that are currently involved in his life.

Evidencing AC2.1 to your assessor:

For AC2.1 you must evidence your skills in identifying with an individual the strengths, skills and existing networks they have that could support them to live at home.

Assessment Method:

Direct Observation of your work practices.

- You can **show** your assessor how you identify with an individual the strengths, skills and existing networks they have that could support them to live at home.

REMEMBER TO:

- Make arrangements for **observation** of **your work practices**.
- Include evidence of you identifying with an individual the strengths, skills and existing networks they have.
- Ensure the evidence you include relates to supporting an individual to live at home.
- Think about **your work setting** and how you identify with an individual the strengths, skills and existing networks they have that could support them to live at home.

Learning Outcome 2: Be able to contribute to planning support for living at home

Assessment Criterion 2.2: Identify with an individual their needs that may require additional support and their preferences for how their needs may be met

What does AC2.2 mean?

- ○ The lead word **identify** means that you must **make clear** through **your work practices** how to establish with an individual their needs that may require additional support and their preferences for how their needs may be met.
- ○ Your **observations** of your work practices must include you identifying with an individual their needs and their preferences.
- ○ For the key word **needs** you can think about an individual's requirements that may require additional support, in relation to their physical, emotional, personal, social, environmental and/or financial well-being and safety.
- ○ For the key word **preferences** you can think about how an individual may choose to have their individual requirements met.

Read the following **Real Work Setting** scenario and think about how it relates to your work setting and role:

Real Work Setting

Name: Andrea

Job role: Senior Reablement Officer for individuals living in their own homes

(See page 236 for a description of the role.)

Identifying an individual's needs: Andrea begins her meeting with Sean by asking him to tell her all about how he is enjoying living in his own home and all the areas he is able to manage well in, as well as any areas with which he feels he may require additional support. Sean explains that he feels that he manages to live at home on his own very well but that his family are concerned about the cleanliness levels of his home when they visit.

Evidencing AC2.2 to your assessor:

For AC2.2 you must evidence your skills in identifying with an individual their needs that may require additional support and their preferences for how their needs may be met.

Assessment Method:

Direct Observation of your work practices.

- You can **show** your assessor how you identify with an individual their needs that may require additional support and their preferences for how their needs may be met.

REMEMBER TO:

- Make arrangements for **observation of your work practices**.
- Include evidence of you identifying with an individual their needs that may require additional support.
- Ensure the evidence you provide also includes you identifying with an individual their preferences for how their needs may be met.
- Think about **your work setting** and how you identify with an individual their needs that may require additional support and their preferences for how their needs may be met.

Learning Outcome 2: Be able to contribute to planning support for living at home

Assessment Criterion 2.3: Agree with the individual and others the risks that need to be managed in living at home and ways to address them

What does AC2.3 mean?

- The lead words **agree with** mean that you must **be able to show** through **your work practices** how to establish with an individual and others the risks that need to be managed in living at home and ways to address them.
- Your **observations** of your work practices must include you identifying with an individual and others the risks that need to be managed and how to address them.
- For the key words **risks that need to be managed** you can think about how to establish with an individual and others how to identify, control and minimise risks that may occur when living at home.

Read the following **Real Work Setting** scenario and think about how it relates to your work setting and role:

Real Work Setting
Name: Andrea
Job role: Senior Reablement Officer for individuals living in their own homes
(See page 236 for a description of the role.)
Managing risks: Andrea asks Sean during their meeting why he thinks that his family have concerns about the cleanliness levels of his home. Sean explains that they are worried mainly about the hygiene levels in the kitchen, because this is where his two dogs sleep and because if he is feeling tired he does not always do the cleaning.

Evidencing AC2.3 to your assessor:

For AC2.3 you must evidence your skills in agreeing with an individual and others the risks that need to be managed in living at home and ways to address them.

Assessment Method:
Direct Observation of your work practices.
- You can **show** your assessor how you agree with an individual and others the risks that need to be managed in living at home and ways to address them.

REMEMBER TO:
- Make arrangements for **observation** of **your work practices**.
- Include evidence of you agreeing with an individual and others the risks that need to be managed in living at home and ways to address them.
- Ensure the evidence you provide includes you establishing the risks and ways to manage them with both the individual and others.
- Think about **your work setting** and how you agree with an individual and others the risks that need to be managed in living at home and ways to address them.

Learning Outcome 3: Be able to work with individuals to secure additional services and facilities to enable them to live at home

Assessment Criterion 3.1: Support the individual and others to access and understand information about resources, services and facilities available to support the individual to live at home

What does AC3.1 mean?

○ The lead word **support** means that you must **be able to show** through **your work practices** how to assist the individual and others in accessing and understanding information about resources, services and facilities available to support the individual to live at home.

○ Your **observations** of your work practices must include you supporting the individual and others to access and understand information about resources, services and facilities available.

○ For the key word **resources** you can think about the personnel, support, finances, equipment and aids available to support the individual to live at home.

○ For the key words **services and facilities** you can think about the organisations, systems, equipment and places available in the community to support the individual to live at home.

Read the following **Real Work Setting** scenario and think about how it relates to your work setting and role:

Real Work Setting

Name: Alan

Job role: Senior Home Carer for older people

Alan has been working as a Senior Home Carer for five years. His Senior responsibilities include: supervising a team of Home Carers; setting up and monitoring care packages for individuals; updating individuals' care plans; attending review meetings; liaising with individuals, their families and other professionals.

Accessing and understanding information: Alan has arranged to meet with Doris, her daughter and son-in-law to discuss the support that the home care agency can provide, as well as other local services and facilities that are available to support Doris to continue living at home.

Evidencing AC3.1 to your assessor:

For AC3.1 you must evidence your skills in supporting the individual and others to access and understand information about resources, services and facilities available to support the individual to live at home.

Assessment Method:

Direct Observation of your work practices.

● You can **show** your assessor how you support the individual and others to access and understand information about resources, services and facilities available to support the individual to live at home.

REMEMBER TO:

● Make arrangements for **observation of your work practices**.

● Include evidence of you supporting the individual and others to access and understand information.

● Ensure the evidence you provide relates to resources, services and facilities available to support the individual to live at home.

● Think about **your work setting** and how you support the individual and others to access and understand information about resources, services and facilities available to support the individual to live at home.

Learning Outcome 3: Be able to work with individuals to secure additional services and facilities to enable them to live at home

Assessment Criterion 3.2: Work with the individual and others to select resources, facilities and services that will meet the individual's needs and minimise risks

What does AC3.2 mean?

○ The lead words **work with** mean that you must **be able to show** through **your work practices** how to support the individual and others to select resources, facilities and services that will meet the individual's needs and minimise risks.

○ Your **observations** of your work practices must include you supporting the individual and others to select resources, facilities and services.

○ For the key word **resources** you can think about the personnel, support, finances, equipment and aids available to meet the individual's needs and minimise risks.

○ For the key words **services and facilities** you can think about the organisations, systems, equipment and places available in the community to meet the individual's needs and minimise risks.

Read the following **Real Work Setting** scenario and think about how it relates to your work setting and role:

Real Work Setting

Name: Alan

Job role: Senior Home Carer for older people

(See page 239 for a description of the role.)

Selecting resources, facilities and services: During his meeting with Doris, her daughter and son-in-law, Alan asks each in turn whether there is any specific support, services or facilities that they either have heard or read about that they think would meet Doris's needs and minimise the risks of her living at home on her own. All agree that Doris would benefit from an additional hour of support from a Carer in the evenings, who could be more involved in arranging her health care appointments.

Evidencing AC3.2 to your assessor:

For AC3.2 you must evidence your skills in working with the individual and others to select resources, facilities and services that will meet the individual's needs and minimise risks.

Assessment Method:

Direct Observation of your work practices.

● You can **show** your assessor how you work with the individual and others to select resources, facilities and services that will meet the individual's needs and minimise risks.

REMEMBER TO:

● Make arrangements for **observation of your work practices**.
● Include evidence of you supporting the individual and others to select resources, facilities and services.
● Ensure the evidence you provide relates to meeting the individual's needs and minimising risks.
● Think about **your work setting** and how you work with an individual and others to select resources, facilities and services that will meet the individual's needs and minimise risks.

Learning Outcome 3: Be able to work with individuals to secure additional services and facilities to enable them to live at home

Assessment Criterion 3.3: Contribute to completing paperwork to apply for required resources, facilities and services, in a way that promotes active participation

What does AC3.3 mean?

○ The lead words **contribute to** mean that you must **be able to show** through **your work practices** how to promote active participation when completing paperwork to apply for required resources, facilities and services.

○ Your **observations** of your work practices must include you promoting active participation.

○ For the key word **resources** you can think about the personnel, support, finances, equipment and aids that need to be applied for.

○ For the key words **facilities and services** you can think about the organisations, systems, equipment and places available in the community that need to be applied for.

○ For the key words **active participation** you can think about how the way you complete paperwork can ensure that you support individuals to live their lives as they wish.

Read the following **Real Work Setting** scenario and think about how it relates to your work setting and role:

Real Work Setting

Name: Alan

Job role: Senior Home Carer for older people

(See page 239 for a description of the role.)

Contributing to completing paperwork: Alan suggests to Doris that he can support her with filling out the documentation for requesting additional support from a Carer and with identifying the additional areas of support with which she would like support in the evenings. With respect to being involved in arranging her health care appointments, Alan and Doris's daughter have agreed that they will support her to register with a new GP and dentist and to complete all the relevant documentation.

Evidencing AC3.3 to your assessor:

For AC3.3 you must evidence your skills in contributing to completing paperwork to apply for required resources, facilities and services, in a way that promotes active participation.

Assessment Method:

Direct Observation of your work practices.

● You can **show** your assessor how you contribute to completing paperwork to apply for required resources, facilities and services, in a way that promotes active participation.

REMEMBER TO:

● Make arrangements for **observation of your work practices**.

● Include evidence of you contributing to completing paperwork.

● Ensure the evidence you provide relates to applying for required resources, facilities and services, in a way that promotes active participation.

● Think about **your work setting** and how you contribute to completing paperwork to apply for required resources, facilities and services, in a way that promotes active participation.

Learning Outcome 3: Be able to work with individuals to secure additional services and facilities to enable them to live at home

Assessment Criterion 3.4: Obtain permission to provide additional information about the individual in order to secure resources, services and facilities

What does AC3.4 mean?

○ The lead words **obtain permission** mean that you must **be able to show** through **your work practices** how to gain the consent of an individual or a representative to provide additional information about the individual in order to secure resources, services and facilities.

○ Your **observations** of your work practices must include you obtaining permission from the individual or their representative.

○ For the key words **additional information** you can think about the personal details that may be required about an individual's well-being and circumstances.

○ For the key word **resources** you can think about obtaining personnel, support, finances, equipment and aids.

○ For the key words **services and facilities** you can think about obtaining access to organisations, systems, equipment and places available in the community.

Read the following **Real Work Setting** scenario and think about how it relates to your work setting and role:

Real Work Setting
Name: Alan
Job role: Senior Home Carer for older people
(See page 239 for a description of the role.)
Obtaining permission to provide additional information: Alan asks Doris whether she would be happy for him and her daughter to provide the Home Carers, the GP's surgery and the dentist with additional information about her mental well-being and how this can affect the way she interacts with others at times. Doris agrees with Alan and her daughter for them to share this information with others who have a need to know.

Evidencing AC3.4 to your assessor:

For AC3.4 you must evidence your skills in obtaining permission to provide additional information about the individual in order to secure resources, services and facilities.

Assessment Method:

Direct Observation of your work practices.

● You can **show** your assessor how you obtain permission to provide additional information about the individual in order to secure resources, services and facilities.

REMEMBER TO:
● Make arrangements for **observation of your work practices**.
● Include evidence of you obtaining permission to provide additional information about the individual.
● Ensure the evidence you provide relates to securing resources, services and facilities.
● Think about **your work setting** and how you obtain permission to provide additional information about the individual in order to secure resources, services and facilities.

Learning Outcome 4: Be able to work in partnership to introduce additional services for individuals living at home

Assessment Criterion 4.1: Agree roles and responsibilities for introducing additional support for an individual to live at home

What does AC4.1 mean?

○ The lead word **agree** means that you must **be able to show** through **your work practices** how to establish roles and responsibilities for introducing additional support for an individual to live at home.

○ Your **observations** of your work practices must include you agreeing roles and responsibilities.

○ For the key words **roles and responsibilities** you can think about how to establish the agreed duties and areas of responsibility for introducing additional support for an individual to live at home.

Read the following **Real Work Setting** scenario and think about how it relates to your work setting and role:

Real Work Setting
Name: Sabria
Job role: Senior Community Carer for young adults
Sabria has been working as a Senior Community Carer for one year. Her Senior responsibilities include: supporting and supervising Community Carers; mentoring new Community Carers; carrying out risk assessments; updating individuals' care plans; being part of the on-call rota for the delivery of a person-centred service.
Agreeing roles and responsibilities: Kathryn has been living at home with her husband, who until recently had been her main carer since she sustained a head injury. As her husband is no longer able to carry out tasks that require moving or lifting, Kathryn has contacted Sabria to see if additional support can be provided to enable her to continue to live in her own home. Kathryn has never used the services of employed Carers before, and both she and her husband are concerned that their home will no longer feel like their own and that Kathryn will not feel comfortable being supported by a stranger, in particular with personal care tasks. Sabria reassures Kathryn that her team of Carers has many years of experience and that Carers are carefully matched to individuals to ensure that all parties are in agreement about who is providing the support and how this will be done, and that everyone's roles and responsibilities are agreed and discussed before the support package commences.

Evidencing AC4.1 to your assessor:

For AC4.1 you must evidence your skills in agreeing roles and responsibilities for introducing additional support for an individual to live at home.

Assessment Method:

Direct Observation of your work practices.

● You can **show** your assessor how you agree roles and responsibilities for introducing additional support for an individual to live at home.

REMEMBER TO:

● Make arrangements for **observation** of **your work practices**.

● Include evidence of you agreeing roles and responsibilities.

● Ensure the evidence you provide relates to introducing additional support for an individual to live at home.

● Think about **your work setting** and how you agree roles and responsibilities for introducing additional support for an individual to live at home.

Learning Outcome 4: Be able to work in partnership to introduce additional services for individuals living at home

Assessment Criterion 4.2: Introduce the individual to new resources, services and facilities or support groups

What does AC4.2 mean?

○ The lead word **introduce** means that you must **be able to show** through **your work practices** how to support an individual to consider new resources, services, facilities or support groups.

○ Your **observations** of your work practices must include you introducing an individual to additional resources, services, facilities or support groups.

○ For the key word **resources** you can think about how to introduce an individual to new personnel, support, finances, equipment and aids.

○ For the key words **services and facilities** you can think about how to introduce an individual to new organisations, systems, equipment and places available in the community.

○ For the key words **support groups** you can think about how to introduce an individual to new groups, where members share common concerns and emotions to help each other.

Read the following **Real Work Setting** scenario and think about how it relates to your work setting and role:

Real Work Setting

Name: Sabria

Job role: Senior Community Carer for young adults

(See page 243 for a description of the role.)

Introducing new resources, services and facilities or support groups: Sabria agrees to set up an initial meeting between Kathryn, her husband and the three Home Carers who Sabria thinks would be a good match. Sabria adds that this initial meeting would provide Kathryn and her husband with an opportunity to meet the Home Carers and to ask them any questions they may have about how the support will work in practice. Sabria has also brought with her some leaflets about support groups available in the local area for individuals who have sustained head injuries.

Evidencing AC4.2 to your assessor:

For AC4.2 you must evidence your skills in introducing the individual to new resources, services and facilities or support groups.

Assessment Method:

Direct Observation of your work practices.

● You can **show** your assessor how you introduce the individual to new resources, services and facilities or support groups.

REMEMBER TO:
● Make arrangements for **observation** of **your work practices**.
● Include evidence of you introducing the individual to additional resources, services and facilities or support groups.
● Ensure the evidence you provide relates to new resources, services and facilities or support groups.
● Think about **your work setting** and how you introduce the individual to new resources, services and facilities or support groups.

Learning Outcome 4: Be able to work in partnership to introduce additional services for individuals living at home

Assessment Criterion 4.3: Record and report on the outcomes of additional support measures in required ways

What does AC4.3 mean?

- The lead words **record and report** mean that you must **be able to show** through **your work practices** how to document and share information in required ways on the outcomes of additional support measures.
- Your **observations** of your work practices must include you **recording and reporting**.
- For the key word **outcomes** you can think about how you document and share information on the effectiveness of additional support measures put in place.

Read the following **Real Work Setting** scenario and think about how it relates to your work setting and role:

Real Work Setting

Name: Sabria

Job role: Senior Community Carer for young adults

(See page 243 for a description of the role.)

Recording and reporting on outcomes: Sabria is meeting with Kathryn and her husband to review the effectiveness of the additional support measures that were put in place four weeks ago to enable Kathryn to continue to live at home. Both Kathryn and her husband are very pleased with how the additional support has worked in practice and both confirm that they get on very well with all three Home Carers, as all are very professional and support them in many different ways. Kathryn and her husband explain to Sabria that since having the package of support they both feel they can live their own lives again and be independent once more within their relationship. Kathryn's husband explains how he has noticed that Kathryn seems a lot more confident, and that attending the support group together has also shown them new ways of managing life after a head injury.

Evidencing AC4.3 to your assessor:

For AC4.3 you must evidence your skills in recording and reporting on the outcomes of additional support measures in required ways.

Assessment Method:

Direct Observation of your work practices.

- You can **show** your assessor how you record and report on the outcomes of additional support measures in required ways.

REMEMBER TO:

- Make arrangements for **observation** of **your work practices**.
- Include evidence of you recording and reporting in required ways.
- Ensure the evidence you provide relates to the outcomes of additional support measures.
- Think about **your work setting** and how you record and report on the outcomes of additional support measures in required ways.

Learning Outcome 5: Be able to contribute to reviewing support for living at home

Assessment Criterion 5.1: Work with the individual and others to agree methods and timescales for ongoing review

What does AC5.1 mean?

- The lead words **work with** mean that you must **be able to show** through **your work practices** how to support the individual and others to agree methods and timescales for ongoing review.
- Your **observations** of your work practices must include you working with the individual and others.
- For the key word **methods** you can think about the different ways of reviewing on an ongoing basis how an individual's support is working in practice.
- For the key word **timescales** you can think about the different factors that may determine how often and when an individual's support is reviewed.

Read the following **Real Work Setting** scenario and think about how it relates to your work setting and role:

Real Work Setting

Name: Paulette
Job role: Senior Home Carer for adults who have autism
Paulette has been working as a Senior Home Carer for seven years. Her Senior responsibilities include: day-to-day running of the service and the team of Home Carers; supporting individuals to administer medication; updating care plans and risk assessments; liaising with individuals, their families and other professionals involved in their lives.
Agreeing methods and timescales for ongoing review: Paulette has met with Zara, an individual who has recently started using the service, as well as her Home Care Worker, Weekend Support Worker and Social Worker to discuss how and when to review Zara's support package for living at home. Zara is not keen on continuing to hold meetings at her home on an ongoing basis but does want to meet up with everyone to review the support that has been put in place. Zara suggests that the next meeting could be held in her office; all agree to this. It is agreed that Zara would benefit from having at least twelve weeks to experience the support being delivered as it takes her a little while to become comfortable working with different people and to get used to different working approaches.

Evidencing AC5.1 to your assessor:

For AC5.1 you must evidence your skills in working with the individual and others to agree methods and timescales for ongoing review.

Assessment Method:
Direct Observation of your work practices.
- You can **show** your assessor how you work with the individual and others to agree methods and timescales for ongoing review.

REMEMBER TO:
- Make arrangements for **observation** of **your work practices**.
- Include evidence of you working with the individual and others.
- Ensure the evidence you provide relates to agreeing methods and timescales for ongoing review.
- Think about **your work setting** and how you work with an individual and others to agree methods and timescales for ongoing review.

Learning Outcome 5: Be able to contribute to reviewing support for living at home

Assessment Criterion 5.2: Identify any changes in an individual's circumstances that may indicate a need to adjust the type or level of support

What does AC5.2 mean?

○ The lead word **identify** means that you must **make clear** through **your work practices** how to note any changes in an individual's circumstances that may indicate a need to adjust the type or level of support.

○ Your **observations** of your work practices must include you identifying any changes in an individual's circumstances.

○ For the key word **circumstances** you can think about changes that may occur in an individual's life, for example in their relationships with others, their health, housing situation, social network, finances or legal status.

○ For the key word **adjust** you can think about how an individual's type of support may need to be amended and the level of support increased or reduced.

Read the following **Real Work Setting** scenario and think about how it relates to your work setting and role:

Real Work Setting

Name: Paulette

Job role: Senior Home Carer for adults who have autism

(See page 246 for a description of the role.)

Identifying changes in an individual's circumstances: Paulette has received a phone call from Zara's Social Worker, who has expressed concern over Zara's working relationship with one of the Home Carers. It appears from Zara's conversations with her Social Worker that she is having difficulty getting along with one Home Carer due to a personality clash. Paulette agrees to speak with Zara about the Social Worker's concerns and also with the Home Carer with whom Zara is having difficulties.

Evidencing AC5.2 to your assessor:

For AC5.2 you must evidence your skills in identifying any changes in an individual's circumstances that may indicate a need to adjust the type or level of support.

Assessment Method:

Direct Observation of your work practices.

● You can **show** your assessor or an expert witness how you identify any changes in an individual's circumstances that may indicate a need to adjust the type or level of support.

REMEMBER TO:

● Make arrangements for **observation of your work practices**.

● Include evidence of you identifying any changes in an individual's circumstances.

● Ensure the evidence you provide relates to an indication that there is a need to adjust the type or level of support.

● Think about **your work setting** and how you identify any changes in an individual's circumstances that may indicate a need to adjust the type or level of support.

Learning Outcome 5: Be able to contribute to reviewing support for living at home

Assessment Criterion 5.3: Work with the individual and others to agree revisions to the support provided

What does AC5.3 mean?

○ The lead words **work with** mean that you must **be able to show** through **your work practices** how to support the individual and others to agree revisions to the support provided.

○ Your **observations** of your work practices must include you working with the individual and others.

○ For the key word **revisions** you can think about how an individual's support may need to be updated and altered to fully meet their current needs and preferences.

Read the following **Real Work Setting** scenario and think about how it relates to your work setting and role:

Real Work Setting

Name: Paulette

Job role: Senior Home Carer for adults who have autism

(See page 246 for a description of the role.)

Agreeing revisions to the support provided: Following a meeting with Zara it has been agreed with her that the two Home Carers who currently provide her with support will continue to do so, and that Paulette will allocate a new Home Carer to Zara on a trial basis for one week to see how this works in practice. Paulette has also agreed with Zara to increase the monitoring of her support package with daily phone calls and has informed Zara's Social Worker of this. Paulette then documents the agreed revisions in Zara's support plan, makes Zara aware of these revisions and asks Zara to sign the revised support plan to indicate her agreement to this. Zara does so and thanks Paulette for her support and understanding.

Evidencing AC5.3 to your assessor:

For AC5.3 you must evidence your skills in working with the individual and others to agree revisions to the support provided.

Assessment Method:

Direct Observation of your work practices.

◑ You can **show** your assessor how you work with the individual and others to agree revisions to the support provided.

REMEMBER TO:

● Make arrangements for **observation** of **your work practices**.
● Include evidence of you working with the individual and others.
● Ensure the evidence you provide relates to agreeing revisions to the support provided.
● Think about **your work setting** and how you work with an individual and others to agree revisions to the support provided.

Learning Outcome 1: Understand specific communication needs and factors affecting them

Assessment Criterion 1.1: Explain the importance of meeting an individual's communication needs

What does AC1.1 mean?

- The lead word **explain** means that you must **make clear the reasons why** it is important to meet an individual's communication needs.
- Your **account** must make clear **details** of the importance of meeting an individual's communication needs.
- For the key words **communication needs** you can think about the ways in which individuals' communication needs vary, due to individuals' abilities, cultures and backgrounds, and the reasons why it is important that their needs are met.

Read the following **Real Work Setting** scenario and think about how it relates to your work setting and role:

Real Work Setting

Name: Jake

Job role: Senior Residential Worker for adults who have complex needs

Jake has been working as a Senior Residential Worker for seven years. His Senior responsibilities include: providing support to a team of Residential Workers; assisting the manager with the development of care plans and packages; supervising staff; developing staff rotas; liaising with individuals' families, friends, advocates and other professionals.

Meeting an individual's communication needs: Jake is delivering Day 1 of a six-day training session he has developed for the team of Residential Workers to whom he provides support. Day 1 focuses on the reasons why it is important to meet individuals' communication needs. Jake begins by explaining to the team that the five adults who live in the residential home communicate in different ways in different situations and with different people. Jake encourages the team to split into two groups and together discuss the reasons why it is important to meet individuals' communication needs. Jake suggests that during their discussions they may also like to think about the consequences of not meeting individuals' communication needs. One of the team members indicates that she is finding it very useful to focus her mind on the individuals the team supports and the importance of ensuring that they all meet their specific communication needs.

Evidencing AC1.1 to your assessor:

For AC1.1 you must evidence your understanding of specific communication needs and factors affecting them.

Assessment Methods:

Oral/Written Questioning or **Discussion** or a **Personal Statement** or **Reflection**.

- You can **tell** your assessor about the importance of meeting an individual's communication needs.
- Or, you can **talk** to your assessor about the importance of meeting an individual's communication needs.
- Or, you can write a **personal statement or reflection** about your experience of the importance of meeting an individual's communication needs.

REMEMBER TO:

- Provide an **account** and explain the importance of meeting an individual's communication needs.
- Include **details** about the reasons why meeting an individual's communication needs is important.
- Ensure your evidence relates to an individual's communication needs.
- Think about **your work setting** and the importance of meeting an individual's communication needs.

Learning Outcome 1: Understand specific communication needs and factors affecting them

Assessment Criterion 1.2: Explain how own role and practice can impact on communication with an individual who has specific communication needs

What does AC1.2 mean?

- The lead word **explain** means that you must **make clear how** your role and practice can impact on communication with an individual who has specific communication needs.
- Your **account** must make clear **details** of how your job role and work practices can have an impact.
- For the key words **role and practice** you can think about how the duties that form part of your job role and the way that you carry these out can affect your communication with an individual who has specific communication needs.

Read the following **Real Work Setting** scenario and think about how it relates to your work setting and role:

Real Work Setting
Name: Jake
Job role: Senior Residential Worker for adults who have complex needs
(See page 249 for a description of the role.)
Impact of your role and practice: Jake is delivering Day 2 of a six-day training session he has developed for the team of Residential Workers to whom he provides support. Day 2 focuses on how roles and work practices can have an impact on communication with individuals who have specific communication needs. Jake begins by sharing with the team an extract from his reflective diary about how his role as a Senior and his work practices have had an impact on the range of aids and communication systems that are now available at the home.

Evidencing AC1.2 to your assessor:

For AC1.2 you must evidence your understanding of how your role and practice can impact on communication with an individual who has specific communication needs.

Assessment Methods:

Oral/Written Questioning or **Discussion** or a **Personal Statement** or **Reflection**.

- You can **tell** your assessor how your role and practice can impact on communication with an individual who has specific communication needs.
- Or, you can **talk** to your assessor about how your role and practice can impact on communication with an individual who has specific communication needs.
- Or, you can write a **personal statement or reflection** about your experience of how your role and practice can impact on communication with an individual who has specific communication needs.

REMEMBER TO:

- Provide an **account** of how your role and practice can impact on communication with an individual who has specific communication needs.
- Include **details** and **examples** of how your role and practice can impact on communication with an individual who has specific communication needs.
- Think about **your work setting** and how your role and practice can impact on communication with an individual who has specific communication needs.

Learning Outcome 1: Understand specific communication needs and factors affecting them

Assessment Criterion 1.3: Analyse features of the environment that may help or hinder communication

What does AC1.3 mean?
- ⊙ The lead word **analyse** means that you must **examine in detail** the different features of the environment that may help or hinder communication.
- ⊙ Your **account** must provide an analysis of **different features** of the environment.
- ⊙ For the key words **features of the environment** you can think about how physical and social aspects of the environment may be helpful or obstructive to communication.

Read the following **Real Work Setting** scenario and think about how it relates to your work setting and role:

Real Work Setting

Name: Jake

Job role: Senior Residential Worker for adults who have complex needs

(See page 249 for a description of the role.)

Features of the environment: Jake is delivering Day 3 of a six-day training session he has developed for the team of Residential Workers to whom he provides support. Day 3 focuses on how the environment may help or hinder communication. Jake has devised two role plays for the team to take part in and observe; one involves a meeting between the manager and an individual and takes place in an individual's room, and the other involves a telephone conversation between a Residential Worker and an individual and takes place in the downstairs lounge. At the end of the each role play Jake talks through with the team what aspects of the environment they thought were both helpful and obstructive to the communication with both individuals.

Evidencing AC1.3 to your assessor:

For AC1.3 you must evidence your understanding of the features of the environment that may help or hinder communication.

Assessment Methods:

Oral/Written Questioning or Discussion or a **Personal Statement or Reflection**.

- You can **tell** your assessor about the features of the environment that may help or hinder communication.
- Or, you can **talk** to your assessor about the features of the environment that may help or hinder communication.
- Or, you can write a **personal statement or reflection** about your experience of the features of the environment that may help or hinder communication.

REMEMBER TO:
- Provide an **account** and an analysis of different features of the environment that may help or hinder communication.
- Include **details** about what each feature is, and **how and why** it may help or hinder communication.
- Include **varied examples** of features of the environment that may help or hinder communication.
- Think about **your work setting** and how the features of the environment may help or hinder communication.

Learning Outcome 1: Understand specific communication needs and factors affecting them

Assessment Criterion 1.4: Analyse reasons why an individual may use a form of communication that is not based on a formal language system

What does AC1.4 mean?

- The lead word **analyse** means that you must **examine in detail** the different reasons why an individual may use a form of communication that is not based on a formal language system.
- Your **account** must provide an analysis of **different reasons** why.
- For the key words **formal language system** you can think about the reasons why individuals may communicate using their own system of symbols, pictures, gestures, expressions, words, objects and sounds.

Read the following **Real Work Setting** scenario and think about how it relates to your work setting and role:

Real Work Setting

Name: Jake

Job role: Senior Residential Worker for adults who have complex needs

(See page 249 for a description of the role.)

Communication not based on a formal language system: Jake is delivering Day 4 of a six-day training session he has developed for the team of Residential Workers to whom he provides support. Day 4 focuses on why individuals may use a form of communication that is not based on a formal language system, and for today's training session Jake will be presenting to the team a case study of an individual who has chosen to use a mixture of pictures and facial expressions to communicate with others.

Evidencing AC1.4 to your assessor:

For AC1.4 you must evidence your understanding of the reasons why an individual may use a form of communication that is not based on a formal language system.

Assessment Methods:

Oral/Written Questioning or **Discussion** or a **Personal Statement** or **Reflection.**

- You can **tell** your assessor about the reasons why an individual may use a form of communication that is not based on a formal language system.
- Or, you can **talk** to your assessor about the reasons why an individual may use a form of communication that is not based on a formal language system.
- Or, you can write a **personal statement or reflection** about your experience of the reasons why an individual may use a form of communication that is not based on a formal language system.

REMEMBER TO:

- Provide an **account** and an **analysis** of the reasons why an individual may use a form of communication that is not based on a formal language system.
- Include **varied** examples of the reasons why.
- Think about **your work setting** and why an individual may use a form of communication that is not based on a formal language system.

Learning Outcome 1: Understand specific communication needs and factors affecting them

Assessment Criterion 1.5: Identify a range of communication methods and aids to support individuals to communicate

What does AC1.5 mean?

- The lead word **identify** means that you must **make clear** a range of communication methods and aids to support individuals to communicate.
- Your **list** must make clear a range of **both** communication methods and aids.
- For the key words **communication methods** you can think about the different verbal and non-verbal ways that can be used to support individuals to communicate.
- For the key words **communication aids** you can think about the different technological aids and people that can be used to support individuals to communicate, such as a Dynavox, Lightwriter, Translator, Interpreter or Advocate.

Read the following **Real Work Setting** scenario and think about how it relates to your work setting and role:

Real Work Setting

Name: Jake

Job role: Senior Residential Worker for adults who have complex needs

(See page 249 for a description of the role.)

Communication methods and aids: Jake is delivering Day 5 of a six-day training session he has developed for the team of Residential Workers to whom he provides support. Day 5 focuses on the range of communication methods and aids that are available to support individuals to communicate. For today's session Jake has arranged for a Speech Therapist to visit the team and show them the range of technological aids, people, techniques and methods that can be used to support individuals to communicate.

Evidencing AC1.5 to your assessor:

For AC1.5 you must evidence your understanding of a range of communication methods and aids to support individuals to communicate.

Assessment Methods:

Oral/Written Questioning or Discussion or a Spidergram.

- You can **tell** your assessor about a range of communication methods and aids to support individuals to communicate.
- Or, you can **talk** to your assessor about a range of communication methods and aids to support individuals to communicate.
- Or, you can complete a **spidergram** showing a range of communication methods and aids to support individuals to communicate.

REMEMBER TO:

- Provide a **range** of **both** communication methods and aids.
- Include a **list** of different communication methods and aids that can be used to support individuals to communicate.
- Think about **your work setting** and the range of communication methods and aids to support individuals to communicate.

Learning Outcome 1: Understand specific communication needs and factors affecting them

Assessment Criterion 1.6: Describe the potential effects on an individual of having unmet communication needs

What does AC1.6 mean?

- The lead word **describe** means that you must provide an **account** that **details** the potential effects on an individual of having unmet communication needs.
- Your **account** must detail **different** potential effects on an individual.
- For the key words **unmet communication needs** you can think about the effects on an individual if they are unable to communicate or be understood by others.

Read the following **Real Work Setting** scenario and think about how it relates to your work setting and role:

Real Work Setting

Name: Jake

Job role: Senior Residential Worker for adults who have complex needs

(See page 249 for a description of the role.)

Potential effects of unmet communication needs: Jake is delivering Day 6 of a six-day training session he has developed for the team of Residential Workers to whom he provides support. Day 6 focuses on the potential effects on individuals of having unmet communication needs. Jake has researched and obtained a series of short video clips of individuals living in a range of different settings. In these, the individuals share their experiences of how not having their communication needs met made them feel and how it affected the way they interacted with others and how they lived their lives. One of the individuals the team provides support to has also asked to share his experiences of not having his communication needs met when he visited a friend in hospital.

Evidencing AC1.6 to your assessor:

For AC1.6 you must evidence your understanding of the potential effects on an individual of having unmet communication needs.

Assessment Methods:

Oral/Written Questioning or **Discussion** or a **Personal Statement** or **Reflection**.

- You can **tell** your assessor about the potential effects on an individual of having unmet communication needs.
- Or, you can **talk** to your assessor about the potential effects on an individual of having unmet communication needs.
- Or, you can write a **personal statement or reflection** about your experience of the potential effects on an individual of having unmet communication needs.

REMEMBER TO:

- Provide a detailed **account** of the potential effects on an individual of having unmet communication needs.
- Include **details** about different potential effects.
- Include **varied** examples of how having unmet communication needs may affect an individual.
- Think about **your work setting** and the potential effects on an individual of having unmet communication needs.

Learning Outcome 2: Be able to contribute to establishing the nature of individuals' specific communication needs and ways to address them

Assessment Criterion 2.1: Work in partnership with the individual and others to identify the individual's specific communication needs

What does AC2.1 mean?

- The lead words **work in partnership** mean that you must **be able to show** through **your work practices** how to work together with the individual and others to identify the individual's specific communication needs.
- Your **observations** of your work practices must include you working with the individual and others.
- The key word **others** may include family, advocates, specialist communication professionals or others important to the individual's well-being.
- For the key words **specific communication needs** you can think about the ways in which individuals' communication needs are unique and may vary in different situations and with different people due to individuals' abilities, cultures and backgrounds.

Read the following **Real Work Setting** scenario and think about how it relates to your work setting and role:

Real Work Setting

Name: Margarita

Job role: Senior Day Centre Officer for adults

Margarita has been working as a Senior Day Centre Officer for two years. Her Senior responsibilities include: assessing the needs of the individuals who use the service; monitoring individuals' progress; carrying out reviews, administering medication; providing support and supervision to a team of Care Assistants and volunteers; liaising with external professionals and agencies.

Identifying an individual's specific communication needs: Margarita is meeting with Lorraine today, who would like to attend the day centre three days a week. Lorraine has had a stroke and finds it difficult to express what she wants. Lorraine and her family have developed a set of key words and photographs of objects and people, and Lorraine uses these with them on a daily basis to express what she is feeling, thinking about and/or wants. A Speech and Language Therapist from the stroke rehabilitation unit is also still working with Lorraine to help her overcome communication difficulties. Margarita has arranged for Lorraine's family and her Speech and Language Therapist to also be present today.

Evidencing AC2.1 to your assessor:

For AC2.1 you must evidence your skills in working in partnership with the individual and others to identify the individual's specific communication needs.

Assessment Method:

Direct Observation of your work practices.

- You can **show** your assessor how you work with the individual and others to identify the individual's specific communication needs.

REMEMBER TO:

- Make arrangements for **observation** of **your work practices**.
- Include evidence of you working with the individual and others.
- Ensure the evidence you provide relates to **identifying** the individual's specific communication needs.
- Think about **your work setting** and how you work with an individual and others to identify the individual's specific communication needs.

Learning Outcome 2: Be able to contribute to establishing the nature of individuals' specific communication needs and ways to address them

Assessment Criterion 2.2: Contribute to identifying the communication methods or aids that will best suit the individual

What does AC2.2 mean?

- The lead words **contribute to** mean that you must **be able to show** through **your work practices** how to share your views and ideas for identifying the communication methods or aids that will best suit the individual.
- Your **observations** of your work practices must include you identifying suitable communication methods or aids.
- For the key words **communication methods** you can think about the different verbal and non-verbal ways of communicating that can be used that will best suit the individual.
- For the key words **communication aids** you can think about the different technological aids and people that can be used that will best suit the individual.

Read the following **Real Work Setting** scenario and think about how it relates to your work setting and role:

Real Work Setting

Name: Margarita

Job role: Senior Day Centre Officer for adults

(See page 255 for a description of the role.)

Identifying communication methods or aids: During the meeting arranged with Lorraine, Margarita asks whether she has considered placing the set of key words and photographs of objects and people that she uses with her family in a communication book. Margarita also puts forward the idea of Lorraine using an electronic voice output communication aid with a keyboard so that the words she types can be converted into speech, because although Lorraine has difficulties speaking she can write and enjoys typing.

Evidencing AC2.2 to your assessor:

For AC2.2 you must evidence your skills in contributing to identifying the communication methods or aids that will best suit the individual.

Assessment Method:

Direct Observation of your work practices.

- You can **show** your assessor how you contribute to identifying the communication methods or aids that will best suit the individual.

REMEMBER TO:
- Make arrangements for **observation of your work practices**.
- Include evidence of your contributions to **identifying** communication methods or aids.
- Ensure the evidence you provide relates to the communication methods or aids that will best suit the individual.
- Think about **your work setting** and how you contribute to identifying the communication methods or aids that will best suit the individual.

Learning Outcome 2: Be able to contribute to establishing the nature of individuals' specific communication needs and ways to address them

Assessment Criterion 2.3: Explain how and when to access information and support about identifying and addressing specific communication needs

What does AC2.3 mean?

- ○ The lead word **explain** means that you must **make clear how and when** to access information and support about identifying and addressing specific communication needs.
- ○ Your **account** must make clear **details** of how and when to access information and support.
- ○ For the key word **information** you can think about how to find out about identifying and addressing individuals' specific communication needs and when you may be required to do so.
- ○ For the key word **support** you can think about the informal and formal sources of practical, emotional and financial support that are available for identifying and addressing individuals' specific communication needs, and how and when to access these.

Read the following **Real Work Setting** scenario and think about how it relates to your work setting and role:

Real Work Setting

Name: Margarita

Job role: Senior Day Centre Officer for adults

(See page 255 for a description of the role.)

Accessing information and support: During the meeting with Lorraine, Margarita asks the Speech Therapist present whether she or the stroke unit would be able to provide her with any more specific information about the techniques and methods they use when communicating with Lorraine so that she can then share this information with her team.

Evidencing AC2.3 to your assessor:

For AC2.3 you must evidence your knowledge of how and when to access information and support about identifying and addressing specific communication needs.

Assessment Methods:

Oral/Written Questioning or **Discussion** or a **Personal Statement** or **Reflection**.

- You can **tell** your assessor about how and when to access information and support about identifying and addressing specific communication needs.
- Or, you can **talk** to your assessor about how and when to access information and support about identifying and addressing specific communication needs.
- Or, you can write a **personal statement or reflection** about your experience of how and when to access information and support about identifying and addressing specific communication needs.

REMEMBER TO:

- Provide an **account** and explain how and when to access information and support about identifying and addressing specific communication needs.
- Include **details** and examples of how and when to access both information and support.
- Ensure your evidence relates to identifying and addressing specific communication needs.
- Think about **your work setting** and how and when to access information and support about identifying and addressing specific communication needs.

Learning Outcome 3: Be able to interact with individuals using their preferred method of communication

Assessment Criterion 3.1: Prepare the environment to facilitate communication

What does AC3.1 mean?

- The lead word **prepare** means that you must **be able to show** through **your work practices** how to arrange the environment to facilitate communication.
- Your **observations** of your work practices must include you preparing the environment.
- For the key word **environment** you can think about both the physical and social aspects that you will need to take into consideration to facilitate communication with an individual.

Read the following **Real Work Setting** scenario and think about how it relates to your work setting and role:

Real Work Setting
Name: Boris
Job role: Senior Support Worker for deaf and hard of hearing adults
Boris has been working as a Senior Support Worker for four years. His Senior responsibilities include: supporting a team of Support Workers to deliver a person-centred service; supervising Support Workers; attending management meetings; facilitating meetings to ensure the involvement of all individuals in the running of the service; enabling individuals to plan, implement, monitor and review their support on an ongoing basis.
Preparing the environment: Boris has arranged to meet with Ben to discuss his current support plan, as at the last group meeting Ben indicated that there were some aspects of his support that he wanted to change. In preparation for this meeting Boris has ensured that the private room they are meeting in is well lit and that he has placed their chairs in an area of the room where both their faces will be clearly visible to each other. Boris has also checked that the dishwasher in the kitchen next door is switched off and that he has closed the kitchen door to try and reduce the background noise. Finally, Boris has ensured that the FM System, a wireless assistive hearing device that enhances the use of hearing aids and assists people who are hard of hearing but who do not wear hearing aids, is switched on and working properly.

Evidencing AC3.1 to your assessor:

For AC3.1 you must evidence your skills in preparing the environment to facilitate communication.

Assessment Method:

Direct Observation of your work practices.

- You can **show** your assessor how you prepare the environment to facilitate communication.

REMEMBER TO:
- Make arrangements for **observation** of **your work practices**.
- Include evidence of you preparing the environment.
- Ensure the evidence you provide relates to facilitating communication.
- Think about **your work setting** and how you prepare the environment to facilitate communication.

Learning Outcome 3: Be able to interact with individuals using their preferred method of communication

Assessment Criterion 3.2: Use agreed methods of communication to interact with the individual

What does AC3.2 mean?

- The lead word **use** means that you must **be able to show** through **your work practices** how to put into practice agreed methods of communication to interact with the individual.
- Your **observations** of your work practices must include using agreed methods of communication.
- For the key words **methods of communication** you can think about the different verbal and non-verbal ways that can be used to interact with the individual and why these methods are agreed.

Read the following **Real Work Setting** scenario and think about how it relates to your work setting and role:

Real Work Setting

Name: Boris

Job role: Senior Support Worker for deaf and hard of hearing adults

(See page 258 for a description of the role.)

Using agreed communication methods: Boris begins the meeting with Ben by checking with him that he understands the purpose of today's meeting and can hear what Boris is saying to him. Ben confirms that he can; he then tells Boris that he is unhappy over the hours of support that he is receiving, as he feels that they are insufficient for everything he wants support with in his flat. Boris explains the agreed support hours and how they are to be used to Ben by speaking clearly and not too fast. Boris ensures that he makes eye contact with Ben whilst discussing his support plan with him and gives him time to read and ask questions about what support has been agreed.

Evidencing AC3.2 to your assessor:

For AC3.2 you must evidence your skills in using agreed methods of communication to interact with the individual.

Assessment Method:

Direct Observation of your work practices.

- You can **show** your assessor how you use agreed methods of communication to interact with the individual.

REMEMBER TO:

- Make arrangements for **observation of your work practices**.
- Include evidence of you using agreed methods of communication.
- Ensure the evidence you provide relates to interacting with the individual.
- Think about **your work setting** and how you use agreed methods of communication to interact with the individual.

Learning Outcome 3: Be able to interact with individuals using their preferred method of communication

Assessment Criterion 3.3: Monitor the individual's responses during and after the interaction to check the effectiveness of communication

What does AC3.3 mean?

◯ The lead word **monitor** means that you must **be able to show** through **your work practices** how to observe and check the individual's responses during and after the interaction to check the effectiveness of communication.

◯ Your **observations** of your work practices must include you monitoring the individual's responses during and after the interaction.

◯ For the key words **effectiveness of communication** you can think about the different ways of checking whether an individual has understood the communication.

Read the following **Real Work Setting** scenario and think about how it relates to your work setting and role:

Real Work Setting

Name: Boris

Job role: Senior Support Worker for deaf and hard of hearing adults

(See page 258 for a description of the role.)

Monitoring the individual's responses: Boris is meeting with his manager for supervision and updates him on the concerns that Ben has raised regarding the number of support hours he is receiving. Boris explains to his manager that he thinks the meeting fully addressed his concerns because Ben spoke to him the following day to tell him that their meeting had helped him gain a better understanding of the role of his Support Worker and that he agreed with the support hours that he is receiving. Boris adds that he also noted that during the meeting Ben developed a calm and relaxed posture and seemed to have a positive outlook by the end. Boris concludes that the meeting with Ben and approaching him in the way he did worked well.

Evidencing AC3.3 to your assessor:

For AC3.3 you must evidence your skills in monitoring the individual's responses during and after the interaction to check the effectiveness of communication.

Assessment Method:

Direct Observation of your work practices.

● You can **show** your assessor how you monitor the individual's responses during and after the interaction to check the effectiveness of communication.

REMEMBER TO:

● Make arrangements for **observation** of **your work practices**.
● Include evidence of you monitoring the individual's responses during and after the interaction.
● Ensure the evidence you provide relates to checking the effectiveness of communication.
● Think about **your work setting** and how you monitor the individual's responses during and after the interaction to check the effectiveness of communication.

Learning Outcome 3: Be able to interact with individuals using their preferred method of communication

Assessment Criterion 3.4: Adapt own practice to improve communication with the individual

What does AC3.4 mean?

- The lead word **adapt** means that you must **be able to show** through **your work practices** how to change your practice to improve communication with the individual.
- Your **observations** of your work practices must include you adapting your practice to improve communication with the individual.
- For the key word **practice** you can think about how to change your style, methods and approaches to improve communication with the individual.

Read the following **Real Work Setting** scenario and think about how it relates to your work setting and role:

Real Work Setting

Name: Boris

Job role: Senior Support Worker for deaf and hard of hearing adults

(See page 258 for a description of the role.)

Adapting your practice: Boris concludes his supervision with his manager by reflecting on how he has adapted his practice to improve communications with Ben. His manager provides him with feedback and explains how he has observed Boris change the way he communicates not only with Ben, but also with the other individuals he supports since he attended the residential training course last year on effective communication with people with hearing loss. His manager goes on to explain that examples of how he has changed his practice have related to spending time preparing for communications, being more aware of his facial expressions and hand gestures, as well as listening to and observing other colleagues who are more experienced than him.

Evidencing AC3.4 to your assessor:

For AC3.4 you must evidence your skills in adapting your practice to improve communication with the individual.

Assessment Method:

Direct Observation of your work practices.

- You can **show** your assessor or an expert witness how you adapt your practice to improve communication with the individual.

REMEMBER TO:
- Make arrangements for **observation** of **your work practices**.
- Include evidence of you adapting your practice.
- Ensure the evidence you provide relates to improving communication with the individual.
- Think about **your work setting** and how you adapt your practice to improve communication with the individual.

Learning Outcome 4: Be able to promote communication between individuals and others

Assessment Criterion 4.1: Support the individual to develop communication methods that will help them to understand others and be understood by them

What does AC4.1 mean?

- The lead word **support** means that you must **be able to show** through **your work practices** how to assist the individual in developing communication methods that will help them to understand others and be understood by them.
- Your **observations** of your work practices must include you assisting an individual.
- For the key words **communication methods** you can think about the different verbal and non-verbal ways that will help the individual to understand others and be understood by them.

Read the following **Real Work Setting** scenario and think about how it relates to your work setting and role:

Real Work Setting

Name: Samantha

Job role: Senior Community Worker for adults who have multiple learning disabilities

Samantha has been working as a Senior Community Worker for one year. Her Senior responsibilities include: leading a team of Community Workers to provide a high quality service; enabling individuals to live active lives with greater independence; supervising and guiding the team of Community Workers to implement person-centred planning, communication approaches and positive risk taking; liaising with individuals, their families and all others involved in their lives.

Supporting the individual to develop communication methods: Samantha has spent the last six months working closely with Moira to get to know how she communicates and to find effective ways of communicating with her, as Moira finds it difficult to understand written words and symbols. Samantha has supported Moira to explore the use of objects of reference to help Moira understand what is going to happen next or what is being discussed, by linking the object to a specific activity and thus giving the object a specific meaning. This has meant Moira has been able to be more actively involved in making her own choices and to express what she likes, dislikes and wants.

Evidencing AC4.1 to your assessor:

For AC4.1 you must evidence your skills in supporting the individual to develop communication methods that will help them to understand others and be understood by them.

Assessment Method:

Direct Observation of your work practices.

- You can **show** your assessor how you support the individual to develop communication methods that will help them to understand others and be understood by them.

REMEMBER TO:

- Make arrangements for **observation** of **your work practices**.
- Include evidence of you supporting the individual to develop communication methods.
- Ensure the evidence you provide includes communication methods that will help the individual to understand others and be understood by them.
- Think about **your work setting** and how you support the individual to develop communication methods that will help them to understand others and be understood by them.

Learning Outcome 4: Be able to promote communication between individuals and others

Assessment Criterion 4.2: Provide opportunities for the individual to communicate with others

What does AC4.2 mean?

- The lead words **provide opportunities** mean that you must **be able to show** through **your work practices** how to make available occasions for the individual to communicate with others.
- Your **observations** of your work practices must include you providing opportunities.
- For the key word **others** you can think about the different people with whom individuals may communicate, such as their family, friends, advocate, professionals.

Read the following **Real Work Setting** scenario and think about how it relates to your work setting and role:

Real Work Setting

Name: Samantha

Job role: Senior Community Worker for adults who have multiple learning disabilities

(See page 262 for a description of the role.)

Providing opportunities to communicate with others: Samantha has met with the team of Community Workers. She has updated them on Moira's preferred method of communication involving objects of reference, and also shared with them a digital recording she has completed so that they can see how Moira uses objects of reference to communicate her choices, wishes, likes and dislikes. Samantha has also written a guide for use by the Community Workers to help them understand the purpose and use of objects of reference for Moira. Samantha has also met with Moira's sister, mother and father and all three have observed Samantha use objects of reference with Moira. Samantha has noted that Moira seems less frustrated and happier in herself and is beginning to lead communications with others.

Evidencing AC4.2 to your assessor:

For AC4.2 you must evidence your skills in providing opportunities for the individual to communicate with others.

Assessment Method:

Direct Observation of your work practices.

- You can **show** your assessor how you provide opportunities for the individual to communicate with others.

REMEMBER TO:

- Make arrangements for **observation** of **your work practices**.
- Include evidence of you providing opportunities for the individual to communicate with others.
- Ensure the evidence you provide includes communication with others.
- Think about **your work setting** and how you provide opportunities for the individual to communicate with others.

Learning Outcome 4: Be able to promote communication between individuals and others

Assessment Criterion 4.3: Support others to understand and interpret the individual's communication

What does AC4.3 mean?

- The lead word **support** means that you must **be able to show** through **your work practices** how to assist others to understand and interpret the individual's communication.
- Your **observations** of your work practices must include you supporting others.
- For the key word **others** you can think about the different people with whom individuals may communicate, such as their family, friends, advocate or professionals.
- For the key words **understand and interpret** you can think about the different ways you can support the different people with whom individuals may communicate to comprehend the meaning of the individual's communication.

Read the following **Real Work Setting** scenario and think about how it relates to your work setting and role:

Real Work Setting

Name: Samantha

Job role: Senior Community Worker for adults who have multiple learning disabilities

(See page 262 for a description of the role.)

Supporting others to understand and interpret: Samantha has agreed for each member of the team to shadow her when working with Moira so that they can experience how to use the objects of reference effectively with Moira. Samantha has also spent some more time with Moira's family and talked through with them the digital recording of Moira using objects of reference so that she can fully explain the interactions to members of the team. These methods have proved to be very effective as Samantha has noticed how all those involved in Moira's life are beginning to have more effective communications with her.

Evidencing AC4.3 to your assessor:

For AC4.3 you must evidence your skills in supporting others to understand and interpret the individual's communication.

Assessment Method:

Direct Observation of your work practices.

- You can **show** your assessor how you support others to understand and interpret the individual's communication.

REMEMBER TO:

- Make arrangements for **observation** of **your work practices**.
- Include evidence of you supporting others.
- Ensure the evidence includes providing support to others so that they can understand and interpret the individual's communication.
- Think about **your work setting** and how you support others to understand and interpret the individual's communication.

Learning Outcome 4: Be able to promote communication between individuals and others

Assessment Criterion 4.4: Support others to be understood by the individual by use of agreed communication methods

What does AC4.4 mean?

- The lead word **support** means that you must **be able to show** through **your work practices** how to assist others to be understood by the individual by use of agreed communication methods.
- Your **observations** of your work practices must include you supporting others.
- For the key word **others** you can think about the different people with whom individuals may communicate, such as their family, friends, advocate, professionals.
- For the key words **agreed communication methods** you can think about the different ways that you can support others to be understood by the individual.

Read the following **Real Work Setting** scenario and think about how it relates to your work setting and role:

Real Work Setting

Name: Samantha

Job role: Senior Community Worker for adults who have multiple learning disabilities

(See page 262 for a description of the role.)

Supporting others to be understood by the individual: Samantha continues to work on an ongoing basis with both her team and Moira's family to ensure that they are able to use the objects of reference in a way that is understood by Moira so that their communications are effective and fully engage Moira as an active participant.

Evidencing AC4.4 to your assessor:

For AC4.4 you must evidence your skills in supporting others to be understood by the individual by use of agreed communication methods.

Assessment Method:

Direct Observation of your work practices.

- You can **show** your assessor how you support others to be understood by the individual by use of agreed communication methods.

REMEMBER TO:

- Make arrangements for **observation** of **your work practices**.
- Include evidence of you supporting others.
- Ensure the evidence includes you supporting others to be understood by the individual by use of agreed communication methods.
- Think about **your work setting** and how you support others to be understood by the individual by use of agreed communication methods.

Learning Outcome 5: Know how to support the use of communication technology and aids

Assessment Criterion 5.1: Identify specialist services relating to communication technology and aids

What does AC5.1 mean?

- The lead word **identify** means that you must **make clear** the different specialist services that exist relating to communication technology and aids.
- Your **list** must make clear services relating to **both communication technology and aids**.
- For the key words **specialist services** you can think about different organisations that may provide information, equipment and support relating to communication technology and aids.
- For the key words **communication technology** you can think about the different services that are available to support individuals to communicate using technology such as audio and visual media, telephones, mobiles and e-mail.
- For the key words **communication aids** you can think about the different services that are available to support individuals to communicate with technological and human aids, such as a Dynavox, a Lightwriter, a Translator, an Interpreter or Advocate.

Read the following **Real Work Setting** scenario and think about how it relates to your work setting and role:

Real Work Setting

Name: Kevin

Job role: Senior Care Assistant for older people

Kevin has been working as a Senior Care Assistant for eleven years. His Senior responsibilities include: leading shifts; allocating and monitoring tasks completed by Care Assistants; updating individuals' service plans; administering medication; supporting individuals with daily activities; liaising with individuals' families.

Specialist services: Kevin is reviewing the service's capacity for supporting the use of communication technology and aids, and begins by enquiring with the Assistive Technology Team about the range of services they provide. Kevin is informed that the service is open to individuals of all ages and that services provided include training for both individuals and staff, the provision of equipment and support with applications for funding for equipment, assessment, and ongoing advice and support. To raise awareness amongst the team of other specialist services that are available relating to communication technology and aids, Kevin has asked each member of the team to find out what is available and bring their findings with them to the team meeting this week.

Evidencing AC5.1 to your assessor:

For AC5.1 you must evidence your knowledge of the different specialist services relating to communication technology and aids.

Assessment Methods:

Oral/Written Questioning or Discussion or a **Spidergram**.

- You can **tell** your assessor about the different specialist services relating to communication technology and aids.
- Or, you can **talk** to your assessor about the different specialist services relating to communication technology and aids.
- Or, you can complete a **spidergram** showing the different specialist services relating to communication technology and aids.

REMEMBER TO:

- Provide examples of **different** specialist services.
- Ensure that the examples you provide relate to communication technology and aids.
- Think about the specialist services relating to communication technology and aids accessible from **your work setting** and in the local authority in which you work.

Learning Outcome 5: Know how to support the use of communication technology and aids

Assessment Criterion 5.2: Describe types of support that an individual may need in order to use communication technology and aids

What does AC5.2 mean?

- The lead word **describe** means that you must provide an **account** that **details** the types of support that an individual may need in order to use communication technology and aids.
- Your **account** must detail **different** types of support that an individual may need.
- For the key words **types of support** you can think about the formal and informal types of practical, emotional and financial support that an individual may need in order to use communication technology and aids.
- For the key words **communication technology and aids** you can think about the types of support that an individual may need in order to use electronic devices such as audiobooks, tablets and apps, and non-electronic equipment such as picture communication cards, communication books or an E-tran frame to facilitate communication and independence.

Read the following **Real Work Setting** scenario and think about how it relates to your work setting and role:

Real Work Setting

Name: Kevin

Job role: Senior Care Assistant for older people

(See page 266 for a description of the role.)

Types of support: Kevin has met with the Assistive Technology Team to gain a better understanding of the types of support that an individual may need in order to be able to use communication technology and aids. Kevin plans to share this information with his team at their next meeting.

Evidencing AC5.2 to your assessor:

For AC5.2 you must evidence your knowledge of how to support the use of communication technology and aids.

Assessment Methods:

Oral/Written Questioning or **Discussion** or a **Personal Statement** or **Reflection**.

- You can **tell** your assessor about the types of support that an individual may need in order to use communication technology and aids.
- Or, you can **talk** to your assessor about the types of support that an individual may need in order to use communication technology and aids.
- Or, you can write a **personal statement or reflection** about your experience of the types of support that an individual may need in order to use communication technology and aids.

REMEMBER TO:

- Provide a detailed **account** of how to support the use of communication technology and aids.
- Include **details** about different types of support that an individual may need in order to use communication technology and aids.
- Think about **your work setting** and the types of support that an individual may need in order to use communication technology and aids.

AC 5.3

Learning Outcome 5: Know how to support the use of communication technology and aids

Assessment Criterion 5.3: Explain the importance of ensuring that communication equipment is correctly set up and working properly

What does AC5.3 mean?

- The lead word **explain** means that you must **make clear** the importance of ensuring that communication equipment is correctly set up and working properly.
- Your **account** must make clear the reasons why it is important to ensure that communication equipment is correctly set up and working properly.
- For the key words **communication equipment** you can think about virtually operated communication equipment, as well as electronic devices such as audiobooks, tablets and apps, and non-electronic communication equipment such as picture communication cards, communication books or an E-tran frame to facilitate communication and independence.

Read the following **Real Work Setting** scenario and think about how it relates to your work setting and role:

Real Work Setting

Name: Kevin

Job role: Senior Care Assistant for older people

(See page 266 for a description of the role.)

Communication equipment: Kevin holds a team meeting and allocates the first half of this to information sharing about how the team can support individuals with the use of technology and aids. Kevin begins by explaining why it is important that each member of the team understands how to set up the communication equipment correctly and the checks to carry out to ensure that it is working properly.

Evidencing AC5.3 to your assessor:

For AC5.3 you must evidence your knowledge of the importance of ensuring that communication equipment is correctly set up and working properly.

Assessment Methods:

Oral/Written Questioning or Discussion or a Personal Statement or Reflection.

- You can **tell** your assessor about the importance of ensuring that communication equipment is correctly set up and working properly.
- Or, you can **talk** to your assessor about the importance of ensuring that communication equipment is correctly set up and working properly.
- Or, you can write a **personal statement or reflection** about your experience of the importance of ensuring that communication equipment is correctly set up and working properly.

REMEMBER TO:

- Provide an **account** and explain the **reasons** why it is important to ensure that communication equipment is correctly set up and working properly.
- Include **details** and examples of the importance of ensuring that communication equipment is correctly set up and working properly.
- Ensure your evidence relates to communication equipment.
- Think about **your work setting** and the importance of ensuring that communication equipment is correctly set up and working properly.

Learning Outcome 6: Be able to review an individual's communication needs and the support provided to address them

Assessment Criterion 6.1: Collate information about an individual's communication and the support provided

What does AC6.1 mean?

- The lead word **collate** means that you must **be able to show** through **your work practices** how to gather information about an individual's communication and the support provided.
- Your **observations** of your work practices must include you collating information.
- For the key word **information** you can think about how you would obtain the necessary details about how an individual communicates and the support that is required through maintaining records, observing the individual and asking for feedback from the individual and others involved in their lives.

Read the following **Real Work Setting** scenario and think about how it relates to your work setting and role:

Real Work Setting

Name: Sue

Job role: Senior Carer for young adults

Sue has been working as a Senior Carer for nine months. Her Senior responsibilities include: supervising a small team of Carers; providing support to individuals; assisting in updating individuals' care plans; maintaining accurate records; liaising with individuals, their families, other professionals and external agencies.

Collating information: Ruby's care review is due next month and Sue will be supporting Ruby to organise this. In preparation for this Sue has been collating information over the last six months about Ruby's communication needs and the support she receives. Sue has collated different types of information from a variety of sources. She has met with Ruby regularly to establish directly with her what her current communication needs are and the support she is receiving. Sue and her team have kept detailed records about Ruby's preferred communication methods, including how communications are facilitated to promote Ruby's independence. Observations have also been completed at the day service that Ruby attends, and Ruby's family and advocate have also shared their observations, views and ideas.

Evidencing AC6.1 to your assessor:

For AC6.1 you must evidence your skills in collating information about an individual's communication and the support provided.

Assessment Method:

Direct Observation of your work practices.

- You can **show** your assessor how you collate information about an individual's communication and the support provided.

REMEMBER TO:

- Make arrangements for **observation** of **your work practices**.
- Include evidence of you collating information.
- Ensure the evidence relates to an individual's communication and the support provided.
- Think about **your work setting** and how you collate information about an individual's communication and the support provided.

Learning Outcome 6: Be able to review an individual's communication needs and the support provided to address them

Assessment Criterion 6.2: Contribute to evaluating the effectiveness of agreed methods of communication and support provided

What does AC6.2 mean?

- The lead word **contribute** means that you must **be able to show** through **your work practices** how to share your views and ideas for evaluating the effectiveness of agreed methods of communication and support provided.
- Your **observations** of your work practices must include you contributing to evaluating.
- For the key word **evaluating** you can think about how to assess the effectiveness of agreed methods of communication and support provided.

Read the following **Real Work Setting** scenario and think about how it relates to your work setting and role:

Real Work Setting

Name: Sue

Job role: Senior Carer for young adults

(See page 269 for a description of the role.)

Evaluating communication methods and support: As part of Ruby's review, Sue shares with Ruby and those in attendance the communication methods that she feels have worked well and have facilitated Ruby's independence in communicating with others. Sue encourages Ruby to share the digital recordings that show how effective the communication passport she is using has been when communicating with others at home, in the day service she attends and when out and about in the community. Sue then details all those involved in supporting Ruby with her communication and talks about the value of having an independent source of support in Ruby's advocate, who has been very good at ensuring Ruby's needs and preferences remain at the centre of all support provided.

Evidencing AC6.2 to your assessor:

For AC6.2 you must evidence your skills in contributing to evaluating the effectiveness of agreed methods of communication and support provided.

Assessment Method:

Direct Observation of your work practices.

- You can **show** your assessor how you contribute to evaluating the effectiveness of agreed methods of communication and support provided.

REMEMBER TO:
- Make arrangements for **observation** of **your work practices**.
- Include evidence of you contributing to evaluating the effectiveness of agreed methods of communication and support provided.
- Ensure the evidence relates to **both** communication methods and support provided.
- Think about **your work setting** and how you contribute to evaluating the effectiveness of agreed methods of communication and support provided.

Learning Outcome 6: Be able to review an individual's communication needs and the support provided to address them

Assessment Criterion 6.3: Work with others to identify ways to support the continued development of communication

What does AC6.3 mean?

- The lead words **work with** mean that you must **be able to show** through **your work practices** how to support and partner others to identify ways to support the continued development of communication.
- Your **observations** of your work practices must include you working with others to identify ways.
- For the key words **continued development** you can think about how you and others can work together to ensure the progress of an individual's communication needs and support.

Read the following **Real Work Setting** scenario and think about how it relates to your work setting and role:

Real Work Setting

Name: Sue

Job role: Senior Carer for young adults

(See page 269 for a description of the role.)

Supporting the continued development of communication: Sue and Ruby agree that, together with her family, advocate, and care and communication professionals, they will continue to observe and check Ruby's progress with her communication passport as well as explore other communication methods and support that may meet her needs. Ruby has also given her permission for the team to share with her family, advocate and other professionals all the digital recordings they complete so that they can better understand her communication needs and the type of support that is required to meet these effectively.

Evidencing AC6.3 to your assessor:

For AC6.3 you must evidence your skills in working with others to identify ways to support the continued development of communication.

Assessment method:

Direct Observation of your work practices.

- You can **show** your assessor how you work with others to identify ways to support the continued development of communication.

REMEMBER TO:

- Make arrangements for **observation** of **your work practices**.
- Include evidence of you working with others and identifying different ways to support the continued development of communication.
- Ensure the evidence relates to identifying ways to support the continued development of communication.
- Think about **your work setting** and how you work with others to identify ways to support the continued development of communication.

Learning Outcome 1: Understand the legislative framework for the use of medication in social care settings

Assessment Criterion 1.1: Identify legislation that governs the use of medication in social care settings

What does AC1.1 mean?

- The lead word **identify** means that you must **make clear** the legislation that governs the use of medication in social care settings.
- Your **list** must make clear **different** pieces of legislation.
- For the key word **legislation** you can think about the relevant laws in place that relate to ordering, receiving, administering, storing, recording and disposing of medication.

Read the following **Real Work Setting** scenario and think about how it relates to your work setting and role:

Real Work Setting

Name: Emma

Job role: Senior Carer for older people

Emma has been working as a Senior Carer for two years. Her Senior responsibilities include: ensuring the smooth running of the home; supporting individuals to lead fulfilling lives; leading a team of Carers; providing support, guidance and supervision to staff; administering medication; developing, updating and reviewing individuals' person-centred plans; liaising with individuals, their families, friends, and other professionals and agencies involved in their lives.

Legislation to govern use of medication: Emma is putting together for the team of Carers an information update on the legislative framework for the use of medication. Emma begins by thinking about the current legislation in place that governs the use of medication in social care settings. First she spends some time looking at the guidance available on the website of the National Institute for Health and Care Excellence (NICE), as well as reading through the Nursing and Midwifery Council's (NMC) standards for the management of medicines. Following this research Emma puts together a list of the main pieces of legislation governing the use of medication in social care settings.

Evidencing AC1.1 to your assessor:

For AC1.1 you must evidence your knowledge of the different legislation that governs the use of medication in social care settings.

Assessment Methods:

Oral/Written Questioning or **Discussion** or a **Spidergram**.

- You can **tell** your assessor about the different legislation that governs the use of medication in social care settings.
- Or, you can **talk** to your assessor about the different legislation that governs the use of medication in social care settings.
- Or, you can complete a **spidergram** showing the different legislation that governs the use of medication in social care settings.

REMEMBER TO:

- Provide examples of **different** legislation that governs the use of medication in social care settings.
- Ensure that the examples you provide relate to the use of medication in social care settings.
- Think about the legislation that governs the use of medication in **your work setting**.

Learning Outcome 1: Understand the legislative framework for the use of medication in social care settings

Assessment Criterion 1.2: Outline the legal classification system for medication

What does AC1.2 mean?

- The lead word **outline** means that you must provide an **account** that briefly details the legal classification system for medication.
- Your account must provide **brief details** of the legal classification system for medication.
- For the key words **legal classification system** you can think about how the Medicines Act 1968 classifies medications into different groups.

Read the following **Real Work Setting** scenario and think about how it relates to your work setting and role:

Real Work Setting

Name: Emma

Job role: Senior Carer for older people

(See page 272 for a description of the role.)

Legal classification system for medication: Emma is developing a quiz on the legal classification system for medication for the team of Carers to complete after they read the information update she has put together for them. Emma decides that she would like to ask the Carers to research the Medicines Act 1968 and find out more about the three classes of medicines: general sale list (GSL); pharmacy medicines (P); prescription-only medicines (POMs). Emma has put together a few questions on each class of medicines that aim to develop the Carers' knowledge of the differences between the classes of medicines, examples of medicines that can be found in each class and any restrictions that apply to how they are obtained.

Evidencing AC1.2 to your assessor:

For AC1.2 you must evidence your understanding of the legal classification system for medication.

Assessment Methods:

Oral/Written Questioning or **Discussion** or **Personal Statement**.

- You can **tell** your assessor about the legal classification system for medication.
- Or, you can **talk** to your assessor about the legal classification system for medication.
- Or, you can write a **personal statement** about the legal classification system for medication.

REMEMBER TO:

- Provide an **account** that includes **brief details** of the legal classification system for medication.
- Ensure that your **account** provides an outline of the legal classification system for medication.
- Think about the legal classification system for medication as it is used in **your work setting**.

Learning Outcome 1: Understand the legislative framework for the use of medication in social care settings

Assessment Criterion 1.3: Explain how and why policies and procedures or agreed ways of working must reflect and incorporate legislative requirements

What does AC1.3 mean?

- ○ The lead word **explain** means that you must **make clear** how as well as the reasons why policies and procedures or agreed ways of working must reflect and incorporate legislative requirements.
- ○ Your **account** must make clear **details** of both how and why.
- ○ For the key words **policies and procedures** and **agreed ways of working** you can think about your work setting's formal processes, as well as the specific guidelines that are in place for reflecting and including legislative requirements for the use of medication.

Read the following **Real Work Setting** scenario and think about how it relates to your work setting and role:

Real Work Setting

Name: Emma
Job role: Senior Carer for older people
(See page 272 for a description of the role.)
Policies and procedures and agreed ways of working: Emma plans to end the information update she is putting together for the team with a discussion around how and why the home's medication policies and procedures and agreed ways of working must reflect and include legislative requirements for the use of medication.

Evidencing AC1.3 to your assessor:

For AC1.3 you must evidence your understanding of how and why policies and procedures or agreed ways of working must reflect and incorporate legislative requirements.

Assessment Methods:

Oral/Written Questioning or **Discussion** or a **Personal Statement.**

- You can **tell** your assessor about how and why policies and procedures or agreed ways of working must reflect and incorporate legislative requirements.
- *Or*, you can **talk** to your assessor about how and why policies and procedures or agreed ways of working must reflect and incorporate legislative requirements.
- *Or*, you can write a **personal statement** about how and why policies and procedures or agreed ways of working must reflect and incorporate legislative requirements.

REMEMBER TO:

- Provide an **account** and explain **both** how and the reasons why policies and procedures or agreed ways of working must reflect and incorporate legislative requirements.
- Include **details** and examples of **how**.
- Include **details** and examples of the reasons **why**.
- Think about **your work setting** and how and why policies and procedures or agreed ways of working must reflect and incorporate legislative requirements.

Learning Outcome 2: Know about common types of medication and their use

Assessment Criterion 2.1: Identify common types of medication

What does AC2.1 mean?

- ○ The lead word **identify** means that you must **make clear** the common types of medication that exist.
- ○ Your **list** must make clear common types of medication.
- ○ For the key words **common types** you can think about the purposes and effects of different medications.

Read the following **Real Work Setting** scenario and think about how it relates to your work setting and role:

Real Work Setting

Name: Hal

Job role: Senior Home Carer for adults who have disabilities

Hal has been working as a Senior Home Carer for adults who have disabilities for five months. His Senior responsibilities include: providing support and guidance to a team of five Home Carers; delivering high quality one-to-one care and support in individuals' homes; administering and supporting individuals with the use of medication; updating and reviewing individuals' plans of care and support; developing working relationships with individuals, individuals' families, friends, advocates and other professionals and agencies.

Types of medication: As part of Hal's induction period as a Senior Home Carer, he completed an open learning course on the safe handling of medication. The second module focused on developing his knowledge of the most common types of medication. Hal found it really useful whilst completing this module to think about the medications used by the individuals he supports and then to consider which common category of medications they belong to. Hal found that the medicines found under each type are used in different ways, such as to provide treatment, for prevention, for relief from ailments and to change chemical balances.

Evidencing AC2.1 to your assessor:

For AC2.1 you must evidence your knowledge of the common types of medication.

Assessment Methods:

Oral/Written Questioning or **Discussion** or a **Spidergram**.

- You can **tell** your assessor about the common types of medication.
- Or, you can **talk** to your assessor about the common types of medication.
- Or, you can complete a **spidergram** showing the common types of medication.

REMEMBER TO:

- Provide a list of **different** types of medication.
- Ensure that the examples you provide relate to common types of medication.
- Think about the common types of medication that are used in **your work setting**.

AC 2.2

Learning Outcome 2: Know about common types of medication and their use

Assessment Criterion 2.2: List conditions for which each type of medication may be prescribed

What does AC2.2 mean?

- The lead word **list** means that you must **make clear** the conditions for which each type of medication may be prescribed.
- Your **list** must make clear **different** conditions.
- For the key word **conditions** you can think about the common types of medication and the reasons why they are prescribed.
- For the key words **type of medication** you can think about the purposes and effects of different medications.

Read the following **Real Work Setting** scenario and think about how it relates to your work setting and role:

Real Work Setting

Name: Hal

Job role: Senior Home Carer for adults who have disabilities

(See page 275 for a description of the role.)

Conditions prescribed for: As part of Hal's open learning course on the safe handling of medication he was asked to evidence his knowledge of the conditions for which each type of medicine may be prescribed. To do this Hal drew up a chart and identified on this the common types of medication he had found out about, examples of medicines from each type, as well as the different conditions for which each of these medicines may be prescribed.

Evidencing AC2.2 to your assessor:

For AC2.2 you must evidence your knowledge of the conditions for which each type of medication may be prescribed.

Assessment Methods:

Oral/Written Questioning or **Discussion** or a **Spidergram**.

- You can **tell** your assessor about the conditions for which each type of medication may be prescribed.
- *Or*, you can **talk** to your assessor about the conditions for which each type of medication may be prescribed.
- *Or*, you can complete a **spidergram** showing the conditions for which each type of medication may be prescribed.

REMEMBER TO:

- Provide a list of different **conditions** for which each type of medication may be prescribed.
- Ensure that the examples of conditions you provide relate to common types of medication.
- Think about **your work setting** and the individuals you provide care and support to as well as the conditions they have for which each type of medication may be prescribed.

Learning Outcome 2: Know about common types of medication and their use

Assessment Criterion 2.3: Describe changes to an individual's physical or mental well-being that may indicate an adverse reaction to a medication

What does AC2.3 mean?

- The lead word **describe** means that you must provide an **account** that **details** the changes to an individual's physical or mental well-being that may indicate an adverse reaction to a medication.
- Your **account** must detail **different** changes that may arise in an individual's physical or mental well-being.
- For the key words **physical or mental well-being** you can think about how a medication may affect an individual's health, their body, how they are feeling and how they manage day-to-day activities.
- For the key words **adverse reactions** you can think about the negative side effects that a medication may have on an individual's physical or mental well-being.

Read the following **Real Work Setting** scenario and think about how it relates to your work setting and role:

Real Work Setting

Name: Hal

Job role: Senior Home Carer for adults who have disabilities

(See page 275 for a description of the role.)

Changes to an individual's physical or mental well-being: For the final part of his open learning course on the safe handling of medication, Hal developed case studies of three individuals he provided care and support to and considered changes to their physical or mental well-being that could have indicated an adverse reaction to a medication. In doing this, Hal found it useful to reference the British National Formulary pharmaceutical book available in his workplace.

Evidencing AC2.3 to your assessor:

For AC2.3 you must evidence your knowledge of changes to an individual's physical or mental well-being that may indicate an adverse reaction to a medication.

Assessment Methods:

Oral/Written Questioning or **Discussion** or a **Personal Statement or Reflection**.

- You can **tell** your assessor about the changes to an individual's physical or mental well-being that may indicate an adverse reaction to a medication.
- Or, you can **talk** to your assessor about the changes to an individual's physical or mental well-being that may indicate an adverse reaction to a medication.
- Or, you can write a **personal statement or reflection** about your experience of the changes to an individual's physical or mental well-being that may indicate an adverse reaction to a medication.

REMEMBER TO:

- Provide a detailed **account** of the changes to an individual's physical or mental well-being.
- Include **details** about changes to an individual's physical or mental well-being that may indicate an adverse reaction to a medication.
- Think about **your work setting** and the changes to an individual's physical or mental well-being that may indicate an adverse reaction to a medication.

Learning Outcome 3: Understand roles and responsibilities in the use of medication in social care settings

Assessment Criterion 3.1: Describe the roles and responsibilities of those involved in prescribing, dispensing and supporting use of medication

What does AC3.1 mean?

- The lead word **describe** means that you must provide an **account** that **details** the roles and responsibilities of those involved in prescribing, dispensing and supporting use of medication.
- Your **account** must detail the roles and responsibilities of **different** people involved in prescribing, dispensing and supporting use of medication.
- For the key words **roles and responsibilities** you can think about how different people's job tasks involve prescribing, dispensing and supporting the use of medication.
- For the key word **prescribing** you can think about the health care professionals whose jobs involve writing prescriptions, such as doctors and dentists.
- For the key word **dispensing** you can think about the health care professionals who supply medication, such as pharmacists.
- For the key words **supporting use** you can think about the health and social care professionals who provide support to use medication, such as nurses, doctors, consultants, Care Workers, Senior Care Workers, managers, advocates, family and friends.

Read the following **Real Work Setting** scenario and think about how it relates to your work setting and role:

Real Work Setting

Name: Monica

Job role: Senior Carer for adults who have mental health needs

Monica has been working as a Senior Carer for adults who have mental health needs for one year. Her Senior responsibilities include: working with registered nursing staff to provide individualised care to individuals; leading on individuals' support plans and daily activities; supporting individuals to use medication; liaising with a network of professionals and agencies.

Roles and responsibilities: Further to an individual's request for information about his medication plan, Monica has prepared a list of the roles and responsibilities of those involved in prescribing, dispensing and supporting Al's use of medication.

Evidencing AC3.1 to your assessor:

For AC3.1 you must evidence your knowledge of the roles and responsibilities of those involved in prescribing, dispensing and supporting use of medication.

Assessment Methods:

Oral/Written Questioning or **Discussion** or **Personal Statement**.

- You can **tell** your assessor about the roles and responsibilities of those involved in prescribing, dispensing and supporting use of medication.
- Or, you can **talk** to your assessor about the roles and responsibilities of those involved in prescribing, dispensing and supporting use of medication.
- Or, you can write a **personal statement** about the roles and responsibilities of those involved in prescribing, dispensing and supporting use of medication.

REMEMBER TO:

- Provide a detailed **account** of the roles and responsibilities of those involved in prescribing, dispensing and supporting use of medication.
- Include **details** about the roles and responsibilities of the different people involved.
- Ensure the **evidence** you provide relates to those involved in prescribing, dispensing and supporting use of medication.
- Think about **your work setting** and roles and responsibilities of those involved in prescribing, dispensing and supporting use of medication.

Learning Outcome 3: Understand roles and responsibilities in the use of medication in social care settings

Assessment Criterion 3.2: Explain where responsibilities lie in relation to use of over-the-counter remedies and supplements

What does AC3.2 mean?

○ The lead word **explain** means that you must **make clear** the responsibilities when an individual uses over-the-counter remedies and supplements.

○ Your account must make clear **details** of both **where** these responsibilities lie and **why**.

○ For the key words **over-the-counter remedies and supplements** you can think about whose responsibility it is when an individual uses remedies and supplements for which a prescription is not needed.

Read the following **Real Work Setting** scenario and think about how it relates to your work setting and role:

Real Work Setting

Name: Monica

Job role: Senior Carer for adults who have mental health needs

(See page 278 for a description of the role.)

Responsibilities relating to using over-the-counter remedies and supplements: During Monica's meeting with Al about his medication plan, Al discloses to Monica that when he has been going to the local shops he has been purchasing a herbal remedy, St John's Wort, to help with his arthritis. Monica asks him whether he knows what this remedy contains; Al tells Monica that he thought that all herbal remedies were safe and that he did not need to know its ingredients. Monica explains to Al that just because herbal remedies occur naturally does not mean that they are all safe, and she suggests to him that she can accompany him to the pharmacist tomorrow to ask some more questions about its use and also to the doctors to explore other treatment options available for Al's arthritis.

Evidencing AC3.2 to your assessor:

For AC3.2 you must evidence your understanding of where responsibilities lie in relation to the use of over-the-counter remedies and supplements.

Assessment Methods:

Oral/Written Questioning or **Discussion** or **Personal Statement**.

● You can **tell** your assessor about where responsibilities lie in relation to the use of over-the-counter remedies and supplements.

● Or, you can **talk** to your assessor about where responsibilities lie in relation to the use of over-the-counter remedies and supplements.

● Or, you can write a **personal statement** about where responsibilities lie in relation to the use of over-the-counter remedies and supplements.

REMEMBER TO:

● Provide an **account** and explain **both where** responsibilities lie and **why**.

● Include **details** and examples of over-the-counter remedies and supplements.

● Include **details** and examples of **where** responsibilities lie and the reasons **why**.

● Think about **your work setting** and where responsibilities lie in relation to the use of over-the-counter remedies and supplements.

Learning Outcome 4: Understand techniques for administering medication

Assessment Criterion 4.1: Describe the routes by which medication can be administered

What does AC4.1 mean?

- The lead word **describe** means that you must provide an **account** that **details** the routes by which medication can be administered.
- Your **account** must detail the **different** routes.
- For the key word **routes** you can think about how medication can be administered in different ways, such as via inhalation, instillation, orally, transdermally, topically, intravenously, rectally, vaginally, subcutaneously and intramuscularly.

Read the following **Real Work Setting** scenario and think about how it relates to your work setting and role:

Real Work Setting

Name: Lee

Job role: Senior Personal Assistant to a young adult

Lee has been working as a Senior Personal Assistant for two years. His Senior responsibilities include: supporting the physical, emotional and social care of individuals; contributing to assessments and individual plans; maintaining and updating records; assisting the manager in the induction, training and development of Personal Assistants.

Routes of administration of medication: Lee has prepared a training session for the team of Personal Assistants that focuses on the different techniques to use for administering medication. Lee will begin the training session by reviewing with the team their knowledge of the different routes by which medication can be administered, by asking them to name as many different routes as they can. Lee will then reveal all the different routes that exist to the team and ask them to compare their findings with his. A final activity around understanding more about the different routes by which medication can be administered will also be completed and will involve the team conducting some research of their own.

Evidencing AC4.1 to your assessor:

For AC4.1 you must evidence your understanding of the routes by which medication can be administered.

Assessment Methods:

Oral/Written Questioning or Discussion or Personal Statement.

- You can **tell** your assessor about the routes by which medication can be administered.
- Or, you can **talk** to your assessor about the routes by which medication can be administered.
- Or, you can write a **personal statement** about the routes by which medication can be administered.

REMEMBER TO:

- Provide a detailed **account** of the routes by which medication can be administered.
- Include **details** about the routes by which medication can be administered.
- Ensure the evidence you provide relates to **different** routes of administration.
- Think about **your work setting** and the routes by which medication can be administered to and by individuals.

Learning Outcome 4: Understand techniques for administering medication

Assessment Criterion 4.2: Describe different forms in which medication may be presented

What does AC4.2 mean?

- The lead word **describe** means that you must provide an **account** that **details** the different forms in which medication may be presented.
- Your **account** must detail the **different** forms of medication.
- For the key word **forms** you can think about how medication can be presented in different ways, such as tablets, injections, liquids, inhalants, creams, suppositories and pessaries.

Read the following **Real Work Setting** scenario and think about how it relates to your work setting and role:

Real Work Setting

Name: Lee

Job role: Senior Personal Assistant to a young adult

(See page 280 for a description of the role.)

Forms of medication: Lee is meeting today with the nurse who has agreed to attend the team's training session and to make a short presentation about the different forms in which medication may be presented. The nurse plans to use examples of medicines so that the team can develop a greater understanding of how different medications may be presented. Lee has agreed with the nurse for the team to have an opportunity at the end of the presentation to ask her any questions they may have. After the nurse's presentation Lee plans to conduct a question-and-answer session with each team member to ascertain their understanding of the different forms in which medication may be presented.

Evidencing AC4.2 to your assessor:

For AC4.2 you must evidence your understanding of the different forms in which medication may be presented.

Assessment Methods:

Oral/Written Questioning or Discussion or Personal Statement.

- You can **tell** your assessor about the different forms in which medication may be presented.
- Or, you can **talk** to your assessor about the different forms in which medication may be presented.
- Or, you can write a **personal statement** about the different forms in which medication may be presented.

REMEMBER TO:

- Provide a detailed **account** of the different forms in which medication may be presented.
- Include **details** about the different forms.
- Ensure the evidence you provide relates to **different** forms of medication.
- Think about **your work setting** and the different forms in which medication may be presented.

Learning Outcome 4: Understand techniques for administering medication

Assessment Criterion 4.3: Describe materials and equipment that can assist in administering medication

What does AC4.3 mean?

○ The lead word **describe** means that you must provide an **account** that **details** the different materials and equipment that can assist in administering medication.

○ Your **account** must detail the **different** materials and equipment that can assist in administering medication.

○ For the key words **materials and equipment** you can think about the range of items that can help in administering medication, such as gloves, inhalers, nebulisers, medication cups and spoons.

Read the following **Real Work Setting** scenario and think about how it relates to your work setting and role:

Real Work Setting

Name: Lee

Job role: Senior Personal Assistant to a young adult

(See page 280 for a description of the role.)

Materials and equipment when administering medication: Lee is inducting a newly recruited Personal Assistant and is talking through with him each of the individuals he will be providing care and support to, so that he can gain a good insight and understanding into their needs and agreed ways of working before he meets them. As part of the induction Lee shows the new Personal Assistant each individual's medication profile and plan of care, and then discusses with him how each individual's medication is administered, including the different materials and equipment available to assist in administering medication for each individual, as well as how these are to be used with each individual.

Evidencing AC4.3 to your assessor:

For AC4.3 you must evidence your understanding of the materials and equipment that can assist in administering medication.

Assessment Methods:

Oral/Written Questioning or **Discussion** or a **Personal Statement** or **Reflection**.

● You can **tell** your assessor about the different materials and equipment that can assist in administering medication.

● Or, you can **talk** to your assessor about the different materials and equipment that can assist in administering medication.

● Or, you can write a **personal statement or reflection** about your experience of the materials and equipment that can assist in administering medication.

REMEMBER TO:

● Provide a detailed **account** of the materials and equipment that can assist in administering medication.

● Include **details** about both materials and equipment.

● Ensure the evidence you provide relates to materials and equipment that can assist in administering medication.

● Think about **your work setting** and the materials and equipment that can assist in administering medication.

Learning Outcome 5: Be able to receive, store and dispose of medication supplies safely

Assessment Criterion 5.1: Demonstrate how to receive supplies of medication in line with agreed ways of working

What does AC5.1 mean?
- The lead word **demonstrate** means that you must **be able to show** through **your work practices** how to receive supplies of medication in line with agreed ways of working.
- Your **observations** of your work practices must include you receiving supplies of medication.
- For the key words **agreed ways of working** you can think about the procedures you must follow in your work setting when receiving supplies of medication.

Read the following **Real Work Setting** scenario and think about how it relates to your work setting and role:

Real Work Setting

Name: Christine

Job role: Senior Support Worker for adults who have learning disabilities

Christine has been working as a Senior Support Worker for two years. Her Senior responsibilities include: coordinating and reviewing packages of care and support for individuals; promoting individuals' well-being and independence; carrying out supervisions and appraisals for a team of Support Workers; handling medication, including ordering, receiving, administering, storing, recording and disposing of medication; maintaining accurate records.

Receiving supplies of medication: Christine is the designated responsible person for taking receipt of medication delivered to the registered care home. This morning the pharmacy delivered to the home some medication for different individuals and on receipt of this Christine completed her checks as per the home's policy, to include the details of the medication delivered and the dosage and instructions on each of the medications delivered. Christine then proceeded to count the quantities of each medication and then entered this in the medication stock book, indicating clearly the stocks received and the total stocks now held at the home. Christine also took receipt this morning of medication for an individual who had returned to the home after a holiday. Christine ensured that the full details of the medication were provided by the GP, that the medication was in its original containers and was in date, before recording the quantities that were received.

Evidencing AC5.1 to your assessor:
For AC5.1 you must evidence your skills in receiving supplies of medication in line with agreed ways of working.

Assessment Method:
Direct Observation of your work practices.
- You can **show** your assessor or an expert witness how you receive supplies of medication in line with agreed ways of working.

REMEMBER TO:
- Make arrangements for **observation of your work practices**.
- Include evidence of you receiving supplies of medication.
- Ensure the evidence you provide is in line with agreed ways of working in your work setting.
- Think about **your work setting** and the procedures you must follow when receiving supplies of medication.

Learning Outcome 5: Be able to receive, store and dispose of medication supplies safely

Assessment Criterion 5.2: Demonstrate how to store medication safely

What does AC5.2 mean?
- The lead word **demonstrate** means that you must **be able to show** through **your work practices** how to store medication safely.
- Your **observations** of your work practices must include you storing medication.
- For the key word **safely** you can think about the procedures you must follow in your work setting when storing medication so that the medication continues to be effective, is secure and cannot be accessed by those unauthorised to do so.

Read the following **Real Work Setting** scenario and think about how it relates to your work setting and role:

Real Work Setting

Name: Christine

Job role: Senior Support Worker for adults who have learning disabilities

(See page 283 for a description of the role.)

Storing medication safely: Christine ensures that she checks all stock levels at the home when medication is received, usually on a weekly basis. As part of her checks Christine monitors the expiration dates of all medications, and also ensures that medications that have been opened and are being used have not expired. When taking receipt of medication at the home Christine rotates the stock so that older medication is placed at the front so it is used before the new supplies of medication. In addition, when Christine administers medication to individuals she ensures that it is stored away safely afterwards; some medications are locked in the medicine cupboard attached to the wall and others in the lockable box located in the fridge. When Christine is administering medication she ensures she carries both sets of keys on her and that only she has access to them. As part of the safe storage of medications Christine is aware of the importance of ensuring that the temperatures of the medicine cupboard and the medicines fridge are maintained correctly at all times to ensure the effectiveness of all medicines.

Evidencing AC5.2 to your assessor:
For AC5.2 you must evidence your skills in how to store medication safely.

Assessment Method:

Direct Observation of your work practices.

- You can **show** your assessor or an expert witness how you store medication safely.

REMEMBER TO:
- Make arrangements for **observation** of **your work practices**.
- Include evidence of you storing medication.
- Ensure the evidence you provide is related to storing medication safely.
- Think about **your work setting** and the procedures you must follow when storing medication safely.

Learning Outcome 5: Be able to receive, store and dispose of medication supplies safely

Assessment Criterion 5.3: Demonstrate how to dispose of unused or unwanted medication safely

What does AC5.3 mean?

○ The lead word **demonstrate** means that you must **be able to show** through **your work practices** how to dispose of unused or unwanted medication safely.

○ Your **observations** of your work practices must include you disposing of unused or unwanted medication safely.

○ For the key words **unused or unwanted medication** you can think about the procedures you must follow in your work setting when medication received has either not been used by an individual or is no longer wanted by an individual. This may be due to an individual leaving or dying, or the individual's medication being discontinued or changed, or the expiration date of the medication being reached.

Read the following **Real Work Setting** scenario and think about how it relates to your work setting and role:

Real Work Setting

Name: Christine

Job role: Senior Support Worker for adults who have learning disabilities

(See page 283 for a description of the role.)

Disposing of unused or unwanted medication safely: Christine ensures that all unused and unwanted medication is returned to the pharmacy for safe disposal. Christine completes the stock levels medication book in the home as well as the medication disposal book; both are checked by the Home Manager and then signed and checked by the pharmacy. One individual in the home self-administers medication and the syringes he uses are disposed of in a sharps box, which is kept secure in the home and disposed of in line with the home's procedures.

Evidencing AC5.3 to your assessor:

For AC5.3 you must evidence your skills in how to dispose of unused or unwanted medication safely.

Assessment Method:

Direct Observation of your work practices.

● You can **show** your assessor or an expert witness how to dispose of unused or unwanted medication safely.

REMEMBER TO:

● Make arrangements for **observation** of **your work practices**.
● Include evidence of you disposing of unused or unwanted medication.
● Ensure the evidence you provide relates to disposing of medication safely.
● Think about **your work setting** and the procedures you must follow to dispose of unused or unwanted medication safely.

Learning Outcome 6: Know how to promote the rights of the individual when managing medication

Assessment Criterion 6.1: Explain the importance of the following principles in the use of medication: consent; self-medication or active participation; dignity and privacy; confidentiality

What does AC6.1 mean?

○ The lead word **explain** means that you must **make clear** the importance of the following principles in the use of medication: consent; self-medication or active participation; dignity and privacy; confidentiality.

○ Your **account** must make clear **details** of the importance of these principles in the use of medication.

○ For the key word **consent** you can think about how to obtain an individual's agreement to the use of medication.

○ For the key words **self-medication or active participation** you can think about how an individual can be fully involved in the use of their medication.

○ For the key word **dignity** you can think about how to maintain an individual's self-respect in the use of their medication.

○ For the key word **privacy** you can think about how to maintain restricted an individual's use of medication.

○ For the key word **confidentiality** you can think about how to maintain secure an individual's use of medication.

Read the following **Real Work Setting** scenario and think about how it relates to your work setting and role:

Real Work Setting

Name: Francesco

Job role: Senior Carer for adults who have dementia

Francesco has been working as a Senior Carer for adults who have dementia for six years. His Senior responsibilities include: day-to-day coordination of a person-centred service; providing support, guidance and training to a team of Carers; assisting the manager with referrals, care plans and reviews; supporting individuals with the use of medication; liaising with individuals' families, other professionals and agencies.

Principles in the use of medication: Francesco is delivering a training update to the team of Carers to refresh their knowledge of the main principles in the use of medication and how to promote the rights of individuals who have dementia.

Evidencing AC6.1 to your assessor:

For AC6.1 you must evidence your knowledge of the importance of the following principles in the use of medication: consent; self-medication or active participation; dignity and privacy; confidentiality.

Assessment Methods:

Oral/Written Questioning or **Discussion** or a **Personal Statement** or **Reflection**.

● You can **tell** your assessor about the importance of principles in the use of medication.

● Or, you can **talk** to your assessor about the importance of principles in the use of medication.

● Or, you can write a **personal statement or reflection** about your experience of the importance of principles in the use of medication.

REMEMBER TO:

● Provide an **account** and explain the **importance** of principles in the use of medication.

● Include **details** and examples of why each of the following principles is important in the use of medication: consent; self-medication or active participation; dignity and privacy; confidentiality.

● Think about **your work setting** and the importance of principles in the use of medication.

Learning Outcome 6: Know how to promote the rights of the individual when managing medication

Assessment Criterion 6.2: Explain how risk assessment can be used to promote an individual's independence in managing medication

What does AC6.2 mean?

- ○ The lead word **explain** means that you must **make clear** how risk assessment can be used to promote an individual's independence in managing medication.
- ○ Your **account** must make clear **details** of how risk assessment can be used.
- ○ For the key words **risk assessment** you can think about how the process of evaluating the risks identified with respect to an individual managing their medication can promote an individual's independence.
- ○ For the key word **independence** you can think about the role of risk assessment in enabling an individual to manage their medication effectively.

Read the following **Real Work Setting** scenario and think about how it relates to your work setting and role:

Real Work Setting

Name: Francesco

Job role: Senior Carer for adults who have dementia

(See page 286 for a description of the role.)

Risk assessment and promoting independence: Francesco is meeting with one Carer for supervision. The Carer has raised her anxiety over an individual with dementia whom she supports who is finding it difficult to continue to self-medicate as she cannot always remember what medication she has taken in the mornings. Francesco discusses with the Carer the various options available to the individual, including the use of colour-coded dosette boxes that make it clearly visible which medications have been taken and which remain.

Evidencing AC6.2 to your assessor:

For AC6.2 you must evidence your knowledge of how risk assessment can be used to promote an individual's independence in managing medication.

Assessment Methods:

Oral/Written Questioning or **Discussion** or a **Personal Statement or Reflection**.

- You can **tell** your assessor about how risk assessment can be used to promote an individual's independence in managing medication.
- Or, you can **talk** to your assessor about how risk assessment can be used to promote an individual's independence in managing medication.
- Or, you can write a **personal statement or reflection** about your experience of how risk assessment can be used to promote an individual's independence in managing medication.

REMEMBER TO:

- Provide an **account** of how risk assessment can be used to promote an individual's independence in managing medication.
- Include **details** and examples of how risk assessment can be used.
- Ensure your evidence relates to the use of risk assessment to promote an individual's independence in managing medication.
- Think about **your work setting** and how risk assessment can be used to promote an individual's independence in managing medication.

Learning Outcome 6: Know how to promote the rights of the individual when managing medication

Assessment Criterion 6.3: Describe how ethical issues that may arise over the use of medication can be addressed

What does AC6.3 mean?

- The lead word **describe** means that you must provide an **account** that **details** how to address ethical issues that may arise over the use of medication.
- Your **account** must detail **how** to address different ethical issues that may arise over the use of medication.
- For the key words **ethical issues** you can think about how these may be related to the individual's ability, health, change in needs, rights and/or wishes, and to those of others involved in individuals' lives.

Read the following **Real Work Setting** scenario and think about how it relates to your work setting and role:

Real Work Setting

Name: Francesco

Job role: Senior Carer for adults who have dementia

(See page 286 for a description of the role.)

Ethical issues: Francesco is carrying out a review with an individual, at which the individual's wife expresses concerns over her husband continuing to use medication in tablet form and thinks that due to his dementia he should be prescribed this in liquid form as he will find it easier to take this way. Francesco explains to the individual's wife that at present her husband is refusing to change the form in which he takes his medication as he feels that he has no difficulties with taking tablets. Francesco agrees to monitor the individual and his needs closely to ensure that he can continue to take his medication safely and according to his wishes.

Evidencing AC6.3 to your assessor:

For AC6.3 you must evidence your knowledge of how ethical issues that may arise over the use of medication can be addressed.

Assessment Methods:

Oral/Written Questioning or **Discussion** or a **Personal Statement** or **Reflection**.

- You can **tell** your assessor about how ethical issues that may arise over the use of medication can be addressed.
- Or, you can **talk** to your assessor about how ethical issues that may arise over the use of medication can be addressed.
- Or, you can write a **personal statement or reflection** about your experience of how ethical issues that may arise over the use of medication can be addressed.

REMEMBER TO:

- Provide a detailed **account** of how ethical issues that may arise over the use of medication can be addressed.
- Include **details** and examples of how ethical issues can be addressed.
- Ensure your evidence relates to the use of medication.
- Think about **your work setting** and how ethical issues that may arise over the use of medication can be addressed.

AC 7.1

Learning Outcome 7: Be able to support use of medication

Assessment Criterion 7.1: Demonstrate how to access information about an individual's medication

What does AC7.1 mean?

- ○ The lead word **demonstrate** means that you must **be able to show** through **your work practices** how to access information about an individual's medication.
- ○ Your **observations** of your work practices must include you accessing information.
- ○ For the key words **accessing medication** you can think about the procedures you must follow in your work setting when obtaining written, verbal or electronic information about an individual's medication.

Read the following **Real Work Setting** scenario and think about how it relates to your work setting and role:

Real Work Setting

Name: Michael

Job role: Senior Support Worker for adults who have autism

Michael has been working as a Senior Support Worker for four years. His Senior responsibilities include: assessing and reviewing individuals' needs; supervising a team of Support Workers; providing support to and working with individuals with autism; developing and leading group activities; administering medication; maintaining accurate records.

Accessing information about an individual's medication: Michael has agreed with his assessor to be observed by him following the correct procedures for accessing information about an individual's medication. Michael has agreed this both with his manager and with an individual he supports with his medication. Prior to administering this individual's medication Michael checks the individual's medication administration record for details of the medication he is about to administer, and also reads through the individual's medication profile to confirm that there have been no changes to his medication or any adverse effects experienced. Michael also checks with the individual that he is ready to have his medication and asks him to confirm his details, and then discusses with him the purpose of the medication.

Evidencing AC7.1 to your assessor:

For AC7.1 you must evidence your skills in accessing information about an individual's medication.

Assessment Method:
Direct Observation of your work practices.

- ● You can **show** your assessor how you access information about an individual's medication.

REMEMBER TO:
- ● Make arrangements for **observation** of **your work practices**.
- ● Include evidence of you accessing information.
- ● Ensure the evidence you provide is related to an individual's medication.
- ● Think about **your work setting** and the procedures you must follow to access information about an individual's medication.

Learning Outcome 7: Be able to support use of medication

Assessment Criterion 7.2: Demonstrate how to support an individual to use medication in ways that promote hygiene, safety, dignity and active participation

What does AC7.2 mean?

- The lead word **demonstrate** means that you must **be able to show** through **your work practices** how to support individuals to use medication in ways that promote hygiene, safety, dignity and active participation.
- Your **observations** of your work practices must include supporting an individual to use medication.
- For the key word **hygiene** you can think about how to support an individual to keep themselves, their surroundings and the equipment that is used when using medication clean.
- For the key word **safety** you can think about how to support an individual to use medication in ways that protect the individual, you and others from potential dangers, risks and injuries.
- For the key word **dignity** you can think about how to maintain an individual's self-respect in the use of their medication.
- For the key words **active participation** you can think about how to support an individual to be fully involved and in control of their use of medication.

Read the following **Real Work Setting** scenario and think about how it relates to your work setting and role:

Real Work Setting

| **Name:** Michael |
| **Job role:** Senior Support Worker for adults who have autism |
| (See page 289 for a description of the role.) |
| **Supporting an individual's use of medication:** Michael has arranged to be observed supporting an individual to use medication in ways that are hygienic, safe and dignified, and that encourage the individual to be actively involved in and lead the process. |

Evidencing AC7.2 to your assessor:

For AC7.2 you must evidence your skills in supporting an individual to use medication in ways that promote hygiene, safety, dignity and active participation.

Assessment Method:
Direct Observation of your work practices.

- You can **show** your assessor how you support an individual to use medication in ways that promote hygiene, safety, dignity and active participation.

REMEMBER TO:
- Make arrangements for **observation** of **your work practices**.
- Include evidence of you supporting an individual to use medication.
- Ensure the evidence you provide is related to using medication in ways that promote hygiene, safety, dignity and active participation.
- Think about **your work setting** and how to support an individual to use medication in ways that promote hygiene, safety, dignity and active participation.

Learning Outcome 7: Be able to support use of medication

Assessment Criterion 7.3: Demonstrate strategies to ensure that medication is used or administered correctly

What does AC7.3 mean?

- ○ The lead word **demonstrate** means that you must **be able to show** through **your work practices** how to use strategies to ensure that medication is used or administered correctly.
- ○ Your **observations** of your work practices must include you using strategies to ensure that medication is used or administered correctly.
- ○ For the key word **strategies** you can think about different ways to ensure that the individual receives the **correct** medication, the correct dose, by the correct route, at the correct time, with agreed support, in line with the individual's guidelines and medication plan and the individual's rights to active participation, dignity, privacy, respect and confidentiality.

Read the following **Real Work Setting** scenario and think about how it relates to your work setting and role:

Real Work Setting

Name: Michael

Job role: Senior Support Worker for adults who have autism

(See page 289 for a description of the role.)

Strategies to ensure the correct use or administration of medication: Michael is being shadowed today by another Senior Support Worker. First, Michael checks that the medication containers and the medication administration record (MAR) include the name of the individual, and also asks the individual to identify himself. To ensure that Michael has the correct medication he checks the name, route and dose of the medication against the label on the container and the individual's MAR. Michael then reads through the most recent entry made on the individual's MAR to check when the last dose was given. Michael then explains to the individual the purpose of his medication, what it is and seeks his consent to administer it to him. Once Michael observes the individual take his medication he records that he has done so in the MAR. Michael explains to the Senior shadowing him that he will continue to monitor the individual in case of any adverse reactions to his medication.

Evidencing AC7.3 to your assessor:

For AC7.3 you must evidence your skills in using strategies to ensure that medication is used or administered correctly.

Assessment Method:
Direct Observation of your work practices.

- ● You can **show** your assessor how you use strategies to ensure that medication is used or administered correctly.

REMEMBER TO:
- ● Make arrangements for **observation** of **your work practices**.
- ● Include evidence of you using different strategies.
- ● Ensure the evidence you provide is related to ensuring that medication is used or administered correctly.
- ● Think about **your work setting** and how to use strategies to ensure that medication is used or administered correctly.

Learning Outcome 7: Be able to support use of medication

Assessment Criterion 7.4: Demonstrate how to address any practical difficulties that may arise when medication is used

What does AC7.4 mean?

- The lead word **demonstrate** means that you must **be able to show** through **your work practices** how to address any practical difficulties that may arise when medication is used.
- Your **observations** of your work practices must include you addressing practical difficulties that arise when medication is used.
- For the key words **practical difficulties** you can think about problems that may arise when medication is used, such as: missed, lost, incorrect and split medication; an individual's decision to refuse medication; an individual's inability or refusal to take medication in its prescribed form; anomalies in records or instructions for use of the medication; any adverse reactions or vomiting that the individual may experience.

Read the following **Real Work Setting** scenario and think about how it relates to your work setting and role:

Real Work Setting

Name: Michael

Job role: Senior Support Worker for adults who have autism

(See page 289 for a description of the role.)

Addressing practical difficulties that may arise when medication is used: Michael and his assessor have arranged to meet and discuss Michael's evidence collection to date. Michael's assessor provides him with some constructive and developmental feedback and then talks through with him how he plans to collect evidence of dealing with practical difficulties, as although he has observed Michael several times now supporting individuals in their use of medication, he has not observed him deal with any practical difficulties. Michael explains to his assessor that he has recently experienced a number of different problems and that he dealt with all of these himself. Michael's assessor asks him whether his manager will be able to provide him with an expert witness testimony of the different practical difficulties he addressed whilst administering medication; Michael agrees to ask his manager about this as his manager did observe him on all the occasions when practical difficulties arose.

Evidencing AC7.4 to your assessor:

For AC7.4 you must evidence your skills in addressing any practical difficulties that may arise when medication is used.

Assessment Method:

Direct Observation of your work practices.

- You can **show** your assessor or an expert witness how to address any practical difficulties that may arise when medication is used.

REMEMBER TO:

- Make arrangements for **observation of your work practices**.
- Include evidence of you addressing any practical difficulties.
- Ensure the evidence you provide is related to difficulties that may arise when medication is used.
- Think about **your work setting** and how to address any practical difficulties that may arise when medication is used.

Learning Outcome 7: Be able to support use of medication

Assessment Criterion 7.5: Demonstrate how and when to access further information or support about the use of medication

What does AC7.5 mean?

○ The lead word **demonstrate** means that you must **be able to show** through **your work practices** how and when to access further information or support about the use of medication.

○ Your **observations** of your work practices must include you accessing further information or support about the use of medication.

○ For the key words **access further information or support** you can think about the occasions when you may require additional information or support from others, such as from the individual, the GP, nurse, pharmacist or your manager, and the procedures you would follow to access these sources.

Read the following **Real Work Setting** scenario and think about how it relates to your work setting and role:

Real Work Setting

Name: Michael
Job role: Senior Support Worker for adults who have autism
(See page 289 for a description of the role.)
Accessing further information or support: At the end of Michael's meeting with his assessor he asks him whether he will need also to collect an expert witness testimony. This would be to support the occasions when he asked his manager about additional support for an individual who did not understand why they needed to take their medication and wanted to know more details about its purpose and its potential side effects. Michael's assessor agrees with him that this would be a good source of evidence, particularly as this evidence occurred naturally and was observed by his line manager. His assessor agrees that it may be difficult for him to observe this occurring naturally when he observes Michael in his work setting.

Evidencing AC7.5 to your assessor:

For AC7.5 you must evidence your skills in showing how and when to access further information or support about the use of medication.

Assessment Method:

Direct Observation of your work practices.

● You can **show** your assessor or an expert witness how and when to access further information or support about the use of medication.

REMEMBER TO:

● Make arrangements for **observation** of **your work practices**.
● Include evidence of you accessing further information or support.
● Ensure the evidence you provide is related to **both** the process you followed and when you followed it.
● Think about **your work setting** and how and when to access further information or support about the use of medication.

Learning Outcome 8: Be able to record and report on use of medication

Assessment Criterion 8.1: Demonstrate how to record use of medication and any changes in an individual associated with it

What does AC8.1 mean?

○ The lead word **demonstrate** means that you must **be able to show** through **your work practices** how to record use of medication and any changes in an individual associated with it.

○ Your **observations** of your work practices must include you recording the use of medication and any changes in an individual.

○ For the key words **changes in an individual** you can think about positive changes as well as adverse reactions that may occur in an individual, such as positive or negative changes to an individual's physical, emotional, mental and social well-being.

Read the following **Real Work Setting** scenario and think about how it relates to your work setting and role:

Real Work Setting

Name: Chloe

Job role: Senior Personal Assistant to an adult who has a learning disability and mental health needs

Chloe has been working as a Senior Personal Assistant for two years. Her Senior responsibilities include: supporting, mentoring and supervising a team of Personal Assistants; supporting the induction and training of a team of Personal Assistants; reviewing individuals' needs; supporting the individual to lead a fulfilling life; supporting the individual with personal care tasks, including supporting the use of medication.

Recording use of medication and changes: Chloe is working the evening shift tonight and has just observed the individual she supports take her medication. Due to the individual experiencing drowsiness when taking this new medication, Chloe observes the individual closely for some time afterwards and agrees with the individual to document in full what she observes. Chloe also asks the individual whether she has experienced any other side effects since she has been taking this new medication. The individual confirms to Chloe that she has been feeling a little dizzy and seems to be having increased balance problems; Chloe agrees with the individual to record this information in full also.

Evidencing AC8.1 to your assessor:

For AC8.1 you must evidence your skills in recording use of medication and any changes in an individual associated with it.

Assessment Method:
Direct Observation of your work practices.

● You can **show** your assessor or an expert witness how to record use of medication and any changes in an individual associated with it.

REMEMBER TO:
● Make arrangements for **observation** of **your work practices**.
● Include evidence of you recording use of medication and any changes in an individual.
● Ensure the evidence you provide is related to the medication the individual has taken.
● Think about **your work setting** and how to record use of medication and any changes in an individual associated with it.

Learning Outcome 8: Be able to record and report on use of medication

Assessment Criterion 8.2: Demonstrate how to report on use of medication and problems associated with medication, in line with agreed ways of working

What does AC8.2 mean?

○ The lead word **demonstrate** means that you must **be able to show** through **your work practices** how to report on use of medication and problems associated with it, in line with agreed ways of working.

○ Your **observations** of your work practices must include you reporting on use of medication and problems associated with it, in line with agreed ways of working.

○ For the key words **problems associated with medication** you can think about adverse reactions and side effects that may occur in an individual, such as changes to their physical, emotional, mental and social well-being.

○ For the key words **agreed ways of working** you can think about the procedures you must follow in your work setting when reporting on the use of medication and the problems associated with an individual's use of medication.

Read the following **Real Work Setting** scenario and think about how it relates to your work setting and role:

Real Work Setting

Name: Chloe
Job role: Senior Personal Assistant to an adult who has a learning disability and mental health needs
(See page 294 for a description of the role.)
Reporting on use of medication and any problems: Chloe has reported to her line manager her observations of the changes she has observed in the individual and the changes about which the individual has informed her. Her line manager advises her to report her observations to the individual's GP.

Evidencing AC8.2 to your assessor:

For AC8.2 you must evidence your skills in how to report on use of medication and problems associated with medication, in line with agreed ways of working.

Assessment Method:

Direct Observation of your work practices.

● You can **show** your assessor or an expert witness how to report on use of medication and problems associated with medication, in line with agreed ways of working.

REMEMBER TO:

● Make arrangements for **observation of your work practices**.
● Include evidence of you reporting on use of medication and problems associated with medication.
● Ensure the evidence you provide is in line with agreed ways of working.
● Think about **your work setting** and how to report in line with the agreed ways of working on use of medication and problems associated with medication.

Learning Outcome 1: Understand the importance of good personal hygiene

Assessment Criterion 1.1: Explain why personal hygiene is important

What does AC1.1 mean?

- The lead word **explain** means that you must **make clear** the reasons why personal hygiene is important.
- Your **account** must **detail** the reasons why.
- For the key words **personal hygiene** you can think about the reasons why it is important to care for your body and keep it clean and healthy.

Read the following **Real Work Setting** scenario and think about how it relates to your work setting and role:

Real Work Setting

Name: Graeme
Job role: Senior Residential Carer for adults who have learning disabilities
Graeme has been working as a Senior Residential Carer for one year. His Senior responsibilities include: inducting, training, mentoring and supervising a team of Residential Carers; updating and reviewing individuals' person-centred plans; providing care and support to individuals with daily activities; supporting individuals to access a range of facilities and services; maintaining accurate records and reporting directly to the manager.
The importance of maintaining personal hygiene: As part of the annual training updates provided to all the team, Graeme will be delivering a training session to Carers focused on the importance of good personal hygiene. Graeme begins by asking the team what good personal hygiene means to each of them; Graeme finds it interesting to note that what is important to each team member in terms of personal hygiene is influenced by their culture, religious beliefs and upbringing. Graeme then asks the team to read through a case study of an individual who has learning disabilities who was not encouraged by those supporting him to maintain his personal hygiene. Graeme uses this case study as a basis for asking the team to consider the consequences of not maintaining good personal hygiene, before discussing together the reasons why personal hygiene is important and giving examples. Graeme asks the team during their discussions to think about why good personal hygiene is important not only for individuals who have learning disabilities, but also for those involved in supporting them.

Evidencing AC1.1 to your assessor:

For AC1.1 you must evidence your understanding of why personal hygiene is important.

Assessment Methods:
Oral/Written Questioning or **Discussion** or a **Personal Statement** or **Reflection**.

- You can **tell** your assessor about why personal hygiene is important.
- Or, you can **talk** to your assessor about why personal hygiene is important.
- Or, you can write a **personal statement or reflection** about your experience of why personal hygiene is important.

REMEMBER TO:
- Provide an **account** and **explain** why personal hygiene is important.
- Include **details** of different reasons why.
- Include examples of why personal hygiene is important.
- Think about **your work setting** and why personal hygiene is important.

Learning Outcome 1: Understand the importance of good personal hygiene

Assessment Criterion 1.2: Describe the effects of poor personal hygiene on health and well-being

What does AC1.2 mean?

- The lead word **describe** means that you must provide an **account** that **details** the effects of poor personal hygiene.
- Your **account** must detail the effects of poor personal hygiene on health and well-being.
- For the key words **poor personal hygiene** you can think about the effects of not caring for your body or keeping it clean and healthy.
- For the key words **health and well-being** you can think about the effects on your and others' physical, emotional, mental and social health and well-being of not caring for your body or keeping it clean and healthy.

Read the following **Real Work Setting** scenario and think about how it relates to your work setting and role:

Real Work Setting

Name: Graeme

Job role: Senior Residential Carer for adults who have learning disabilities

(See page 296 for a description of the role.)

The effects of poor personal hygiene: In the afternoon session of Graeme's training for Carers focused on the importance of good personal hygiene, he asks the team to revisit the case study of an individual who has learning disabilities who was not encouraged by those supporting him to maintain his personal hygiene. They watch a short film put together by this individual and his partner before discussing together the effects of personal hygiene on the individual and others involved in his life. Graeme asks the team to consider the effects on their physical, emotional, mental and social health and well-being.

Evidencing AC1.2 to your assessor:

For AC1.2 you must evidence your understanding of the effects of poor personal hygiene on health and well-being.

Assessment Methods:

Oral/Written Questioning or **Discussion** or a **Personal Statement** or **Reflection**.

- You can **tell** your assessor about the effects of poor personal hygiene on health and well-being.
- Or, you can **talk** to your assessor about the effects of poor personal hygiene on health and well-being.
- Or, you can write a **personal statement or reflection** about your experience of the effects of poor personal hygiene on health and well-being.

REMEMBER TO:

- Provide a detailed **account** of the effects of poor personal hygiene on health and well-being.
- Include **details** and examples of the effects of poor personal hygiene on health and well-being.
- Ensure your evidence relates to the effects of poor personal hygiene on different aspects of health and well-being.
- Think about **your work setting** and examples of the effects of poor personal hygiene on health and well-being.

Learning Outcome 2: Be able to support individuals to maintain personal hygiene

Assessment Criterion 2.1: Support an individual to understand factors that contribute to good personal hygiene

What does AC2.1 mean?

- The lead word **support** means that you must **be able to show** through **your work practices** how to assist an individual in understanding factors that contribute to good personal hygiene.
- Your **observations** of your work practices must include you supporting an individual to understand factors that contribute to good personal hygiene.
- For the key word **factors** you can think about washing before and/or after high risk activities, such as preparing food, using the toilet, eating, showering and bathing (including frequency and equipment used), washing and grooming hair, cleaning and trimming nails, moisturising skin, washing and changing clothes (including frequency and equipment used), treating promptly and correctly any infections or skin allergies.
- For the key words **good personal hygiene** you can think about how you can support an individual to understand different aspects of keeping one's body clean and healthy.

Read the following **Real Work Setting** scenario and think about how it relates to your work setting and role:

Real Work Setting

Name: Malcolm

Job role: Senior Residential Carer for older adults who have learning disabilities

Malcolm has been working as a Senior Residential Carer for ten years. His Senior responsibilities include: assisting the manager to coordinate, develop and review the service; developing, implementing and reviewing individuals' person-centred plans; supporting and training new and existing Residential Carers; carrying out supervisions and appraisals with the team; communicating with and developing positive relationships with individuals, their families, friends, advocates, Carers, other professionals and services.

Factors that contribute to good personal hygiene: Malcolm provides day-to-day support to John, who is finding it difficult to understand why and how to maintain good personal hygiene. As part of John's person-centred plan, Malcom and John meet to talk about why personal hygiene is important and what it means to have good personal hygiene. Malcolm decides to begin the discussion with John by drawing a body map and exploring together the different aspects of keeping the body clean and healthy.

Evidencing AC2.1 to your assessor:

For AC2.1 you must evidence your skills in supporting an individual to understand factors that contribute to good personal hygiene.

Assessment Method:
Direct Observation of your work practices.

- You can **show** your assessor or an expert witness how to support an individual to understand factors that contribute to good personal hygiene.

REMEMBER TO:
- Make arrangements for **observation of your work practices**.
- Include evidence of you demonstrating how to support an individual.
- Ensure your evidence relates to understanding factors that contribute to good personal hygiene.
- Think about **your work setting** and how to support an individual to understand factors that contribute to good personal hygiene.

Learning Outcome 2: Be able to support individuals to maintain personal hygiene

Assessment Criterion 2.2: Address personal hygiene issues with the individual in a sensitive manner without imposing own values

What does AC2.2 mean?

○ The lead word **address** means that you must **be able to show** through **your work practices** how to think about and deal with personal hygiene issues with the individual in a sensitive manner without imposing your own values.

○ Your **observations** of your work practices must include you dealing with personal hygiene issues with the individual.

○ For the key words **personal hygiene issues** you can think about aspects in relation to not washing, frequency of washing, inconsistency when washing, regularity of grooming hair and cleaning and trimming nails, frequency of moisturising skin, frequency of washing and changing clothes, precautions taken with infections or skin allergies, and body odour.

○ For the key words **sensitive manner** you can think about how you speak with an individual, the language, pictures and words you use, where you meet to speak about this with an individual, how you respond to an individual's questions and feelings.

○ For the key words **own values** you can think about how, when thinking about and dealing with personal hygiene issues with the individual, you do not impose your personal thoughts, ideas, principles and beliefs on the individual.

Read the following **Real Work Setting** scenario and think about how it relates to your work setting and role:

Real Work Setting

Name: Malcolm

Job role: Senior Residential Carer for older adults who have learning disabilities

(See page 298 for a description of the role.)

Sensitively addressing personal hygiene issues: During Malcolm's meeting with John both explore through the use of the drawn body map the different parts of the body that can smell if they are not cleaned regularly.

Evidencing AC2.2 to your assessor:

For AC2.2 you must evidence your skills in addressing personal hygiene issues with the individual in a sensitive manner without imposing your own values.

Assessment Method:

Direct Observation of your work practices.

● You can **show** your assessor or an expert witness how to address personal hygiene issues with the individual in a sensitive manner without imposing your own values.

REMEMBER TO:

● Make arrangements for **observation** of **your work practices**.
● Include evidence of you addressing personal hygiene issues with the individual.
● Ensure your evidence relates to you doing this in a sensitive manner and without imposing your own values.
● Think about **your work setting** and how to address personal hygiene issues with the individual in a sensitive manner without imposing your own values.

Learning Outcome 2: Be able to support individuals to maintain personal hygiene

Assessment Criterion 2.3: Support the individual to develop awareness of the effects of poor hygiene on others

What does AC2.3 mean?

○ The lead word **support** means that you must **be able to show** through **your work practices** how to assist an individual in developing awareness of the effects of poor hygiene on others.

○ Your **observations** of your work practices must include you supporting an individual to develop awareness of the effects of poor hygiene on others.

○ For the key word **effects** you can think about the impact on others' physical, emotional, mental and social health and well-being of individuals not caring for their body or keeping it clean and healthy.

○ For the key words **poor hygiene** you can think about the effects of not caring for your body or keeping it clean and healthy.

Read the following **Real Work Setting** scenario and think about how it relates to your work setting and role:

Real Work Setting

Name: Malcolm

Job role: Senior Residential Carer for older adults who have learning disabilities

(See page 298 for a description of the role.)

Developing awareness of the effects of poor hygiene on others: After John successfully uses the drawn body map to identify the different parts of the body that can smell if they are not cleaned regularly, Malcolm raises with John how this can affect other people in different ways. They both think about and discuss all the other people involved in John's life and how he may unintentionally affect them through not maintaining good personal hygiene.

Evidencing AC2.3 to your assessor:

For AC2.3 you must evidence your skills in supporting the individual to develop awareness of the effects of poor hygiene on others.

Assessment Method:

Direct Observation of your work practices.

● You can **show** your assessor or an expert witness how to support the individual to develop awareness of the effects of poor hygiene on others.

REMEMBER TO:

● Make arrangements for **observation** of **your work practices**.

● Include evidence of you supporting the individual to develop awareness of the effects of poor hygiene.

● Ensure your evidence relates to the effects of poor hygiene on others.

● Think about **your work setting** and how to support the individual to develop awareness of the effects of poor hygiene on others.

Learning Outcome 2: Be able to support individuals to maintain personal hygiene

Assessment Criterion 2.4: Support the preferences and needs of the individual while maintaining their independence

What does AC2.4 mean?

- The lead word **support** means that you must **be able to show** through **your work practices** how to promote the preferences and needs of the individual while maintaining their independence.
- Your **observations** of your work practices must include you supporting the preferences and needs of the individual and maintaining their independence.
- For the key word **preferences** you can think about the different ways individuals keep their bodies clean and healthy, according to their background, beliefs, culture and faith.
- For the key word **needs** you can think about the different support that individuals may require, depending on their strengths, abilities and preferences.
- For the key word **independence** you can think about how to provide support to an individual by assisting them to manage their personal hygiene rather than doing it for them.

Read the following **Real Work Setting** scenario and think about how it relates to your work setting and role:

Real Work Setting

Name: Malcolm

Job role: Senior Residential Carer for older adults who have learning disabilities

(See page 298 for a description of the role.)

Individuals' preferences and needs: John explains to Malcolm that he would prefer to have showers rather than baths, and would like to have these in the evenings before going to bed rather than in the mornings. John also shows Malcolm the new deodorant he has bought, which is a roll-on type rather than a spray, and the new linen basket he has bought to place all his used clothes in to remind him to wash these regularly. Malcolm praises John for acting on their agreed actions to maintain a good personal hygiene.

Evidencing AC2.4 to your assessor:

For AC2.4 you must evidence your skills in supporting the preferences and needs of the individual while maintaining their independence.

Assessment Method:

Direct Observation of your work practices.

- You can **show** your assessor or an expert witness how to support the preferences and needs of the individual while maintaining their independence.

REMEMBER TO:

- Make arrangements for **observation** of **your work practices**.
- Include evidence of you supporting the preferences and needs of the individual.
- Ensure your evidence relates to maintaining good personal hygiene and maintaining their independence.
- Think about **your work setting** and how to support the preferences and needs of the individual while maintaining their independence.

Learning Outcome 2: Be able to support individuals to maintain personal hygiene

Assessment Criterion 2.5: Describe how to maintain the dignity of an individual when supporting intimate personal hygiene

What does AC2.5 mean?

- The lead word **describe** means that you must provide an **account** that **details** how to maintain the dignity of an individual when supporting intimate personal hygiene.
- Your **account** must detail **how** to maintain the dignity of an individual.
- For the key word **dignity** you can think about how this involves showing your respect to the individual, empathising when individuals are supported with intimate personal hygiene. **Maintaining dignity** includes privacy, having trust on both sides, being professional, being aware of abuse, averting eye contact to avoid embarrassment, being gentle and being able to empathise. It also means using appropriate language that is suitable for the individual.

Read the following **Real Work Setting** scenario and think about how it relates to your work setting and role:

Real Work Setting

Name: Malcolm

Job role: Senior Residential Carer for older adults who have learning disabilities

(See page 298 for a description of the role.)

Maintaining dignity when supporting intimate personal hygiene: John has agreed to a shower this evening and has chosen Malcolm to support him with this. Malcolm agrees to give John some time alone to get undressed and waits outside the bathroom door until John calls him into the bathroom to assist him with the shower. Whilst John is under the shower Malcolm remains on the other side of the shower door and assists him when John requests this. Each time Malcolm does so he averts eye contact with John so as to avoid embarrassment.

Evidencing AC2.5 to your assessor:

For AC2.5 you must describe how to maintain the dignity of an individual when supporting intimate personal hygiene.

Assessment Methods:

Oral/Written Questioning or **Discussion** or a **Personal Statement or Reflection**.

- You can **tell** your assessor about how to maintain the dignity of an individual when supporting intimate personal hygiene.
- Or, you can **talk** to your assessor about how to maintain the dignity of an individual when supporting intimate personal hygiene.
- Or, you can write a **personal statement or reflection** about your experience of how to maintain the dignity of an individual when supporting intimate personal hygiene.

REMEMBER TO:

- Provide a detailed **account** of how to maintain the dignity of an individual when supporting intimate personal hygiene.
- Include **details** and examples of how to maintain the dignity of an individual when supporting intimate personal hygiene.
- Ensure your evidence relates to supporting intimate personal hygiene.
- Think about **your work setting** and how to maintain the dignity of an individual when supporting intimate personal hygiene.

Learning Outcome 2: Be able to support individuals to maintain personal hygiene

Assessment Criterion 2.6: Identify risks to your health in supporting an individual with personal hygiene routines

What does AC2.6 mean?

- The lead word **identify** means that you must **make clear** risks to your health in supporting an individual with personal hygiene routines.
- Your **list** must make clear the risks to your health.
- For the key word **risks** you can think about how to identify and reduce the potential danger, harm and hazards that may arise in supporting an individual with personal hygiene routines, such as in relation to personal and general health and safety, infection control and abuse.
- For the key words **personal hygiene routines** you can think about how to identify risks in supporting an individual with activities including washing, showering, bathing, using the toilet, dressing, undressing and grooming.

Read the following **Real Work Setting** scenario and think about how it relates to your work setting and role:

Real Work Setting

Name: Malcolm

Job role: Senior Residential Carer for older adults who have learning disabilities

(See page 298 for a description of the role.)

Identifying risks to your health: Prior to supporting John to have a shower this evening Malcolm completed a risk assessment in line with his work setting's procedures for supporting John with this activity. Malcolm identified there being two areas of risk: 1) John becoming physically and/or verbally abusive towards Malcolm; 2) John slipping whilst in the shower.

Evidencing AC2.6 to your assessor:

For AC2.6 you must evidence your knowledge of identifying risks to your health in supporting an individual with personal hygiene routines.

Assessment Methods:

Oral/Written Questioning or **Discussion** or a **Spidergram**.

- You can **tell** your assessor about identifying risks to your health in supporting an individual with personal hygiene routines.
- Or, you can **talk** to your assessor about identifying risks to your health in supporting an individual with personal hygiene routines.
- Or, you can complete a **spidergram** showing risks to your health in supporting an individual with personal hygiene routines.
- You can also use a risk assessment you have completed at work that identifies risks to your health in supporting an individual with personal hygiene routines as a supporting piece of **work product evidence**.

REMEMBER TO:

- Include a **list** of different risks to your health.
- Ensure the list relates to supporting an individual with personal hygiene routines.
- Think about **your work setting** and identify risks to your health in supporting an individual with personal hygiene routines.

Learning Outcome 2: Be able to support individuals to maintain personal hygiene

Assessment Criterion 2.7: Reduce risks to your health when supporting the individual with personal hygiene routines

What does AC2.7 mean?

- The lead word **reduce** means that you must **be able to show** through **your work practices** how to minimise the risks to your health when supporting the individual with personal hygiene routines.
- Your **observations** of your work practices must include you minimising the risks to your health.
- For the key word **risks** you can think about how to minimise the potential danger, harm and hazards that may arise in supporting an individual with personal hygiene routines, such as in relation to personal and general health and safety, infection control and abuse.
- For the key words **personal hygiene routines** you can think about activities including washing, showering, bathing, using the toilet, dressing, undressing and grooming, and how to minimise the risks to your health that these may present.

Read the following **Real Work Setting** scenario and think about how it relates to your work setting and role:

Real Work Setting

Name: Malcolm

Job role: Senior Residential Carer for older adults who have learning disabilities

(See page 298 for a description of the role.)

Reduce risks to your health: As part of Malcolm's risk assessment he has put in a series of controls to reduce the risks to his own health. Malcolm knows that the trigger for John to become physically and/or verbally abusive towards him is when John gets embarrassed by being supported with his personal hygiene. For this reason, waiting outside the bathroom door and on the other side of the shower door and averting eye contact are all ways of working that Malcolm uses to reduce this risk. For the second area of risk, that of John slipping whilst in the shower, a non-slip shower mat is used, hand rails have been installed in the shower and Malcolm also ensures that sufficient time and support are provided to John.

Evidencing AC2.7 to your assessor:

For AC2.7 you must evidence your skills in reducing risks to your health when supporting the individual with personal hygiene routines.

Assessment Method:
Direct Observation of your work practices.

- You can **show** your assessor or an expert witness how to reduce risks to your health when supporting the individual with personal hygiene routines.

REMEMBER TO:
- Make arrangements for **observation** of **your work practices**.
- Include evidence of you reducing risks to your health when supporting the individual with personal hygiene routines.
- Think about **your work setting** and how to reduce risks to your health.

Learning Outcome 2: Be able to support individuals to maintain personal hygiene

Assessment Criterion 2.8: Identify others who may be involved in supporting the individual to maintain personal hygiene

What does AC2.8 mean?

- The lead word **identify** means that you must **make clear** others who may be involved in supporting an individual to maintain personal hygiene.
- Your **list** must make clear others who may be involved in supporting the individual.
- For the key word **others** you can think about how the people who can support the individual may include the individual themselves, your colleagues, the individual's family, carers and friends, members of the public, advocates and other professionals.
- For the key words **personal hygiene** you can think about activities including washing, showering, bathing, using the toilet, dressing, undressing and grooming.

Read the following **Real Work Setting** scenario and think about how it relates to your work setting and role:

Real Work Setting

Name: Malcolm

Job role: Senior Residential Carer for older adults who have learning disabilities

(See page 298 for a description of the role.)

Identifying others who may be involved in supporting the individual: When completing his risk assessment to support John with a shower this evening Malcolm also considered the risks posed to others who may be involved in this activity.

Evidencing AC2.8 to your assessor:

For AC2.8 you must evidence your knowledge of identifying others who may be involved in supporting an individual to maintain personal hygiene.

Assessment Methods:

Oral/Written Questioning or **Discussion** or a **Spidergram.**

- You can **tell** your assessor about identifying others who may be involved in supporting an individual to maintain personal hygiene.
- Or, you can **talk** to your assessor about identifying others who may be involved in supporting an individual to maintain personal hygiene.
- Or, you can complete a **spidergram** showing others who may be involved in supporting an individual to maintain personal hygiene.
- You can also use a risk assessment you have completed at work that identifies others who may be involved in supporting an individual to maintain personal hygiene as a supporting piece of **work product evidence.**

REMEMBER TO:

- Include a **list** of others who may be involved in supporting an individual.
- Ensure the list relates to maintaining personal hygiene.
- Think about **your work setting** and who may be involved in supporting an individual to maintain personal hygiene.

Learning Outcome 3: Understand when poor hygiene may be an indicator of other underlying personal issues

Assessment Criterion 3.1: Identify underlying personal issues that may be a cause of poor personal hygiene

What does AC3.1 mean?

- The lead word **identify** means that you must **make clear** underlying personal issues that may be a cause of poor personal hygiene.
- Your **list** must make clear issues that may cause poor personal hygiene.
- For the key words **personal issues** you can think about how these may relate to an individual's physical, emotional or social well-being, or to abuse or financial issues.
- For the key words **poor personal hygiene** you can think about the underlying reasons there may be for the individual not caring for their body or keeping it clean and healthy.

Read the following **Real Work Setting** scenario and think about how it relates to your work setting and role:

Real Work Setting
Name: Lorraine
Job role: Senior Home Carer for an adult who has learning disabilities
Lorraine has been working as a Senior Home Carer for three years. Her Senior responsibilities include: monitoring and reviewing the support in place for an adult with learning disabilities who lives on her own; supporting and managing a team of Carers; working with the individual to live as independently as possible and learn new life skills.
Identifying underlying personal issues: Lorraine and the other Carers who support Tracey have noticed that over the last few days Tracey has been reluctant to change her clothes or wash her hair; this is unusual for Tracey as she takes a lot of pride in her appearance, enjoys changing her clothes several times a day and spends a lot of time ensuring her hair always looks nice. Lorraine thinks that these changes usually occur in Tracey when she is feeling anxious or worried about an aspect of her life.

Evidencing AC3.1 to your assessor:

For AC3.1 you must evidence your understanding of identifying underlying personal issues that may be a cause of poor personal hygiene.

Assessment Methods:

Oral/Written Questioning or Discussion or a Spidergram.

- You can **tell** your assessor about identifying underlying personal issues that may be a cause of poor personal hygiene.
- Or, you can **talk** to your assessor about identifying underlying personal issues that may be a cause of poor personal hygiene.
- Or, you can complete a **spidergram** showing underlying personal issues that may be a cause of poor personal hygiene.

REMEMBER TO:
- Include a **list** of underlying personal issues that may be a cause of poor personal hygiene.
- Ensure the list relates to poor personal hygiene.
- Think about underlying personal issues that may be a cause of poor personal hygiene in **your work setting**.

Learning Outcome 3: Understand when poor hygiene may be an indicator of other underlying personal issues

Assessment Criterion 3.2: Describe how underlying personal issues might be addressed

What does AC3.2 mean?

- The lead word **describe** means that you must provide an **account** that **details** how underlying personal issues might be addressed.
- Your **account** must detail underlying personal issues.
- For the key words **personal issues** you can think about how these may relate to an individual's physical, emotional or social well-being, or to abuse or financial issues.
- For the key word **addressed** you can think about the different ways to deal with underlying personal issues, depending on what they are, the individual's needs and the agreed support in place.

Read the following **Real Work Setting** scenario and think about how it relates to your work setting and role:

Real Work Setting

Name: Lorraine

Job role: Senior Home Carer for an adult who has learning disabilities

(See page 306 for a description of the role.)

Addressing underlying personal issues: Lorraine visits Tracey and over a coffee raises the issue of her noticing that Tracey does not seem her usual self these days and that she is concerned over her well-being. Tracey gets very upset and leaves the lounge and goes to her room. Lorraine gives her some time alone and after about twenty minutes Tracey comes out of her room. She says that she is very worried about her sister as she has not heard from her for five days; as she usually phones her every day she is afraid that something has happened to her. Lorraine reassures Tracey and supports her to think about what she can do; Tracey decides that she will ring her sister. Tracey finds out that her sister hasn't been in contact as she hasn't been very well, but is feeling much better now and is looking forward to seeing her as usual at the weekend.

Evidencing AC3.2 to your assessor:

For AC3.2 you must evidence your understanding of addressing underlying personal issues that may be a cause of poor personal hygiene.

Assessment Methods:

Oral/Written Questioning or Discussion or Personal Statement or Reflection.

- You can **tell** your assessor about addressing underlying personal issues that may be a cause of poor personal hygiene.
- Or, you can **talk** to your assessor about addressing underlying personal issues that may be a cause of poor personal hygiene.
- Or, you can complete a **personal statement or reflection** about your experience of addressing underlying personal issues that may be a cause of poor personal hygiene.

REMEMBER TO:

- Provide an **account** that details how to address underlying personal issues that may be a cause of poor personal hygiene.
- Think about **your work setting** and underlying personal issues that may be a cause of poor personal hygiene.

Learning Outcome 1: Understand the principles and practice of person-centred thinking, planning and reviews

Assessment Criterion 1.1: Explain what person-centred thinking is, and how it relates to person-centred reviews and person-centred planning

What does AC1.1 mean?

- The lead word **explain** means that you must **make clear** what person-centred thinking is, and how it relates to person-centred reviews and person-centred planning.
- Your **account** must **detail** what person-centred thinking is.
- For the key words **person-centred thinking** you can think about how to support an individual to decide what is important to them, how to support an individual's rights whilst balancing risks, and how to ensure the people providing support are the most suitable for the individual.
- For the key words **person-centred reviews** you can think about how to involve an individual, how to use the review to focus on the individual's strengths and wishes, and how to support the individual to achieve their goals.
- For the key words **person-centred planning** you can think about how to support an individual to live their life as they wish, how to promote an individual's rights to independence, dignity and choice, how to include the individual's support network and provide support that meets the individual's needs and wishes.

Read the following **Real Work Setting** scenario and think about how it relates to your work setting and role:

Real Work Setting

Name: Sophie
Job role: Senior Support Worker for adults who have learning disabilities
Sophie has been working as a Senior Support Worker for one year. Her Senior responsibilities include: leading a team of Support Workers to support three adults with learning disabilities to live in their communities; providing ongoing support, training and supervision of the team.
Person-centred thinking: Sophie is inducting two volunteers today and begins by explaining to them what person-centred thinking is and how it is based on the principles of supporting individuals to lead their lives how they wish and to plan for the future.

Evidencing AC1.1 to your assessor:

For AC1.1 you must evidence your understanding of what person-centred thinking is, and how it relates to person-centred reviews and person-centred planning.

Assessment Methods:
Oral/Written Questioning or **Discussion** or a **Personal Statement or Reflection**.

- You can **tell** your assessor about what person-centred thinking is, and how it relates to person-centred reviews and person-centred planning.
- Or, you can **talk** to your assessor about what person-centred thinking is, and how it relates to person-centred reviews and person-centred planning.
- Or, you can write a **personal statement or reflection** about your experience of what person-centred thinking is, and how it relates to person-centred reviews and person-centred planning.

REMEMBER TO:
- Provide an **account** and **explain** what person-centred thinking is, and how it relates to person-centred reviews and person-centred planning.
- Include **details** and examples of person-centred thinking and the links to person-centred reviews and person-centred planning.
- Think about **your work setting** and what person-centred thinking is, and how it relates to person-centred reviews and person-centred planning.

Learning Outcome 1: Understand the principles and practice of person-centred thinking, planning and reviews

Assessment Criterion 1.2: Explain the benefits of using person-centred thinking with individuals

What does AC1.2 mean?

- The lead word **explain** means that you must **make clear** the benefits of using person-centred thinking with individuals.
- Your **account** must **detail** the benefits.
- For the key words **person-centred thinking** you can think about how to support an individual to decide what is important to them, how to support an individual's rights whilst balancing risks, and how to ensure the people providing support are the most suitable for the individual.

Read the following **Real Work Setting** scenario and think about how it relates to your work setting and role:

Real Work Setting

Name: Sophie

Job role: Senior Support Worker for adults who have learning disabilities

(See page 308 for a description of the role.)

Benefits of person-centred thinking: During Sophie's induction of the two volunteers she invites one of the individuals with learning disabilities to explain how the team's way of working benefits her. Sally explains that she likes living where she does because the way the staff support her has enabled her to think about her life and what she would like to do in the future; Sally adds that this has also made her feel good about and confident in herself. Sally tells the volunteers that having a support network also helps, as different people can help her out in different ways and at different times, and that she likes it as everyone understands her and what she wants.

Evidencing AC1.2 to your assessor:

For AC1.2 you must evidence your understanding of the benefits of using person-centred thinking with individuals.

Assessment Methods:

Oral/Written Questioning or **Discussion** or a **Personal Statement** or **Reflection**.

- You can **tell** your assessor about the benefits of using person-centred thinking with individuals.
- Or, you can **talk** to your assessor about the benefits of using person-centred thinking with individuals.
- Or, you can write a **personal statement or reflection** about your experience of the benefits of using person-centred thinking with individuals.

REMEMBER TO:

- Provide an **account** and **explain** the benefits of using person-centred thinking with individuals.
- Include **details** and examples of the benefits of using person-centred thinking.
- Think about **your work setting** and the benefits of using person-centred thinking with individuals.

Learning Outcome 1: Understand the principles and practice of person-centred thinking, planning and reviews

Assessment Criterion 1.3: Explain the beliefs and values on which person-centred thinking and planning are based

What does AC1.3 mean?

- The lead word **explain** means that you must **make clear** the beliefs and values on which person-centred thinking and planning are based.
- Your **account** must **detail** the beliefs and values.
- For the key words **person-centred thinking** you can think about how to support an individual to decide what is important to them, how to support an individual's rights whilst balancing risks, and how to ensure the people providing support are the most suitable for the individual.
- For the key words **person-centred planning** you can think about: how to support an individual to live their life as they wish; how to promote an individual's rights to independence, dignity and choice; how to include the individual's support network and plan support with them that meets the individual's needs and wishes.

Read the following **Real Work Setting** scenario and think about how it relates to your work setting and role:

Real Work Setting

Name: Sophie

Job role: Senior Support Worker for adults who have learning disabilities

(See page 308 for a description of the role.)

Beliefs and values: At the end of the shift Sophie reflects on her discussions with the volunteers she inducted today and then provides a short summary to them both about the beliefs and values that underpin person-centred thinking and planning. This includes supporting individuals to make their own decisions, to lead their own lives, to make plans for the future and to have support in place that works for the individual by meeting their needs and their preferences.

Evidencing AC1.3 to your assessor:

For AC1.3 you must evidence your understanding of the beliefs and values on which person-centred thinking and planning are based.

Assessment Methods:

Oral/Written Questioning or **Discussion** or a **Personal Statement** or **Reflection**.

- You can **tell** your assessor about the beliefs and values on which person-centred thinking and planning are based.
- Or, you can **talk** to your assessor about the beliefs and values on which person-centred thinking and planning are based.
- Or, you can write a **personal statement or reflection** about the beliefs and values on which person-centred thinking and planning are based.

REMEMBER TO:

- Provide an **account** and **explain** the beliefs and values on which person-centred thinking and planning are based.
- Include **details** and examples of beliefs and values.
- Think about **your work setting** and the beliefs and values on which person-centred thinking and planning are based.

Learning Outcome 1: Understand the principles and practice of person-centred thinking, planning and reviews

Assessment Criterion 1.4: Explain how the beliefs and values on which person-centred thinking is based differ from assessment and other approaches to planning

What does AC1.4 mean?

- The lead word **explain** means that you must **make clear** how the beliefs and values on which person-centred thinking is based differ from assessment and other approaches to planning.
- Your **account** must **detail** how person-centred thinking differs from assessment and other approaches to planning.
- For the key words **person-centred thinking** you can think about how to support an individual to decide what is important to them, how to support an individual's rights whilst balancing risks, and how to ensure the people providing support are the most suitable for the individual.
- For the key word **assessment** you can think about how this involves determining an individual's eligibility for a service or equipment or additional funding.
- For the key word **planning** you can think about how to support an individual using care or support planning, and how decisions are made based on their needs.

Read the following **Real Work Setting** scenario and think about how it relates to your work setting and role:

Real Work Setting

Name: Sophie

Job role: Senior Support Worker for adults who have learning disabilities

(See page 308 for a description of the role.)

How person-centred thinking differs from assessment and planning: Sophie then explains to both volunteers that they must remember that the person-centred thinking way of working is not the same as assessment and other planning approaches. It is a way of working with the individual to achieve the lives they want to lead.

Evidencing AC1.4 to your assessor:

For AC1.4 you must evidence your understanding of how the beliefs and values on which person-centred thinking is based differ from assessment and other approaches to planning.

Assessment Methods:
Oral/Written Questioning or **Discussion** or a **Personal Statement** or **Reflection**.

- You can **tell** your assessor about how the beliefs and values on which person-centred thinking is based differ from assessment and other approaches to planning.
- Or, you can **talk** to your assessor about how the beliefs and values on which person-centred thinking is based differ from assessment and other approaches to planning.
- Or, you can write a **personal statement or reflection** about your experience of how the beliefs and values on which person-centred thinking is based differ from assessment and other approaches to planning.

REMEMBER TO:
- Provide an **account** of the beliefs and values on which person-centred thinking is based.
- Include **details** and examples of the difference between person-centred thinking and assessment and other planning approaches.
- Think about **your work setting** and how the beliefs and values on which person-centred thinking is based differ from assessment and other approaches to planning.

Learning Outcome 1: Understand the principles and practice of person-centred thinking, planning and reviews

Assessment Criterion 1.5: Explain how person-centred thinking tools can form the basis of a person-centred plan

What does AC1.5 mean?

- The lead word **explain** means that you must **make clear** how person-centred thinking tools can form the basis of a person-centred plan.
- Your **account** must **detail** different person-centred thinking tools and how they form the basis of a person-centred plan.
- For the key words **person-centred thinking tools** you can think about what processes are available to support individuals to be active partners, recognise what's important to them and central to making plans for their futures. These include: Making Action Plans (MAPS), to learn about a person's history in order to plan for the future; One-Page Profiles, to find out more about what is important to the individual and what support is needed; Essential Lifestyle Planning, to make improvements to an individual's day-to-day life.
- For the key words **person-centred plan** you can think about how to enable an individual to lead their lives as they wish and ensure what they want is listened to and acted on.

Read the following **Real Work Setting** scenario and think about how it relates to your work setting and role:

Real Work Setting

Name: Sophie

Job role: Senior Support Worker for adults who have learning disabilities

(See page 308 for a description of the role.)

Person-centred thinking tools: Sophie has recently attended a person-centred thinking workshop led by another service in the organisation, which wanted to discuss and share the person-centred thinking tools it uses with individuals.

Evidencing AC1.5 to your assessor:

For AC1.5 you must evidence your understanding of how person-centred thinking tools can form the basis of a person-centred plan.

Assessment Methods:

Oral/Written Questioning or **Discussion** or a **Personal Statement** or **Reflection**.

- You can **tell** your assessor about how person-centred thinking tools can form the basis of a person-centred plan.
- Or, you can **talk** to your assessor about how person-centred thinking tools can form the basis of a person-centred plan.
- Or, you can write a **personal statement or reflection** about your experience of how person-centred thinking tools can form the basis of a person-centred plan.

REMEMBER TO:

- Provide an **account** of how person-centred thinking tools can form the basis of a person-centred plan.
- Include **details** and examples of person-centred thinking tools.
- Include how these tools can form the basis of a person-centred plan.
- Think about **your work setting** and how person-centred thinking tools can form the basis of a person-centred plan.

Learning Outcome 1: Understand the principles and practice of person-centred thinking, planning and reviews

Assessment Criterion 1.6: Describe the key features of different styles of person-centred planning and the contexts in which they are most useful

What does AC1.6 mean?

- ○ The lead word **describe** means that you must provide an **account** that **details** the key features of different styles of person-centred planning and the contexts in which they are most useful.
- ○ Your **account** must detail **different** styles of person-centred planning.
- ○ For the key words **styles of person-centred planning** you can think about how these ways of working involve supporting an individual to live their life as they wish, promoting an individual's rights, including the individual's support network as active partners and planning support with them that meets what the individual wants and is important to them.

Read the following **Real Work Setting** scenario and think about how it relates to your work setting and role:

Real Work Setting

Name: Sophie

Job role: Senior Support Worker for adults who have learning disabilities

(See page 308 for a description of the role.)

Person-centred planning styles: In the training workshop Sophie attended she learnt more about the main features of person-centred planning styles, which all involve enabling individuals to find out what is important to them and then acting on this to achieve their wishes and goals in life. This process is achieved by working with the individual and with the other people who are in their support network and involved in their lives.

Evidencing AC1.6 to your assessor:

For AC1.6 you must evidence your understanding of the key features of different styles of person-centred planning and the contexts in which they are most useful.

Assessment Methods:

Oral/Written Questioning or **Discussion** or a **Personal Statement** or **Reflection.**

- You can **tell** your assessor about the key features of different styles of person-centred planning and the contexts in which they are most useful.
- Or, you can **talk** to your assessor about the key features of different styles of person-centred planning and the contexts in which they are most useful.
- Or, you can write a **personal statement or reflection** about your experience of the key features of different styles of person-centred planning and the contexts in which they are most useful.

REMEMBER TO:

- Provide a detailed **account** of the key features of different styles of person-centred planning and the contexts in which they are most useful.
- Include **details** and examples of the key features of different styles of person-centred planning.
- Include the contexts in which they are most useful.
- Think about **your work setting** and the key features of different styles of person-centred planning and the contexts in which they are most useful.

Learning Outcome 1: Understand the principles and practice of person-centred thinking, planning and reviews

Assessment Criterion 1.7: Describe examples of person-centred thinking tools, their purpose, and how and when each one might be used

What does AC1.7 mean?

- The lead word **describe** means that you must provide an **account** that **details** examples of person-centred thinking tools, their purpose, and how and when each one might be used.
- Your **account** must detail **different** person-centred thinking tools.
- For the key words **person-centred thinking tools** you can think about: the processes that are available; how, why and when they are used to support individuals to be active partners; what's important to individuals that can be central to making plans for their futures, such as using MAPS to learn about a person's history in order to plan for the future, or One-Page Profiles to find out more about what is important to the individual and what support is needed, and Essential Lifestyle Planning to make improvements to an individual's day-to-day life.

Read the following **Real Work Setting** scenario and think about how it relates to your work setting and role:

Real Work Setting
Name: Sophie
Job role: Senior Support Worker for adults who have learning disabilities
(See page 308 for a description of the role.)
Person-centred thinking tools: Sophie plans to share the information she obtained on different person-centred thinking tools with the rest of her team so that they can together consider what each tool involves, its purpose, how and when it is to be used. Sophie thinks this will help the team to develop their knowledge in this area so that tools used with individuals are carefully matched to who they are and their life.

Evidencing AC1.7 to your assessor:

For AC1.7 you must evidence your understanding of examples of person-centred thinking tools, their purpose, and how and when each one might be used.

Assessment Methods:

Oral/Written Questioning or Discussion or a Personal Statement or Reflection.

- You can **tell** your assessor about examples of person-centred thinking tools, their purpose, and how and when each one might be used.
- Or, you can **talk** to your assessor about examples of person-centred thinking tools, their purpose, and how and when each one might be used.
- Or, you can write a **personal statement or reflection** about your experience of examples of person-centred thinking tools, their purpose, and how and when each one might be used.

REMEMBER TO:

- Provide a detailed **account** of examples of person-centred thinking tools.
- Include **details** and examples of person-centred thinking tools.
- Include details about their purpose, and how and when each one might be used.
- Think about **your work setting** and examples of person-centred thinking tools, their purpose, and how and when each one might be used.

Learning Outcome 1: Understand the principles and practice of person-centred thinking, planning and reviews

Assessment Criterion 1.8: Explain the different ways that One-Page Profiles are used

What does AC1.8 mean?

- The lead word **explain** means that you **must make** clear different ways that One-Page Profiles are used.
- Your **account** must **detail** the different ways in which One-Page Profiles are used.
- For the key words **One-Page Profiles** you can think about how an individual sees themselves and how others see the individual, what is important to an individual, what needs to be known about the individual to provide good quality support.

Read the following **Real Work Setting** scenario and think about how it relates to your work setting and role:

Real Work Setting

Name: Sophie

Job role: Senior Support Worker for adults who have learning disabilities

(See page 308 for a description of the role.)

One-Page Profiles: Sophie will be working with Jamie, an individual with learning disabilities who has recently moved to his own flat. As part of her getting to know Jamie, his family and advocate have put together with him a One-Page Profile. This includes words, symbols and photographs showing what he likes and dislikes about himself, what others like about him, what activities he enjoys doing, what is important to him in his life and what he values most, as well as the support that he needs on a day-to-day basis. Jamie is meeting with Sophie today for the first time in his flat and is going to share his One-Page Profile with her. Jamie would like his brother and father to also be present, as he has a very close relationship with both, to help tell Sophie more about him and answer any questions or provide any additional information she may require.

Evidencing AC1.8 to your assessor:

For AC1.8 you must evidence your understanding of the different ways that One-Page Profiles are used.

Assessment Methods:

Oral/Written Questioning or Discussion or a Personal Statement or Reflection.

- You can **tell** your assessor about the different ways that One-Page Profiles are used.
- Or, you can **talk** to your assessor about the different ways that One-Page Profiles are used.
- Or, you can write a **personal statement or reflection** about your experience of the different ways that One-Page Profiles are used.

REMEMBER TO:

- Provide an **account** and **explain** the different ways that One-Page Profiles are used.
- Include **details** and examples of the different ways that One-Page Profiles are used.
- Think about **your work setting** and the different ways that One-Page Profiles are used.

Learning Outcome 2: Understand the context within which person-centred thinking and planning takes place

Assessment Criterion 2.1: Interpret current policy, legislation and guidance underpinning person-centred thinking and planning

What does AC2.1 mean?

○ The lead word **interpret** means that you must provide an **account** that details how current policy, legislation and guidance underpin person-centred thinking and planning.

○ Your **account** must **detail** the current policy, legislation and guidance in place.

○ For the key word **policy** you can think about the principles and rules available in your work setting as well as those available nationally and how they underpin person-centred thinking and planning, such as those that promote inclusion and citizenship of people who have learning disabilities.

○ For the key word **legislation** you can think about the laws in place that underpin person-centred thinking and planning, such as the Human Rights Act 1998, the Equality Act 2010 and the Mental Capacity Act 2005.

○ For the key word **guidance** you can think about the guidelines available in your work setting as well as those available nationally and how they underpin person-centred thinking and planning, such as the national strategy 'Valuing People Now'.

Read the following **Real Work Setting** scenario and think about how it relates to your work setting and role:

Real Work Setting

Name: Carl

Job role: Senior Personal Assistant for adults who have learning disabilities

Carl has been working as a Senior Personal Assistant for three years. His Senior responsibilities include: providing support, training and guidance to a team of Personal Assistants; working closely with individuals, their families and advocates; building on the support in place to ensure all support provided is planned with individuals and reflects their current and future needs.

Policy, legislation and guidance underpinning person-centred thinking and planning: Carl has been spending time reading through current policy, legislation and guidance that is particularly relevant to people who have learning disabilities. He has been thinking about how the purpose and outcomes of these underpins person-centred thinking and planning as they place the individual at the forefront and are based on giving individuals and those important to them more choice, control and power.

Evidencing AC2.1 to your assessor:

For AC2.1 you must evidence your understanding of current policy, legislation and guidance underpinning person-centred thinking and planning.

Assessment Methods:

Oral/Written Questioning or Discussion or a Personal Statement.

● You can **tell** your assessor about the current policy, legislation and guidance underpinning person-centred thinking and planning.

● Or, you can **talk** to your assessor about the current policy, legislation and guidance underpinning person-centred thinking and planning.

● Or, you can write a **personal statement** about the current policy, legislation and guidance underpinning person-centred thinking and planning.

REMEMBER TO:

● Provide an **account** of current policy, legislation and guidance underpinning person-centred thinking and planning.

● Include **details** and examples of current policy, legislation and guidance.

● Include details about how these underpin person-centred thinking and planning.

● Think about **your work setting** and the current policy, legislation and guidance underpinning person-centred thinking and planning.

Learning Outcome 2: Understand the context within which person-centred thinking and planning takes place

Assessment Criterion 2.2: Analyse the relationship between person-centred planning and the commissioning and delivery of services

What does AC2.2 mean?

- The lead word **analyse** means that you must **examine in detail** the relationship between person-centred planning and the commissioning and delivery of services.
- Your **account** must provide an analysis of the relationship.
- For the key word **relationship** you can think about the links between person-centred planning and the commissioning and delivery of services.
- For the key words **person-centred planning** you can think about how to support an individual to live their life as they wish, promote an individual's rights, include the individual's support network as active partners, and plan support with them that meets what the individual wants and is important to them.
- For the key words **commissioning and delivery of services** you can think about the process of developing and providing effective services.

Read the following **Real Work Setting** scenario and think about how it relates to your work setting and role:

Real Work Setting

Name: Carl

Job role: Senior Personal Assistant for adults who have learning disabilities

(See page 316 for a description of the role.)

Relationship between person-centred planning and the commissioning and delivery of services: Carl strongly believes that involving individuals and those important to them not only helps them to live their lives fully, but is also essential for identifying the priorities and needs of people who have learning disabilities, and ensuring services are planned and delivered to meet these priorities and needs.

Evidencing AC2.2 to your assessor:

For AC2.2 you must evidence your understanding of the relationship between person-centred planning and the commissioning and delivery of services.

Assessment Methods:

Oral/Written Questioning or Discussion or a Personal Statement.

- You can **tell** your assessor about the relationship between person-centred planning and the commissioning and delivery of services.
- Or, you can **talk** to your assessor about the relationship between person-centred planning and the commissioning and delivery of services.
- Or, you can write a **personal statement** about the relationship between person-centred planning and the commissioning and delivery of services.

REMEMBER TO:

- Provide an **account** and an analysis of the relationship between person-centred planning and the commissioning and delivery of services.
- Include **details** about how person-centred planning and the commissioning and delivery of services are linked.
- Include **varied** examples of how the relationship works in practice.
- Think about **your work setting** and the relationship between person-centred planning and the commissioning and delivery of services.

Learning Outcome 2: Understand the context within which person-centred thinking and planning takes place

Assessment Criterion 2.3: Describe how person-centred planning and person-centred reviews influence strategic commissioning

What does AC2.3 mean?

- The lead word **describe** means that you must provide an **account** that **details** how person-centred planning and person-centred reviews influence strategic commissioning.
- Your **account** must detail **how** person-centred planning and person-centred reviews influence strategic commissioning.
- For the key words **person-centred planning** you can think about how to support an individual to live their life as they wish, promote an individual's rights, include the individual's support network as active partners and plan support with them that meets what the individual wants and what is important to them.
- For the key words **person-centred reviews** you can think about involving an individual and using the review to focus on the individual's strengths and wishes and on supporting the individual to achieve their goals.
- For the key words **strategic commissioning** you can think about how person-centred planning and person-centred reviews influence the process of developing effective and good quality services.

Read the following **Real Work Setting** scenario and think about how it relates to your work setting and role:

Real Work Setting

Name: Carl

Job role: Senior Personal Assistant for adults who have learning disabilities

(See page 316 for a description of the role.)

Influencing strategic commissioning: Carl has been involved in empowering individuals who have learning disabilities to share their views and ideas about the gaps that there are in services, and how services can be better planned and delivered around individuals.

Evidencing AC2.3 to your assessor:

For AC2.3 you must evidence your understanding of how person-centred planning and person-centred reviews influence strategic commissioning.

Assessment Methods:

Oral/Written Questioning or **Discussion** or a **Personal Statement.**

- You can **tell** your assessor about how person-centred planning and person-centred reviews influence strategic commissioning.
- Or, you can **talk** to your assessor about how person-centred planning and person-centred reviews influence strategic commissioning.
- Or, you can write a **personal statement** about how person-centred planning and person-centred reviews influence strategic commissioning.

REMEMBER TO:

- Provide a detailed **account** of how person-centred planning and person-centred reviews influence strategic commissioning.
- Include **details** and examples of how person-centred planning and person-centred reviews influence strategic commissioning.
- Think about **your work setting** and how person-centred planning and person-centred reviews influence strategic commissioning.

Learning Outcome 2: Understand the context within which person-centred thinking and planning takes place

Assessment Criterion 2.4: Explain what a person-centred team is

What does AC2.4 mean?
- The lead word **explain** means that you must **make clear** what is meant by a person-centred team.
- Your **account** must **detail** what a person-centred team is and what it involves.
- For the key words **person-centred team** you can think about how person-centred thinking is a useful tool to enable a team to work together effectively and strongly by agreeing on the purpose of the team, what is important to the team and what support team members need, and how and when they need this.

Read the following **Real Work Setting** scenario and think about how it relates to your work setting and role:

Real Work Setting

Name: Carl
Job role: Senior Personal Assistant for adults who have learning disabilities
(See page 316 for a description of the role.)
Person-centred team: Carl is meeting with the team today and together they will be exploring how they can become a person-centred team by working through the following seven questions together. 1) Why are we here? To clarify what is expected from team members and the team as a whole. 2) Who are you and how do we work together? To get to know each other and build up trust and understanding. 3) What are we here to do? To clarify roles and responsibilities. 4) Who is going to do what, when and where? To agree on the actions that need to be taken and implemented. 5) How are we doing? To identify strengths and areas for improvement. 6) What else can we try? To build on what the team is learning and what is working. 7) How can we record and share what we are learning? To agree on how to record and present what the team is learning.

Evidencing AC2.4 to your assessor:

For AC2.4 you must evidence your understanding of what a person-centred team is.

Assessment Methods:
Oral/Written Questioning or **Discussion** or a **Personal Statement** or **Reflection**.
- You can **tell** your assessor about what a person-centred team is.
- Or, you can **talk** to your assessor about what a person-centred team is.
- Or, you can write a **personal statement or reflection** about what a person-centred team is.

REMEMBER TO:
- Provide an **account** and **explain** what a person-centred team is.
- Include **details** and examples of the meaning of a person-centred team.
- Think about **your work setting** and what a person-centred team is.

Learning Outcome 2: Understand the context within which person-centred thinking and planning takes place

Assessment Criterion 2.5: Explain how person-centred thinking can be used within a team

What does AC2.5 mean?

- The lead word **explain** means that you must **make clear** how person-centred thinking can be used within a team.
- Your **account** must **detail** how person-centred thinking can be used.
- For the key words **person-centred thinking** you can think about how this is a useful tool to enable a team to work together effectively and strongly by agreeing on the purpose of the team, what is important to the team and what support team members need, and how and when they need this.

Read the following **Real Work Setting** scenario and think about how it relates to your work setting and role:

Real Work Setting

Name: Carl

Job role: Senior Personal Assistant for adults who have learning disabilities

(See page 316 for a description of the role.)

Use of person-centred thinking in a team: In his Senior role, Carl sees himself as being the person to develop the established team further by encouraging, leading and motivating them to use person-centred thinking to revisit how effective the team is in achieving its aims and goals, and how team members are ensuring that their approaches and support are enabling individuals to live their lives fully and in the ways they want to. Carl also plans to use person-centred thinking to support the team to spend more time reflecting on: what they have achieved; which approaches have worked and which haven't; how they can use this learning to develop the ways they work as a team with the individuals to whom they provide support, with each other and with other teams.

Evidencing AC2.5 to your assessor:

For AC2.5 you must evidence your understanding of how person-centred thinking can be used within a team.

Assessment Methods:
Oral/Written Questioning or **Discussion** or a **Personal Statement or Reflection**.

- You can **tell** your assessor about how person-centred thinking can be used within a team.
- Or, you can **talk** to your assessor about how person-centred thinking can be used within a team.
- Or, you can write a **personal statement or reflection** about your experience of how person-centred thinking can be used within a team.

REMEMBER TO:
- Provide an **account** of how person-centred thinking can be used within a team.
- Include **details** and examples of how person-centred thinking can be used within a team.
- Think about **your work setting** and how person-centred thinking can be used within a team.

Learning Outcome 2: Understand the context within which person-centred thinking and planning takes place

Assessment Criterion 2.6: Analyse how to achieve successful implementation of person-centred thinking and planning across an organisation

What does AC2.6 mean?

- The lead word **analyse** means that you must **examine in detail** how to achieve successful implementation of person-centred thinking and planning across an organisation.
- Your **account** must provide an analysis of how to achieve successful implementation of person-centred thinking and planning across an organisation.
- For the key words **person-centred thinking and planning** you can think about how to put into practice these ways of working across an organisation, such as: working alongside and with staff; getting to know each member of staff, including their skills, their strengths, their abilities and the support they need; involving staff in decisions that are made; seeking their views and opinions.

Read the following **Real Work Setting** scenario and think about how it relates to your work setting and role:

Real Work Setting

Name: Carl

Job role: Senior Personal Assistant for adults who have learning disabilities

(See page 316 for a description of the role.)

Successful implementation of person-centred thinking and planning: Carl is attending a senior management meeting this afternoon and has prepared a short presentation of digitally recorded testimonies of the Personal Assistants in his team focusing on the benefit of person-centred thinking and planning to the service's outcomes, the team members' lives and the lives of the individuals they support. It is hoped that in this way Carl's team will be used as a model of good practice to replicate across other services in the organisation.

Evidencing AC2.6 to your assessor:

For AC2.6 you must evidence your understanding of how to achieve successful implementation of person-centred thinking and planning across an organisation.

Assessment Methods:

Oral/Written Questioning or Discussion or a Personal Statement.

- You can **tell** your assessor about how to achieve successful implementation of person-centred thinking and planning across an organisation.
- Or, you can **talk** to your assessor about how to achieve successful implementation of person-centred thinking and planning across an organisation.
- Or, you can write a **personal statement** about your experience of how to achieve successful implementation of person-centred thinking and planning across an organisation.

REMEMBER TO:

- Provide an **account** and an **analysis** of how to achieve successful implementation of person-centred thinking and planning across an organisation.
- Include **details** about how to achieve successful implementation of person-centred thinking and planning.
- Include examples of how to achieve this across an organisation.
- Think about **your work setting** and how to achieve successful implementation of person-centred thinking and planning across an organisation.

Learning Outcome 2: Understand the context within which person-centred thinking and planning takes place

Assessment Criterion 2.7: Describe the role of the manager in implementing person-centred thinking and planning

What does AC2.7 mean?

- The lead word **describe** means that you must provide an **account** that **details** the role of the manager in implementing person-centred thinking and planning.
- Your **account** must detail the role of the manager.
- For the key words **person-centred thinking and planning** you can think about the role of the manager in relation to putting these ways of working into practice across an organisation, such as: working alongside and with staff; getting to know each member of staff, including their skills, their strengths, their abilities, the support they need; involving staff in decisions that are made by seeking their views and opinions.

Read the following **Real Work Setting** scenario and think about how it relates to your work setting and role:

Real Work Setting

Name: Carl

Job role: Senior Personal Assistant for adults who have learning disabilities

(See page 316 for a description of the role.)

Role of the manager in person-centred thinking and planning: Carl works closely with his line manager, Dean, who has been not only very supportive, but also Carl's role model in implementing person-centred thinking and planning across his team and the organisation as a whole. Dean knows each team member's strengths and is an excellent coach and mentor to Carl as he always enables him to bring out the very best in himself and his team. Team meetings and open forums are held regularly with the team to actively encourage them to discuss openly, listen to each other and share any ideas, concerns and difficulties they are having working together.

Evidencing AC2.7 to your assessor:

For AC2.7 you must evidence your understanding of the role of the manager in implementing person-centred thinking and planning.

Assessment Methods:

Oral/Written Questioning or **Discussion** or a **Personal Statement or Reflection.**

- You can **tell** your assessor about the role of the manager in implementing person-centred thinking and planning.
- Or, you can **talk** to your assessor about the role of the manager in implementing person-centred thinking and planning.
- Or, you can write a **personal statement or reflection** about your experience of the role of the manager in implementing person-centred thinking and planning.

REMEMBER TO:

- Provide a detailed **account** of the role of the manager.
- Include **details** and examples of the role of the manager in implementing person-centred thinking and planning.
- Think about **your work setting** and the role of the manager in implementing person-centred thinking and planning.

Learning Outcome 2: Understand the context within which person-centred thinking and planning takes place

Assessment Criterion 2.8: Explain how this relates to the role of a facilitator

What does AC2.8 mean?

- The lead word **explain** means that you must **make clear** how implementing person-centred thinking and planning relates to the role of a facilitator.
- Your **account** must **detail** how this relates to the role of a facilitator.
- For the key word **facilitator** you can think about who manages the person-centred thinking and planning process in terms of working with the individual and others involved in their lives.

Read the following **Real Work Setting** scenario and think about how it relates to your work setting and role:

Real Work Setting

Name: Carl

Job role: Senior Personal Assistant for adults who have learning disabilities

(See page 316 for a description of the role.)

Role of a facilitator: As a Senior, Carl regularly facilitates meetings with his team members and with the individuals to whom his team provides support. He also ensures that all information discussed and shared in these forums is recorded in meaningful ways and in a variety of different formats so that all information is understandable and provided in a way that meets each person's unique needs. In his role as a facilitator Carl is provided with many opportunities to implement person-centred thinking and planning with team members and individuals, and also to reflect on and build on his own professional and training needs. Carl's close working relationship with his manager, along with the guidance and support he receives from him is central to his and the team's achievements.

Evidencing AC2.8 to your assessor:

For AC2.8 you must evidence your understanding of how implementing person-centred thinking and planning relates to the role of a facilitator.

Assessment Methods:

Oral/Written Questioning or **Discussion** or a **Personal Statement** or **Reflection**.

- You can **tell** your assessor about how implementing person-centred thinking and planning relates to the role of a facilitator.
- Or, you can **talk** to your assessor about how implementing person-centred thinking and planning relates to the role of a facilitator.
- Or, you can write a **personal statement or reflection** about how implementing person-centred thinking and planning relates to the role of a facilitator.

REMEMBER TO:

- Provide an **account** of how implementing person-centred thinking and planning relates to the role of a facilitator.
- Include **details** about the role of a facilitator.
- Include **details** about how a facilitator is involved in implementing person-centred thinking and planning.
- Think about **your work setting** and the role of a facilitator in relation to implementing person-centred thinking and planning.

Learning Outcome 3: Understand own role in person-centred planning

Assessment Criterion 3.1: Explain the range of ways to use person-centred thinking, planning and reviews in your role: with individuals; as a team member; as part of an organisation

What does AC3.1 mean?

- ⦿ The lead word **explain** means that you must **make clear** the range of ways to use person-centred thinking, planning and reviews in your role.
- ⦿ Your **account** must **detail** the range of ways involved in your role, with individuals, as a team member and as part of an organisation.
- ⦿ For the key words **person-centred thinking and planning** you can think about how your role involves putting into practice these ways of working with individuals, as a member of a team and as part of an organisation.
- ⦿ For the key words **person-centred reviews** you can think about how your role includes using the reviews to focus on individuals' and team members' strengths and wishes, and on supporting individuals and team members to achieve their goals as well as the goals of the organisation.

Read the following **Real Work Setting** scenario and think about how it relates to your work setting and role:

Real Work Setting

Name: Amina

Job role: Senior Care Assistant for adults who have learning disabilities

Amina has been working as a Senior Care Assistant for five years. Her Senior responsibilities include: providing mentoring, guidance and support to Care Assistants; inducting new Care Assistants; developing and reviewing support plans with individuals and others involved in their lives.

Using person-centred thinking, planning and reviews in your role: Amina discusses with her manager in supervision how she has used person-centred thinking, planning and reviews in her role as a team member, as a member of senior management and with the individuals with whom she works.

Evidencing AC3.1 to your assessor:

For AC3.1 you must evidence your understanding of the range of ways to use person-centred thinking, planning and reviews in your role: with individuals; as a team member; as part of an organisation.

Assessment Methods:

Oral/Written Questioning or **Discussion** or a **Personal Statement** or **Reflection.**

- You can **tell** your assessor about the range of ways to use person-centred thinking, planning and reviews in your role.
- Or, you can **talk** to your assessor about the range of ways to use person-centred thinking, planning and reviews in your role.
- Or, you can write a **personal statement or reflection** about your experience of the range of ways to use person-centred thinking, planning and reviews in your role.

REMEMBER TO:

- Provide an **account** and **explain** the range of ways to use person-centred thinking, planning and reviews in your role: with individuals; as a team member; as part of an organisation.
- Include **details** about different ways to use person-centred thinking, planning and reviews in your role.
- Think about **your work setting** and the range of ways to use person-centred thinking, planning and reviews in your role.

Learning Outcome 3: Understand own role in person-centred planning

Assessment Criterion 3.2: Explain the different person-centred thinking skills required to support individuals

What does AC3.2 mean?

- The lead word **explain** means that you must make clear the different person-centred thinking skills required to support individuals.
- Your **account** must **detail** the different person-centred thinking skills.
- For the key words **person-centred thinking skills** you can think about the skills required to be able to work alongside and with individuals, to get to know each individual, to involve individuals in decisions and to seek their views and opinions.

Read the following **Real Work Setting** scenario and think about how it relates to your work setting and role:

Real Work Setting

Name: Amina

Job role: Senior Care Assistant for adults who have learning disabilities

(See page 324 for a description of the role.)

Person-centred thinking skills required to support individuals: During Amina's supervision, her manager asks her about the main person-centred thinking skills she feels are required to support individuals. Amina explains that there are many skills that are necessary, such as being approachable, having an interest in getting to know individuals, being committed to involving them in their local communities, being a good listener, being able to support individuals without taking over, being able to communicate with individuals and all the others involved in their lives, being able to empower individuals to take control of their lives by showing them how to share the responsibilities for this, as well as being flexible when an individual's preferences, wishes or needs change.

Evidencing AC3.2 to your assessor:

For AC3.2 you must evidence your understanding of the different person-centred thinking skills required to support individuals.

Assessment Methods:

Oral/Written Questioning or **Discussion** or a **Personal Statement** or **Reflection**.

- You can **tell** your assessor about the different person-centred thinking skills required to support individuals.
- Or, you can **talk** to your assessor about the different person-centred thinking skills required to support individuals.
- Or, you can write a **personal statement or reflection** about your experience of the different person-centred thinking skills required to support individuals.

REMEMBER TO:

- Provide an **account** and **explain** the different person-centred thinking skills required.
- Include **details** about different person-centred thinking skills.
- Think about **your work setting** and the different person-centred thinking skills required to support individuals.

Learning Outcome 3: Understand own role in person-centred planning

Assessment Criterion 3.3: Identify challenges that may be faced in implementing person-centred thinking, planning and reviews in your work

What does AC3.3 mean?

○ The lead word **identify** means that you must **make clear** the challenges that may be faced in implementing person-centred thinking, planning and reviews in your work.

○ Your **list** must include different examples of challenges that may be faced.

○ For the key words **person-centred thinking** you can think about the challenges that may be faced in enabling a team to work together effectively and strongly, by agreeing on what is important to the team, and what support team members and individuals need, how and when.

○ For the key words **person-centred planning** you can think about the challenges that may be involved in working with individuals and others to support individuals to live their lives as they wish, in promoting an individual's rights, and in including the individual's support network as active partners and planning support with them that meets what the individual wants and is important to them.

○ For the key words **person-centred reviews** you can think about the challenges that may be faced in involving individuals, using reviews to focus on individuals' strengths and wishes, and supporting individuals to achieve their goals.

Read the following **Real Work Setting** scenario and think about how it relates to your work setting and role:

Real Work Setting

Name: Amina

Job role: Senior Care Assistant for adults who have learning disabilities

(See page 324 for a description of the role.)

Challenges in implementing person-centred thinking, planning and reviews in your work: Amina then shares with her manager some of the challenges she has experienced, both within the team and externally, with individuals and others involved in their lives when putting into practice person-centred thinking, planning and reviews in her work setting.

Evidencing AC3.3 to your assessor:

For AC3.3 you must evidence your understanding of challenges that may be faced in implementing person-centred thinking, planning and reviews in your work.

Assessment Methods:

Oral/Written Questioning or **Discussion** or a **Spidergram**.

● You can **tell** your assessor about challenges that may be faced in implementing person-centred thinking, planning and reviews in your work.

● *Or*, you can **talk** to your assessor about challenges that may be faced in implementing person-centred thinking, planning and reviews in your work.

● *Or*, you can complete a **spidergram** showing the challenges that may be faced in implementing person-centred thinking, planning and reviews in your work.

REMEMBER TO:

● **List** specific challenges that may be faced in implementing person-centred thinking, planning and reviews in your work.

● Include **different** examples of challenges.

● Ensure they relate to implementing person-centred thinking, planning and reviews in your work.

● Think about **your work setting** and the challenges that may be faced in implementing person-centred thinking, planning and reviews in your work.

Learning Outcome 3: Understand own role in person-centred planning

Assessment Criterion 3.4: Describe how challenges that may be faced in implementing person-centred thinking, planning and reviews might be overcome

What does AC3.4 mean?

○ The lead word **describe** means that you must provide an **account** that **details** how challenges that may be faced in implementing person-centred thinking, planning and reviews might be overcome.

○ Your **account** must detail how challenges might be overcome.

○ For the key words **person-centred thinking** you can think about how to overcome the challenges that may be faced in enabling a team to work together effectively and strongly, by agreeing on what is important to the team, and what support team members and individuals need, how and when.

○ For the key words **person-centred planning** you can think about how to overcome the challenges that may be involved in working with individuals and others to support individuals to live their lives as they wish, in promoting an individual's rights, and in including the individual's support network as active partners and planning support with them that meets what the individual wants and is important to them.

○ For the key words **person-centred reviews** you can think about how to overcome the challenges that may be faced in involving individuals, using reviews to focus on individuals' strengths and wishes and supporting individuals to achieve their goals.

Read the following **Real Work Setting** scenario and think about how it relates to your work setting and role:

Real Work Setting

Name: Amina

Job role: Senior Care Assistant for adults who have learning disabilities

(See page 324 for a description of the role.)

Overcoming challenges in implementing person-centred thinking, planning and reviews in your work: Amina and her manager discuss some of the strategies Amina has used to effectively overcome the challenges that she has faced when working with the team, providing support to individuals and involving others involved in individuals' lives.

Evidencing AC3.4 to your assessor:

For AC3.4 you must evidence your understanding of how challenges that may be faced in implementing person-centred thinking, planning and reviews might be overcome.

Assessment Methods:

Oral/Written Questioning or Discussion or a Personal Statement or Reflection.

● You can **tell** your assessor about how to overcome challenges that may be faced.

● Or, you can **talk** to your assessor about how to overcome challenges that may be faced.

● Or, you can write a **personal statement or reflection** about your experience of how to overcome challenges that may be faced.

REMEMBER TO:

● Provide a detailed **account** of how challenges that may be faced in implementing person-centred thinking, planning and reviews might be overcome.

● Include **details** and examples of how to overcome challenges.

● Think about **your work setting** and how to overcome challenges that may be faced in implementing person-centred thinking, planning and reviews.

Learning Outcome 4: Be able to apply person-centred planning in relation to your life

Assessment Criterion 4.1: Demonstrate how to use a person-centred thinking tool in relation to your life to identify what is working and not working

What does AC4.1 mean?

- ○ The lead word **demonstrate** means that you must **be able to show** through **your work practices** how to use a person-centred thinking tool in relation to your life to identify what is working and not working.
- ○ Your **observations** of your work practices must include you using a person-centred thinking tool in relation to your life.
- ○ For the key words **person-centred thinking tool** you can think about how tools such as MAPS can be used to identify your strengths and what is working in your life, as well as how to move away from what is not working in your life, and achieve your dreams for the future, or a tool such as Important To/For to distinguish what's important *to* you from what's important *for* you.

Read the following **Real Work Setting** scenario and think about how it relates to your work setting and role:

Real Work Setting

Name: Shane

Job role: Senior Community Worker for adults who have learning disabilities

Shane has been working as a Senior Community Worker for two years. His Senior responsibilities include: coordinating packages of support with individuals; supporting individuals to engage with others involved in their lives; carrying out supervisions and appraisals for a team of Community Workers; providing them with advice and guidance.

Using a person-centred thinking tool: Shane has been having some personal difficulties at home as well as some difficulties working with a new team member. Shane's manager has suggested that he needs to take a step back from his situation and use a person-centred thinking tool that he finds suitable to identify what is working and what is not working in both his home life and his work life. He suggests that he begin with using the Important To/For tool.

Evidencing AC4.1 to your assessor:

For AC4.1 you must evidence your skills in how to use a person-centred thinking tool in relation to your life to identify what is working and not working.

Assessment Method:
Direct Observation of your work practices.

- You can **show** your assessor or an expert witness how to use a person-centred thinking tool in relation to your life to identify what is working and not working.

REMEMBER TO:
- Make arrangements for **observation** of **your work practices**.
- Include evidence of you using a person-centred thinking tool in relation to your life to identify what is working and not working.
- Ensure the evidence you provide is related to using a person-centred thinking tool in relation to your life.
- Think about **your work setting** and how to use a person-centred thinking tool in relation to your life to identify what is working and not working.

Learning Outcome 4: Be able to apply person-centred planning in relation to your life

Assessment Criterion 4.2: Describe what other person-centred thinking tools would be useful in your life

What does AC4.2 mean?
- The lead word **describe** means that you must provide an **account** that **details** what other person-centred thinking tools would be useful in your life.
- Your **account** must detail other person-centred thinking tools.
- For the key words **person-centred thinking tools** you can think about other tools, such as: the Doughnut, which looks at roles and responsibilities; Matching Support, which looks at matching staff's skills, strengths and personalities to particular individuals; Circles of Support, which looks at identifying who is important in your life.

Read the following **Real Work Setting** scenario and think about how it relates to your work setting and role:

Real Work Setting

Name: Shane

Job role: Senior Community Worker for adults who have learning disabilities

(See page 328 for a description of the role.)

Using other person-centred thinking tools: Shane has also spent some time discussing with his manager other person-centred tools that may be useful to him in terms of the areas of work and home he wishes to address, and thinks that the Doughnut will be useful for work and Circles of Support for home. Shane begins by finding out more about each tool and how relevant each will be to helping him address the areas that are not working well, as well as identifying where his strengths lie and how he can build on these for the future. Shane has found using person-centred thinking tools a good way to see his life, hopes and dreams objectively and in ways that are understandable.

Evidencing AC4.2 to your assessor:
For AC4.2 you must evidence your understanding of what other person-centred thinking tools would be useful in your life.

Assessment Methods:
Oral/Written Questioning or Discussion or a Personal Statement or Reflection.
- You can **tell** your assessor about other person-centred thinking tools that would be useful in your life.
- Or, you can **talk** to your assessor about other person-centred thinking tools that would be useful in your life.
- Or, you can write a **personal statement or reflection** about other person-centred thinking tools that would be useful in your life.

REMEMBER TO:
- Provide a detailed **account** of what other person-centred thinking tools would be useful in your life.
- Include **details** and examples of other person-centred thinking tools that would be useful in your life.
- Think about other person-centred thinking tools that would be useful in **your life**.

Learning Outcome 4: Be able to apply person-centred planning in relation to your life

Assessment Criterion 4.3: Evaluate which person-centred thinking tools could be used to think more about own community connections

What does AC4.3 mean?

- The lead word **evaluate** means that you must **be able to show** through **your work practices** how you assess which person-centred thinking tools could be used to think more about your own community connections.
- Your **observations** of your work practices must include an assessment of which person-centred thinking tools could be used to think more about your community connections.
- For the key words **person-centred thinking tools** you can think about other tools, such as: Who Am I? My Gifts and Capacities, to build up a picture of you as an individual; or Who Am I? My Places, to build up a profile of your interests, where you go and access to think more about how you are involved and part of a community or different communities.
- For the key words **community connections** you can think about the people and services you know, that know you and that you access, and how you are involved in and part of a community or different communities.

Read the following **Real Work Setting** scenario and think about how it relates to your work setting and role:

Real Work Setting

Name: Shane

Job role: Senior Community Worker for adults who have learning disabilities

(See page 328 for a description of the role.)

Using other person-centred thinking tools to think about your community connections: Shane has been mapping out his network of connections in his community at work and at home. Completing this activity has made Shane realise just how many different people and services he comes into contact with for different reasons and for different lengths of time. It has also helped him think about how involved he is in both his communities and why this is very important to him and the way he lives his life and carries out his role as a Senior Community Worker.

Evidencing AC4.3 to your assessor:

For AC4.3 you must evidence your skills in how to evaluate which person-centred thinking tools could be used to think more about your community connections.

Assessment Method:

Direct Observation of your work practices.

- You can **show** your assessor or an expert witness how to evaluate which person-centred thinking tools could be used to think more about your community connections.

REMEMBER TO:

- Make arrangements for **observation of your work practices**.
- Include **evidence** of you evaluating which person-centred thinking tools could be used to think more about your community connections.
- Think about which person-centred thinking tools could be used to think more about **your community connections**.

Learning Outcome 4: Be able to apply person-centred planning in relation to your life

Assessment Criterion 4.4: Evaluate which person-centred thinking tools or person-centred planning styles could be used to think more about your future aspirations

What does AC4.4 mean?

- The lead word **evaluate** means that you must **be able to show** through **your work practices** how you assess which person-centred thinking tools or planning styles could be used to think more about your future aspirations.
- Your **observations** of your work practices must include you assessing which person-centred thinking tools or planning styles could be used to think more about your future aspirations.
- For the key words **person-centred thinking tools or person-centred planning styles** you can think about tools, such as: Essential Lifestyle Planning, which focuses on how to build on your current life to achieve your hopes and dreams for the future; Hopes and Fears, which identifies what is stopping you from achieving your hopes and how to overcome these barriers; Planning Alternate Tomorrows with Hope (PATH), to help you think about identifying short-term and long-term goals to achieve your future aspirations.
- For the key words **future aspirations** you can think about these in relation to your career or your personal life.

Read the following **Real Work Setting** scenario and think about how it relates to your work setting and role:

Real Work Setting

Name: Shane

Job role: Senior Community Worker for adults who have learning disabilities

(See page 328 for a description of the role.)

Using person-centred thinking tools for future aspirations: Shane has decided to use the PATH person-centred thinking tool to help him move forward and stop seeing his future aspirations as unrealistic. Using this tool has helped Shane to refocus on his future hopes and dreams and to map out a path of how he can realistically achieve these hopes and dreams and make steps towards both his short-term and long-term goals. Shane also plans to look into developing an Essential Lifestyle Plan for himself.

Evidencing AC4.4 to your assessor:

For AC4.4 you must evidence your skills in how to evaluate which person-centred thinking tools or person-centred planning styles could be used to think more about your future aspirations.

Assessment Method:	**REMEMBER TO:**
Direct Observation of your work practices. • You can **show** your assessor or an expert witness how to evaluate which person-centred thinking tools or planning styles could be used to think more about your future aspirations.	• Make arrangements for **observation** of **your work practices**. • Include evidence of you evaluating person-centred thinking tools or person-centred planning styles. • Think about **which** person-centred thinking tools or planning styles could be used to think more about **your future aspirations**.

Learning Outcome 5: Be able to implement person-centred thinking, planning and reviews

Assessment Criterion 5.1: Demonstrate the person-centred thinking and styles of person-centred planning that can be used to help individuals move towards their dreams

What does AC5.1 mean?

- The lead word **demonstrate** means that you must **be able to show** through **your work practices** the person-centred thinking and styles of person-centred planning that can be used to help individuals move towards their dreams.
- Your **observations** of your work practices must include you using person-centred thinking and styles of person-centred planning with individuals.
- For the key words **person-centred thinking and styles of person-centred planning** you can think about how working approaches, good quality support and tools – such as Essential Lifestyle Planning, Hopes and Fears and PATH – help individuals to think about identifying short-term and long-term goals to achieve their dreams.

Read the following **Real Work Setting** scenario and think about how it relates to your work setting and role:

Real Work Setting

Name: Ria

Job role: Senior Carer for young adults who have learning disabilities

Ria has been working as a Senior Carer for five years. Her Senior responsibilities include: day-to-day support to individuals and a team of Carers; assessing individuals' changing support needs; developing, implementing and evaluating person-centred care and support; liaising with other agencies and services to maximise individuals' involvement in their local communities; supporting the manager to manage the service.

Using person-centred thinking and styles of person-centred planning: Ria is currently supporting her team to work closely with an individual who is moving to live in a shared house after living in his own flat for a year as he found that he was unable to manage living on his own and maintaining his own flat. Ria and the team have empowered the individual to use his experience of living in his own flat to help him identify what he didn't like, as well as what he discovered about himself, his abilities, likes and strengths, to help him express what he needs from the team and others involved in his life to put together an action plan to help him achieve his dream of living on his own.

Evidencing AC5.1 to your assessor:

For AC5.1 you must evidence your skills in using person-centred thinking and styles of person-centred planning to help individuals move towards their dreams.

Assessment Method:	REMEMBER TO:
Direct Observation of your work practices. • You can **show** your assessor the person-centred thinking and styles of person-centred planning that can be used to help individuals move towards their dreams.	• Make arrangements for **observation** of **your work practices**. • Include evidence of you using person-centred thinking and styles of person-centred planning. • Ensure the evidence you provide relates to helping individuals move towards their dreams. • Think about **your work setting** and the person-centred thinking and styles of person-centred planning that can be used to help individuals move towards their dreams.

Learning Outcome 5: Be able to implement person-centred thinking, planning and reviews

Assessment Criterion 5.2: Show that the plan and process are owned by the individual

What does AC5.2 mean?

- The lead word **show** means that you must be able to **demonstrate** through **your work practices** that the plan and process are owned by the individual.
- Your **observations** of your work practices must include you showing that the individual owns the plan and process.
- For the key words **plan and process** you can think about how a person-centred plan or an Essential Lifestyle Plan, as well as the detailed process undertaken to develop either of these, is actively led by the individual, who is in control of it and owns it.

Read the following **Real Work Setting** scenario and think about how it relates to your work setting and role:

Real Work Setting

Name: Ria

Job role: Senior Carer for young adults who have learning disabilities

(See page 332 for a description of the role.)

Showing that the plan and process are owned by the individual: Ria has supported Sara to put together an Essential Lifestyle Plan with her and all the people involved in her life, including her family, friends, advocate and other professionals; this has been a very detailed process and has taken place over a period of two months. It has involved Sara being enabled to explore what is important to her, which she has not done before, as in the past she has instead expressed what others involved in her life think is important for her. Sara has found it very empowering to be listened to about how she wants to live her life and the support she will need to do this. In addition, she has had an opportunity for the first time to discuss with her family and friends areas on which they disagree about what will improve her quality of life, and to agree with them how to resolve these challenges and move forward together.

Evidencing AC5.2 to your assessor:

For AC5.2 you must evidence your skills in showing that the plan and process are owned by the individual.

Assessment Method:
Direct Observation of your work practices.

- You can **show** your assessor that the plan and process are owned by the individual.

REMEMBER TO:
- Make arrangements for **observation** of **your work practices**.
- Include evidence of you showing that the plan and process are owned by the individual.
- Ensure the evidence you provide relates to the individual's ownership.
- Think about **your work setting** and how the plan and process are owned by the individual.

Learning Outcome 5: Be able to implement person-centred thinking, planning and reviews

Assessment Criterion 5.3: Demonstrate how person-centred thinking tools can be used to develop a person-centred plan

What does AC5.3 mean?

- The lead word **demonstrate** means that you must be able to **show** through **your work practices** how person-centred thinking tools can be used to develop a person-centred plan.
- Your **observations** of your work practices must include you using person-centred thinking tools to develop a person-centred plan.
- For the key words **person-centred thinking tools** you can think about the role of tools – such as MAPS, PATH, Who Am I? My Gifts and Capacities and Who Am I? My Places – in developing person-centred plans that belong to and are owned by individuals.
- For the key words **person-centred plan** you can think about what is involved in developing a person-centred plan or an Essential Lifestyle Plan.

Read the following **Real Work Setting** scenario and think about how it relates to your work setting and role:

Real Work Setting

Name: Ria
Job role: Senior Carer for young adults who have learning disabilities
(See page 332 for a description of the role.)
Using person-centred thinking tools to develop a person-centred plan: Supporting Sara in putting together her own Essential Lifestyle Plan involved exploring together several different person-centred thinking tools. Using MAPS was very useful as this tool helped Sara to think about who she is, what is important to her, what she likes, what others like and admire about her, and what her dreams and hopes for the future are. For Sara this involved expressing herself in words, pictures and sounds. Using the Circles of Support tool enabled Sara to think about who is involved in her life, why and how.

Evidencing AC5.3 to your assessor:

For AC5.3 you must evidence your skills in demonstrating how person-centred thinking tools can be used to develop a person-centred plan.

Assessment Method:

Direct Observation of your work practices.

- You can **show** your assessor how person-centred thinking tools can be used to develop a person-centred plan.

REMEMBER TO:

- Make arrangements for **observation** of **your work practices**.
- Include evidence of you showing how person-centred thinking tools can be used.
- Ensure your evidence relates to developing a person-centred plan.
- Think about **your work setting** and how person-centred thinking tools can be used to develop a person-centred plan.

Learning Outcome 5: Be able to implement person-centred thinking, planning and reviews

Assessment Criterion 5.4: Using information from a person-centred review to start a person-centred plan

What does AC5.4 mean?

○ The lead word **using** means that you must be able to **demonstrate** through **your work practices** how to access information obtained from a person-centred review to start a person-centred plan.

○ Your **observations** of your work practices must include you using information from a person-centred review to start a person-centred plan.

○ For the key words **person-centred review** you can think about the information that can be obtained on individuals' strengths and wishes, and the support individuals would like to receive to achieve their goals.

○ For the key words **person-centred plan** you can think about what is involved in starting a person-centred plan or an Essential Lifestyle Plan.

Read the following **Real Work Setting** scenario and think about how it relates to your work setting and role:

Real Work Setting

Name: Ria

Job role: Senior Carer for young adults who have learning disabilities

(See page 332 for a description of the role.)

Using information from a person-centred review: Ria is meeting with one of the Carers on the team this morning to talk her through how to use information gained from person-centred reviews to start person-centred plans. As the Carer has not used this approach before, Ria has suggested she shadow her when she does this with one of the individuals she supports. She has sought permission from an individual to do this. Ria meets with Tom, who has recently had a person-centred review, at which Tom, his family, advocate, Personal Assistant and Carer were present, and he has brought along the information discussed and obtained at this meeting. Ria and Tom begin by looking through the information collated; this includes pictures hand drawn by Tom about his likes, photographs of people who support him and with whom he enjoys doing different activities, and digitally recorded film of times spent with his family.

Evidencing AC5.4 to your assessor:

For AC5.4 you must evidence your skills in how to use information from a person-centred review to start a person-centred plan.

Assessment Method:

Direct Observation of your work practices.

○ You can **show** your assessor how you use information from a person-centred review to start a person-centred plan.

REMEMBER TO:

● Make arrangements for **observation** of **your work practices**.

● Include evidence of you using information from a person-centred review.

● Ensure your evidence relates to starting a person-centred plan.

● Think about **your work setting** and how to use information from a person-centred review to start a person-centred plan.

Learning Outcome 5: Be able to implement person-centred thinking, planning and reviews

Assessment Criterion 5.5: Use person-centred thinking to enable individuals to choose those who support them

What does AC5.5 mean?

- The lead word **use** means that you must be able to **demonstrate** through **your work practices** how to apply person-centred thinking to enable individuals to choose those who support them.
- Your **observations** of your work practices must include you using person-centred thinking.
- For the key words **person-centred thinking** you can think about how to support an individual to decide what is important to them, how to support their choices and how to ensure the people providing the support are the most suitable for the individual.

Read the following **Real Work Setting** scenario and think about how it relates to your work setting and role:

Real Work Setting

Name: Ria

Job role: Senior Carer for young adults who have learning disabilities

(See page 332 for a description of the role.)

Enabling individuals to choose whom to support them: During Ria's meeting with Tom to develop his person-centred plan, they discuss the activities that Tom would like to try at the weekends. Tom chooses the photographs showing Boccia, Golf and Drama. Ria and Tom then talk through what each activity involves, the support that Tom may need to participate in these activities, and the qualities and skills he thinks those who support him may need. Ria enables Tom then to think about whom he would like to support him with each activity by looking at the photographs of the people in his circles of support. Ria and Tom then agree to approach each person he has chosen to find out if they are able to support him with each activity and to agree a plan of action for each activity.

Evidencing AC5.5 to your assessor:

For AC5.5 you must evidence your skills in using person-centred thinking to enable individuals to choose those who support them.

Assessment Method:

Direct Observation of your work practices.

- You can **show** your assessor how you use person-centred thinking to enable individuals to choose those who support them.

REMEMBER TO:

- Make arrangements for **observation** of **your work practices**.
- Include evidence of you showing how to use person-centred thinking.
- Ensure your evidence relates to enabling individuals to choose those who support them.
- Think about **your work setting** and how to use person-centred thinking to enable individuals to choose those who support them.

Learning Outcome 5: Be able to implement person-centred thinking, planning and reviews

Assessment Criterion 5.6: Support the individual and others involved to understand their responsibilities in achieving actions agreed

What does AC5.6 mean?

- The lead word **support** means that you must be able to **demonstrate** through **your work practices** how to assist the individual and others in understanding their responsibilities in achieving actions agreed.
- Your **observations** of your work practices must include you supporting the individual and others involved to understand their responsibilities.
- For the key words **others** you can think about how the people involved in sharing the responsibilities for achieving actions agreed may include the individual's partner, family, friends, advocate, carers, members of the public, your colleagues and/or professionals.

Read the following **Real Work Setting** scenario and think about how it relates to your work setting and role:

Real Work Setting

Name: Ria

Job role: Senior Carer for young adults who have learning disabilities

(See page 332 for a description of the role.)

Supporting the individual and others to understand their responsibilities: Ria and Tom then arrange to meet the people involved in supporting him with each activity and Ria empowers Tom to express the support he will need in order to be able to participate fully in each activity. A set of clear responsibilities is then drawn up by Tom and all those involved, and recorded by Ria; this includes responsibility for booking the activities, participating in the activities and reviewing each one afterwards to include Tom's experience of these, as well as the quality and level of support provided. Tom, along with each person involved in the process, agrees when and how to carry out these responsibilities to achieve his wish to try each of these activities for the first time this summer.

Evidencing AC5.6 to your assessor:

For AC5.6 you must evidence your skills in supporting the individual and others involved to understand their responsibilities in achieving actions agreed.

Assessment Method:

Direct Observation of your work practices.

- You can **show** your assessor how you support the individual and others involved to understand their responsibilities in achieving actions agreed.

REMEMBER TO:

- Make arrangements for **observation** of **your work practices**.
- Include evidence of you supporting the individual and others involved to understand their responsibilities.
- Ensure your evidence relates to achieving actions agreed.
- Think about **your work setting** and how to support the individual and others involved to understand their responsibilities in achieving actions agreed.

Learning Outcome 5: Be able to implement person-centred thinking, planning and reviews

Assessment Criterion 5.7: Demonstrate a successful person-centred review

What does AC5.7 mean?

- The lead word **demonstrate** means that you must **be able to show** through **your work practices** a successful person-centred review.
- Your **observations** of your work practices must include you demonstrating a successful person-centred review.
- For the key words **person-centred review** you can think about the information that can be obtained on individuals' strengths and wishes, and the support individuals would like in order to achieve their goals and how the person is involved in the whole process.

Read the following **Real Work Setting** scenario and think about how it relates to your work setting and role:

Real Work Setting

Name: Ria

Job role: Senior Carer for young adults who have learning disabilities

(See page 332 for a description of the role.)

A successful person-centred review: At the end of Tom's person-centred review, Ria asks each person involved for their views and contributions about how the meeting worked in practice. This includes the arrangements made in preparation for the review, the facilities and support provided, how the review was facilitated, the quality and relevance of discussions, the quality and relevance of the information shared, and the quality and level of involvement of each participant. Tom gives Ria a thumbs-up and says that he feels good and enjoyed being the leader of his review. Tom's brother thanks Tom for running the review so well and for making him a part of it. Tom's advocate thought it was a very good idea to make use of the digital recorded film in the way they did. Tom's Carer and Personal Assistant confirm that this was the first time they'd been involved in a person-centred review, that they thought it was very informative and enjoyed feeling part of Tom's circle of support. Ria thanks everyone for their contributions and explains that she has found the process very informative and feels that she has got a better insight into everyone's views and how to continue to improve on the quality of support available to Tom.

Evidencing AC5.7 to your assessor:

For AC5.7 you must evidence your skills in demonstrating a successful person-centred review.

Assessment Method:

Direct Observation of your work practices.

- You can **show** your assessor how you demonstrate a successful person-centred review.

REMEMBER TO:

- Make arrangements for **observation of your work practices**.
- Include evidence of you demonstrating a successful person-centred review.
- Think about **your work setting** and how to demonstrate a successful person-centred review.

Learning Outcome 1: Understand how active support translates values into person-centred practical action with an individual

Assessment Criterion 1.1: Compare the characteristics associated with active support and the hotel model in relation to an individual's support

What does AC1.1 mean?

- The lead word **compare** means that you must **make clear** the similarities and differences associated with the active support model and the hotel model in relation to an individual's support.
- Your **account** must make clear **both the similarities and the differences** between these two models.
- For the key words **active support** you can think about how this involves interacting with individuals in a person-centred way, including day-to-day planning with individuals that promotes their participation and enhances their quality of life. For example, this may mean Carers supporting individuals to plan for activities they wish to participate in, including providing opportunities for individuals to lead these activities.
- For the key words **hotel model** you can think about how this involves institutional-style settings that are organised according to staff needs rather than individuals' needs; they are not person-centred and they offer a poor quality of life to individuals. For example, this may mean Carers carrying out all the domestic tasks and not providing opportunities for individuals to participate in activities.

Read the following **Real Work Setting** scenario and think about how it relates to your work setting and role:

Real Work Setting

Name: Miguel

Job Role: Senior Care Assistant for older people

Miguel's Senior responsibilities include: supporting a team of Care Assistants to provide high quality, person-centred and individualised support to all individuals; leading on care planning and reviews.

Comparing the active support and hotel models: At Miguel's team meeting this week he plans to update the team on new ways of working to ensure more effective person-centred support to individuals. He will be referring to active support and the hotel model of support.

Evidencing AC1.1 to your assessor:

For AC1.1 you must evidence your understanding of comparing the characteristics associated with active support and the hotel model in relation to an individual's support.

Assessment Methods:

Oral/Written Questioning or **Discussion** or a **Personal Statement.**

- You can **tell** your assessor about the similarities and differences associated with active support and the hotel model in relation to an individual's support.
- Or, you can **talk** to your assessor about the similarities and differences associated with active support and the hotel model in relation to an individual's support.
- Or, you can write a **personal statement** about the similarities and differences associated with active support and the hotel model in relation to an individual's support.

REMEMBER TO:

- Provide an **account** and **compare** the characteristics associated with active support and the hotel model in relation to an individual's support.
- Include varied examples of characteristics of both active support and the hotel model.
- Include details about the similarities and differences associated with active support and the hotel model.
- Ensure your evidence relates to an individual's support.
- Think about **your work setting** and the characteristics associated with active support and the hotel model in relation to an individual's support.

Learning Outcome 1: Understand how active support translates values into person-centred practical action with an individual

Assessment Criterion 1.2: Identify practical changes that could be made within a service setting to: promote an individual's independence; support informed choices; improve quality of life

What does AC1.2 mean?

○ The lead word **identify** means that you must **make clear** the practical changes that could be made within a service setting to: promote an individual's independence; support informed choices; improve quality of life.

○ Your **list** must make clear **different** practical changes that could be made within a service setting.

○ For the key words **practical changes** you can think about how this involves ensuring services and their settings are responsive to individuals' needs, are able to accommodate changes that individuals may wish to make in their lives, and are able to provide opportunities for individuals to lead their lives as they wish.

Read the following **Real Work Setting** scenario and think about how it relates to your work setting and role:

Real Work Setting

Name: Miguel

Job Role: Senior Care Assistant for older people

(See page 339 for a description of the role.)

Identifying practical changes: Miguel also plans to involve the team this week in discussing and agreeing new ways of working that they will adopt as a whole team in order to promote individuals' independence in all daily activities, support individuals to make informed choices and improve individuals' quality of life. Miguel is hoping that the team will share their ideas for how they can do this as part of their day-to-day work activities, and that together they can plan when and how to do this and also identify any resources that may be required to make this happen.

Evidencing AC1.2 to your assessor:

For AC1.2 you must evidence your understanding of practical changes that could be made within a service setting to: promote an individual's independence; support informed choices; improve quality of life.

Assessment Methods:

Oral/Written Questioning or Discussion or a **Spidergram**.

● You can **tell** your assessor about the practical changes that could be made within a service setting.

● Or, you can **talk** to your assessor about the practical changes that could be made within a service setting.

● Or, you can complete a **spidergram** showing the practical changes that could be made within a service setting.

REMEMBER TO:

● Provide the different **practical changes** that could be made within a service.

● Include **varied** examples of practical changes that could be made.

● Ensure your evidence relates to promoting an individual's independence, supporting informed choices and improving quality of life.

● Think about **your work setting** and the practical changes that could be made to promote individuals' independence, support informed choices and improve quality of life.

Learning Outcome 2: Be able to interact positively with individuals to promote participation

Assessment Criterion 2.1: Assess the levels of help an individual would need to participate in a range of new activities

What does AC2.1 mean?

○ The lead word **assess** means that you must **be able to show** through **your work practices** how you determine the levels of help an individual would need in order to participate in a range of new activities.

○ Your **observations of your work practices** must include you determining the levels of help an individual would need.

○ For the key words **levels of help** you can think about varying levels of assistance to individuals – from verbal reminders providing the lowest level of support, to actual physical guidance providing the highest level of support. Support to individuals should be given flexibly according to the individual's need for help, and should be focused on encouraging as much independence as possible.

○ For the key words **range of new activities** you can think about how individuals can be assessed to be supported to participate in a range of social, leisure, educational and work activities.

Read the following **Real Work Setting** scenario and think about how it relates to your work setting and role:

Real Work Setting

Name: Julia

Job Role: Senior Support Worker for adults who have learning disabilities

Julia's Senior responsibilities include: ensuring all individuals receive high quality, individualised and person-centred support; supporting and developing the team's working practices; coaching and mentoring team members; maintaining up-to-date support plans for all individuals.

Assessing levels of help needed: Julia is meeting with Anna for the first time. She will be assessing from the referral information and from speaking with this individual, her advocate and family how much support will be required for her to take part in two new activities she has never tried before: rock climbing and canoeing.

Evidencing AC2.1 to your assessor:

For AC2.1 you must evidence your skills in assessing the levels of help an individual would need to participate in a range of new activities.

Assessment Method:

Direct Observation of your work practices.

● You can **show** your assessor or an expert witness how to assess the **levels of help** an individual would need to participate in a range of new activities.

● You can use the information you have found out about an individual, in relation to the levels of help needed, and documented in their plan of support as a supporting piece of **work product evidence**.

REMEMBER TO:

● Make arrangements for **observation of your work practices**.

● Include evidence of how you assessed the levels of help an individual would need.

● Include evidence of the **support** an individual would need to participate in a range of new activities.

● Think about **your work setting** and how you assess the levels of help an individual would need to participate in a range of new activities.

Learning Outcome 2: Be able to interact positively with individuals to promote participation

Assessment Criterion 2.2: Use task analysis to break down a range of new activities into manageable steps for an individual

What does AC2.2 mean?

- The lead word **use** means that you must **be able to show** through **your work practices** how you opt for task analysis to break down a range of new activities into manageable steps for an individual.
- Your **observations** of your work practices must include you using task analysis.
- For the key words **task analysis** you can think about how this involves breaking tasks down into small, manageable steps, as is done in DIY guides and cookbooks. The size of each step or the number of steps for a specific task should vary according to the individual's ability or need for support.
- For the key words **range of new activities** you can think about how task analysis can be used to support individuals to participate in a range of social, leisure, educational and work activities.

Read the following **Real Work Setting** scenario and think about how it relates to your work setting and role:

Real Work Setting

Name: Julia

Job Role: Senior Support Worker for adults who have learning disabilities

(See page 341 for a description of the role.)

Using task analysis: Julia has prepared with Anna a series of photographs, drawings and media clips of both rock climbing and canoeing in order to prepare Anna for what each of these activities will involve. Julia has also prepared with Anna a series of steps to complete prior to Anna participating in both activities. Step 1 will be visiting the location where each activity is held; Step 2 will be meeting the instructors who lead on each activity; Step 3 will be booking in the activity; Step 4 will involve Anna selecting whom she would like to be supported by on each activity. Anna's advocate will provide additional support as and when required throughout the whole process.

Evidencing AC2.2 to your assessor:

For AC2.2 you must evidence your skills in using task analysis to break down a range of new activities into manageable steps for an individual.

Assessment Method:
Direct Observation of your work practices.

- You can **show** your assessor or an expert witness how to use task analysis to break down a range of new activities into manageable steps for an individual.

REMEMBER TO:
- Make arrangements for **observation** of **your work practices**.
- Include evidence of how you use task analysis.
- Include evidence of how you break down a range of new activities into manageable steps for an individual.
- Think about **your work setting** and how you use task analysis to break down a range of new activities into manageable steps for an individual.

Learning Outcome 2: Be able to interact positively with individuals to promote participation

Assessment Criterion 2.3: Evaluate different ways of positively reinforcing an individual's participation in a range of new activities

What does AC2.3 mean?

- ○ The lead word **evaluate** means that you must **be able to show** how you assess different ways in which an individual's participation in a range of new activities can be positively reinforced.
- ○ Your **evaluation** must include considering different ways of positively reinforcing an individual's participation.
- ○ For the key words **positively reinforcing** you can think about how this involves recognising what an individual gains from undertaking a specific task. Positive reinforcements can include: naturally occurring rewards, such as drinking a cup of tea an individual has made for you; things that the individual likes, such as praise or attention; offering a preferred activity as an encouragement or reward for participating in a specified activity.
- ○ For the key words **range of new activities** you can think about the different ways that can be used to positively reinforce an individual's participation in a range of social, leisure, educational and work activities.

Read the following **Real Work Setting** scenario and think about how it relates to your work setting and role:

Real Work Setting

Name: Julia

Job Role: Senior Support Worker for adults who have learning disabilities

(See page 341 for a description of the role.)

Positively reinforcing an individual's participation: Julia and the team use a variety of positive reinforcements before, during and after Anna's participation in each of the new planned activities. At the end of Anna's successful active participation in both activities, Julia holds a meeting with all those involved to discuss the positive reinforcements that worked well and those that didn't, including the reasons why.

Evidencing AC2.3 to your assessor:

For AC2.3 you must evidence your knowledge of different ways of positively reinforcing an individual's participation in a range of new activities.

Assessment Methods:

Oral/Written Questioning or **Discussion** or a **Personal Statement** or **Reflection**.

- You can **tell** your assessor about different ways of positively reinforcing an individual's participation in a range of new activities.
- *Or*, you can **talk** to your assessor about different ways of positively reinforcing an individual's participation in a range of new activities.
- *Or*, you can write a **personal statement or reflection** about your experience of positively reinforcing an individual's participation in a range of new activities.

REMEMBER TO:

- Provide an **account** and an **evaluation** of different ways of positively reinforcing an individual's participation in a range of new activities.
- Include **varied** examples of different ways.
- Include **details** about how effective each way is.
- Ensure your evidence relates to positively reinforcing an individual's participation in a range of new activities.
- Think about **your work setting** and the different ways of positively reinforcing an individual's participation in a range of new activities.

Learning Outcome 2: Be able to interact positively with individuals to promote participation

Assessment Criterion 2.4: Demonstrate positive interaction with an individual to promote successful participation in a range of new activities

What does AC2.4 mean?

- The lead word **demonstrate** means that you must **be able to show** through **your work practices** how to show positive interaction with an individual to promote successful participation in a range of new activities.
- Your **observations** of your work practices must include you demonstrating positive interaction with an individual.
- For the key words **positive interaction** you can think about how you interact with an individual in a supportive manner, using levels of assistance, task analysis and positive reinforcement to help an individual participate in a range of new activities constructively and successfully.
- For the key words **range of new activities** you can think about the different ways that can be used to positively reinforce (*see AC2.3*) and support an individual's participation in a range of social, leisure, educational and work activities.

Read the following **Real Work Setting** scenario and think about how it relates to your work setting and role:

Real Work Setting

Name: Julia
Job Role: Senior Support Worker for adults who have learning disabilities
(See page 341 for a description of the role.)

Demonstrating positive interaction with an individual: During the meeting to discuss Anna's participation in two new activities, Anna and all those involved in supporting her share their observations of various different positive interactions that worked well and enabled Anna to fully participate and enjoy experiencing these two new activities. It is agreed that providing Anna with more verbal prompts and fewer physical prompts enabled her to develop her skills in different areas; using photographs and media clips enabled Anna to understand what each activity involved and how she could contribute to each; using naturally occurring reinforcements from others who Anna did not know, such as the instructors and other participants, motivated her to take part, be more independent and enjoy herself.

Evidencing AC2.4 to your assessor:

For AC2.4 you must evidence your skills of how to demonstrate positive interaction with an individual to promote successful participation in a range of new activities.

Assessment Method:
Direct Observation of your work practices.

- You can **show** your assessor or an expert witness how to demonstrate positive interaction with an individual to promote successful participation in a range of new activities.

REMEMBER TO:
- Make arrangements for **observation** of **your work practices**.
- Include evidence of how you positively interact with an individual.
- Include evidence of how your interaction promotes an individual's successful participation in a range of new activities.
- Think about **your work setting** and how to positively interact with an individual to promote successful participation in a range of new activities.

Learning Outcome 3: Be able to develop and implement person-centred daily plans to promote participation

Assessment Criterion 3.1: Develop daily plans with the individual and others to ensure a valued range of activities for an individual is available throughout the day, avoiding lengthy periods of disengagement

What does AC3.1 mean?

- The lead word **develop** means that you must **be able to show** through **your work practices** how to establish daily plans with the individual and others to ensure a valid range of activities is available for an individual throughout the day, avoiding lengthy periods of disengagement.
- Your **observations** of your work practices must include you showing how to establish daily plans with an individual and others, such as your colleagues, the individual's family or carers, friends, other professionals, members of the public and advocates.
- For the key words **valued range of activities** you can think about how to ensure a balance of activities is made available to individuals that contribute to good quality of life. Activities may include a range of voluntary, domestic, personal, leisure, work, educational and social activities.
- For the key word **disengagement** you can think about how individuals can avoid lengthy periods without constructive or meaningful activity. Disengaged individuals may wander about aimlessly, pace, stare, sit, lie down, purposefully fiddle with items and/or avoid social contact.

Read the following **Real Work Setting** scenario and think about how it relates to your work setting and role:

Real Work Setting
Name: Dio
Job Role: Senior Home Carer
Dio has been working as a Senior Home Carer for three years. His Senior responsibilities include coordinating and delivering individualised care to adults with learning and physical disabilities in their own homes. Dio also provides support to a team of Home Carers who support individuals with a range of daily activities both inside and outside their homes.
Developing daily plans: Dio is supporting Harold to lead his care review to agree on and plan a range of activities in which Harold would like to participate; his key worker, uncle and Physiotherapist are also present.

Evidencing AC3.1 to your assessor:

For AC3.1 you must evidence your skills in developing daily plans with the individual and others.

Assessment Method:

Direct Observation of your work practices.

- You can **show** your assessor or an expert witness how to develop daily plans with the individual and others to ensure a valid range of activities is available for an individual throughout the day, avoiding lengthy periods of disengagement.

REMEMBER TO:

- Make arrangements for **observation of your work practices**.
- Include evidence of developing daily plans with an individual and others.
- Include evidence of making a valued range of activities available throughout the day.
- Include evidence of how to avoid lengthy periods of disengagement.
- Think about **your work setting** and how to develop daily plans with the individual and others to ensure a valued range of activities is available for an individual throughout the day, avoiding lengthy periods of disengagement.

Learning Outcome 3: Be able to develop and implement person-centred daily plans to promote participation

Assessment Criterion 3.2: Support the implementation of daily plans that promote an individual's participation in a range of activities

What does AC3.2 mean?

- The lead word **support** means that you must **be able to show** through **your work practices** how to assist and work with the individual and others to implement daily plans that promote the individual's participation in a range of activities.
- Your **observations** of your work practices must include you supporting the implementation of daily plans.
- For the key word **range of activities** you can think about how to ensure a balance of activities that contribute to good quality of life is made available to individuals. Activities may include a range of voluntary, domestic, personal, leisure, work, educational and social activities.

Read the following **Real Work Setting** scenario and think about how it relates to your work setting and role:

Real Work Setting

Name: Dio

Job Role: Senior Home Carer

(See page 345 for a description of the role.)

Supporting the implementation of daily plans: Dio and his colleagues are actively supporting Harold to carry out his plans to participate in a range of activities, both when at home and when in his local community. Dio provides regular support to Harold's key worker in relation to how to encourage Harold to motivate himself every morning. He has advised Harold's uncle on some of the leisure centres Harold enjoys going to and why, and he has arranged for the Physiotherapist to show him and the team how best to support Harold to participate in his mobility activities every morning and evening. Dio has found providing consistent and high quality support and information to the team to be very effective in enabling Harold to be an active participant in a range of activities, and to make his own choices and decisions about his preferred ways to spend each day.

Evidencing AC3.2 to your assessor:

For AC3.2 you must evidence your skills in supporting the implementation of daily plans that promote an individual's participation in a range of activities.

Assessment Method:

Direct Observation of your work practices.

- You can **show** your assessor or an expert witness how to support the implementation of daily plans that promote an individual's participation in a range of activities.

REMEMBER TO:

- Make arrangements for **observation** of **your work practices**.
- Include evidence of supporting the implementation of daily plans.
- Include evidence of a range of activities.
- Include evidence of daily plans that promote an individual's participation in a range of activities.
- Think about **your work setting** and how to support the implementation of daily plans that promote an individual's participation in a range of activities.

Learning Outcome 3: Be able to develop and implement person-centred daily plans to promote participation

Assessment Criterion 3.3: Review and revise an individual's daily plan with the individual and others to increase the opportunities for participation

What does AC3.3 mean?

○ The lead words **review and revise** mean that you must **be able to show** through **your work practices** how to monitor and update an individual's daily plan with the individual and others in order to increase the opportunities for participation.

○ Your **observations** of your work practices must include you reviewing and revising an individual's daily plan with the individual and others.

○ For the key words **individual and others** you can think about how to review and revise an individual's daily plan with the individual, your colleagues, the individual's families, friends or carers, other professionals, members of the public and advocates.

Read the following **Real Work Setting** scenario and think about how it relates to your work setting and role:

Real Work Setting

Name: Dio

Job Role: Senior Home Carer

(See page 345 for a description of the role.)

Reviewing and revising an individual's daily plan: Dio discusses with Harold how he thinks his daily plans are working; Harold says to Dio that he is enjoying them but feels that he wants to try different activities, where he can make some new friends. Dio has also agreed with Harold's key worker to try some different techniques for motivating Harold in the mornings, including suggesting he has a shower in the morning rather than the evening and using music to wake up to rather than the sound of his alarm clock. Dio is exploring in more detail with Harold and his Physiotherapist the possibility of Harold undertaking his mobility exercises in a hydrotherapy pool, as Harold thoroughly enjoys swimming.

Evidencing AC3.3 to your assessor:

For AC3.3 you must evidence your skills in reviewing and revising an individual's daily plan with the individual and others to increase the opportunities for participation.

Assessment Method:

Direct Observation of your work practices.

● You can **show** your assessor or an expert witness how to review and revise an individual's daily plan with the individual and others to increase the opportunities for participation.

REMEMBER TO:

● Make arrangements for **observation** of **your work practices**.
● Include evidence of reviewing and revising an individual's daily plan.
● Include evidence of how to do this with an individual and others.
● Include evidence of how to increase the opportunities for participation.
● Think about **your work setting** and how to review and revise an individual's daily plan with the individual and others to increase the opportunities for participation.

Learning Outcome 4: Be able to use person-centred records to evaluate an individual's participation in activities

Assessment Criterion 4.1: Develop a person-centred record to monitor an individual's participation in activities

What does AC4.1 mean?

○ The lead word **develop** means that you must **be able to show** through **your work practices** how to establish a person-centred record to monitor an individual's participation in activities.

○ Your **observations** of your work practices must include you showing how to establish a person-centred record.

○ For the key words **person-centred record** you can think about how to develop a record that reflects what is important to individuals and helps them to live the life they choose.

Read the following **Real Work Setting** scenario and think about how it relates to your work setting and role:

Real Work Setting

Name: Patricia

Job Role: Senior Support Worker to an adult who has autism

Patricia has been working as a Senior Support Worker for two years. Her Senior responsibilities include leading a small team of Support Workers to enable an adult to live her life as she chooses. Patricia is responsible for coordinating this individual's plan of support and for reviewing it on a regular basis to monitor its effectiveness.

Developing a person-centred record: Patricia has developed a range of ways to monitor how actively Suzy is participating in activities agreed with her, including observing Suzy's reactions whilst participating in activities and noting the duration of her participation and interest in different activities. Patricia also collects monitoring information from the rest of the team and from Suzy's family and friends, in particular from her brother, with whom she has a close relationship, and from one of her best friends, who has known her for many years. Patricia then ensures that she captures all this information in Suzy's individual support plan, which is focused on whether Suzy enjoys the activity and has an interest in the activity, and if her involvement is important to her.

Evidencing AC4.1 to your assessor:

For AC4.1 you must evidence your skills in developing a person-centred record to monitor an individual's participation in activities.

Assessment Method:

Direct Observation of your work practices.

● You can **show** your assessor or an expert witness how to develop a person-centred record to monitor an individual's participation in activities.

● You can also use the person-centred record you have developed to monitor an individual's participation in activities as a supporting piece of **work product evidence**.

REMEMBER TO:

● Make arrangements for **observation** of **your work practices**.

● Include evidence of **developing** a person-centred record.

● Include evidence of how to monitor an individual's participation in activities.

● Think about **your work setting** and how to develop a person-centred record to monitor an individual's participation in activities.

Learning Outcome 4: Be able to use person-centred records to evaluate an individual's participation in activities

Assessment Criterion 4.2: Review an individual's participation in activities to assess changes over time

What does AC4.2 mean?

- The lead word **review** means that you must **be able to show** through **your work practices** how to monitor an individual's participation in activities to assess changes over time.
- Your **observations** of your work practices must include you reviewing an individual's participation in activities.
- For the key word **changes** you can think about how an individual's participation in activities may be affected by changes in an individual's physical, mental, emotional, social or financial well-being.

Read the following **Real Work Setting** scenario and think about how it relates to your work setting and role:

Real Work Setting

| **Name:** Patricia |
| **Job Role:** Senior Support Worker to an adult who has autism |
| (See page 348 for a description of the role.) |

Reviewing an individual's participation in activities: This month Patricia has completed her review of Suzy's participation in activities, using the monitoring information made available to her from a variety of sources. These include Suzy, other Support Workers who work with Suzy, and Suzy's parents, brother and best friend. Patricia has also spent a considerable amount of time working closely with Suzy and observing her participation in and responses to different activities. Over time Patricia has noted that Suzy's level of active participation has increased for the activities she has taken part in at home, and that areas of her independent living skills have also developed as a direct result of her active participation. For the activities Suzy has taken part in in her local community, her level of participation has been variable and this has largely been due to Suzy feeling anxious about being in a new space away from home and being surrounded in a public place by people she doesn't know.

Evidencing AC4.2 to your assessor:

For AC4.2 you must evidence your skills in reviewing an individual's participation in activities to assess changes over time.

Assessment Method:

Direct Observation of your work practices.

- You can **show** your assessor or an expert witness how to review an individual's participation in activities to assess changes over time.

REMEMBER TO:
- Make arrangements for **observation** of **your work practices**.
- Include evidence of you **reviewing** an individual's participation in activities.
- Include evidence of how to assess changes over time.
- Think about **your work setting** and how to review an individual's participation in activities to assess changes over time.

Learning Outcome 4: Be able to use person-centred records to evaluate an individual's participation in activities

Assessment Criterion 4.3: Evaluate the extent to which an individual's participation over time represents the balance of activity that is associated with a valued lifestyle

What does AC4.3 mean?

- The lead word **evaluate** means that you must **be able to show** how you assess to what extent an individual's participation over time represents the balance of activity that is associated with a valued lifestyle.
- Your **evaluation** must include considering the extent to which an individual's participation over time is associated with a valued lifestyle.
- For the key words **valued lifestyle** you can think about the balance of activities that contributes to a good quality of life for individuals, such as voluntary, domestic, work, personal, leisure, educational and social activities.

Read the following **Real Work Setting** scenario and think about how it relates to your work setting and role:

Real Work Setting

Name: Patricia

Job Role: Senior Support Worker to an adult who has autism

(See page 348 for a description of the role.)

Activities associated with a valued lifestyle: Patricia reflects on Suzy's quality of life and considers how it has changed and improved over the last six months as a result of her active participation in a range of domestic and leisure activities. Suzy still finds it very difficult to participate in activities where there are numerous other people present whom she does not know, and at the moment has shown no interest in engaging in any educational or work-based activities.

Evidencing AC4.3 to your assessor:

For AC4.3 you must evidence your knowledge of the extent to which an individual's participation over time represents the balance of activity that is associated with a valued lifestyle.

Assessment Methods:
Oral/Written Questioning or **Discussion** or a **Personal Statement** or **Reflection**.

- You can **tell** your assessor about the extent to which an individual's participation over time represents the balance of activity that is associated with a valued lifestyle.
- Or, you can **talk** to your assessor about the extent to which an individual's participation over time represents the balance of activity that is associated with a valued lifestyle.
- Or, you can write a **personal statement or reflection** about your experience of the extent to which an individual's participation over time represents the balance of activity that is associated with a valued lifestyle.

REMEMBER TO:
- Provide an **account** and an **evaluation** of the extent to which an individual's participation over time represents the balance of activity that is associated with a valued lifestyle.
- Include **varied** examples of the extent to which an individual's participation over time is representative.
- Include **details** about the balance of activity that is associated with a valued lifestyle.
- Think about **your work setting** and the extent to which an individual's participation over time represents the balance of activity that is associated with a valued lifestyle.

Learning Outcome 4: Be able to use person-centred records to evaluate an individual's participation in activities

Assessment Criterion 4.4: Explain the changes required to improve the quality of an individual's participation in order to promote independence, informed choice and a valued life

What does AC4.4 mean?

- The lead word **explain** means that you must **make clear** the changes required to improve the quality of an individual's participation in order to promote independence, informed choice and a valued life.
- Your **account** must make clear the changes required to improve the quality of an individual's participation.
- For the key word **changes** you can think about how these may be related to the individual, the setting, the activities, the support, or the services and resources being used.

Real Work Setting

Name: Patricia

Job Role: Senior Support Worker to an adult who has autism

(See page 348 for a description of the role.)

The changes required to improve the quality of an individual's participation: Patricia discusses with Suzy and all those involved in her life how the team plans to support Suzy in developing her confidence when she is outside her home and around people she does not know. Patricia has developed a plan with Suzy to gradually increase day by day and step by step the new places she visits, as well as the members of the public she comes across whom she does not know. Suzy is also going to speak with a counsellor, who will also be providing her with independent support during this process.

Evidencing AC4.4 to your assessor:

For AC4.4 you must evidence your knowledge of the changes required to improve the quality of an individual's participation in order to promote independence, informed choice and a valued life.

Assessment Method:

Oral/Written Questioning or **Discussion** or a **Personal Statement** or **Reflection**.

- You can **tell** your assessor about the changes required to improve the quality of an individual's participation in order to promote independence, informed choice and a valued life.
- Or, you can **talk** to your assessor about the changes required to improve the quality of an individual's participation in order to promote independence, informed choice and a valued life.
- Or, you can write a **personal statement or reflection** about your experience of the changes required to improve the quality of an individual's participation in order to promote independence, informed choice and a valued life.

REMEMBER TO:

- Provide an **account** and **explain** the changes required to improve the quality of an individual's participation in order to promote independence, informed choice and a valued life.
- Include **varied** examples of how to improve the quality of an individual's participation.
- Include details about how to promote independence, informed choice and a valued life.
- Think about **your work setting** and the changes required to improve the quality of an individual's participation in order to promote independence, informed choice and a valued life.

Glossary

Active participation – is a way of working that recognises an individual's right to participate in the activities and relationships of everyday life as independently as possible; the individual is regarded as an active partner in their own care or support, rather than a passive recipient

Agreed ways of working – include policies and procedures where these exist, they may be less formally documented with micro-employers

Carers – refers to partner, family, friends, neighbours

Community connecting related tools – Who am I? My gifts and capacities, Hopes and Fears, mapping our network, Passion audit, Capacity mapping and Who am I – My places

Consent – means informed agreement to an action or decision; the process of establishing consent will vary according to an individual's assessed capacity to consent

Individual (in the context of safeguarding – Unit HSC24) – will usually mean the person supported by the learner but may include those for whom there is no formal duty of care

Individual (in the context of person centred working – Unit HSC36) – refers to someone requiring care or support; it will usually mean the person or people supported by the learner

Individual (in the context of person centred assessment and care planning – HSC3020) – is the person requiring care or support. An advocate may act on behalf of an individual

Individual (in the context of specific communication needs – Unit HSC3029) – is someone with specific communication needs who requires care or support

Others (in the context of personal development – Unit SHC32) – may include the individual, carers, advocates, supervisor, line manager or employer, other professionals

Others (in the context of planning support for living at home – Unit HSC3022) may include, family, friends, advocates, others who are important to the individual's well-being

Person-centred – reflects what is important to individual and helps them to live the life they choose

Person-centred teams – a person-centred team uses person-centred thinking within the team context, to clarify the purpose of the team, what is important to the team and what support team members need. Teams can work through seven questions to explore becoming a person-centred team. Each question uses a range of person-centred thinking tools to answer it. Information about purpose, what is important to the team, action and reflection is recorded and updated in a person-centred team plan.

Person-centred thinking tools – include Important to/for (recorded as a one page profile), Working/Not Working, The doughnut, Matching staff, Relationship circle, Communication charts, 4 plus 1 questions, citizenship tool, Decision making agreement, Presence to contribution and Dreaming

Person-centred values – may include individuality, rights, choice, privacy, independence, dignity, respect, partnership

Policies and procedures – may include other agreed ways of working as well as formal policies or procedures

Preferences and needs – will include any particular requirements and personal hygiene determined by an individual's culture, faith, belief, religion

Revisions – may include: closing the plan if all objectives have been met, reducing the level of support to reflect increased independence, increasing the level of support to address unmet needs, changing the type of support, changing the method of delivering support

Stress – can have positive as well as negative effects, but in this unit (HSC37) it is used to refer to negative stress